Exploring Communication Law

A Socratic Approach

Randy Bobbitt
University of West Florida

PEARSON

Boston   New York   San Francisco
Mexico City   Montreal   Toronto   London   Madrid   Munich   Paris
Hong Kong   Singapore   Tokyo   Cape Town   Sydney

Editor-in-Chief: *Karon Bowers*
Acquisitions Editor: *Jeanne Zalesky*
Assistant Editor: *Jenny Lupica*
Marketing Manager: *Suzan Czajkowski*
Production Editor: *Claudine Bellanton*
Editorial Production Service: *Elm Street Publishing Services, Inc.*
Composition Buyer: *Linda Cox*
Manufacturing Buyer: *JoAnne Sweeney*
Electronic Composition: *Elm Street Publishing Services, Inc.*
Photo Researcher: *Annie Pickert*
Cover Administrator: *Kristina Mose-Libon*

For related titles and support materials, visit our online catalog at www.ablongman.com.

Between the time website information is gathered and then published, it is not unusual for some sites to have closed. Also, the transcription of URLs can result in typographical errors. The Publisher would appreciate notification where these errors occur so that they may be corrected in subsequent editions.

ISBN-13: 978-0-205-46231-5   ISBN-10: 0-205-46231-6

Library of Congress Cataloging-in-Publication Data

Bobbitt, William R. (William Randy)
  Exploring communication law : a Socratic approach / Randy Bobbitt.
      p. cm.
  Includes bibliographical references and indexes.
    ISBN 978-0-205-46231-5 (alk. paper)
    1. Mass media—Law and legislation—United States. 2. Freedom of speech—United States.
  3. Freedom of expression—United States. 4. United States. Constitution. 1st Amendment.
  1. Title.

  KF2750.B63 2008   2007022986
    343.7309'9—dc22

Printed in the United States of America

10 9 8 7 6 5 4 3 2 1   11 10 09 08 07

Credits appear on page 305, which constitutes an extension of the copyright page.

CONTENTS

PART THREE   Communication in Business

11 Intellectual Property   214

PREFACE

Exploring Communication Law is the culmination of a decade's worth of work in researching, teaching, and writing about communication law. It is based on my teaching style, which has changed dramatically since I began as a graduate teaching assistant.

For the first ten years or so of my teaching career, I used the traditional lecture/note-taking model of instruction. While I enjoyed the process of preparing lecture notes and students seemed to enjoy my classes, I always believed there might be a better way to use our class time. While I was in my doctoral program I took a number of courses in communication law and constitutional law that were taught by professors who had taught in law schools in addition to communication programs. I was fascinated with their Socratic dialogue approach to teaching—one that required students to thoroughly prepare for each class meeting and challenged them to think about controversial issues, develop positions, and then publicly defend their views.

I have been very pleased with the students' reactions to this teaching method. I can tell from their comments made to me directly, as well as those on student evaluations, that they agree that it leads to a more thorough learning of the material, as opposed to just memorizing definitions for a test. While some students are initially uncomfortable speaking about controversial subjects in front of their peers, most of them warm up to it eventually. Much of the positive reinforcement for this teaching method comes from transfer and transient students, who are quick to compare it to the lecture/note-taking model they have encountered at other institutions.

Communication law is often a difficult subject for students to grasp, but it is important for those who plan on careers in journalism, broadcasting, advertising, and public relations. Basic knowledge of the law will often help you to safeguard the legal rights of yourself or your employer. Other times it involves respecting the legal rights of others.

Nearly all aspects of the law are complex, and communication law is especially so because of the rapidly changing nature of the technology with which professional communicators work. That means encountering many questions for which there are no simple answers. As one of my favorite graduate school professors often told his constitutional law classes, sometimes the safest answer to legal questions is "sometimes . . . maybe . . . it depends."

Like many textbooks written by college professors, this book began as a collection of lecture notes and handouts. Many of those lecture notes and handouts came from five professors who were influential in my teaching career: Donna Dickerson, former director of the School of Mass Communications at the University of South Florida, now dean of the College of Arts and Sciences at the University of Texas at Tyler; Barbara Petersen, professor of media law at USF; and three professors at Bowling Green State University: Dennis Hale and Jim Foust in the School of Communication Studies, and Steven Ludd in the Department of Political Science.

In addition to those professors, I thank the following individuals at the University of North Carolina—Wilmington: Frank Trimble, chair of the Department of Communication Studies; Patsy Odom and Linda Peay, department administrative assistants; Courtney Hill, Nathan Wolf, and Hayley Lovitt, research assistants and expert proofreaders; and Lisa Williams, reference librarian. At the University of West Florida, I thank department chair Bruce Swain and colleagues Eileen Perrigo and Rick Scott.

I also thank the hundreds of students who have taken my classes over the last decade and provided valuable feedback on preliminary versions of this book.

Finally, we would like to thank the following individuals, who reviewed this book for Allyn and Bacon and offered their comments: Carol Atkinson, Central Missouri State University; Tamara Kay Baldwin, Missouri State University; Genelle Belmas, California State University, Fullerton; Hugh S. Fullerton, Sam Houston State University; Jane S. McConnell, Minnesota State University; Carole McNall, St. Bonaventure University; Bruce L. Plopper, University of Arkansas, Little Rock; David W. Scott, University of South Carolina; Darryl. C. Smith, University of West Florida; and Kirk Wolf, Delta College.

ABOUT THE AUTHOR

Randy Bobbitt is an assistant professor in the Department of Communication Arts at the University of West Florida (UWF), where he directs the public relations program at UWF's Fort Walton Beach Campus. In addition to public relations, he has taught courses in journalism, communication law, and communication ethics. Prior to going to UWF, he taught at the University of North Carolina at Wilmington, Marshall University, and the University of South Florida.

His research interests include public relations, political communication, popular culture, and communication law and ethics. Prior to teaching, he worked professionally in both journalism and public relations. He is a past president of the West Virginia Chapter of the Public Relations Society of America and is a frequent speaker at professional and student public relations conferences. He holds a Ph.D. in communication law and policy from Bowling Green State University.

His monographs include *A Big Idea and a Shirt-Tail Full of Type: The Life and Work of Wallace F. Stovall* (1995) and *Who Owns What's Inside the Professor's Head: Universities, Faculty, and the Battle Over Intellectual Property* (2006). His other textbooks include *Developing the Public Relations Campaign* (2005, co-authored with Ruth Sullivan) and *Exploring Communication Law* (2008). He is currently working on a new book, *Us Against Them: The Political Culture of Talk Radio,* which he hopes to publish in 2008.

1 Getting Started:

Basic Concepts and Definitions

LEARNING OBJECTIVES

As a result of reading this chapter, students should:

- Have a general understanding of the four theoretical models of media regulation in use around the world and how the American system of regulating media differs from that of other countries.

- Understand the six sources of communication law and how responsibility for various forms of communication regulation and policy is distributed among federal, state, and local governments.

- Understand the constitutional amendments that affect communication law.

- Have a basic understanding of the federal and state court systems and how the appeals process works, including how cases reach the U.S. Supreme Court.

- Have a basic understanding of the Socratic Dialogue format for class discussion and what will be expected of students in this class.

Freedom of Expression around the World

Around the world, governments that recognize the value of free speech are rare. The best examples are the governments of the United States, Canada, New Zealand, Uruguay, and most countries in Western Europe. Many of those countries have government documents similar to our Bill of Rights. Germany's Article 5 of Basic Law and Canada's Charter of Rights and Freedoms, for example, provide for both freedom of speech and freedom of the press in those countries. South Africa's relatively new constitution provides that its citizens have freedom of speech, press, artistic creativity, academic discourse, and scientific research, but disallows speech that includes war propaganda, incitement of imminent violence, or advocacy of hatred based on race, ethnicity, gender, or religion (what the American legal system refers to as *hate speech*).

In other countries, free speech is assumed as a right without being specified by law. In Australia and England, for example, freedom of expression is not mentioned in government documents, but courts typically recognize it as an important part of representative democracy.

By contrast, many countries ruled by military dictators or heavily influenced by religious doctrine allow for little or no freedom of speech or press. In many countries in Asia, Africa, Central America, South America, and Eastern Europe, cultural norms dictate that individual rights are subservient to the welfare of the society as a whole and can therefore be limited with little or no justification.

In terms of media regulation specifically, there are four formal models that describe how various governments around the world choose to regulate their newspaper, magazine, broadcasting, and book publishing industries. In their 1956 book, *Four Theories of the Press*, journalism historians and theorists Fred Siebert, Theodore Peterson, and Wilbur Schramm identified the four models as the authoritarian model, libertarian model, social responsibility model, and Soviet-Communist model.[1]

The oldest of the four models is the **authoritarian model,** which evolved during the late Renaissance in sixteenth- and seventeenth-century Europe, shortly after the invention of the printing press. At that time, truth was not considered to be a societal value of great importance to the people, and was instead a higher virtue available only to those in power. In this model, the media are privately owned but regulated by the government, usually through a licensing requirement. Publishers of newspapers whose editorial positions are inconsistent with the views of the government will see their licenses revoked or simply not renewed. Today, the authoritarian model is found mainly in Asia and Africa.

The **libertarian model** evolved in Great Britain in the late 1600s and was adopted by the United States in the years leading up to the Revolutionary War. When it began in Europe, the model was espoused by liberal thinkers such as John Stuart Mill, who was against government censorship in all of its forms. In the United States, a similar view was advocated by Thomas Jefferson and many of the founding fathers who saw a free and robust press as a cornerstone of an emerging democracy. The libertarian model provides for no media regulation at all. It is based on the belief that a free press is a partner in the search for truth and that society benefits from the widest possible diversity of ideas from the widest possible diversity of sources. When this model was used, even libel went unpunished in extreme cases.

The libertarian model was employed in the United States until the early 1900s, when it was replaced by the **social responsibility model,** which grew out of the muckraking era of the 1920s. The difference between the latter two models is that in the libertarian model the media provide the information but leave it up to the audience to interpret the information, whereas in the social responsibility model the media provide the same volume and diversity of information but also help audiences sort through it. This model, which is still in effect today, features two forces that are sometimes in conflict: (1) competition among media outlets for news, which often motivates them to take chances in their pursuit or dissemination of information, and (2) a population that is often skeptical or cynical about the information the media present or the tactics they use to gather it.

The Constitution of the United States. While many of the original articles affect communication indirectly, the amendments (especially the First Amendment) have more direct effect.

And unlike the libertarian model, the social responsibility model provides legal recourse (such as libel and invasion-of-privacy lawsuits) to serve as a check on overzealous media.

Since the demise of the Soviet Union, the **Soviet-Communist model** (sometimes referred to as the "Marxist" model) is almost non-existent. Instead of being licensed by the government as in the authoritarian model, media operating in the Soviet-Communist model are actually an integral part of the government, as publishers and broadcasters work in "information bureaus" that promote the prevailing political ideology. There is no freedom of speech for individuals and little tolerance for dissenting viewpoints published in underground newspapers. Since the fall of the Soviet-Communist empire, however, Cuba is the only remaining country in which this model is found.

In 1995, a group of eight communication scholars published an updated version of the four theoretical models of media regulation in *Last Rights: Revisiting Four Theories of the Press*, edited by John C. Nerone, a professor at the University of Illinois. In their book, the authors identify Middle Eastern Muslim nations as the newest practitioners of the authoritarian model. The authors point to the Ayatollah Khomeini's condemnation of author Salman Rushdie's 1988 book, *The Satanic Verses*, as an extreme application of the authoritarian model of media regulation. In discussing the social responsibility theory, which is based partly on competition among media, the authors claim that while the American press still operates on that basis, the model is threatened in part by the growth of media monopolies such as newspaper chains and broadcast networks.[2]

Although most scholars agree that the libertarian model has been replaced by the social responsibility model as the primary structure for American media, some also believe that the growth of "personal journalism," such as web logs, or, "blogs," marks a shift back toward the libertarian philosophy. In the original context of the libertarian model, anyone with enough money to purchase a printing press could establish himself or herself as a book or newspaper publisher. Today, when so many individuals can establish their own website and refer to themselves as electronic journalists or publishers, the libertarian philosophy may well be thriving in cyberspace.

Sources of Communication Law

In the United States, there are six sources of communications law: Constitutional, Statutory, administrative, executive, common, and the law of equity.

Constitutional law refers to law that comes directly from the U.S. Constitution and its amendments, and in some cases, the constitutions of the states.

Statutory law refers to laws made by elected governmental bodies such as the U.S. Congress, state legislatures, county commissions, and city councils. On the federal level, the primary influence of congressional action is in areas such as the Freedom of Information Act and copyrights and trademarks. To a lesser degree, Congress has influence in the areas of broadcasting, advertising, media ownership, and political communication. Most federal law is found in a set of documents known as the *United States Code*.

State legislatures are responsible for making laws regarding libel, privacy, open meetings, open records, shield laws, and cameras in the courtroom. State laws are typically called **statutes.**

City and county governments pass local laws—usually referred to as **ordinances**—concerning adult entertainment, cable television (franchising regulations), newspaper distribution (number and location of vending machines), and transit and outdoor advertising (billboards and benches).

One simplified explanation of the difference between constitutional law and statutory law is to say that constitutional law deals with large and abstract issues while statutory law deals with matters that are specific and concrete.

Administrative law refers to the rules and regulations made by administrative or regulatory agencies that are part of the executive branch of the federal government or a state government. At the federal level, these agencies and their areas of responsibility involving communication law include the Federal Communications Commission (broadcasting and advertising), the Federal Trade Commission (advertising and public relations), the U.S. Postal Service (advertising and mailing regulations), the Securities and Exchange Commission (financial disclosure and securities transactions), the Department of Justice (media ownership), and the Federal Elections Commission (political advertising).

Executive actions are those taken by chief executives such as the U.S. president, state governors, city mayors, or county managers. These actions have little effect on communication law, however. For example, there are not many things that a president can do that would have a direct effect on journalism or related professions. Except in a grave national emergency such as a nuclear war, a president has no authority to exercise direct control over the news media; almost any executive order issued in an attempt to influence media content would be declared unconstitutional. The president has an indirect effect on communication law, however, through appointments of judges to federal courts (including the Supreme Court) and appointments of commissioners to administrative bodies such as the Federal Communications Commission and Federal Trade Commission. The president may also indirectly affect communication law through decisions to classify or declassify government documents.

Common law refers to court rulings that are based on an accumulation of decisions made in similar cases in the past. A Latin term associated with this concept is **stare decisis,** which means "let the decision stand." Common law is sometimes referred to as "case law" or "judge-made law." But the idea that common law is "unwritten law" is a misnomer. All of it is written somewhere—just not all in one place.

The **law of equity** is a method of deciding cases in which judges use their wisdom and experience to determine the fairest course of action for not only the parties involved but also society as a whole. The law of equity is often employed in cases for which there are no precedents (as in common law) or for which the precedents are outdated and so no easy resolution can be attained by a strict application of the law. For example, a judge may determine that a newspaper should not be allowed to publish information that would harm national security interests because to allow publication—and then determine if any harm took place—would not be practical. Four states—Arkansas, Delaware, Mississippi, and Tennessee—maintain separate courts to decide equity cases.

Most areas of law are neatly divided among the federal, state, and local (city and county) governments. But because of the broad nature of the communication

	Federal	State	City/County
Access to Information	Freedom of Information Act of 1966	State public meetings (sunshine laws), public records laws, courtroom cameras	
Advertising	Federal Trade Commission and Federal Communications Commission rules (commercial advertising), Federal Elections Commission rules (political advertising)	Statutes regarding false and misleading advertising; statutes regarding political advertising; statutes regarding advertising of physicians, lawyers, and other professionals; statutes regarding advertising of lotteries and other forms of legal gambling	Outdoor advertising (billboards, yard signs) transit advertising
Broadcasting	Federal Communications Commission rules (programming, operations, ownership)		Cable television franchising
Copyrights	Federal copyright laws		
Libel		Libel statutes	
Newspaper Distribution			Local licensing ordinances (vending machines only)
Patents	Federal patent laws		
Privacy	Wiretapping, newsroom searches (Privacy Protection Act of 1980)	Wiretapping, personal privacy (private facts, false light, intrusion, appropriation)	
Securities Transactions	Securities and Exchange Act of 1934		
Sexual Expression	Children's Internet Protection Act, FCC restrictions on broadcast indecency; federal obscenity laws	State obscenity laws	Adult entertainment ordinances (book and video stores, public nudity)
Shield Laws		State shield laws	
Trade Secrets	Federal trade secret laws	State trade secret laws	
Trademarks	Federal trademark Laws (Lanham Act)	State trademark laws	

FIGURE 1.1

business, certain categories of communication are assigned to each of the three levels, and in some cases responsibility is shared. Figure 1.1 gives a general overview of how those responsibilities are assigned or shared.

Constitutional Amendments That Affect Communication Law

First Amendment (1791)

Congress shall make no law respecting an establishment of religion, or prohibiting the free exercise thereof; or abridging the freedom of speech, or of the press; or the right of the people peaceably to assemble, and to petition the government for a redress of grievances.

Effect on communication law: The original intent of the free press clause was to protect newspaper journalists and book publishers from censorship, while also providing similar protections to a variety of non-journalistic forms of expression. Today, the distinction between journalism and other forms of communication is not as clear, as those expressing political opinions in cyberspace (i.e., "bloggers") are claiming to be journalists.

The petition clause applies to journalists as well as to ordinary citizens and has been at the center of cases involving access to information, such as the Freedom of Information Act, and in complaints relating to open records and open meetings.

Fourth Amendment (1791)

The right of the people to be secure in their persons, houses, papers, and effects, against unreasonable searches and seizures, shall not be violated, and no warrants shall issue, but upon probable cause, supported by oath or affirmation, and particularly the place to be searched, and the persons or things to be seized.

Effect on communication law: The search and seizure clause was originally intended to protect citizens from the unlawful search of their homes or seizures of their personal possessions, but today this clause is often cited by media organizations in cases in which their offices are searched and/or news materials (such as notes or tapes) are seized. One such case was *Zurcher v. Stanford Daily* (discussed in Chapter 8), in which law enforcement personnel searched the offices of a student newspaper and seized photographs as part of an investigation of campus violence.[3]

Sixth Amendment (1791)

In all criminal prosecutions, the accused shall enjoy the right to a speedy and public trial, by an impartial jury of the state and district wherein the crime shall have been committed, which district shall have been previously ascertained by law, and to be informed of the nature and cause of the accusation; to be confronted with the witnesses against him; to have compulsory process for obtaining witnesses in his favor, and to have the assistance of counsel for his defense.

Effect on communication law: The defendant's right to a "speedy and public trial" is often mischaracterized as the "right to a fair trial," even though the Sixth Amendment makes no references to fairness. Nonetheless, this Amendment is often cited in discussions regarding alleged unfairness in the legal system caused by pre-trial publicity, cameras in the courtroom, and other factors. These phenomena are discussed in more detail in Chapter 8.

Eighth Amendment (1791)

Excessive bail shall not be required, nor excessive fines imposed, nor cruel and unusual punishments inflicted.

Effect on communication law: In a number of cases in the late 1990s (unrelated to communication law), the U.S. Supreme Court ruled that excessive punitive damages in civil suits violate the Eighth Amendment. Though not yet applied in media cases, legal scholars speculate this ruling may help to limit the size of punitive damage awards in libel and privacy cases.

Tenth Amendment (1791)

The powers not delegated to the United States by the Constitution, nor prohibited by it to the states, are reserved to the states respectively, or to the people.

Effect on communication law: This amendment allows states to establish their own laws regarding libel, privacy, open meetings, open records, shield laws, and courtroom cameras, because those issues are not addressed at the federal level.

Fourteenth Amendment, Section 1 (1868)

All persons born or naturalized in the United States and subject to the jurisdiction thereof, are citizens of the United States and of the state wherein they reside. No state shall make or enforce any law which shall abridge the privileges or immunities of citizens of the United States; nor shall any state deprive any person of life, liberty, or property, without due process of law; nor deny to any person within its jurisdiction the equal protection of the laws.

Effect on communication law: Section 1 of this amendment is also known as the **equal protection clause.** In short, it means that no state law or local government ordinance can invalidate or take priority over any federal law or constitutional right. Passed a few years after the Thirteenth Amendment formally banned slavery, the rationale behind the equal protection clause was to prevent individual states from attempting to re-institute slavery on the state level. Today, the equal protection clause is applied in a variety of cases in which a state law or city or county ordinance limits rights that are provided by federal law or the U.S. Constitution. This concept is also known as "incorporation," meaning that any constitutional right or limitation on government power can be "incorporated" through the Fourteenth Amendment and applied to the states. In cases in which

The United States Supreme Court at the beginning of the 2006–07 session. Seated, left to right: Anthony Kennedy, John Paul Stevens, John Roberts (Chief Justice), Antonin Scalia, David Souter. Back row: Stephen Breyer, Clarence Thomas, Ruth Bader Ginsburg, Samuel Alito.

the federal government cannot limit your free speech rights, no state or local government can, either.

Court Systems

There are fifty-two court systems in the United States: one for each of the fifty states, one for the District of Columbia, and one for the federal system. The federal court system has three responsibilities: (1) interpreting the Constitution, (2) resolving conflicts between the federal government and other parties (including trying defendants accused of committing federal crimes), and (3) resolving conflicts between parties from different states.

Each court system is divided into three levels. The bottom level of the federal system consists of trial courts known as Federal District Courts. Above the trial courts are Circuit Courts of Appeal, which consider appeals from the district courts. Circuit Courts were so named because in the early years of the American judiciary, Supreme Court justices would travel prescribed "circuits" in order to preside over the appeals process. At the top level is the U.S. Supreme Court.

Federal Courts
U.S. Supreme Court

Circuit Courts of Appeal

Federal District Court

State Courts
State supreme court or court of appeal*

State appeals court*

Trial courts, municipal courts, county courts, superior courts, courts of common pleas*

*Titles of state courts vary greatly.

One of the main differences between Circuit Courts of Appeal and the U.S. Supreme Court is that the Circuit Courts of Appeal are governed by the process of **mandatory review,** meaning they must review every case that is appealed to them; the U.S. Supreme Court operates on the principle of **discretionary review** and can decline to review a case if it believes the core issue involved is not significant enough.

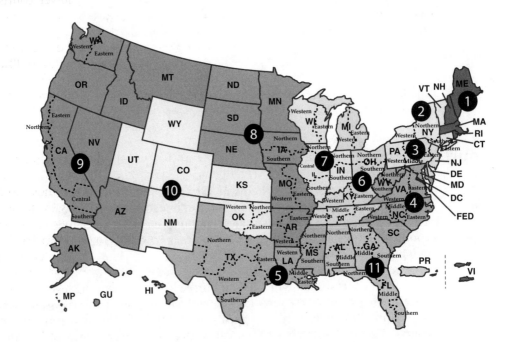

FIGURE 1.2   Geographic boundaries of United States Circuit Courts of Appeals; numbers refer to the number of each Circuit.

After an appeals court hears a case, it typically takes one of three actions. It may **uphold** or **affirm** the finding of the lower court, meaning that it agrees with the ruling of the trial court. It may **overturn** or **reverse** the lower court, meaning that it disagrees with the ruling of the lower court. In some cases it may **remand** the case, meaning that it requires the lower court to re-try the case. Most cases are remanded not because of disagreement over the outcome but because of an error in procedure or legal principle.

When a Circuit Court rules on a case, that ruling is binding only on lower courts from states within that Circuit. The ruling is not binding in lower courts outside of the states that comprise that Circuit, although the case may be cited to support the position of a party involved in a lower-court action or appeal.

Conversely, decisions of the U.S. Supreme Court are binding on all lower courts in the country. The Supreme Court reviews about one hundred cases per year—fewer than 5 percent of all of the appeals it receives. When the Supreme Court agrees to review a case, it issues a **writ of certiorari,** which is a formal document that orders a lower court to send up the written records of a case. Court records and legal publications use the terms "certiorari granted" and "certiorari denied."

When the Supreme Court agrees to hear a case, it does not necessarily mean that it disagrees with the finding of the lower courts and is eager to overturn it. More often the Court agrees to hear a case because (1) a significant right is at stake (such as freedom of speech or equal protection), (2) lower courts have issued contradictory rulings, or (3) a procedural error has occurred (a lower court has applied the law incorrectly).

Conversely, the Supreme Court's decision not to hear a case does not necessarily mean that it agrees with the decision of the lower court. More likely the court has decided not to hear a case because the issue at the core of the case is not significant enough to deserve the attention of the Supreme Court. In some cases, the Court may actually agree with the ruling of a lower court, but order a new trial nevertheless because of some error or oversight in the process employed at lower levels.

When the Supreme Court issues its ruling, it is announced in the form of a **majority opinion** that is written by one or more of the justices voting in favor. Justices who agree with the ruling but for different reasons than those authoring the majority opinion may issue a **concurring opinion.** Justices in the minority may issue a **dissenting opinion.** While not as significant as majority opinions, dissenting opinions play an important part in the legal system because they are often cited in future cases.

Two other terms often heard in the court system are "criminal law" and "civil law." **Criminal law** refers to the field of law dealing with the government prosecuting an individual for crimes against society. Such cases get labels such as *United States v. Wilson, California v. Smith, State v. Jones,* or *The People v. Brown.* **Civil law** involves individuals or parties suing each other for violations known as **torts.** Such cases receive labels such as *Smith v. Jones* or *Brown v. Daily Tribune.*

Understanding the Socratic Dialogue

Although sometimes (and understandably) attributed to the Greek philosopher Socrates, the **Socratic Dialogue** was actually developed by Plato, one of his star pupils, who dutifully named it in honor of his mentor.

The Socratic Dialogue is sometimes confused with the **Socratic Method,** which was indeed the creation of Socrates. In the Socratic Method, Socrates would force students to jump through a series of intellectual hoops in order to defend what they believed to be the "truth." The objective of this sometimes confrontational method was to engage an individual student in a series of back-and-forth exchanges, repeatedly confronting the student with information that contradicted his or her beliefs. Many times the result was the student's concession that his or her original idea was incorrect. Today, a formal application of the Socratic Method is typically used in law school classes, not to embarrass or humiliate students but rather to sharpen their ability to "think on their feet" and prepare them for the rigors of courtroom debate. An informal application of the Socratic Method is found in the format of political talk shows on radio and television, where the moderator attempts to embarrass or intimidate guests and assert his or her own intellectual superiority.

A true Socratic Dialogue, however, is less confrontational and more constructive than the Socratic Method. Developed by Plato after years of study under Socrates, the Socratic Dialogue involves more than just a back-and-forth dialogue between professor and student. Instead, it involves a group of students or other participants discussing a topic in an atmosphere in which participants are encouraged to express their own opinions, agree with or add to the opinions expressed by others, or respectfully disagree with or challenge others' opinions. A successful Socratic Dialogue requires a skilled moderator or facilitator, as well as sincere and enthusiastic participants. As James M. Lang wrote in his 2005 book, *Life on the Tenure Track*, when the professor calls upon a student in a class discussion, it should be framed as "an invitation to participate in an intellectual feast, not as challenging the student to a duel."[4]

Contrary to popular belief, the desired objective of a Socratic Dialogue is not consensus. Instead, the objectives are to motivate participants to examine their own beliefs, develop the self-confidence to express them, and encourage them to consider the opinions of others.

If your professor has chosen this textbook, he or she is likely to be an advocate of the Socratic Dialogue method of teaching. His or her role will be to choose which questions from this book will be used (class time or student interest may limit the number of questions that can be used), assign the appropriate background reading, and keep the discussion on track. The role of the students is to prepare for the discussion in advance, participate enthusiastically, and answer challenging questions asked by the professor and by classmates. Each class will build on those that came before it in a logical manner, making consistent attendance and punctuality a necessity. Both the professor and students must also be open to and respectful of divergent viewpoints. It is possible to criticize another person's ideas without criticizing the person. In an effective Socratic dialogue, there are no "right" or "wrong" answers.

Your professor will likely use the Socratic Dialogue for both the discussion questions (sprinkled throughout the chapters) and the case problems at the end of the chapters.

Some discussion questions ask you to think about broad, philosophical questions

(continued)

Understanding the Socratic Dialogue (*Continued*)

and to be prepared to express your opinion. Others involve a specific case or group of cases. For those questions, it will be helpful to understand each of the following: (1) What was the central issue debated in this case or cases? (2) What was the court decision and how was it reached? (3) How does the outcome of that case affect us today?

Most of the case problems begin with fictional scenarios. Here are some examples:

> You're the attorney for the *Mudville Daily Tribune* and have just learned that the local police chief is suing the paper for libel because . . .
> You're the chief legal counsel at Mudville State University, and university administrators want to censor the school's newspaper . . .
> You're an attorney and have been approached by both sides in a case . . .

Most of the case problems will provide two or more possible courses of action and then ask you to choose one and be prepared to defend your decision. Much like the discussion questions, there are no right or wrong answers for case problems. Which side you take will not affect your course grade or how the professor evaluates your level of preparation—what is much more important is how well you are able to support your answer.

In determining which side to take (and preparing your answer), you may find the following steps helpful:

1. Identify what kind of speech is involved and how that type of speech is generally viewed in society (for example, where it falls on the First Amendment hierarchy discussed in Chapter 2). Is it political speech or commercial speech? Is it truthful advertising or false advertising? Obscenity or non-obscene sexual expression? The hierarchy may not apply to all of the case problems, but it will apply to most of them.

2. Consider the legal principles involved. These are the headings, subheadings, and boldfaced terms in the chapters.

3. Find appropriate case law. You will need to find at least one real-world case for each case problem, but for most you should be able to find two or more cases. In some instances you will find cases that are similar to yours, and your argument would include an explanation of why the fictional case should be treated the same as the real-world case you're citing. In other instances, you may wish to distinguish the fictional case from the real-world case, explaining why it is different and therefore deserves to be treated differently.

SOCRATIC DIALOGUE QUESTIONS

1. Suppose you were a government official in a newly formed country and were put in charge of setting up a system by which media in the new country would be regulated. Which of the four models described in this chapter would you choose, and why?

2. Of the six constitutional amendments listed in this chapter, which do you believe should be modified to account for advances in technology and other changes in American society?

GLOSSARY OF TERMS

Administrative law   A system of rules and regulations made by administrative or regulatory agencies that are part of the executive branch of the federal government or a state government.

Affirm   A court's decision to confirm or validate the decision of a lower court.

Authoritarian model   A regulatory system in which the media are privately owned but are regulated by the government, most often through a licensing procedure.

Civil law   The field of law that involves individuals or parties suing each other for damages. Also known as tort law.

Common law   A system of deciding cases based on an accumulation of decisions made in similar cases in the past.

Concurring opinion   An opinion written by one or more Supreme Court justices who agree with the majority opinion but wish to offer a different perspective.

Constitutional law   Law that comes directly from the U.S. Constitution and its amendments, and in some cases, the constitutions of the states.

Criminal law   The field of law dealing with the government prosecuting an individual for crimes against society.

Discretionary review   The rule that allows the U.S. Supreme Court to choose only those cases involving significant constitutional issues.

Dissenting opinion   An opinion written by one or more Supreme Court justices voting in the minority.

Equal protection clause   A term used to describe Section 1 of the Fourteenth Amendment. The clause provides that no state law or local government ordinance can invalidate or take priority over any federal law or constitutional right.

Executive actions   Actions taken by chief executives such as the U.S. president, state governors, city mayors, or county managers.

Law of equity   A system of deciding cases in which judges use their wisdom and experience to determine the fairest course of action for not only the parties involved but also society as a whole.

Libertarian model   A system under which media operate with little or no government regulation.

Majority opinion   A summary of the Supreme Court's decision, written by one or more justices voting in favor.

Mandatory review   The rule that requires Circuit Courts of Appeal to review every case coming to them from lower courts.

Ordinances   A term often used to refer to laws made by local elected bodies such as city councils and county commissions.

Overturn   A court's decision to invalidate or reverse the decision of a lower court.

Remand   A court's decision to send a case back to a lower court to be tried again, usually because of a procedural error.

Reverse   A court's decision to invalidate or overturn the decision of a lower court.

Social responsibility model   A regulatory model in which the media provide a wide variety of information but also help their audiences process and understand it and in which legal recourse exists as a check on overzealous media.

Socratic Dialogue   A method of teaching in which students or other individuals discuss various aspects of a controversial issue. Less confrontational than the Socratic Method, Socratic Dialogue was developed by Plato and named in honor of Socrates, his mentor.

Socratic Method   A method of teaching in which an instructor engages his or her students in back-and-forth exchanges, sometimes confrontational in nature.

Soviet-Communist model   A regulatory system in which the media operate as a department within a country's government. This system is sometimes referred to as the "Marxist" model.

Stare decisis   Often associated with common law, this Latin term means "let the decision stand."

Statutes   A term often used to refer to laws made by elected bodies such as state legislatures.

Statutory law   Laws made by elected governmental bodies such as the U.S. Congress, state legislatures, county commissions, and city councils.

Torts   The field of law that involves individuals or parties suing each other for damages. Also known as civil law.

Uphold   A court's decision to confirm or validate the decision of a lower court.

Writ of certiorari   A formal document issued by the U.S. Supreme Court that orders a lower court to send up the written records of a case, an indication to the parties that the Court intends to review the case.

NOTES

1. Fred Siebert, Theodore Peterson, and Wilbur Schramm. *Four Theories of the Press.* Freeport, N.Y.: Books for Libraries Press, 1973.

2. John C. Nerone, ed., *Last Rights: Revisiting Four Theories of the Press.* Urbana, Ill.: University of Illinois Press, 1995.

3. *Zurcher v. Stanford Daily*, 436 U.S. 547 (1978).

4. James M. Lang, *Life on the Tenure Track: Lessons from the First Year.* Baltimore, Md.: Johns Hopkins University Press, 2005, p. 28.

2 An Overview of the First Amendment

Congress shall make no law respecting an establishment of religion, or prohibiting the free exercise thereof; or abridging the freedom of speech, or of the press; or the right of the people peaceably to assemble, and to petition the government for a redress of grievances.

The First Amendment
Ratified December 15, 1791

Even in a conservative era, the principle of free speech in America stands as solidly as one of the marble pillars that prop up the Supreme Court building.

David Savage
Supreme Court correspondent
Los Angeles Times

Protection of free speech is not needed for inoffensive, popular speech with which all or most members of a community agree. Such speech is not threatened. Freedom is required precisely for unpopular speech, the toleration of which is one of the marks of a free society.

Alan Charles Kors and
Harvey A. Silverglate
The Shadow University, 1998

LEARNING OBJECTIVES

As a result of reading this chapter, students should:

- Understand that the First Amendment is a controversial and often misunderstood part of the Constitution that is subject to a variety of interpretations.
- Understand and be prepared to discuss the values that are often associated with First Amendment freedoms.
- Understand the First Amendment hierarchy and the rationale for providing some forms of expression with more constitutional protection than others.
- Understand the differences between various concepts associated with the First Amendment that are often found in opposing pairs, such as obtrusive and non-obtrusive speech, political speech and commercial speech, hate speech and fighting words, and obscenity and non-obscene sexual expression.

The First Amendment in the Abstract

When you hear the word *speech*, you probably think about the type of oral communication you practiced in your public speaking class. But in a First Amendment context, the term *speech* means much more. Legally, **speech** is defined as an "oral, written, pictorial, or other expression of an idea or opinion." Based on that definition, speech can take the form of oral communication, letters to the editor of a newspaper or magazine, posters, videotapes, bumper stickers, yard signs, billboards, documentary films, public parades, political and commercial advertising in the print or broadcast media, and dozens of other forms of communication. Throughout this book and in legal discussions in general, the terms *freedom of speech, freedom of expression,* and *First Amendment freedoms* are typically used interchangeably.

Occasionally, speech is divided into **pure speech** and **symbolic speech,** the latter including displays such as wearing a black ribbon on your clothing to demonstrate grief over someone's death or burning the American flag to demonstrate contempt for the government. As Justice William Brennan wrote in his opinion in a case involving symbolic speech, "The First Amendment literally forbids the abridgement only of 'speech,' but we have long recognized that its protection does not end at the spoken or written word."[1]

Factors to Keep in Mind When Studying the First Amendment

Here are some general principles to keep in mind while considering First Amendment issues:

1. *A common misconception is that the First Amendment exists only for journalists, and only journalists can benefit from it.* When James Madison sat down to write the First Amendment in 1791, he wasn't thinking about journalists as much as he was thinking about the ordinary citizen on the street. He did include a clause about freedom of the press, but he was much more concerned about freedom of speech in general—the right of citizens to express opinions on political, social, and religious issues—than the rights of the journalism profession. And he certainly wasn't thinking about issues such as flag-burning, rap music, pornography, and the Internet.

2. *The First Amendment is not just for the benefit of people or organizations that want to disseminate information—it's also for the benefit of the people who want or need to receive that information.* Even if you never work in journalism or broadcasting, write a letter to the editor, work in the entertainment industry, or stand up in front of the city council and make a political speech, you still benefit from the First Amendment because you are a potential receiver of information disseminated by others.

The Supreme Court has made this point several times in recent cases dealing with the rights of advertisers. The court has ruled that the First Amendment is not there only to protect the rights of the advertisers to send you that information— it also protects your right to receive that information if you choose to. This is a fairly recent development in First Amendment theory, and whether the concept of "press freedom" can be interpreted in such a way is worthy of discussion. (Cases in this area are discussed in Chapter 12.)

The telemarketing industry has tried, with less success, to make a similar argument. Consumer protection groups that want to restrict the telemarketing business say that as many as 95 percent of the people don't want to be bothered by these telephone calls. The industry has responded that while restrictions on telemarketing may be intended to protect the privacy of those 95 percent, they are also limiting the First Amendment rights of the 5 percent who want to receive that information.

3. *The First Amendment cannot be superseded by state or local laws or government actions.* Because of the Fourteenth Amendment's equal protection clause, an individual's national citizenship takes priority over his or her citizenship of a state, county, or city. Therefore, no state or local law can invalidate or take priority over any federal law or constitutional right. In the case of free speech, this means that just as the federal government cannot restrict one's free speech rights, neither can a state, county, or city government agency.

Many states have free speech clauses in their constitutions, but most simply reinforce rights already guaranteed by the U.S. Constitution. The constitution of Arizona, for example, states that citizens of that state "may freely speak, write, and publish on all subjects, being responsible for the abuse of that right." The latter clause clarifies that free-speech rights do not protect a person from libel suits or other consequences, perhaps based on the Blackstonian Doctrine (explained in the following chapter).

While the Fourteenth Amendment expands the scope of the First Amendment to include all levels and forms of government—not just Congress—the First Amendment does not apply to private organizations and employers. Therefore, when individuals accuse their employers or the associations to which they belong of violating their First Amendment rights, they are incorrect.

4. *Free speech cases are more interesting if they are examined against the backdrop of what else is happening in the country at the time.* Some of the more significant First Amendment cases in Supreme Court history date back to the 1920s, when America entered the "roaring twenties," was basking in the glow of military success in World War I, was beginning to expand its influence around the world, and was witnessing the rise of Communism in Russia.

Highlights of other decades, and their impact on First Amendment cases, include:

1930s—The Great Depression.
1940s—World War II.
1950s—Communist witch hunt; beginning of the Cold War.

1960s—The era of anti-Vietnam war protests and the beginning of the modern civil rights movement.

1970s—Watergate and the era of political corruption and subsequent campaign finance reform. During this era, the federal government attempted to suppress criticism of the establishment, a practice that has continued throughout the past decades.

1980s—The Reagan era and resurgence of patriotism; acknowledgment that society should allow for some level of discontent.

1990s—America enters the age of the Internet and realizes the free speech issues that come with it.

2000s—Post–September 11; the age of terrorism.

5. *Many provisions of the First Amendment are not supported by public opinion.* When researchers conduct opinion surveys on freedom of speech, they find that the public tends to support free speech in the abstract, but not in the specifics such as flag-burning, pornography, or other matters dealing with decisions of taste. In the years following the September 11, 2001, terrorist attacks, support for First Amendment freedoms such as the rights of individuals to criticize the government and the rights of journalists to scrutinize American military operations overseas dropped dramatically. More recent surveys indicate support for the First Amendment has rebounded somewhat. But a surprising number of Americans still say the press has too much freedom (39 percent), the Constitution should be amended to prohibit burning the American flag as a sign of political protest (35 percent), newspapers should not be allowed to criticize the U.S. military about its strategy and performance (38 percent), and public school students should not be allowed to wear clothing bearing photographs or messages that others may find offensive (67 percent). In areas related to broadcasting, 66 percent of Americans said they would like to see the government restrict sexually explicit content on broadcast television, and 35 percent said that the government should provide stricter regulation of content on cable television.[2]

Levels of Speech

Most speech can be classified as either obtrusive or non-obtrusive (or unobtrusive). **Obtrusive speech** means the material is forced onto children or uninterested adults; a type of speech that cannot be easily avoided. An example would be a speech in a public place amplified by a megaphone or other device that makes it difficult for those nearby to avoid. **Non-obtrusive speech** is that which can easily be avoided, such as what takes place in an indoor movie theater or video rental store.

The majority of speech falls somewhere between the two extremes. Examples include broadcasting or outdoor advertising. While some would argue that both are intrusive (and the Supreme Court has ruled that television and radio have the potential to be obtrusive), they are easier to avoid than some of the examples listed above.

First Amendment Values

Legal scholars have established five values to explain the need for the First Amendment's free speech and free press clauses:

   1. *Search for the truth.* Also known as the "marketplace of ideas," this value states that free speech is necessary for society to discuss and evaluate conflicting political ideas. In the 1919 case of *Abrams v. United States*, Justice Oliver Wendell Holmes wrote in his dissenting opinion that "the best test of truth is the power of the thought to get itself accepted in the competition of the market."[3]

   This value has been a common theme of philosophical literature for centuries. In 1644, English poet and essayist John Milton, accused of violating his country's laws against unlicensed publication, responded with a lengthy work titled *Areopagitica*, in which he argued that licensing deprives citizens of knowledge and ideas that could improve their lives.[4] In his 1859 essay *On Liberty*, English philosopher John Stuart Mill wrote that he supported free expression because he believed people should always be open to new ideas instead of being inclined to censor them without a fair hearing. He added that people need to be exposed to false ideas in order to value those that are true.[5]

   Today, free speech advocacy organizations such as the Freedom Forum First Amendment Center at Vanderbilt University claim that the First Amendment gives Americans the right to be wrong. "If we're free to be wrong, we're also free to be right," the center explains in one of its informational brochures. "The First Amendment allows us to judge the difference between good ideas and bad ones by providing a protected, public space in which competing ideas can prove their worth—and within which equally valuable ideas can co-exist. It gives us the right to hear all sides of every issue and to make our own judgments without governmental interference or control."[6]

   Other defenders of freedom of expression worry that any limitation on such rights might open the door to more restrictions in the future. Using an argumentative technique called the **slippery slope,** they use the example of book banning in school libraries. School board officials sometimes decide that it is permissible to remove a controversial book because it is "just one book" and ask "what's the harm?" Civil liberties groups and other opponents of such action claim that if such a precedent is set, other less controversial books may be at risk in the future.

   2. *An informed electorate.* This value states that free speech and a free press are necessary in order to help citizens make informed decisions about which candidates and issues to vote for and against. Free press advocates claim that journalists need First Amendment protections in order to effectively investigate the qualifications and backgrounds of political candidates and to gather background information on critical public issues.

   3. *Check on government power.* This value states that the media need a free press guarantee in order to fulfill their role of "watchdogs" of government. Free press advocates claim that investigative journalism is necessary to prevent and uncover government corruption and that such aggressive journalism is only possible under the protection of the First Amendment. When explaining the importance of this function of the media, free press advocates often point to the Watergate scandal of the early 1970s. Without First Amendment protections, they claim, the political corruption of that era might not have been uncovered.

4. *Orderly societal change.* This value states that free speech represents a "safety valve" through which ideas can be debated and evaluated, and conflicts can be resolved peacefully rather than violently. Examples include the opportunity to "blow off steam" by participating in displays of hate speech, writing letters to the editor of a newspaper, making public speeches or debates, or staging peaceful demonstrations, instead of choosing more violent and less constructive alternatives. Observers point to countries without free speech protection, where change takes place only as a result of the violent overthrow of a repressive government, as evidence to support the need for free speech protections.

5. *Personal fulfillment and artistic expression.* This value refers to providing an outlet for forms of creative expression, even those that may be controversial in nature, such as pornography. Although this value was likely not part of the founding fathers' discussion of the First Amendment more than two centuries ago, it is often cited today. The expansion of the First Amendment's scope to include entertainment is discussed in Chapter 4; there is some concern that stripping the entertainment industry of its First Amendment protections may also weaken the degree to which the First Amendment protects political expression.

Hierarchy of First Amendment Protection

Legal scholars who track the decisions of the U.S. Supreme Court have documented that certain types of expression consistently get treated in certain ways, providing some degree of predictability. The various forms of communication can be placed into one of three levels, known as the First Amendment hierarchy, with case law traditionally providing some forms of expression with more constitutional protection than others.

At the highest level of protection—nearly absolute—are categories called political speech and religious expression. **Political speech** is defined as "news or opinion about government or public affairs." **Religious expression** is any communication related to a person's spiritual beliefs, or lack thereof. Like any other form of speech, political speech and religious expression can be spoken, written, or broadcast, and may take the form of leaflets, posters, or public speeches.[7]

At the middle level on the hierarchy are forms of speech that receive some (but not absolute) protection. Those forms of expression include **commercial speech** (truthful advertising), **hate speech,** (defined in the following section), and **non-obscene sexual expression** (entertainment of a sexual nature that does not meet the definition of obscenity).

A 2006 anti-abortion protest near the U.S. Capitol in Washington, D.C.

Jehovah's Witnesses spread their message on a University campus. Under the First Amendment, religious communication receives a high degree of protection.

At the bottom of the hierarchy are forms of expression that receive no protection at all—**defamation, obscenity, false advertising,** and **fighting words.**

Most Protection	Political speech
	Religious expression
Some Protection	Hate speech
	Commercial speech
	Non-obscene sexual expression
No Protection	Defamation
	Fighting words
	False advertising
	Obscenity

What Does Freedom of the Press Mean?

For the first 160 years of First Amendment court cases (most of which were argued in the federal court system), "freedom of the press" was interpreted to refer only to the rights of individuals and the media to disseminate information. In numerous cases, such as *Near v. Minnesota* (1931) and *New York Times v. United States* (1971), the Supreme Court has ruled in favor of the media's right to disseminate truthful information without fear of punishment.[8] In many such cases, the Supreme Court cites one or more of the traditional First Amendment values discussed earlier in this chapter, such as encouraging the free exchange of ideas or protecting the media's role as "government watchdogs."

Today, one of the issues tangential to the discussion of a free press is whether terms such as *press, media,* and *journalism* should be limited to their traditional connotations (such as newspapers, magazines, radio, and television) or should be expanded to included Internet-based publications, personal web pages, and blogs.

When any government agency or official takes legal action in an attempt to limit your free speech rights, the burden of proof is always on the government agency or official to explain why your rights should be limited, as opposed to you bearing the burden of proof to explain why those rights should not be limited.

In addition to the right to disseminate information, two other aspects of the First Amendment were debated beginning in the middle of the twentieth century: the First Amendment right of confidentiality and the First Amendment right of access.

"Right of confidentiality" is the media's claim that they have the right to protect the identity of their sources. It was first raised in the 1958 case of *Garland v. Torre,* in which a federal appeals court ruled against a reporter who refused to testify in a criminal trial, but acknowledged the merit of the reporter's claim. "Compulsory disclosure of a journalist's confidential sources of information may entail an abridgement of press freedom by imposing some limitation upon the availability of news," the court admitted.[9]

Today, many states have "shield laws" that protect this privilege, but the right is not absolute. In *Branzburg v. Hayes* (1972), for example, the Supreme Court ruled that a state's shield law does not allow reporters to protect the identity of their sources in cases in which the needs of law enforcement outweigh the reporters' right to protect their confidential relationships.[10]

"Right of access" is the media's claim that they should have nearly unlimited access to news events and locations. The courts agree that as a general principle, the media must have access to news events and locations in order to do an effective job of gathering news. But the courts have also ruled that such rights can be limited in certain situations. For example, the media do not have unlimited access to cover criminal trials and other legal proceedings, and judges have the right to bar the media from parts of a trial in order to protect the privacy of witnesses and prevent excessive pre-trial publicity that might harm the defendant's right to a fair trial. The courts have also ruled that journalists cannot have unlimited access to the sites of automobile accidents[11] or airplane crashes,[12] for the safety of both the journalists and the general public. Examples are discussed in Chapter 8.

Clarifications on the Hierarchy

Corporate Advertising: Political or Commercial Speech?

Many forms of communication are difficult to categorize, as they may contain elements of both political and commercial speech. When the courts must decide if a specific communication is political speech or commercial speech, it does so based on the content—not on who is speaking or in what format. For example, private companies often use paid advertising to encourage voters to approve or reject issues at the ballot box. But just because the company is a commercial interest doesn't automatically make its paid advertising commercial speech—the company still has the right to political speech. And the fact that the company had to pay to put the information in the form of an advertisement does not disqualify it from being political speech.

Hate Speech vs. Fighting Words

The categories of hate speech and fighting words are commonly confused, but are quite different in the eyes of the Supreme Court. **Hate speech** is defined as hostile (but non-violent) speech aimed at a group of people (not specific individuals) based on race, religion, ethnicity, sex, or sexual orientation.[13] **Fighting words** are direct personal insults made against a specific person or persons in their presence, those words "which by their very utterance inflict injury or tend to incite an immediate breach of the peace."[14] The First Amendment, the courts ruled in a 1994 case, "does not protect a speaker who eggs his audience on to commit a violent act, whether against himself or against others.[15]

In *Terminiello v. Chicago* (1949), believed to be one of the first legal cases to differentiate between hate speech and fighting words (even though the term *hate speech* did not yet exist), the Supreme Court overturned the conviction of a Catholic priest who had criticized Jews and African Americans while addressing a group of World War II veterans at a public meeting. The priest had been arrested for violating a city ordinance that prohibited speech that "stirs the public to anger, invites dispute, brings about a condition of unrest, or creates a disturbance." The Court, noting that many forms of speech could fall into that category, ruled that the law was too broad because it included speech that *might lead to injury,* while the fighting words doctrine applied only to words that *inflicted injury.*[16]

Another significant "hate speech" case was *Brandenburg v. Ohio* (1969). The case began with a Ku Klux Klan rally held on private property in Hamilton County, Ohio, far outside the metropolitan area of Cincinnati. A local television station sent a film crew to prepare a news story about the event, and the resulting interviews included anti-black and anti-Jewish language and criticism of the federal government. The state of Ohio had a law that made it illegal to advocate violence against any particular group, and Clarence Brandenburg, one of the individuals interviewed for the news story, was arrested and convicted under the Ohio law for making racial threats. When the case was appealed, the Supreme Court ruled in Brandenburg's favor and invalidated the Ohio law because it dealt with threats that were neither immediate nor specific.[17]

In *Nelson v. Streeter* (1994), the Supreme Court described hate speech as "words or symbols that are offensive, hurtful, or wounding and are directed at racial or ethnic characteristics, gender, religious affiliation, or sexual preference." The case involved an art student who entered his provocative painting—portraying deceased Chicago Mayor Harold Washington in women's underwear—in an art exhibition. After the incident sparked threats (but no actual violence), several city officials attempted to have the painting removed, claiming it constituted fighting words. The court, instead, deemed it to be hate speech.[18] In that case and several that came before and after, the courts determined that hate speech, while objectionable, must be protected as part of the "rough and tumble" discourse that is part of a democratic, open society. These rulings fall in line with the last two First Amendment values discussed earlier in this chapter—the importance of free speech as a "safety valve" through which citizens can "blow off steam" and as an outlet for personal fulfillment and expression.

Significant "fighting words" cases were *Chaplinsky v. New Hampshire* (1942) and *Cohen v. California* (1971). The Chaplinsky case began when Walter Chaplinsky, a Jehovah's Witness, was preaching on a downtown street corner. He made outrageous comments about other religions and handed out literature that was critical of those religions. The police did not try to arrest him; they only tried to warn him that the crowd appeared threatening and that his personal safety was at risk.

Chaplinsky then began to call one of the officers names, so the officer arrested him for violating a New Hampshire law that prohibited name-calling of police officers. A trial court found Chaplinsky guilty, finding that because he was

A Ku Klux Klan march in Washington D.C. The KKK is one of numerous controversial groups whose objectionable public communication is protected as "hate speech" by the First Amendment.

arrested for his name-calling and not for his preaching, his First Amendment rights of free speech and free exercise of religion had not been violated. This U.S. Supreme Court agreed and issued what became known as the fighting words doctrine.[19] The fighting words doctrine is still cited in court cases today and serves as a reminder that free speech rights are not absolute; types of speech that promote or advocate violence fall outside of First Amendment protection.

Almost thirty years later, the court determined that the fighting words doctrine did not apply in *Cohen v. California*. The case began when Paul Cohen walked through a courthouse in Los Angeles wearing a leather jacket, the back of which carried the phrase, "fuck the draft." Cohen was arrested and charged with vulgarity in public, but on appeal, the Supreme Court ruled that the words on his jacket were considered political expression, were not a direct personal insult, and did not meet the definition of fighting words as established by *Chaplinsky*. In its written decision, the court ruled that "one man's vulgarity is another man's lyric," and that logic has subsequently been applied in a variety of cases over the last three decades.[20]

A recent application of the hate speech and fighting words definitions can be found in the debate over the threatening tactics employed by anti-abortion protestors. Vicki A. Saporta, executive director of the National Abortion Federation, points to the example of an anti-abortion group that uses its website to encourage its members to murder physicians as a case of speech that crosses the line from hateful speech to fighting words. "When speech goes beyond advocating hateful beliefs to advocating violent, criminal acts, such as the murder of physicians, it crosses the line and becomes unacceptable," Saporta says.[21]

In numerous cases, the Supreme Court has struggled with the question: *Is cross-burning a form of hate speech or fighting words?* As discussed earlier, the first cross-burning case to reach the U.S. Supreme Court was *Brandenburg v. Ohio* (1969). Although the law regarding "racial threats" did not specifically mention cross-burning, the state of Ohio cited it as an example of the behavior that the statute was intended to address. Since the Brandenburg case, many states have enacted laws that outlaw cross-burning as a form of racial intimidation, but the courts have not been consistent in how those laws are applied.

In the 1992 case of *RAV v. City of St. Paul,* the Supreme Court struck down a city ordinance that banned cross-burning because it was too specific—instead of banning fighting words in general, it banned only those based on race, color, creed, religion, or gender. By implication, the Court ruled, the ordinance would have allowed fighting words aimed at other groups. In questioning city attorneys during oral arguments, Justice Antonin Scalia said, "If you want to prohibit fighting words, prohibit fighting words. But why pick only these particular purposes— race, color, creed, religion, and gender? What about other fighting words?"

The Court also determined that the city should have prosecuted the defendant for more tangible offenses such as trespassing or arson rather than the content or the expression of the acts, which carries a significantly higher burden of proof. The court determined that the statute allowed too much opportunity for viewpoint discrimination; local officials, for example, could take advantage of the vagueness of the law to punish only those forms of objectionable speech that served their interests, while allowing other forms of objectionable speech to go unpunished. In writing the majority opinion, Scalia pointed out that "burning a cross in someone's front yard is reprehensible . . . But the city of St. Paul has sufficient means at its disposal to prevent such behavior without adding the First Amendment to the fire."[22]

The majority decision also implied that the trial court in Minnesota, which originally upheld the defendant's conviction, may have relied too much on the Chaplinsky definition of fighting words and should have instead applied the "clear and present danger" standard previously applied in cases in which citizens were punished for speech that advocated others to conduct violent acts (explained in more detail in Chapter 3).

A decade later, the Supreme Court dealt with the cross-burning issue again. In the 2003 case of *Virginia v. Black*, the Court upheld Virginia's cross-burning law, supporting the state's claim that its purpose was to prevent racial intimidation, not to limit speech. Some legal experts contend that the ruling in *Virginia v. Black* means that cross-burning is now considered fighting words rather than hate speech—especially if it is meant to intimidate or threaten a specific individual or family—but this issue is still subject to debate.[23]

An individual or group wishing to burn a cross still has a valid free speech claim, provided the act is not combined with an overt threat of violence to a specific person or family. For example, if you were to burn a cross on the lawn of an African American family in your neighborhood and attach a note saying "your house will be next," that would be considered a "hate crime," which is different from "hate speech."

Commercial Speech vs. False Advertising

Commercial speech—a euphemism for truthful advertising—receives some degree of First Amendment protection because, while not as important as political speech, it is nevertheless a source of information.

How does our society regulate advertising and not violate the First Amendment? Tobacco companies are not allowed to advertise their products on television. The Federal Trade Commission (FTC) enforces rules about the advertising on television and radio. The U.S. Postal Service enforces rules about direct mail advertising. City and county governments enforce rules about the size, location, and content of outdoor advertising. The courts have looked at all of those actions as limitations on commercial speech that do not violate the First Amendment.

False advertising, however, receives no First Amendment protection. In legal discussions of the advertising business, however, we tend to give advertising the benefit of the doubt regarding its truthfulness. Unless the FTC, a consumer advocacy group, or another party has accused an advertisement of being false, when the term *advertising* is used in a general sense, it is assumed to be truthful.

Obscenity vs. Non-Obscene Sexual Expression

Chapter 4 deals with the difference between *pornography* and *obscenity*, as the terms are often confused. Those terms will be discussed in more detail in that chapter, but for now, just remember that pornography is an artistic term rather than a legal term. Despite what your personal opinions may be about the issue, the courts look at pornography as a form of art—just like music, sculpture, painting, and ballet. In most cases, it falls under the category of non-obscene sexual expression—meaning that the government can regulate it but cannot prohibit it altogether. In several cases, the Supreme Court has referred to pornography as being "protected speech, but only marginally so"[24] and as speech that deserves a place "on the outer fringes of First Amendment protection."[25]

How do we regulate non-obscene sexual expression and not violate the First Amendment? City and county governments have zoning rules regarding the location of adult businesses. Publishers of adult magazines must abide by U.S. Postal Service rules about how the magazines are mailed. Many states also have rules about the sale of adult magazines and videos to minors.

Frequently Asked Questions about the First Amendment

1. *Why is the First Amendment so vague?* This is a question that political scientists and historians have debated for almost two centuries. Some believe that when James Madison penned the First Amendment to the Constitution in 1791, he was simply naïve in not anticipating the controversies and conflicts that would result from how the amendment would be interpreted in years to come. Other experts, however, believe that Madison knew exactly what he was doing: He wanted to create an amendment that could be flexible enough to be interpreted based on issues and technologies that would come along in the future. He probably did not anticipate issues such as flag-burning, cross-burning, rap music, and pornography, however. But that's why we have the U.S. Supreme Court.

2. *If defamatory content receives no First Amendment protection, why are defamation cases so difficult to win?* There are two reasons behind this. First, there is a high burden of proof in cases involving alleged defamation—some say the burden is much higher than in communication law in general. So it's not as simple as suing your local daily newspaper, television station, or Internet service provider after being offended by its content. Court rulings have found that even when they make a mistake that embarrasses an individual, the media's First Amendment right to report on matters of public interest allows them the "benefit of the doubt" in cases in which the individual affected cannot prove significant harm.

Second, the Supreme Court has determined that libel is a natural by-product of free speech. For example, in the 1964 case of *New York Times v. Sullivan*—the most famous libel suit in history—the Court recognized that during any discussion of a controversial or emotional issue, individuals are likely to offend others in the content of their speech or publications. The Court ruled that the First Amendment should allow individuals and organizations the opportunity to "blow off steam" without fear of litigation.[26] In their 1997 book, *Freedom of Speech in the Marketplace of Ideas,* communication law professors Douglas M. Fraleigh and Joseph S. Tuman wrote that "when the government allows the target of defamatory speech to recover damages, it is discouraging that speech from entering the marketplace of ideas."[27]

Others disagree with the "blowing off steam" metaphor, however, and claim that a more appropriate metaphor is "journalistic malpractice"—the need for strong libel law to serve as a deterrent to sloppy journalism. That concept will be addressed in Chapter 6.

3. *The First Amendment says that "Congress shall make no law . . ." But what about the state legislature, the county commission, or the city government?* The Fourteenth Amendment, passed in 1868, includes the "equal protection clause" that says that your status as an American takes priority over your status as a citizen of a state, county, or city. Therefore, just as the First Amendment does not allow the federal government to limit your rights, it also means that no state, county, or city government, agency, or official can limit your rights.

4. *Are my First Amendment rights absolute?* No. In numerous Supreme Court cases (the most famous of which is *Cox v. New Hampshire* in 1941), the Court has ruled that the government can make reasonable "time, place, and manner" restrictions on speech. A current example of this distinction is the limitation on protests outside of abortion clinics. While protestors do have the First Amendment right to express their opinions, they cannot do so at 2 a.m. if the clinic is located in a residential neighborhood (a limitation based on time). They also cannot protest on private property (a limitation on place) and cannot block the entrance to the clinic (a limitation on manner).

5. *Does my child have First Amendment rights at school?* Somewhat. Even though a 1969 Supreme Court case (*Tinker v. Des Moines Independent Community School District*)[28] established the principle that students do not "shed their constitutional rights to freedom of speech or expression at the schoolhouse gate," these rights were essentially weakened in two cases in the 1980s. In the 1986 case of *Bethel v. Fraser*[29] the court ruled that students' rights are not "co-existent" with those of adults, and that the school was not required to tolerate expression that was "inconsistent with its educational mission." Two years later, in *Hazelwood v. Kuhlmeier*[30], the Court ruled that principals of public schools may censor student newspapers if the censorship is "done in a reasonable manner" and "serves a valid purpose." The Court determined that a high school newspaper, produced in a laboratory environment and under the supervision of a school employee, is not a public forum and is therefore not analogous to a daily newspaper with regard to First Amendment protections. Today, courts give principals of public schools broad authority to limit expression by enforcing dress codes and censoring student newspapers. These issues are discussed in more detail in Chapter 5.

Point/Counterpoint: Punishing Hate Speech

Why Hate Speech Should be Punished

Advocates of hate-speech legislation, such as that outlawing cross-burning, point out that an expression of hate need not reach the stage of physical violence to deserve punishment; actions such as racial intimidation are enough to warrant law-enforcement intervention.

Those advocates claim that the prohibition of cross-burning and other expressions of hate are not attempts to limit speech, only to prevent intimidation that may lead to violence. "A burning cross—standing alone and without explanation—is understood in our society as a message of intimidation," prosecutors argued in the 2003 Supreme Court case of *Virginia v. Black*. In an *amicus curiae* ("friend of the court") brief submitted on behalf of the state, the U.S. Solicitor General added that, "A person has no First Amendment right to burn a cross in order to intimidate others . . . intimidation is not protected speech."[31]

Why Hate Speech Should Not be Punished

Because of the First Amendment values of "orderly societal change" and "blowing off steam" discussed earlier in this chapter, opponents of efforts to ban hate speech claim that such efforts would not eliminate the problem—they would only hide it from view. "Abolishing the language reflecting hate will not change the way people think, but instead will force racial and ethnic hatred underground and into the dark, where it is the most comfortable," claims civil libertarian Nat Hentoff.[32]

In their 2004 book, *The Four Freedoms of the First Amendment,* authors Craig R. Smith and David M. Hunsaker identify hate speech as a "pervasive problem" for racial, religious, and sexual minorities that can "undermine self-esteem, cause isolation, and result in violence . . . words can injure reputations and reinforce and/or maintain social inequality in the home, in the classroom, in the workplace, and in the nation." They stop short of advocating its abolishment, however. Instead, they claim the First Amendment does not impose a "good taste" standard on the nation. Using the example of speech codes and computer usage policies intended to eliminate hate speech on college campuses, Smith and Hunsaker claim that such actions "invade privacy, violate rights of association, and chill free speech."[33]

The Supreme Court calls burning a cross and similar expressions of contempt as "symbolic speech" that are protected under the First Amendment, especially when they take place out of view of the general public (such as the case in *Brandenburg v. Ohio*). While such expression is offensive to many, the Court believes it is important to allow groups to express ideas such as contempt for minorities or dissatisfaction with the government by "blowing off steam" rather than through violent alternatives.

Chapter Summary

The First Amendment is a controversial and often misunderstood document that is subject to a variety of interpretations—by both courts and citizens. There are a number of values associated with First Amendment freedoms, including helping citizens to evaluate conflicting ideas in their search for the "truth," protecting the press as it carries out its role as "government watchdog," and providing citizens with the opportunity to "blow off steam" while discussing and debating controversial public issues.

The First Amendment can be viewed as either an abstract document or a blueprint for resolving real-world conflicts involving free speech. As a result, public opinion polls often show that citizens support the First Amendment in terms of its abstract components, such as "free speech" and "free press," but are often reluctant to support it in terms of specific forms of speech that may be controversial or objectionable. In addition, polls show support for the First Amendment waxes and wanes based largely on what is happening in society at the time, such as war, economic crises, or social and political unrest.

The First Amendment applies to a number of communication categories, including political speech, religious expression, hate speech, commercial speech, non-obscene sexual expression, defamation, fighting words, obscenity, and false advertising. These nine forms of communication can be placed on a hierarchy that provides a graphic illustration of their relative importance, and case law provides a number of rationale for providing some forms of expression with more constitutional protection than others.

SOCRATIC DIALOGUE QUESTIONS

1. If a "vote of confidence" were to be taken on the First Amendment today, would the American people vote to keep it or abolish it? Provide examples to support your answer.

2. Of the five theories to explain the need for the First Amendment, which one(s) do you believe are most important? Are there any that could be discarded?

3. Do you agree with the distribution of the various types of expression found on the First Amendment hierarchy? If you had the opportunity to revise the model, what changes would you make?

4. You work for a public utility (telephone or electric company) and purchase advertising space in the local newspaper. Your ads are not designed to promote your services but to encourage voters to pass a new state law that will change how your industry is regulated. Is the advertisement commercial speech or political speech? Should those two types of advertising be treated the same in terms of First Amendment protection?

5. By providing some degree of First Amendment protection to controversial forms of speech such as flag-burning, hate speech, defamation, and non-obscene sexual expression, the Supreme Court is in effect determining that these forms of speech have some social value. What social values do you think the Supreme Court has in mind when it makes those determinations?

6. Find at least one case in Chapter 2 with which you strongly disagree with the court ruling (in the final resolution of the case) and be prepared to share your opinion with the class.

GLOSSARY OF TERMS

Commercial speech   Advertising and other forms of communication intended to promote a product, service, or other commercial idea. Unless otherwise indicated, the terms *advertising* and *commercial speech* are used with the presumption that the messages contained within are truthful.

Defamation   Published or broadcast communication that harms a person's or organization's reputation or financial standing (covered in more detail in Chapter 6).

False advertising   Commercial messages that are untruthful (explained in more detail in Chapter 12).

Fighting words   Communication intended by the speaker to frighten, intimidate, harass, or threaten individuals, usually targeted at members of minority groups. A more formal definition came out of the 1942 Supreme Court case, *Chaplinsky v. New Hampshire.*[34]

Hate speech   Hostile (but non-violent) speech aimed at a group of people (not specific individuals) based on race, religion, ethnicity, sex, or sexual orientation.

Non-obscene sexual expression   Communication of a sexual nature, such as nude dancing, topless dancing, adult magazines, and videos, that may be objectionable but which are not offensive enough to be considered obscene.

Non-obtrusive speech   Speech that can be easily avoided by uninterested persons. Same as "unobtrusive."

Obscenity   Literature or photographic images of a sexual nature that are so offensive as to receive no First Amendment protection.

Obtrusive speech   Speech that is so pervasive that it cannot be avoided by uninterested persons.

Political speech   Communication consisting of news or opinion about government or public affairs.

Pure speech   Communication in any form that overtly expresses an idea or opinion (as opposed to symbolic speech).

Religious expression   Any communication related to a person's spiritual beliefs, or lack thereof.

Slippery slope   An argumentative technique in which an individual or group opposing an idea claims that adoption of that idea may lead to a gradual drift toward a negative outcome.

Speech   Any oral, written, pictorial, or other expression of an idea or opinion.

Symbolic speech   Communication in any form that expresses an idea or opinion through the use of action rather than words, such as wearing a black ribbon to show grief for a deceased person or burning the flag to demonstrate contempt for the government.

NOTES

1. *Texas v. Johnson,* 491 U.S. 397 (1989).
2. "The State of the First Amendment 2005." Nashville, Tenn.: The Freedom Forum First Amendment Center, 2005.
3. *Abrams v. United States,* 250 U.S. 616 (1919).
4. George H. Sabine, ed., John Milton's *Areopagatica* and *On Education.* Northbrook, Ill.: AHM Publishing, 1951.
5. Peter J. Woolley and Albert J. Papa, ed. *American Politics: Core Arguments and Current Controversies.* Upper Saddle River, N.J.: Prentice Hall, 2002, pp. 312–14.
6. "The First Amendment: The Amendment That Keeps Us Free." Nashville, Tenn.: The Freedom Forum First Amendment Center, 1996.
7. The definitions of political speech and religious expression are condensed and paraphrased from numerous sources.
8. *Near v. Minnesota,* 283 U.S. 697 (1931) and *New York Times v. United States,* 403 U.S. 713. (1971).
9. *Garland v. Torre,* 259 F.2d 545 (1958).
10. *Branzburg v. Hayes,* 408 U.S. 665 (1972).
11. *State of New Jersey v. Lashinsky,* 401 A.2d 1121 (1979).
12. *City of Oak Creek, Wisconsin v. King,* 436 N.W. 2d 285 (1989).
13. This definition is condensed and paraphrased from numerous sources.
14. *Chaplinsky v. New Hampshire,* 315 U.S. 568 (1942).
15. *Nelson v. Streeter,* 16 F.3d 145 (1994).
16. *Terminiello v. Chicago,* 337 U.S. 1 (1949).
17. *Brandenburg v. Ohio,* 395 U.S. 444 (1969).
18. *Nelson v. Streeter,* 16 F.3d 145 (1994).
19. *Chaplinsky v. New Hampshire,* 315 U.S. 568 (1942).
20. *Cohen v. California,* 403 U.S. 15 (1971).
21. "Yes or No." *First Amendment News* (February 1998): 7.
22. *RAV v. City of St. Paul,* 505 U.S. 377 (1992).
23. *Virginia v. Black,* 538 U.S. 343 (2003).
24. *Barnes v. Glen Theatre,* 501 U.S. 560 (1991).
25. *Pope v. Illinois,* 107 S.Ct. 1918 (1987).
26. *New York Times v. Sullivan,* 376 U.S. 254 (1964).
27. Douglas M. Fraleigh and Joseph S. Tuman, *Freedom of Speech in the Marketplace of Ideas.* New York, N.Y.: St. Martin's Press, 1987, p. 196.
28. *Tinker v. Des Moines Independent Community School District,* 393 U.S. 503 (1969).
29. *Bethel School District v. Fraser,* 478 U.S. 675 (1986).
30. *Hazelwood School District v. Kuhlmeier,* 484 U.S. 260 (1988).
31. *Virginia v. Black,* 538 U.S. 343 (2003).
32. Nat Hentoff, *Free Speech for Me—But Not for Thee.* New York, N.Y.: Harper Collins, 1992, p. 370.
33. Craig R. Smith and David M. Hunsaker, *The Four Freedoms of the First Amendment.* Long Grove, Ill.: Waveland Press, 2004, p.161.
34. *Chaplinsky v. New Hampshire,* 315 U.S. 568 (1942).

CHAPTER
3

The First Amendment and Political Speech

A free press is a liberty that cannot be limited without being lost.

Thomas Jefferson

Even the most stringent protection of free speech would not protect a man who falsely shouts "fire" in a crowded theatre.

Justice Oliver Wendell Holmes
Schenck v. United States, 1919

At the heart of the First Amendment is the recognition of the fundamental importance of the free flow of ideas and opinions on matters of public interest and concern . . . . In the world of debate about public affairs, many things done with motives that are less than admirable are nevertheless protected by the First Amendment.

Chief Justice William Rehnquist
Hustler v. Falwell, 1988

I recall a news story about a man who spread manure across a downtown street on the morning of a parade. When he was arrested, his defense was that he was protesting the theme of the parade and was simply exercising his First Amendment right of free speech. When one of our reporters asked me if a person had a First Amendment right to spread manure in public, I replied, "only if you're a politician."

Philip Gailey
Editorial Page Editor
St. Petersburg Times

LEARNING OBJECTIVES

As a result of reading this chapter, students should:

- Understand why some categories of speech are given more First Amendment protection than others and the Supreme Court's rationale in providing varying levels of protection.
- Understand the various types of prior restraint, as well as the history of prior restraint cases, and how Supreme Court decisions continue to affect the rights of journalists as well as those of ordinary citizens.

- Understand how common-law rules such as those involving different types of forums (traditional public forums, limited public forums, and nonpublic forums) and equivalent function rules affect our free speech rights.
- Understand the four tests that have been applied to evaluate conflicts involving political speech.

First Amendment Tests

In the early and mid-1900s, the U.S. Supreme Court developed four tests for evaluating political speech: the bad tendency test, the clear and present danger test, and a pair of tests known as balancing tests.

Bad Tendency Test

Applying the **bad tendency test,** developed in the early 1900s against the backdrop of World War I and the years that followed, speech could be restricted if there was any credible evidence that it could result in violent acts.

One example of a case involving the bad tendency test was *Gitlow v. New York* (1925). Benjamin Gitlow was producing anti-government pamphlets and distributing them on street corners in New York. The pamphlets advocated "striking against all capitalistic businesses" and suggested an overthrow of the federal government. Gitlow was accused of violating a New York law that made it illegal to advocate violence against the U.S. government, even though there was no evidence that anyone was taking Gitlow's ideas seriously. Gitlow was prosecuted and convicted in a trial court and appealed his case to the U.S. Supreme Court. The high court ruled that the New York law did not violate the First Amendment and that the government was justified in suppressing speech or utterances "that by their very nature involve danger to the public peace and to the security of the state." Applying the "bad tendency test," the court said that although the leaflets themselves might not be harmful, they might become the starting point for something larger and more dangerous.[1]

Because of its potential to be used to limit legitimate criticism of the government, the bad tendency test is no longer applied.

Clear and Present Danger Test

During World War I, Congress passed the Espionage Act of 1917 in order to limit the activities of citizens protesting American involvement in the war. As a result, more than 2,000 citizens were prosecuted under the law, with more than half being convicted. Some of the charges were based on comments that would be judged as rather harmless by today's standards, such as those claiming the war violated religious doctrine or criticizing the involvement of the Red Cross. These prosecutions were troubling because they sought to punish citizens not only for what they did but for what they thought, and legal historians have concluded that the law resulted in few, if any, convictions for sustentative interference with the war effort.[2]

Against this backdrop, the Supreme Court developed the **clear and present danger test,** which established a higher burden of proof for restricting speech. Under this test, political speech must do more than create a bad tendency; it must present a "clear and present danger," that is, a person's speech must create a "high likelihood of harm," such as that which motivates the audience to carry out violent acts. The clear and present danger test was first applied in 1919 and was commonly applied in free speech cases up to and including the 1950s and 1960s, even though it was last successfully used to limit speech in 1951.

The conflict that created the standard was the 1919 case of *Schenck v. United States*. Plaintiff Charles Schenck was an officer of the Socialist Party in Philadelphia during World War I. A local newspaper published lists of men who had passed their draft board examinations, and Schenck and his associates printed 15,000 leaflets and mailed them to men on the list. The leaflets argued that the war was wrong and that the draft was a violation of the Thirteenth Amendment ban on slavery and involuntary servitude.

The federal government alleged that the anti-draft literature violated the Espionage Act, and Schenck was convicted and sentenced to six months in prison. The case went to the Supreme Court, which upheld the conviction of Schenck because it ruled a "clear and present danger" existed. Justice Oliver Wendell Holmes coined the term "clear and present danger" and wrote that "even the most stringent protection of free speech would not protect a man who falsely shouts fire in a crowded theatre." He further argued that criticisms of the government or the military that might be considered harmless during peacetime should not be tolerated during times of war, and that such comments were not constitutionally protected.[3]

The same year, the court made a similar ruling in *Abrams v. United States*, another case that began during World War I. Plaintiff Jacob Abrams and some of his friends were convicted of distributing anti-war literature (again, in violation of the Espionage Act) and appealed the case to the Supreme Court. But the Supreme Court upheld the conviction of Abrams because it ruled a "clear and present danger" existed. It reiterated its opinion in the *Schenck* case, determining that during war time, the government is given more discretion to punish speech it deems to be potentially harmful to the war effort. Ironically, those disagreeing with the majority opinion included Holmes, the same justice who took the opposite view in *Schenck*. Holmes, in a dissenting opinion co-authored by Justice Louis Brandeis, wrote that the government could not "forbid all effort to change the mind of the country" and there was no immediate danger posed by the distribution of what they called "a silly leaflet by an unknown man."[4]

The "clear and present danger" was last used to uphold a conviction in the 1951 case of *Dennis v. United States*. The plaintiff was Eugene Dennis, a member of the American Communist Party, who advocated the overthrow of the U.S. government. He was arrested and convicted under the Smith Act, a World War II–era law that prohibited such advocacy. The Supreme Court upheld the conviction because it determined that a "clear and present danger" existed. The case was argued against the backdrop of the Cold War between the United States and Russia, and in upholding his conviction, the Court cited the specificity of Dennis's comments and potential for violence should he and his cohorts be successful in convincing others to join them and carry out his proposal.[5]

The first major case in which the Supreme Court ruled that the "clear and present danger" standard was not met was the 1957 case of *Yates v. United States*. Plaintiff Oleta Yates and other members of the Communist Party of California were convicted of conspiring to overthrow the federal government, but the Supreme Court overturned their convictions because no direct illegal action was advocated and the government was unable to prove that a "clear and present danger" existed. Further, the Court distinguished the *Yates* case from previous cases in that her plans were not as well-developed and merely discussed, in an abstract way, what could be achieved by overthrowing the government, whereas previous cases, especially *Dennis*, dealt with more concrete plans.[6]

The Supreme Court made a similar ruling in *Brandenburg v. Ohio* (1969), determining that no "clear and present danger" was involved in the case of Ku Klux Klan members involved in vague and non-specific "hate speech" (see previous chapter) that took place at a Ku Klux Klan rally.[7]

Balancing Tests

Today, the tests most commonly applied are the **balancing tests,** meaning that the courts must find a balance between the needs of the citizens to exercise their free speech rights and the government's need to regulate speech that may be harmful. As applied to the field of journalism, this test requires the courts to balance the rights of reporters to cover the news with the rights of individuals to protect themselves through libel law, privacy law, and other civil actions.

In specific or **ad hoc balancing,** courts begin with a "clean slate" in evaluating specific and localized issues and judge each case on its own merits without preconceived notions of which side should prevail. This test is applied in cases such as an attempt to balance a newspaper's rights to cover the meetings of the city council or school board and the rights of those governmental bodies to claim the need to conduct certain aspects of their business in secret.

The **preferred position theory of balancing** states that rights protected by the Constitution take priority over other rights. For example, a political group's right to protest in a public park would take priority over the citizens' rights to use the park for more traditional (i.e., quieter) purposes because the political group's free speech rights originate within the Constitution, whereas the rights of the citizens to enjoy the peace and serenity of the park do not.

Supreme Court Tendencies in Cases Involving Political Speech

In addition to the "hierarchy of First Amendment protection" explained in the previous chapter, the Supreme Court also looks at six general characteristics of speech and expression when deciding First Amendment cases, especially those cases involving political speech: (1) the application of strict scrutiny, (2) a preference for content neutrality, (3) a bias against overbreadth and vagueness, (4) a recognition of the difference between regulating conduct and regulating speech, (5) the application of different standards for broadcast media and print media, and (6) a prohibition against "compelled speech."

Strict Scrutiny

Also called "heavy burden of proof," **strict scrutiny** refers to the court's tendency to place the burden of proof on the government to explain why it needs to restrict speech, as opposed to a citizen's obligation to explain why his or her speech should not be restricted.

Such rules did not exist early in the nation's history, however. Less than a decade after the states ratified the Bill of Rights, the United States was facing the threat of war from France, and Americans were divided as to how the country should respond to the threat. Because of the volatility of the public debate, Congress passed the Sedition Act of 1798, a law that was somewhat at odds with the First Amendment. The Sedition Act of 1798 established criminal penalties for anyone who "wrote, uttered, or published" any false, scandalous, or malicious writings against the government, Congress, or the president. For the next three years, the law was used to punish newspaper publishers, politicians, and common citizens. Fortunately the law came with an expiration date of March 4, 1801, and by that time war had been avoided. That same day Thomas Jefferson became president, and in his inaugural address he called for greater tolerance for freedom of expression.

The Fourteenth Amendment's equal protection clause, enacted three years after the Thirteenth Amendment formally abolished slavery, was intended in part to reinforce the Thirteenth Amendment and prevent individual states from re-instituting slavery on their own. But the clause also had a significant impact on newspaper publishers. Prior to the Civil War, many southern states had laws on the books that punished citizens for speaking or writing any words critical of slavery or in favor of its abolition, and the town council in Alton, Illinois, passed a resolution stating that the First Amendment did not apply to newspapers and magazines that published articles supporting abolition. Even without the Thirteenth and Fourteenth Amendments, those actions would have been found to violate the First Amendment if challenged. There is no case law to indicate this law was challenged in court. It did, however, create an atmosphere of hostility in the community and resulted in the editor of one Alton newspaper being murdered after continuing to publish anti-slavery editorials.

A state legislature may have good intentions when it attempts to prohibit controversial forms of expression such as pornography, exhibitions of hate speech, and flag-burning (as a form of political protest), but when those laws are challenged, lawyers defending the statutes will likely be unable to prove to the satisfaction of the court that the state's interest in limiting speech outweighs the First Amendment values at stake. In the 1963 case of *Bantam Books v. Sullivan*, for example, the Supreme Court ruled against the state of Rhode Island in its attempt to limit sales of literature it deemed to harm the state's youth because the state failed to meet its burden of proof. The court's majority decision claimed that "any system of prior restraints of expression comes to the court bearing heavy presumption against its constitutionality."[8]

Content Neutrality

The principle of **content neutrality** means that government restrictions on speech cannot be based on content but can be based on the **time, place, or manner** of the speech.

Although the concept of time, place, and manner was used in the free speech cases in the late 1930s, it is more commonly associated with the 1941 case of *Cox v. New Hampshire*. The conflict started when sixty-eight Jehovah's Witnesses were arrested for parading through a downtown area without a parade permit. After their arrest, they challenged the city ordinance that required the parade permit, claiming that it violated three of their First Amendment rights: speech, religion, and assembly. The state of New Hampshire claimed that parade permits were necessary—not to decide who could have a parade and who couldn't—but so local officials could know about the parade ahead of time in order to provide security personnel and trash pickup and to prevent problems caused by two or more groups wanting to have a parade at the same time. The Supreme Court agreed, and in issuing the decision, used a term that would became a major principle in First Amendment cases for the next six decades (and probably beyond)—that of "time, place, and manner." The *Cox* case is significant because it reaffirmed what the Supreme Court had stated in previous cases (including *Schenck* and *Abrams*)—that free speech rights are not absolute and that "reasonable" time, place, and manner restrictions are permissible.[9]

A more recent case with a similar outcome was *Heffron v. Krishna* (1981). The plaintiff was an official with the Minnesota State Agriculture Department, and part of his job was overseeing the Minnesota State Fair. The Hare Krishnas wanted to distribute religious literature and solicit money on the fairgrounds, but the Agriculture Department placed them in the same category with exhibitors, meaning that they had to apply for booth space, pay an exhibitor fee, and be limited to soliciting donations and distributing literature in that contained space. The Krishnas claimed these requirements infringed upon their First Amendment rights of free speech and free exercise of religion.

The Supreme Court, however, ruled in favor of the Agriculture Department and gave it the right to enforce its rules. The court's decision was based on two factors. First, the restriction was content neutral, meaning that the Agriculture Department was not trying to limit the content of the speech, only the place and the manner. Second, the Court ruled that the fairgrounds represented a **limited public forum;** because there was a limited amount of space on the property, the government had the right to regulate its use. The Court drew a distinction between a limited public forum and a **traditional public forum,** such as a downtown sidewalk or public park, where speech could not be limited to the same degree.[10]

Today, the concept of a limited public forum (sometimes known as a designated public forum) also applies to airport terminals, where political and religious activity can be limited. Courts sometimes use the term **non-public forum** to refer to prisons, military bases, and other government-supervised venues where expression can be limited with little or no recourse.

Ironically, shortly after the Krishna decision, the Supreme Court was faced with another public forum case—this time concerning the rights of citizens to protest on the steps of the Supreme Court building itself. In *U.S. v. Grace* (1983), the Court ruled that the areas immediately surrounding government buildings are traditional public forums and therefore are appropriate places for political speech, provided the speech does not interfere with persons entering or leaving the buildings or the activities taking place inside.[11]

The case of *Clark v. Community for Creative Non-Violence* [CCNV] began in 1982 when CCNV, a civil rights group attempting to draw attention to the problem of homelessness, planned a demonstration on the National Mall in Washington, a park that stretches between the Lincoln Memorial and the U.S. Capitol. The demonstration took the form of a "tent city" that would be manned twenty-four hours a day, with members of the group sleeping in shifts. The National Park Service (NPS) said that members of the group could occupy the tents at any time but that they were not allowed to sleep there because of the rule forbidding sleeping on any NPS property other than its approved campgrounds.

This case became known as the "sleep speech" case and raised the question of whether sleep could be considered symbolic speech. A federal court in the District of Columbia and the U.S. Court of Appeals both sided with the demonstrators and said the government could not prohibit sleeping on the mall. In 1984, the Supreme Court overturned that decision, however, ruling that the National Park Service had the right to regulate the group's activity because the regulation was content neutral and was a legitimate time, place, and manner restriction.[12]

Ward v. Rock Against Racism (1989) involved a nonprofit organization that planned a fund-raising concert in New York's Central Park. Because of the noise complaints that resulted from previous concerts, the city government established a rule that performers had to use the city's amplification system rather than bringing their own. Because the group believed the city's equipment was inferior to its own, it filed a lawsuit, claiming the rule violated its freedom of expression. But the Supreme Court ruled that the city's requirement did not violate the First Amendment because it was content neutral and was a legitimate manner restriction.[13]

In two cases dealing with the rights of abortion opponents, *Frisby v. Schultz* (1988)[14] and *Schenck v. Pro-Choice Network* (1997),[15] the Court ruled that abortion opponents had the right to protest outside of abortion clinics but could not block entrances or attempt to intimidate employees or patients as they entered or exited the clinics. In 1994, Congress passed the Freedom of Access to Clinic Entrances (FACE) Act, which imposes monetary fines on protestors who violate the provisions of the act.

Early in 2006, groups protesting gays in the military and homosexuality in general turned to a new and controversial tactic—demonstrating at or near the funerals of military personnel killed in the war in Iraq. In response to the protests, many state legislatures passed laws to prohibit such activity. If such laws are challenged on constitutional grounds, courts will likely decide the cases based on a number of factors, including whether the funeral sites are public or private property, whether the protests are obtrusive or non-obtrusive, and whether the protests can be prohibited under the time, place, and manner exception.

The last three time, place, and manner cases discussed here deal with the distribution of literature at shopping centers and other privately owned settings. The case of *Lloyd Corporation v. Tanner* (1972) began in the latter days of the Vietnam War when a shopping center in Portland, Oregon, attempted to prohibit draft protestors from distributing anti-war literature. A trial court ruled the mall owner had infringed on the group's free speech rights, and an appeals court agreed. Both courts determined that even though the shopping center was private property, it served as the "functional equivalent" of a public gathering place, and therefore more speech should be allowed. The owner appealed the case to the Supreme Court, which reversed the decision of the lower courts and ruled 5–4 that private property owners had the right to regulate the distribution of literature on their property as long as they were fair and treated all groups equally.[16]

The dissenting justices in the Lloyd case agreed with lower courts' position that a shopping center is the functional equivalent of public property because it is a gathering place for large numbers of people, and therefore more speech should be allowed.

Partially as a result of the dissent in the Lloyd case, several states have laws—known collectively as **equivalent function rules**—that prohibit shopping centers from limiting speech. The laws, sometimes called **rules of quasi-public places,** are intended to balance the private property rights of the shopping mall owners with the public's right of assembly and free speech.

The rights of states to enact such laws was tested in 1980 in the case of *Pruneyard Shopping Center v. Robins.* A California court had applied the equivalent function concept in ruling in favor of high school students distributing political literature at a shopping mall, so the mall owners appealed to the U.S. Supreme Court, hoping that the Lloyd decision would work in their favor. The Supreme Court, however, ruled that states had the right under the Tenth Amendment to determine their own laws regarding the distribution of literature on private property and that an equivalent function rule was constitutional because it was expanding free speech rights rather than limiting them.[17]

The concept of quasi-public places had its origins in the 1946 case of *Marsh v. Alabama.* A ship-building company that owned most of the property in town barred Jehovah's Witnesses and other religious groups from distributing literature on what it considered private property. The Supreme Court ruled that property that is generally open to the public, such as in a retail shopping center or similar space, served a public function and therefore property owners had to allow for the principle of free speech, provided that such speech posed no threat of property damage or harm to individuals. "Ownership does not always mean absolute dominion," the Court stated in its majority opinion.[18]

Today, many sports stadiums and arenas have similar problems because while they are publicly owned, they are often leased to private interests for events. In those circumstances, most "equivalent function" rules would allow the party leasing the stadium or arena to regulate commercial speech but not political speech.

Overbreadth and Vagueness

The Supreme Court generally upholds laws restricting speech if the laws serve a legitimate objective, but the Court requires that the laws be as narrow and specific as possible. The Court generally invalidates laws that are too open-ended or are based on terms that are too difficult to define. The Court describes such laws as "over-inclusive" or overbroad and vague. While the terms **overbreadth and vagueness** are sometimes lumped together, they are actually different legal concepts. "Overbreadth" refers to those laws that the Supreme Court finds to be in violation of the First Amendment because they restrict speech more than necessary. "Vagueness" refers to laws that the Supreme Court finds to be in violation of the First Amendment because they are so loosely written that potential speakers would not know ahead of time that such speech was prohibited.

The case most often cited to illustrate the overbreadth and vagueness concepts is *Houston v. Hill* (1987), in which the Supreme Court ruled that a city ordinance in Houston, Texas, violated both principles. The conflict began when Raymond Hill became involved in a verbal confrontation with a police officer at a public event. Hill told the officer to "go pick on somebody your own size" and was arrested and charged with violating a city ordinance that prohibited citizens from "interfering with a police officer in execution of his duty." Hill appealed his conviction to the Supreme Court, claiming that because he did not make contact with the officer or resist arrest, his free speech rights had been violated. The Court ruled in Hill's favor, determining that his statement was speech rather than conduct and that the law was unconstitutional because it was both overbroad and vague.[19]

In the years to follow, the Supreme Court struck down many other state laws and city and county ordinances involving freedom of expression based on either the overbreadth or vagueness principles.

Conduct vs. Speech

The Supreme Court generally upholds laws and lower court rulings restricting a person's conduct but strikes down those that attempt to limit speech or expression. Significant cases involving the difference between conduct and speech include *United States v. O'Brien* (1968) and *Texas v. Johnson* (1989).

The *O'Brien* case began on March 31, 1966, when draft protestor David O'Brien and three of his friends were at a Vietnam War protest on the steps of the federal courthouse in Boston. They were being watched by FBI agents, and at one point, as a spontaneous gesture, O'Brien set fire to his Selective Service Registration

Certificate, better known as a draft card. The crowd began to attack him, so the FBI agents escorted him into the courthouse, both for his own safety and also so they could place him under arrest for violating a federal law that prohibited the destruction of the card.

O'Brien was convicted but appealed his case, claiming his actions were protected as political speech under the First Amendment. His appeal eventually reached the U.S. Supreme Court, which rejected his First Amendment argument and upheld the conviction because the government's actions were content neutral—related more to the destruction of government property rather than to his motives in protesting the war.

In issuing its ruling, the Court established the **O'Brien Test,** a three-part standard for evaluating laws dealing with displays of contempt for the government or its policies. According to the test, the law is constitutional provided (1) it advances an important government interest, (2) it does not suppress speech (i.e., it relates to conduct rather than speech), and (3) it is narrowly tailored to the government interest with only an incidental restriction of free speech. In the O'Brien case, the Court determined that the law in question met all three parts of the test.[20]

Twenty-one years later, in the case of *Texas v. Johnson,* the Supreme Court made the opposite ruling regarding flag-burning, determining that it is political speech rather than conduct. Gregory Johnson was part of a group protesting outside the 1984 Republican National Convention in Dallas when he was charged with burning an American flag. The Texas trial court found him guilty and sentenced him to a year in prison and a $2,000 fine. A Texas appeals court overturned the ruling, determining that it was a free speech issue, drawing a distinction between Johnson's "symbolic speech" and the "conduct" determination it made in the O'Brien case. Texas prosecutors appealed the case, and when the Texas Supreme Court refused to hear it, the state appealed to the U.S. Supreme Court.

The Court ruled 5–4 to invalidate the conviction, agreeing with the Texas appeals court that Johnson's actions were a form of political speech and the Texas law limited his First Amendment rights.

At first glance, the Johnson case appeared to be similar to the O'Brien case in that it dealt with the individual's motives behind his conduct—the expression of contempt for the federal government. In the Johnson case, however, the Court determined that the government's motive of protecting the flag did not outweigh Johnson's right of expression. In the O'Brien case, the court determined that the government's motive in protecting the Selective Service Registration System (i.e., the draft) outweighed O'Brien's First Amendment rights.

Writing for the majority in *Johnson,* Justice William Brennan made three significant points: (1) the court cannot find something illegal just because it is objectionable or distasteful; (2) expression of dissatisfaction with the government is at the core of the First Amendment; and (3) the country is strong enough to withstand this type of critical speech. The most significant dissent was written by Chief Justice William Rehnquist, who argued that while Johnson had a First Amendment right to express contempt for the federal government, he had other alternatives and needn't resort to the burning of a national symbol. The choice of that method, Rehnquist wrote, suggested that his true motive was not to "express any particular idea, but to antagonize others."[21]

Shortly after that case was decided, Congress passed the Flag Protection Act of 1989, which stated that anyone who "defaces, physically defiles, burns, maintains on the floor or ground, or tramples upon any flag of the United States shall be fined or imprisoned for not more than one year, or both." Much like state laws prohibiting flag-burning, the Flag Protection Act (FPA) dealt only with the burning of the flag as a form of disrespect or political protest; it did not prohibit the "official" burning of a damaged or faded flag as the method of destruction prescribed by law. President George H. W. Bush allowed the FPA to take effect without his signature, but two more flag-burning cases came up immediately—one in Seattle and the other in Washington, D.C.—that gave the courts another opportunity to rule on the issue. The following year, in the case of *United States v. Eichman* (consolidating the Seattle and Washington, D.C., cases), the Court found the Flag Protection Act unconstitutional for the same reason it invalidated the Texas flag-desecration law in 1988, ruling again that flag-burning is considered political speech rather than conduct.[22]

Differing Standards for Broadcast Media and Print Media

The court system, including the U.S. Supreme Court, recognizes different levels of regulation for broadcast media and print media, allowing the broadcast media to be subject to strict regulation by the Federal Communications Commission while newspapers and magazines are subject to almost no regulation whatsoever. The reasoning behind this policy involves (1) public ownership of the airwaves, (2) the pervasiveness and potential obtrusiveness of broadcast media, and (3) the limited number of channels and frequencies available to television and radio broadcasters. Cases in this area are discussed in Chapter 9.

Compelled Speech

The Supreme Court has ruled that just as the First Amendment does not allow the government to limit an individual's right to speak, it also means that individuals or organizations cannot be required to participate in speech to which they object. The first conflict involving **compelled speech** was resolved in the 1943 case of *West Virginia State Board of Education v. Barnette*, in which the Supreme Court ruled that school children could not be required to recite the Pledge of Allegiance if their families' religious beliefs forbade it.[23]

One of the more interesting compelled speech conflicts to reach the Supreme Court was the 1977 case of *Wooley v. Maynard*, which involved a couple in New Hampshire who objected to the state motto, "Live Free or Die," on their car license plate. They covered the slogan with masking tape and were charged by the state of New Hampshire with defacing the plate. When the case was appealed to the

Supreme Court, the Court ruled in favor of the couple on two grounds: first, because the state failed to prove that the couple's actions were harmful; and second, because the couple was only declining to participate in speech to which they objected.

The Court determined that the state was using automobile license plates as "mobile billboards" to promote the government's views. The court said "The First Amendment protects the right of individuals to hold a point of view different from the majority and to refuse to foster, in the way (the state) commands, an idea they find morally objectionable." State officials claimed the purpose of the plate was to promote "appreciation of history, individualism, and state pride," but the Court ruled that the government could do so through a number of other methods without imposing the speech on its citizens.[24]

Since the *West Virginia State Board of Education* and *Wooley* rulings, many other compelled speech cases have resulted in similar rulings. Government employees cannot be required to sign pledges to support or oppose a political philosophy. Physicians working in government-run health clinics cannot be required to counsel patients against abortion. In *Hurley v. Irish-American Gay, Lesbian, and Bisexual Group of Boston* (1995), the Supreme Court ruled that a private association organizing a community parade could not be required to include in the parade those groups to which the association objected.[25]

The compelled speech rule has also been applied in cases in which persons criticized in the media have requested the opportunity to respond. Courts have ruled that newspapers are not required to publish letters to the editor or similar responses (but most newspapers believe they have an ethical responsibility to do so). In the 1974 case of *Miami Herald Co. v. Tornillo,* for example, the Court ruled that the state of Florida could not require newspapers to publish letters from political candidates in response to the paper's editorials and endorsements.[26]

In terms of advertising, both print media and broadcast media have the right to refuse commercial advertising without stating a reason. Exceptions are spelled out in Chapter 12.

In the 1980s, the Court applied the compelled speech rule to the manner in which labor unions and professional organizations collect money from their members and spend it to support political candidates and issues to which some members object. As a result of such cases, the Federal Election Commission and many state governments have enacted laws requiring groups to segregate the money it collects from members into required contributions (which may not be spent on political activities) and voluntary contributions (which may be spent on political activities).

In the 1990s, the Supreme Court considered whether the compelled speech rule applied in cases in which college students objected to how their student activity fees were used to fund campus activities (such as student newspapers or athletics) in which they had no interest or student organizations involved in controversial causes. These cases are discussed in Chapter 5.

In the early 2000s, the Court applied the compelled speech rule to conflicts that began when the U.S. Department of Agriculture and other government agencies attempted to force agricultural companies to contribute to special funds that would be used to promote products through media campaigns. Attorneys representing the government agencies analogized the fees to general taxes and pointed out that taxpayers as a whole often see their money go to pay for military operations and other expenses they don't agree with, yet they cannot opt out of paying the taxes. Some of the representatives of the cattle industry and other agricultural interests objected to the content of the ads, while others claimed that they did not object to the content but believed that if they were forced to pay for the campaigns, they should have more input into how the ads were produced.

Decisions reached by the courts in compelled speech cases have been inconsistent and are typically decided based on whether the fees collected are spent solely on advertising or are part of a broader regulatory program. In 1997, the Supreme Court ruled in *Glickman v. Wileman & Eliot* that the federal government could collect a fee from producers of citrus products and not be guilty of compelled speech because only a small portion of the funds were used for promotional purposes; the majority of the money was spent on a larger program of regulation.[27] In 2005, the Court reached a similar decision in the case of *Johanns v. Livestock Marketing Association*, determining that the U.S. Department of Agriculture's program of imposing a fee and using a small portion of the revenue for promotional purposes was not a case of compelled speech.[28]

In a 2001 case, however, the Court upheld a compelled speech claim because the sole purpose of the fee collected was to fund an advertising campaign. In *United States v. United Foods*, one of the largest agricultural companies in the country sued the United States Department of Agriculture (USDA) on behalf of the nation's mushroom farmers, claiming that payment of the advertising fee was compelled speech. After a lengthy battle in Federal District Court and in the Circuit Court of Appeals, the Supreme Court ruled in favor of the company in June 2001, agreeing with the company's compelled speech claim.[29]

Federal district courts have also ruled in favor of the dairy cattle farmers who objected to having to pay for the USDA's "Got Milk?" advertising program and pork producers who objected to the industry's program that called their product "the other white meat."[30]

Somewhat related to the issue of compelled speech is the potential for conflict that arises when state governments sponsor controversial forms of speech. In the late 1990s and early 2000s, legislatures in thirteen states dealt with proposals to offer license plates bearing the slogan "Choose Life" and graphics supporting adoption as an alternative to abortion. Most states charge vehicle owners an extra fee for specialty plates (some states offer more than one hundred) and give part of the proceeds to nonprofit organizations and charities associated with the causes being promoted. In the case of the "Choose Life" plates, the funds go to pro-adoption groups, anti-abortion groups, or both. In many of the states, abortion-rights groups such as Planned Parenthood and the National Organization for Women (NOW) challenged the plates under the principle of "equal protection," claiming that "when the state creates a forum for the expression of political views, it cannot promote one opinion and deny the forum to an opposing opinion."[31]

In 2001, a state appeals court in Florida dismissed the first of those suits, claiming that NOW failed to prove the program was unconstitutional. The following year, a Circuit Court of Appeals made a similar ruling in the case of Louisiana's "Choose Life" plates.

In 2004, however, a Circuit Court of Appeals ruled that South Carolina's "Choose Life" plates were unconstitutional. The following year, the U.S. Supreme Court declined to hear an appeal of the case, leaving the lower court ruling in place.[32]

In October 2004, a Federal District Court judge in Tennessee ruled that state's "Choose Life" plate, for which part of the revenue generated was given to an anti-abortion group, violated the constitution because it promoted only one side in the abortion debate and did not allow groups with opposing viewpoints to sponsor their own plates. Lawmakers in Tennessee worried that a strict interpretation of the court ruling might prompt individuals to challenge the appropriateness of the state's other specialty license plates, such as those promoting animal rights and encouraging citizens to protect environmentally sensitive lands, such as the Great Smoky Mountains National Park.[33]

In March 2006, a Circuit Court of Appeals reversed the ruling of the lower courts in Tennessee and determined that the license plate program did not unfairly promote an anti-abortion philosophy. "Although this exercise of government one-sidedness with respect to a very contentious political issue may be ill-advised, we are unable to conclude that the Tennessee statute contravenes the First Amendment," the court decision read.[34]

Prior Restraint vs. Punishment after the Fact

Government regulation of speech takes two forms: **prior restraint** (commonly called "censorship") and **punishment after the fact.**

Punishment after the fact is based on the philosophy of English legal scholar William Blackstone, who believed that speech should never be suppressed (such as in the case of prior restraint), but that the government has the right to punish the source of harmful speech after it takes place under the appropriate laws, such as those involving copyrights, libel, or obscenity. Blackstone, writing in 1769, stated that, "The liberty of the press is indeed essential to the nature of a free state; but this consists in laying no previous restraints upon publication, and not in freedom from censure for criminal matter when published. Every free man has an undoubted right to lay what sentiments he pleases before the public; to forbid this is to destroy the freedom of the press, but if he published what is improper, mischievous, or illegal, he must take the consequences of his own temerity."[35] Today, the principle of not allowing for prior restraint, but allowing instead for punishment after the fact, is known as the **Blackstonian Doctrine.**

One famous example of the doctrine being applied in a prior restraint case was one involving former President Gerald Ford's book, *A Time to Heal. The Nation,* a national news magazine, obtained some of Ford's personal papers and announced

Newspapers roll through the presses. Daily newspapers in the United States traditionally operate with a minimum of prior restraint.

its intention to publish them just prior to the release of the book. Ford objected to the publication because of potential damage to sales of the book and asked a federal district court for an injunction to prohibit the magazine from publishing the papers. The court declined to issue the injunction, ruling instead that Ford would have to prove "after the fact" that sales of the book were harmed before seeking financial damages. While Ford was unsuccessful in his injunction case, his publisher, Harper & Row, later pursued the case (successfully) under copyright law.[36]

The Blackstonian Doctrine is sometimes applied in cases of criminals whose acts were alleged to have been inspired by the media. In the 1997 case of *Rice v. Paladin Enterprises*, for example, the families of three murder victims sued the publisher of a book titled *Hit Man*, which prosecutors believe provided the suspect with instructions on how to commit the murder and destroy the evidence. A lower court denied the publisher's motion to dismiss the suit based on constitutional grounds, but an appeals court labeled the book as a "murder manual" that was not protected by the First Amendment. The publisher appealed the case to the Supreme Court, but the Court refused to hear the case and instructed the trial court to proceed. Before the trial could begin, however, the publisher settled out of court with the plaintiffs for $5 million and took the book off the market.[37]

Examples of Prior Restraint Found to be Constitutional

There are four forms of prior restraint the Supreme Court has consistently determined are justifiable and not violations of the First Amendment: (1) gag orders, (2) pre-publication agreements, (3) limitations on media coverage of military operations, and (4) propaganda labeling.

Gag Orders

A **gag order** is a judge's directive to participants in a legal proceeding not to discuss the case with outside parties, including the media. The purpose is to avoid the details of a case from being reported in the media, thereby contaminating the pool of potential jurors. Some judges also issue gag orders to media covering the trial. Such orders are allowed provided they are for a limited time; they may prohibit media coverage of pre-trial proceedings but are then lifted to allow coverage once the trial begins. But any gag order that attempts to limit media coverage of the trial itself would likely be overturned if appealed.

A gag order is similar to an injunction (see next section) in that they both prohibit a specific form of speech. The main difference is that a gag order is issued by a judge based on his or her opinion; an injunction is issued at the request of a third party. A case involving gag orders in the legal system, *Nebraska Press Association v. Stuart*, is discussed in Chapter 8.

Pre-Publication Agreements

Many federal government agencies require employees to sign **pre-publication agreements** that require employees to submit manuscripts for any books based on their experiences for government approval (and usually censorship). Significant cases involving pre-publication agreements are *United States v. Marchetti* (1972) and *Snepp v. United States* (1980).

The Marchetti case involved Victor Marchetti, a Central Intelligence Agency (CIA) operative who wrote a book titled *The CIA and the Cult of Intelligence* in which he chronicled his experiences in South America. The CIA enforced a pre-publication agreement that he had signed when he joined the agency. The agreement did not bar him from writing a book, but it required that the manuscript be submitted to CIA officials in advance so it could be cleared.

Marchetti accepted the requirement at first and submitted his manuscript for review. The CIA made 339 deletions, which represented almost 20 percent of the manuscript. Marchetti claimed that even though he signed the agreement, deleting 20 percent of his manuscript would constitute prior restraint and violate his First Amendment rights.

Before going to court, Marchetti and his lawyer met with CIA officials, who agreed to drop 171 of the objections, reducing the proportion of deleted material from 20 percent to about 10 percent. Marchetti still was not satisfied and took his claim to Federal District Court and eventually the U.S. Supreme Court, but the High Court upheld the remaining deletions and ruled that pre-publication agreements are a justifiable form of prior restraint. The book appeared in its abridged form, and in each place where material had been deleted, the publisher printed the word "DELETED" in capital letters.[38]

Eight years later, in *Snepp v. United States,* the Supreme Court made a similar ruling on pre-publication agreements. Plaintiff Frank Snepp was a former CIA analyst who had worked in Southeast Asia and was one of the last Americans to be airlifted from Saigon before the North Vietnamese took over in 1975. After Snepp returned to the United States, he resigned from the CIA and wrote a book titled *Decent Interval,* in which he was critical of the agency's operations during the war.

Like Marchetti, Snepp claimed that the pre-publication agreement he had signed was a violation of his First Amendment rights and that once the CIA censors removed anything objectionable, there would not be anything left worth publishing. This case also went to the Supreme Court, which ruled again that pre-publication agreements for government employees were constitutional. By the time the court made its ruling, Snepp's book had already been published. Instead of attempting to recall the book, the Court required that Snepp surrender all of his royalties to the CIA—more of a punitive payment than a compensatory one. The Court paid some attention to the First Amendment values of the case, but decided the issue based largely on the principles of contract law, determining that Snepp had signed away his First Amendment rights when he agreed to the provision in his CIA contract.[39]

A few years after the Snepp case, President Reagan failed in his attempt to apply the pre-publication rule to current employees. His executive order was determined to be unenforceable because under contact law, the rule could only be applied only as a condition of employment at the time of hiring and could not be applied retroactively.

The issue of pre-publication agreements surfaced again in 2005 when twenty-three-year CIA veteran Gary Berntsen published his book, *Jawbreaker,* which detailed his experiences in Afghanistan. He submitted the manuscript to the agency's publication review board, which he later accused of "dragging its feet" and causing him to miss his publisher's deadline for completing his work. He was also angered when the board instructed him to delete details of military operations in

Afghanistan that had already been reported in books written by authors who were not CIA agents. In his court case, he asked to be allowed to include in future editions those details that had been deleted from the 2005 edition. The case was still pending as of late 2006.[40]

Limitations on Media Coverage of Military Operations

Historically, the Supreme Court has upheld the military's right to exercise prior restraint over the dissemination of news coming out of war zones and other military operations. The most recent case in this area was *The Nation v. Department of Defense* (1991).

The case began when *The Nation*, a national news and political magazine, joined with other publications in filing suit against the Pentagon over treatment of the media covering the first Gulf War (1990–91) because of the delay in getting information that resulted from the "media pool" system of reporting. With this system, a select number of journalists were part of a small pool of reporters who covered the war and then shared their stories with other members of the press. Of the approximately 750 media personnel covering the war, only about 100 were allowed access to the front lines. Journalists were also not allowed to use the satellite telephones they had brought with them for fear the calls might be intercepted, and news stories were often reviewed before they were allowed to be transmitted. Journalists did not complain that the deletion of news content was unreasonable, only that the review process delayed the transmission of news.

The suit was filed while the war was still in progress, but by the time it reached the Supreme Court, the war was over and the Court declined to hear it because it would be hypothetical rather than substantive. Even though this case never reached a resolution, it was significant because the lack of a ruling supported the military's right to exercise prior restraint in military operations.[41]

After the failure of *The Nation* case and a similar case filed by a French press agency, media executives requested a meeting with the Secretary of Defense, claiming that "the Gulf War should not become the model for future coverage." Several of the executives met with Pentagon officials in 1992 to negotiate rules for media coverage of military operations in the future. Among the changes agreed to were greater access to the front lines, the elimination of the pool system unless absolutely necessary, and a clarification that military public affairs officers would be available to help reporters but would not interfere with their work.

Later in the 1990s, those rules were tested during American military operations in Somalia, Bosnia, and Kosovo. With only a few exceptions, both military officials and journalists agreed that the rules seemed to work in those three operations.

As the American military entered the war on terrorism in 2001 and the second Gulf War in 2003, access for journalists was expanded even further with the advent of the "embedded reporters" policy in which journalists got even closer to the action, living and working directly alongside military personnel. There were criticisms that some reporters became too involved in the action and that their

CBS News correspondent Scott Pelley reports from Iraq. The work of journalists reporting from war zones has traditionally been subject to government censorship, but in the most recent war in Iraq, the military has allowed for greater media access.

objectivity was compromised, but compared to media pools used in the first Gulf War in the early 1990s, the policy was viewed as successful by most media outlets.

Although censorship of the news during war time is perceived to be a twentieth-century phenomena, such conflicts have existed throughout the history of the nation. During the Civil War, for example, the federal government attempted to censor northern newspapers—known collectively as "the Copperhead press"—that opposed the war or advocated the continuation of slavery.

Propaganda Labeling

The principle of **propaganda labeling** means that the federal government can require political speech coming from sources outside of the United States to be subjected to prior restraint if the U.S. government labels it as "propaganda." The idea is based on a 1938 law called the Foreign Agents Registration Act, which was designed to prevent Nazi propaganda from entering the United States.

One example of this principle occurred in the 1987 case of *Meese v. Keene*. The case began in the early 1980s when a series of documentary films produced in Canada focused on the environmental problems faced by that country—most of them advancing the country's position that air pollution and acid rain affecting Canada's environment were caused by emissions from factories in the northern United States. When the producers tried to get their films shown in the United States, the Reagan administration had the films labeled as "propaganda," meaning that anyone wanting to show them to American audiences had to register with the Justice Department as a foreign agent.

Environmental activist Barry Keene, also a state legislator in California, announced plans to show the films at an environmental film festival. The Justice

Department, headed by Attorney General Edwin Meese, informed him that such films could not be shown unless Keene registered as a foreign agent. Keene sued, claiming that Meese's registration requirement was a form of prior restraint. But the Supreme Court sided with the Justice Department and ruled that prior restraint was acceptable in this case because the material involved was considered propaganda and the labeling process was an acceptable form of prior restraint.[42]

Examples of Prior Restraint Found to be Unconstitutional

There are four forms of prior restraint the Supreme Court has generally determined to be unconstitutional because they violate the First Amendment; therefore those cases are generally decided in favor of the party whose free speech rights were infringed. Those forms of prior restraint are (1) injunctions, (2) discriminatory licensing, (3) discriminatory taxation, and (4) the denial of book royalties to convicted criminals (the so-called "Son of Sam" laws).

Injunctions

An **injunction** is a legal action in which a court issues an order for the offending party to stop a specific activity. While acceptable when applied to behavior or conduct, injunctions are seldom allowed in the case of speech, except in cases of false advertising or obscenity. Examples of unsuccessful government attempts in enforcing injunctions are found in the cases of *Near v. Minnesota* (1931), *New York Times v. United States* (1971), and *United States v. Progressive* (1979).

The *Near* case was argued at the height of the prohibition era, when a weekly paper in Minneapolis criticized local government officials, claiming they were allowing the city of Minneapolis to be run by "Jewish gangsters" who were selling alcohol illegally, organizing prostitution rings, bribing city officials, and fixing elections. City officials attempted to shut down the paper under a Minnesota law that allowed city governments to take such actions against newspapers if they disrupted the processes of government or "created a public nuisance."

Newspaper editor Jay Near filed suit in an attempt to have the law invalidated, and when the case reached the U.S. Supreme Court, it ruled that injunctions were an unacceptable form of prior restraint. Instead, the court cited the Blackstonian Doctrine and determined that the city would instead have to sue the newspaper under existing law—in this case, the state's libel law.

Further, the Supreme Court determined that a heavy burden of proof would be required, and in this case, the state failed to meet that burden of proof. The court ruled that prior restraint was permissible only during war time when that expression would be detrimental to the war effort, but the country was not at war at the time.[43]

Almost forty years later, the Supreme Court made a similar ruling in *New York Times vs. United States* (1971), also known as the "Pentagon Papers" case. The case centered on an investigation into the American involvement in Vietnam, commissioned by Secretary of Defense Robert McNamara. The resulting report documented the belief of military leaders that the war was "unwinable." Pentagon officials were concerned that if the report was published, it would further undermine morale and public support for the war, which was already low.

The *New York Times* obtained a copy of the report and planned to publish the first installment in June, 1971. The Justice Department, headed by Attorney General John Mitchell, obtained an injunction against the newspaper to stop publication of the report. The newspaper appealed the case to the Supreme Court, which agreed to hear it on an expedited basis. The court ruled 6–3 that the government did not meet its burden of proof and that the injunction was an unconstitutional form of prior restraint. Of the six justices voting to allow publication, two were "absolutists" who felt that speech should not be limited under any circumstances. The other four justices said press freedom could sometimes be limited in certain cases but not in this one.[44]

In the 1979 case of *United States v. Progressive*, a magazine announced its intention to publish an article that detailed the construction of an atomic bomb. The article was the work of a freelance writer who claimed that all of the information used to develop the article was available from public sources. The editors sent a copy of the article to a number of scientists and scholars in order to verify its technical accuracy. Government officials learned about the article and claimed it posed a danger to national security and might encourage some countries to develop their own nuclear devices. In addition, they asserted that publication of the article would violate the Atomic Energy Act of 1954. Before the case could be decided, another magazine published a similar article, making the *Progressive* case moot because the information was already publicly available.[45]

Discriminatory Licensing

The Supreme Court recognizes the authority of city and county governments to issue licenses for certain forms of communication, but not those that provide the opportunity for discrimination. The conflict that established this principle of **discriminatory licensing** was the 1938 case of *Lovell v. Griffin*. The case centered on a city ordinance in Griffin, Georgia, that required the licensing of persons wanting to distribute literature or conduct door-to door fund-raising. Alma Lovell, a Jehovah's Witness, was fined for violating the law and challenged its validity. Her complaint, supported by other groups that had been denied licenses, was that the city manager had the sole authority to accept or reject license applications and was not required to state a reason for rejecting applications. Further, the city manager was the only person who could perform the licensing function; when the city manager was on vacation, an applicant had to wait until he or she returned to receive a license. When Lovell's appeal reached the Supreme Court, it ruled that the city ordinance violated free speech rights because it gave the city manager too much discretion and provided too much opportunity for discrimination.[46]

The Supreme Court made a similar determination in the 2002 case of *Watchtower Bible & Tract Society of New York v. Village of Stratton.* The court ruled against the village of Stratton, Ohio, in a lawsuit filed by the Jehovah's Witnesses and supported by other church groups and the American Civil Liberties Union. The court clarified that its ruling applied not only to religious communication but to any form of public discourse, including political communication. Village officials, supported by the National League of Cities, had claimed that its permitting law was intended to protect the privacy of citizens and to discourage burglars from posing as door-to-door solicitors in order to case neighborhoods, but the Court determined that those interests were outweighed by the citizens' First Amendment rights of political and religious expression.[47]

In the 1998 case of *Lakewood v. Plain Dealer Publishing* and the 1993 case of *Cincinnati v. Discovery Network,* the Court ruled that city governments had the right to license newspaper vending machines but had to treat all publications equally. In both cases, city governments allowed major daily newspapers to sell their products through thousands of vending machines but would not allow the same privilege to publishers of cheaper, less prestigious weekly newspapers and real estate magazines. The Court rejected the cities' claim that the cheaper publications were mostly commercial speech and did not deserve equal status with the larger daily publications. The Court ruled that if the city allowed daily newspapers to purchase licenses, it must provide the same opportunity to other publications at the same rate.[48]

Discriminatory Taxation

The Supreme Court's ban on **discriminatory taxation** means that media can be taxed just like any other business but must be treated equally with other businesses. Therefore, no government or governmental agency can apply taxation to certain types of media or media outlets based on content. As examples, the publisher of a pornographic magazine cannot be forced to pay taxes higher than those paid by magazines with less controversial content; adult bookstores cannot be required to charge sales taxes on their merchandise at a different rate than mainstream bookstores.

The major case in this area is *Grosjean v. American Press Co.* (1936). The case began when a newspaper publisher challenged a Louisiana state law that imposed a 2 percent revenue tax on newspapers with a circulation of more than 20,000. When the case reached the Supreme Court, it ruled that the tax was unconstitutional for several reasons. First, the Court noted a similarity between the Louisiana tax and the "stamp tax" that England placed on newspapers in the 1700s, a tax that was one of the conditions that led to the Revolutionary War. Another problem noted by the Court was that the tax was selectively enforced. As the law was written, it required the tax to be imposed on all newspapers with a certain circulation. But in many cases, the state imposed the tax only on larger newspapers that published stories and editorials critical of the state government, while newspapers that published positive stories about the government were not required to pay the tax. In addition to the problem of selective application of the law, the court looked at this as a case of prior restraint because the state was attempting to influence the content of the news by imposition of the tax.[49]

"Son of Sam" Laws

In the 1980s, many states passed laws that prohibit convicted criminals from benefiting financially from books, magazine articles, or movies about their crimes, whether written by them or someone else. Instead, most of the laws require that financial benefits go to the victims of their crimes. Many such measures are called "Son of Sam" laws after David Berkowitz, a serial murderer who created controversy by collecting royalties on a book he wrote about his 1970s crime spree.

In *Simon & Schuster v. New York State Crime Victims Board* (1991), the Court found that New York's law was unconstitutional because it was "over-inclusive" and that the state had failed to demonstrate a compelling reason to have such a law. The case began when the publishing company refused to turn over royalties from the book *Wiseguy*—the memoirs of organized crime boss Henry Hill—to a state agency in charge of collecting such money and using it to compensate crime victims. When the publisher refused to comply, it challenged the law on constitutional grounds. Writing the majority opinion, Justice Sandra Day O'Connor claimed that if such a law had been in effect in an earlier era, it would have prevented Henry David Thoreau from collecting royalties from writing the literary classic *Civil Disobedience*.[50]

California's law was successfully challenged in 2002 by a man who was convicted of the 1963 kidnapping of Frank Sinatra's son and thirty-five years later collected $485,000 for the movie rights to his life story. The California Supreme Court ruled that "expressive works" deserved First Amendment protection, regardless of the conditions under which they were created.[51]

Frequently Asked Questions about Political Speech

1. *Why can't television stations and networks do something about negative political campaign ads?* Under current rules of the Federal Communications Commission (FCC), television stations and networks are required to provide "reasonable access" to political candidates and are not responsible for the accuracy of those ads (see more information on this in Chapter 12). Because of the large volume of political advertisements aired during a political campaign, television stations and networks would be "unreasonably burdened" by a requirement that they verify the accuracy of ads before they aired. Instead, the FCC and other observers suggest that for candidates claiming that their opponents are airing unfair or inaccurate ads, a more practical recourse is to respond with ads of their own rather than expecting the station or network to withdraw their opponent's ad.

2. *If there is a disagreement over whether or not a form of speech needs to be limited or regulated, who bears the burden of proof?* In any free speech conflict, the "benefit of the doubt" generally works in favor of the individual or organization whose rights are at risk for being limited. Therefore, the government bears the burden of proving a specific communication is harmful and should be limited, as opposed to the communicator having to prove that his or her speech is not harmful. This rule, known as the **rational basis standard,** is not absolute, however. The "hierarchy of First Amendment protection" explained in the previous chapter means that the higher the value placed on the speech (such as political speech or religious expression), the higher the burden of proof; the lower the value (such as obscenity and fighting words), the lower the burden.

3. *Why do publishers have the right to sell books that provide instructions on how to commit (and get away with) murder and make bombs?* Book publishers have successfully argued in numerous cases that they are not responsible for the misuse of information. They also claim that such information is already available from other sources, such as the Internet and/or other books already in print. There's also a slippery slope problem: If the government had the right to limit one publisher's book because it determined it to be harmful, it might one day use the same rationale to prohibit the publication of less harmful material.

4. *The equivalent function rule states that I have free speech rights at our local shopping mall. But there are signs on the outside doors and at the entrance to the parking lot that says "no distribution of handbills." Which is correct?* Even though most shopping malls post such signs, those rules would likely be unenforceable if your state has an "equivalent function" law or other provision regarding "quasi-public places." In the absence of a state law, however, the precedent set by the *Lloyd* case would allow private property owners to limit all forms of speech.

If you were to challenge the shopping center management in court, the judge would likely take a number of factors into consideration, including the nature of your handbills (political speech or commercial speech) and to what degree, if any, your distribution of the materials was obtrusive or disruptive.

5. *Is the Patriot Act an abridgement of my free speech rights?* So far, the main concern regarding the Patriot Act has been its effect on privacy, as it includes provisions that make it easier for government officials to eavesdrop on telephone calls and obtain records, such as college transcripts and library circulation records of suspected terrorists. But the Act may eventually be challenged on free speech grounds as well, as some civil libertarians believe that a loose interpretation of the law may allow the government to target individuals and groups for merely disparaging government officials or policies.

The American Civil Liberties Union has criticized the Patriot Act provision that allows the government to gather information such as which library books an individual checks out or which websites he or she visits. Attorney Jameel Jaffer wrote in a 2002 position paper that "If people think that the government is looking over their shoulders to see what books they are reading or what websites they

The Garden State Mall in Paramus, N.J. In most states, shopping malls are considered "quasi-public places," and therefore much of the communication there is protected by the First Amendment.

are visiting, many are not going to read those books or visit those websites. Some of this speech that will be silenced is speech that is important in an open democracy. Many provisions of the Patriot Act are absolutely a First Amendment threat. Often there is a greater chill on free expression not from direct censorship, but from government monitoring."[52]

The official name of the law is the USA Patriot Act, an acronym for "Uniting and Strengthening America by Providing Appropriate Tools Required to Intercept and Obstruct Terrorism." The Act was passed late in 2001 in response to the terrorist attacks of that September.

Point/Counterpoint: Flag Burning

Why Flag-Burning Should be Illegal

Advocates of legislation that would ban flag-burning claim that such desecration of the flag is unpatriotic and offensive to military veterans and American society as a whole. Further, it emulates the actions of protestors in other countries who burn the American flag to demonstrate hate for America.

In his dissenting opinion in *Texas v. Johnson,* Chief Justice William Rehnquist argued that "the American flag, throughout more than 200 years of our history, has come to be the visible symbol embodying our nation . . . The flag is not simply another 'idea' or 'point of view' competing for recognition in the marketplace of ideas. Millions and millions of Americans regard it with almost mystical reverence regardless of what sort of social, political, or philosophical beliefs they may have . . . There are certain well-defined and narrowly limited classes of speech, the prevention and punishment of which have never thought to raise any constitutional problem. These include the lewd and obscene, the profane, the libelous, and the insulting or fighting words . . . (they) are of such slight social value as a step to truth that any benefit that may be derived from them is clearly outweighed by the social interest in order and morality."[53]

Why Flag-Burning Should Not be Punished

The best arguments against flag-burning legislation are found in Justice William Brennan's three-point majority opinion: (1) the court cannot find something illegal just because it is objectionable or distasteful; (2) expression of dissatisfaction with the government is at the core of the First Amendment; and (3) the country is strong enough to withstand this type of critical speech.[54]

Opponents of anti-flag-burning legislation also claim that, like the act of burning a cross, the act of burning a flag is an example of expressing dissatisfaction in a non-violent manner (i.e. "blowing off steam").

There's also a slippery slope problem: Most laws in this regard are not limited to burning of the flag, but rather "desecration" of the flag. How would we define desecration? Would it violate the law to sew an American flag onto the back side of one's pants? What about other questionable commercial uses of the flag, such as in product advertising?

One interesting irony in this conflict: A federal law dealing with the proper treatment of the American flag dictates that the appropriate way to dispose of a worn or damaged flag is by burning it.

Chapter Summary

Some categories of speech are given more First Amendment protection than others, and Supreme Court decisions provide a variety of rationale behind those varying levels of protection. In addition to categorizing the speech and determining where it falls on the First Amendment hierarchy (described in the previous chapter), the Supreme Court looks at the value of the speech to society and the forum in which it takes place. The Court generally does not take into consideration the speakers' motives and strikes down laws that restrict a citizen's speech based on its content.

Through the last century, the Court has used four different tests to evaluate conflicts involving political speech. The bad tendency test (no longer used) required the government to meet a very low burden of proof in order to suppress speech. The clear and present danger test increased the burden so significantly that there are few cases in which the government can meet the burden. Today, the tests most often applied are the balancing tests, in which the Court seeks to find a balance between protecting citizens' free speech rights and the government's interest in regulating potentially harmful speech.

CASE PROBLEMS

Coming to a Bookstore Near You

R. A. Bookwriter, a popular novelist, has just finished a work of fiction based on the American military's involvement in a recent civil war in Elbonia. The settings and background events of the novel are based on known facts, but the story includes fictional characters and dialogue. The general theme of this book is critical of the U.S. government and military leaders, suggesting that their decisions led to an unnecessary loss of life and property damage. The author may make millions of dollars from book sales and movie rights, as will the book's publisher, MegaHype Publishing Company. Afraid that the book may be embarrassing for the military and harmful to recruiting efforts, the Department of Defense has gone to Federal District Court asking for an injunction that would prevent MegaHype Publishing from releasing the book.

You're not directly involved in the legal battle, but as a retired communications lawyer, you have been following news coverage of the case. A weekly political magazine has contacted you and asked you to write a brief op-ed piece for an upcoming issue; it doesn't care which side you take. Would your op-ed piece suggest that the Federal District Court *should* or *should not* issue the injunction? Which legal principles (from the first two chapters) could you cite? Hint: The author has never been a government employee, so no pre-publication agreement is involved.

Roadside Memorials

Your state is considering a law restricting "roadside memorials" (usually a combination of crosses, signs, flowers and other decorative objects) at the sites of highway fatalities. The proposed law prohibits these types of memorials from the medians altogether and requires all memorials to be at least thirty feet from the sides of the road. The state government claims they create a distraction for drivers. Family members who have established the memorials claim their First Amendment rights are being violated. Which side are you on? What legal principles (from Chapters 2 and 3) could you cite?

Free Speech in the Stadium Parking Lot

You're the chief legal counsel for the Mudville County Stadium Authority (MCSA), a unit of Mudville County government. The Treehugger Society is a national environmental advocacy group that has had an active chapter in Mudville County for twelve years.

In order to spread its pro-environment message, the Treehugger Society recently began peaceful demonstrations outside of Mudville County Stadium, when the Mudville Mudfrogs, a minor-league professional baseball team, plays its home games. Members of the group carry signs and hand out literature explaining their cause. Even though the events thus far have been peaceful, fans are complaining to police outside the stadium that the group's members are following them through the parking lots, attempting to talk to them and give them environmental literature. Owners of the team acknowledge that while the stadium is owned by the county and run by the MCSA, it is leased to them for home games and therefore they should have more control over who can and cannot distribute literature.

To add more fuel to the conflict, a pro-business group, People for Economic Expansion, has filed a complaint with the MCSA, claiming that if the Treehugger Society is allowed to distribute literature at the stadium, then its own members should also be allowed to distribute literature promoting their views, which are often in opposition to those of the Treehugger Society.

The MCSA has enforced a policy for many years of prohibiting the distribution of commercial literature (such as restaurant flyers) on the stadium grounds, but it has allowed candidates for public office to distribute campaign literature.

The MCSA will meet one week from tonight to discuss a proposal to ban all forms of literature and speech on stadium grounds. You must recommend to the MCSA one of the following courses of action: (1) to allow all forms of literature and speech, (2) to allow no forms of literature or speech, or (3) to allow only certain forms of speech (specify which). Explain how your recommendation, if it became a new county policy, would affect the two groups described above and how it fits in with generally accepted principles of communication law.

SOCRATIC DIALOGUE QUESTIONS

1. Consider the scenario described earlier in the chapter in which protestors gather at the sites of military funerals in order to express dissatisfaction with homosexuals serving in the war in Iraq. Which rules (from this chapter) should apply, and to what degree?

2. Consider the section titled "Compelled Speech" and the cases involving automobile license plates bearing the phrase

"Choose Life," which has been challenged by abortion rights activists. How are those cases different from the *Wooley v. Maynard* ("Live Free or Die") case? If you were in a position to make the decision, which of the following courses of action would you take: (a) allow only one side in a controversial debate to sponsor license plates, depending on the preference of the legislature; (b) allow both groups to sponsor license plates provided they followed the same guidelines as non-controversial groups; or (c) decide that state license plates should stay out of politics and disallow any political or potentially controversial messages?

Is there a slippery slope problem in this conflict? Suppose you choose (b) and allow both sides in the abortion debates to sponsor their own license plates. What if a white supremacist group and other controversial groups want their own license plates?

3. This chapter includes several cases that illustrate the bad tendency test and clear and present danger tests, but none to illustrate the balancing tests. Why are those examples missing?

4. If you went to the second floor of the university library and began shouting criticisms of the university loud enough to be heard on the first floor, under which legal principles (from Chapters 2 and 3) could the university officials require you to leave?

5. Do you agree with the court rulings in the *Marchetti* and *Snepp* cases? Is it possible for a government employee to "sign away" his or her First Amendment rights as a condition of employment, or are those rights so basic that they cannot be signed away, even if the person was willing? If you were the judge assigned to the case, how would you decide the *Jawbreaker* case?

6. Do you agree with the Supreme Court decisions and legal principles described in this chapter? To what degree should the government be allowed to exercise prior restraint over the news coverage of military operations?

7. In *Meese v. Keene,* the documentary films at issue were clearly examples of political speech. Does the fact that they were produced outside of the United States disqualify them from First Amendment protection as political speech? Which of the following

parties has the strongest claim that its First Amendment rights are being limited by the "propaganda label"—the Canadian organization that produced the films, the coordinator of the film festival (Keene), or the potential audience that may never get to see the films?

8. Re-read the section on the clear and present danger test and consider some of the relevant cases. Now compare and contrast the Espionage Act of 1917 with the USA Patriot Act.

9. The Supreme Court has ruled in *New York Times v. United States* (the Pentagon Papers case described in the previous section) and similar cases that injunctions are an unconstitutional form of prior restraint. But in other cases, the court has ruled that the military can exercise prior restraint over news coverage coming out of war zones and other military operations. Is this a contradiction or inconsistency?

10. Consider the section titled "Discriminatory Licensing" and the cases of *Lovell v. Griffin* (1938) and *Watchtower Bible & Tract Society of New York v. Village of Stratton* (2002). In those cases, the Supreme Court ruled that local governments could not prohibit religious groups and political supporters from door-to-door soliciting. Agree or disagree?

11. Consider the case of anti-war protestors choosing to demonstrate at or near the funerals of military personnel killed in Iraq (or any controversial war). Factoring in concepts such as obtrusive vs. non-obtrusive speech, limited public forums vs. traditional public forums, time-place-manner, and other issues discussed in Chapters 2 and 3, what types of rules should apply?

12. Find at least one case in Chapter 3 with which you strongly disagree with the court ruling (in the final resolution of the case) and be prepared to share your opinion with the class.

GLOSSARY OF TERMS

Ad hoc balancing A test in which courts begin with a "clean slate" in evaluating specific and localized issues and judge each case on its own merits without preconceived notions of which side should prevail.

Bad tendency test A standard, no longer applied, for evaluating the potential danger of political speech. Under this standard, speech could be limited if it presented even the slightest danger of harm.

Balancing tests The standard most often applied today in evaluating the potential danger of political speech. Using this standard, the courts weigh citizens' free speech rights against the government's interest in regulating potentially harmful speech.

Blackstonian Doctrine A policy of not exercising prior restraint but instead punishing the source of harmful speech after it occurs; first suggested by English legal scholar William Blackstone.

Clear and present danger test A standard used during much of the 1900s for evaluating the potential danger of political speech. Under this standard, harmful speech must do more than create a bad tendency, it must result in a high likelihood of harm, such as cases in which audiences exposed to the speech are motivated to conduct violent acts.

Compelled speech The act of forcing someone to participate, either directly or indirectly, in speech to which they object; generally not allowed by the Supreme Court.

Content neutrality The policy of evaluating speech without consideration of its content, usually paying more attention to its time, place, and manner.

Discriminatory licensing The abuse of government discretion in the issuing of licensing for communication. The principle was first applied to door-to-door soliciting, but today is also applied in discussions of broadcasting licenses.

Discriminatory taxation The application of tax policy based on content of the materials involved, such as taxing pornographic literature at a higher rate than literature of a less controversial nature. This type of taxation is unconstitutional as determined by the Supreme Court.

Equivalent function rule A collective term for state laws that require owners of shopping centers and other privately owned property to allow the same free speech opportunities offered by public places. Also known as the **rule of quasi-public-places.**

Gag order A judge's directive to participants in a legal proceeding not to discuss the case with outside parties, including the media.

Injunction A legal action in which a court issues an order for the offending party to stop a specific activity.

Limited public forum A public place in which speech can be limited because of concerns for safety or the potential for congestion.

Non-public forum Government-supervised venues in which speech is customarily not allowed, such as military installations and prisons.

O'Brien Test A three-part standard for evaluating laws dealing with displays of contempt for the government or its policies.

Overbreadth and vagueness Adjectives used to describe laws that are too loosely structured or that use terms too difficult to define; such laws are typically found unconstitutional by the courts.

Preferred position theory of balancing A test in which courts begin to evaluate a case with the assumption that rights protected by the Constitution take priority over other rights.

Pre-publication agreement Part of an employment contract that requires government employees and former employees to submit book manuscripts for approval and censorship.

Prior restraint A formal term for censorship; the act of preventing speech before it takes place.

Propaganda labeling The government's attempt to identify speech critical of the country (see *Meese v. Keene*).

Punishment after the fact As opposed to prior restraint, the policy of waiting until after speech occurs to determine potential harm and decide appropriate punishment.

Rational basis standard A rule that states that when the government attempts to restrict speech, it must have a "rational basis" for doing so; i.e., the burden rests on the government to prove why the speech must be restricted, as opposed to being on the speaker to prove why the speech should not be suppressed.

Strict scrutiny   The tendency of the courts to place a heavy burden on the government to prove why prior restraint or other action is necessary in a particular case.

Time, place, and manner   An extension of content neutrality; a policy of making prior restraint decisions based not on content but on when, where, and how the speech takes place.

Traditional public forum   A public place in which political speech is expected and seldom regulated, such as a public park or the sidewalk outside a government building.

NOTES

1. *Gitlow v. New York*, 268 U.S. 652 (1925).
2. Douglas M. Fraleigh and Joseph S. Tuman, *Freedom of Speech in the Marketplace of Ideas.* New York, N.Y.: St. Martin's Press, 1997, p. 90.
3. *Schenck v. United States*, 249 U.S. 47 (1919).
4. *Abrams v. United States*, 50 U.S. 616 (1919).
5. *Dennis v. United States*, 341 U.S. 494 (1951).
6. *Yates v. United States*, 354 U.S. 298 (1957).
7. *Brandenburg v. Ohio*, 395 U.S. 444 (1969).
8. *Bantam Books v. Sullivan*, 372 U.S. 58 (1963).
9. *Cox v. New Hampshire*, 312 U.S. 569 (1941).
10. *Heffron v. Krishna*, 452 U.S. 640 (1981).
11. *U.S. v. Grace*, 461 U.S. 171 (1983).
12. *Clark v. Community for Creative Non-Violence*, 468 U.S. 288 (1984).
13. *Ward v. Rock Against Racism*, 491 U.S. 781 (1989).
14. *Frisby v. Schultz*, 487 U.S. 474 (1988).
15. *Schenck v. Pro-Choice Network*, 117 S.Ct. 855 (1997).
16. *Lloyd Corporation v. Tanner*, 407 U.S. 551 (1972).
17. *Pruneyard Shopping Center v. Robins*, 447 U.S. 74 (1980).
18. *Marsh v. Alabama*, 326 U.S. 501 (1946).
19. *Houston v. Hill*, 482 U.S. 451 (1987).
20. *United States v. O'Brien*, 391 U.S. 367 (1968).
21. *Texas v. Johnson*, 491 U.S. 397 (1989).
22. *United States v. Eichman*, 496 U.S. 310 (1990).
23. *West Virginia State Board of Education v. Barnette*, 319 U.S. 624 (1943).
24. *Wooley v. Maynard*, 430 U.S. 705 (1977).
25. *Hurley v. Irish-American Gay, Lesbian, and Bisexual Group of Boston*, 115 S.Ct. 1338 (1995).
26. *Miami Herald v. Tornillo*, 418 U.S. 241 (1974).
27. *Glickman v. Wileman & Eliott*, 521 U.S. 457 (1997).
28. *Johanns v. Livestock Marketing Association*, 125 S.Ct. 2055 (2005).
29. *United States v. United Foods*, 533 U.S. 405 (2001).
30. Gina Holland, "Farmers Have a Beef With Paying for Ads." Associated Press report, December 9, 2004.
31. "Courts to Determine if 'Choose Life' Plates are Constitutional." Associated Press report, January 25, 2005.
32. "Appeals Court Denies Rehearing on Anti-Abortion License Plates." Associated Press report, June 28, 2004.
33. Lucas L. Johnson, "Federal Appeals Court Allows 'Choose Life' Plates in Tennessee." *Chattanooga Times Free Press* (March 18, 2006,): A-1.
34. Ibid.
35. Robert Trager, Joseph Russomanno, and Susan Dente Ross, *The Law of Journalism and Mass Communication* (Boston, Mass.: McGraw-Hill, 1007), p.99.
36. *Harper and Row Publishers v. The Nation*, 471 U.S. 539 (1985).
37. *Rice v. Paladin Enterprises*, 128 F.3d 233 (1997).
38. *United States v. Marchetti*, 466 F.2d 1309 (1972).
39. *Snepp v. United States*, 444 U.S. 507 (1980).
40. Dana Priest, "Suing Over the CIA's Red Pen; Retired Operative Says Agency Unfairly Edited His Book." *Washington Post* (October 9, 2006,): A-15.
41. *The Nation v. Department of Defense*, 762 F. Supp. 1558 (1991).
42. *Meese v. Keene*, 481 U.S. 465 (1987).
43. *Near v. Minnesota*, 283 U.S. 697 (1931).
44. *New York Times v. United States*, 403 U.S. 713 (1971).
45. *United States v. Progressive*, 467 F. Supp. 990 (1979).
46. *Lovell v. Griffin*, 303 U.S. 444 (1938).
47. *Watchtower Bible & Tract Society of New York v. Village of Stratton*, 536 U.S. 150 (2002).
48. *Lakewood v. Plain Dealer Publishing*, 486 U.S. 750 (1988); *Cincinnati v. Discovery Network*, 507 U.S. 410 (1993).
49. *Grosjean v. American Press Co.*, 297 U.S. 233 (1936).
50. *Simon & Schuster v. New York State Crime Victims Board*, 502 U.S. 105 (1991).
51. Harriet Chiang, "Son of Sam Law Nullified in California." *San Francisco Chronicle* (January 23, 2002): 7-A.
52. David L. Hudson, "The Patriot Act: An Overview." Freedom Forum First Amendment Center.
53. *Texas v. Johnson*, 491 U.S. 397 (1989).
54. Ibid.

4 The First Amendment and Sexual Expression

I do not know how to define obscenity. But I know it when I see it.

Justice Potter Stewart
Jacobellis v. Ohio, 1964

Just as there is no use arguing about taste, there is no use litigating about it.

Justice Antonin Scalia
Pope v. Illinois, 1987

If the First Amendment means anything, it means that a state has no business telling a man, sitting alone in his own house, what books he may read or what films he may watch.

Justice Thurgood Marshall
Stanley v. Georgia, 1969

The government cannot stand at the gateway to the free market and decide which ideas are worth expressing and which are not.

Norman Siegel
Director, New York Chapter,
American Civil Liberties Union

LEARNING OBJECTIVES

As a result of reading this chapter, students should:

- Understand the three categories used by the Supreme Court to define various types of sexual expression, as well as the Court's rationale behind treating each category differently.

- Understand the history of pornography and obscenity regulation, with an emphasis on the transition of the pornography industry from its beginnings (as "dirty bookstores") to one acknowledged by Wall Street analysts as having a major impact on the American economy.

- Understand the role played by technology in the expansion of the pornography industry.

Defining Sexual Content

The Supreme Court uses three categories—obscenity, non-obscene sexual expression, and indecency—to define various forms of sexual expression, with each category being treated differently by the Court.

Many people use the terms *obscenity* and *pornography* as if they are interchangeable terms, but they are not. **Obscenity**(from the Greek for "filth") is a legal term used to describe sexually explicit material that is so offensive that it does not deserve First Amendment protection. **Pornography** (from the Greek for "writing about prostitutes") is actually an artistic term rather than a legal term and describes a broader category of material that is sexually arousing, but not to the degree of being obscene; pornography still receives limited First Amendment protection. There are many examples of books and movies that could be considered pornographic but not obscene.

Obscenity, the only one of the three categories that is not constitutionally protected, is determined by a standard called the Miller Test, which resulted from the 1973 Supreme Court case, *Miller v. California*[1] (discussed later in this chapter).

At both the federal and state levels, lawmakers and the courts have always considered child pornography (this is one of the few cases in which "pornography" is used in a legal sense) to be in the same category as obscenity and therefore not deserving of First Amendment protection. Nearly every state in the nation has one or more laws dealing with child pornography, and those laws are typically upheld by the courts when challenged.

In 1977, Congress passed the Protection of Children Against Sexual Exploitation Act, which made it illegal to produce, sell, distribute, or possess child pornography in the form of still photographs, motion pictures, or videotapes. The law was upheld in the 1982 case of *New York v. Ferber*, in which the Supreme Court ruled that the constitutional standards for evaluating adult pornography and child pornography are not the same.[2] The Court made a similar ruling in the 1990 case of *Osborne v. Ohio*.[3]

Non-obscene sexual expression is a broader category that deals with material of a sexual nature that does not meet the standards of the Miller Test, a standard for evaluating cases involving material accused of being obscene (discussed later in this chapter). Examples include exotic dancing, adult magazines, and adult videos—expressions that might be objectionable or distasteful but are not offensive enough to be labeled obscene.

While topless dancing is permissible in most communities (subject to zoning laws and other time, place, and manner restrictions), nude dancing is not. In the 1991 case of *Barnes v. Glen Theatre*, the Supreme Court upheld an Indiana law prohibiting nude dancing. While the Court recognized the expressive nature of such dancing, it determined that it was on the "outer fringes" of First Amendment protection and that the state had a compelling interest in enforcing its law, in this case for the safety of the performers.[4] Other states have laws that prohibit nude dancing only within businesses that serve alcohol.

Some states have attempted to further restrict adult businesses with zoning laws based on "secondary effects," such as an increase in crime rates or a decrease in property values, but courts generally find such laws unconstitutional because they claim that crime rates and property values are affected by too many other variables.

The label of "non-obscene sexual expression" typically means that the government can apply time, place, and manner restrictions to the materials in question but cannot ban them altogether. Examples of time, place, and manner restrictions on non-obscene sexual expression are zoning regulations for adult businesses, local ordinances requiring minimum ages for purchases, and limitations on what may be distributed through the mail (as determined by the U.S. Postal Service). These restrictions are sometimes referred to as the brown paper wrapper principle—so named because publishers of adult magazines would often mail their products that way—and are designed to ensure that material is not available to minors or forced onto "unwilling" adults but is still available to adults who voluntarily seek it out.

In the 1968 case of *Ginsberg v. New York* (discussed in more detail later in this chapter), the Supreme Court upheld a state law prohibiting the sale of pornographic magazines to anyone under the age of seventeen.[5]

In the 1986 case of *City of Renton v. Playtime Theatres,* the Court upheld a city ordinance banning adult theatres within 1,000 feet of a residential neighborhood, church, public park, or school. Although not spelled out in the written decisions, both cases involved the Supreme Court applying the time, place, and manner principle in upholding the authority of state and local governments in regulating sexual expression.[6]

The Supreme Court, however, does not subscribe to the belief that individuals can expect absolute protection from offensive material. In the 1975 case of *Erznoznik v. City of Jacksonville,* for example, the Supreme Court invalidated a city ordinance that prohibited drive-in theaters from showing films with nudity if their screens were visible from the street or other public place.[7]

Feminist writer Andrea Dworkin and law school professor Catharine MacKinnon have co-authored a number of academic articles in which they argue that pornography and adult businesses should be illegal (as obscenity is now) because such materials and commercial enterprises subordinate and dehumanize women and contribute to violent acts such as rape, incest, and abuse.[8] Law school professor Marianne Wesson doesn't necessarily agree with an outright ban but argues that sexual assault victims should be able to sue those who made and distributed the harmful material or activities. She does not cite the Blackstonian Doctrine, but the premise is the same.[9]

Indecency (from the Latin for "the opposite of something that is fitting") is an even broader term than non-obscene sexual expression. It is used mainly to refer to broadcasting and musical performances. While most indecency has sexual connotations, this category also includes profanity and references to bodily functions. Much like non-obscene sexual expression, material labeled "indecent" may be offensive to many audiences but is not offensive enough to qualify for the "obscenity" label as determined by the Miller Test.

The definitions for obscenity, non-obscene sexual expression, and indecency are important because each time the Supreme Court (or other court) evaluates a case involving offensive material, it first uses those three definitions to categorize it. Generally, the courts are reluctant to limit any type of sexual expression because so much art includes sexual expression, and vice versa.

History of Obscenity Laws

The Hicklin Rule and the Comstock Act

The history of obscenity regulation begins with the English law case *Regina v. Hicklin*(1868), which resulted in the **Hicklin Rule.** The Hicklin Rule stated that a work was obscene if it "had the tendency to deprave and corrupt those whose minds are open to such immoral influences," such as children.[10] Without a standard of their own, American courts depended on the Hicklin Rule for the five-year period that followed.

In the United States, the first law aimed at regulating sexual expression was a federal statute called the **Comstock Act,** passed in 1873. The law was named after Anthony Comstock, a New York grocer and social activist who worked with the Young Men's Christian Association (YMCA) in New York to form the Committee for the Suppression of Vice. In 1873, the committee persuaded Congress to pass a law prohibiting the mailing of obscene books, pamphlets, newspapers, and periodicals.

The major weakness of the Comstock Act was similar to that of the Hicklin Rule—vagueness and overbreadth. With no specific definition, obscenity was deemed to be anything related to sex that offended the values of the person or groups making the charges. The law also allowed the terms *obscenity* and *indecency* to be used as though they were synonymous—a problem that would not be clarified for almost a century. As a result, the law was used to ban many classic literary works, including Aristophanes's *Lysistrata* and George Bernard Shaw's *Mrs. Warren's Profession.*

The Early 1900s

In the early 1900s, politicians feared that the newly developed technology of motion picture film would lead to the downfall of public morals—and not just because of the sexual content of films but because of other reasons as well. For example, Congress banned the interstate transport of prizefighting films after African American boxer Jack Johnson defeated Jim Jeffries, a white former heavyweight champion; and in some communities, politicians expressed concern that films such as *The Great Train Robbery* would lead to an increase in violent crime.

Many communities created film censorship boards to determine which films were acceptable for the public to see. In the 1915 case of *Mutual Film Corporation v. Industrial Commission of Ohio,* the Supreme Court upheld the authority of such a committee in Ohio, which had claimed it would approve of only those films that were of a "moral, educational, or amusing and harmless character." At that time, films received no First Amendment protection because they were considered entertainment products rather than forms of speech, and therefore the Court did not apply First Amendment values in evaluating the Ohio case.[11]

The 1950s: The Roth Test

In 1952, the Supreme Court heard an appeal of a case that was unrelated to the Comstock Act but which was significant because it put motion picture film under First Amendment protection. The case of *Joseph Burstyn Inc. v. Wilson* originated with a movie titled *The Miracle*, which was never accused of being obscene but was banned in New York state because it was considered sacrilegious.

The case resulted in the first application of the First Amendment to entertainment. Prior to that case, **censorship** of movies was generally accepted because society and the courts interpreted the First Amendment as applying only to political speech and not entertainment. But in this case, the Supreme Court put entertainment in the same category with political speech in terms of First Amendment protection and ruled that movies could not be censored.[12]

The Supreme Court first attempted to define obscenity in the 1957 case of *Butler v. Michigan*, in which the Court invalidated a state law prohibiting the sale of printed matter that tended to "incite minors to violent or depraved or immoral acts." Justice Felix Frankfurter, writing the majority opinion, expressed concern about the breadth of the Michigan law, stating that while protecting youth, it also limited access to the same material by adults. The *Butler* case helped to make the distinction between obscenity and non-obscene sexual expression. The Court ruled that while the objective of protecting youth was admirable, the Michigan statute was overbroad because it also restricted access to the same material for adults and was analogous to "burning down the house in order to roast the pig."[13]

Shortly after the *Butler* case came a similar case, *Roth v. United States*, in which the Supreme Court determined that there was no constitutional protection for obscenity.[14] The case involved Samuel Roth, who was prosecuted under the Comstock Act for mailing obscenity. The Supreme Court upheld his conviction and provided a four-part standard for evaluating obscenity cases, called the **Roth Test:**

> Material is obscene if the **average person** finds the **dominant theme** appeals to **prurient interests** and is **without redeeming social importance.**

The Roth Test was the standard for deciding obscenity cases from 1957 through 1973, but it was modified in the 1966 case of *Memoirs v. Massachusetts,*[15] when the Supreme Court added the phrase "utterly without redeeming social value" as the third prong of the Roth Test, making it nearly impossible for prosecutors to obtain obscenity convictions.

One of the most significant cases of that era was *Stanley v. Georgia* (1969), which began when police entered the private home of an alleged bookmaker.

During the search, the police found an 8mm film, which they viewed and labeled as obscenity. The owner of the home was convicted, but when his appeal reached the Supreme Court, the justices ruled that mere possession of obscene material, with no intent to sell or distribute, could not be declared illegal and was not subject to government action because it was a matter of personal privacy. (In 1990, however, the Court clarified that the ruling does not apply to possession of child pornography, which remains illegal to possess.[16]) In its majority opinion, the Court determined that, "If the First Amendment means anything, it means that a state has no business telling a man, sitting alone in his own house, what books he may read or what films he may watch. Our whole constitutional heritage rebels at the thought of giving government the power to control men's minds."[17]

The 1970s: The Miller Test

Shortly before the *Stanley* ruling, President Lyndon Johnson ordered a government study to investigate the issue of obscenity. The committee determined that there was no relationship between sexually explicit material and anti-social behavior, and in its final report, issued in 1970, the committee recommended that the government "give up" on trying to eliminate obscenity altogether. As alternatives, the committee recommended the government (1) concentrate on limiting access to sexually explicit material by minors, and (2) encourage local school systems to develop comprehensive sex education programs for students in public elementary and secondary schools. Richard Nixon, a more conservative president than his predecessors, did not accept the findings of the study, and after taking office in 1969, he appointed more conservative justices to the Supreme Court in an attempt to curtail obscenity.

The Court got its first chance to deal with the obscenity issue in 1973 with the case of *Miller v. California*.The case began when pornographer Marvin Miller was convicted under a California law regarding the mailing of obscenity. The Supreme Court did not decide on Miller's guilt or innocence; it merely reviewed the constitutionality of the California law under which he was prosecuted. The Court sent Miller's case back to the California court to be re-tried, but in its written opinion ruled that obscenity should "not be available to minors or unwilling participants." The Court also developed what later became known as the **Miller Test** that established a three-part standard for determining whether material was obscene. The Miller Test is not an obscenity law per se, but rather a guideline for courts to use to determine if state laws or city or county ordinances are constitutional.

According to the Miller Test, material is obscene if:

1. The average person, applying contemporary community standards, finds the dominant theme appeals on a whole to prurient interests.
2. The material depicts in a patently offensive way sexual conduct specifically defined by a state law.
3. The work, as a whole, lacks serious artistic, literary, political, or scientific value.[18]

A video store offering sexually explicit material near the Port Authority Bus Terminal in New York, March, 2005. Ten years after Mayor Rudolph Giuliani declared war on Times Square's X-rated peep shows, strip joints and video stores, shops selling sexually explicit materials have slowly begun to creep back into the area, adroitly exploiting loopholes in the low and property-owners' demand for high-paying tenants to stage their comeback.

In essence, in developing the Miller Test, the Supreme Court abandoned the idea of a national standard for obscenity and instead emphasized the components—"contemporary community standards" and "defined by a state law."

While it is not without its critics, the Miller Test has been a valuable guideline for more than three decades. Any time the Supreme Court or any other court has to decide a case involving a book, film, or videotape accused of being obscene, it first uses the Miller Test to categorize the material. Community leaders often disagree about what constitutes "contemporary community standards," but in the 1974 case of *Jenkins v. Georgia,* which involved the film *Carnal Knowledge,* the Court ruled that nudity by itself is not obscene. Other cases have made other distinctions, such as rulings that images of people having sex are not obscene, nor are images of homosexual acts. In the 1987 case of *Pope v. Illinois,* which involved the prosecution of store clerks for selling allegedly obscene materials to undercover police officers, the Court struck down a state law as unconstitutionally vague and clarified that the third prong of the Miller Test should be judged by a "reasonable person" rather than an "average person." In writing a concurring opinion, Justice Antonin Scalia distinguished the case as one involving matters of taste rather than law and declared that "just as it is useless to argue about taste, it is useless to litigate about it."[19]

Today, the term *community standards* presents a number of problems and has prompted many legal experts to argue that the Miller Test has outlived its usefulness. When the Supreme Court developed the test, it was assumed that the term *community* described a physical place with finite boundaries, such as a city or a county. Today, with controversial material being produced in one city and distributed by cable systems and the Internet across the country and around the world, legal experts worry that the difficulty in defining what constitutes a "community" makes the Miller Test outdated. Is the "online community" a community?

But debate over the term *community* is not a new one. As far back as 1989, a federal judge in California dismissed a case against an adult video distributor because the judge said that in Los Angeles alone, the population was so diverse as to prevent anyone from producing "positive evidence of what the entire community believes in."

In addition to allowing individual cities, counties, and state governments to set their own criteria for determining what constitutes obscenity in a general sense, the courts also allow individual communities to set different standards for different audiences, a concept known as **variable obscenity.** The most common example is a local ordinance that states that material that falls into the "indecency" or "non-obscene sexual expression" category when consumed by an adult audience may be classified as "obscenity" when consumed by minors. One of the notable cases in this area was *Ginsberg v. New York* (1968), which began when a convenience store operator on Long Island, New York, was charged with selling adult magazines to a minor. The conflict eventually reached the U.S. Supreme Court, which ruled that material suitable for adults (although objectionable) was far more harmful in the hands of children.[20]

The legitimacy of variable obscenity clauses in local and state obscenity statutes is not guaranteed, however. In the 1994 case of *Soundgarden v. Eikenberry*, a federal court found unconstitutional a Washington state law that prohibited music stores and other retailers from selling "sexually explicit" music to minors. In striking down the law, the court ruled that with no labeling procedure in place (at the time), retailers had no way to determine which recordings were covered by the law, and if they restricted the sale of all material with which they had concerns, the result would be to limit access to adults.[21]

The 1980s: The Meese Commission

In the 1980s, the central focus of the anti-pornography movement was the elimination of child pornography. In the 1982 case of *New York v. Ferber*, for example, the Supreme Court upheld a state statute prohibiting child pornography even if the material was not deemed to be obscene. The Court determined that contrary to the findings of the 1970 report that concluded there was no connection between sexual explicit material and anti-social behavior, child pornography indeed had a detrimental effect on both the audience and on the child performers, who in many cases were forced into participating. Further, the Court stated, child pornography had little social or artistic value, based on the third part of the Miller Test.[22]

In 1984, Congress passed the Child Protection Act, which placed child pornography under the umbrella of obscenity and thereby authorized government officials to prosecute such cases. It also broadened the U.S. Postal Service's authority to inspect mail and seize materials suspected of being child pornography.

In the 1985 case of *American Booksellers Association v. Hudnut,* a federal appeals court invalidated an Indianapolis ordinance outlawing the sale of pornography. The court determined the material in question did not meet the Miller Test definition of obscenity and cited the "slippery slope" problem that would result if a city government was allowed to regulate any form of speech it determined to carry the potential for harm. The Court drew a distinction in this case between so-called "adult pornography" (which it classified as non-obscene sexual expression) and the child pornography involved in the *Ferber* case.[23]

In 1986, a second presidential commission—this time appointed by President Ronald Reagan and headed by Attorney General Edwin Meese—held six hearings and considered the testimony of 208 witnesses. The commission's 1,960-page report concluded that pornography harms both the individual and society. The report stopped short of expanding the definition of obscenity; instead, it encouraged federal and state governments to enact tougher obscenity laws and to create a task force within the Justice Department to enforce existing laws.

Social scientists disputed the findings of the Meese Commission, while legal scholars, free speech advocates, and representatives of the pornography industry criticized the report as biased because it depended too much on the testimony of sexual assault victims, wives complaining about their husbands' addiction to pornography, and even former *Playboy* centerfold models who told of their experiences. Soon after completion of the report, the Justice Department doubled the number of investigators assigned to work on obscenity and child pornography cases, and as a result, the number of prosecutions and convictions also doubled.

Because of the negative connotation the report attached to soft-core magazines such as *Playboy* and *Penthouse,* many bookstores, convenience stores, and newsstands stopped carrying such publications. Circulation of such publications dropped temporarily but later recovered after an increase in mail subscriptions.

The 1990s and 2000s: The Era of Cable and the Internet

In 1992, the Cable Television and Consumer Protection Act was passed, with several provisions relating to obscene and indecent programming. In general, however, the Justice Department chose a new list of priorities in the early- and mid-1990s: domestic terrorism, white-collar crime, anti-trust litigation, and civil rights issues, such as employment discrimination and racial profiling. Under Attorney General Janet Reno, obscenity was moved to the back burner on the Department of Justice's list of law enforcement priorities, and it remained there for the duration of the Clinton Administration.

Even though the Justice Department was lax in prosecuting obscenity cases during this era, new laws were still being enacted. One significant law was the Child Pornography Prevention Act (CPPA) of 1996, which made it a federal crime to reproduce, distribute, sell, receive, or possess child pornography. The law expanded previous child pornography legislation by prohibiting not only those materials using actual children, but also those using "adults that appear to be children" and computer-generated images of children, which lawmakers referred to as "virtual porn." The law was challenged by the adult film industry, which used the pseudonym "Free Speech Coalition." In 2002, in the case of *Ashcroft v. Free Speech Coalition*, the U.S. Supreme Court ruled that the CPPA was overbroad because it went past the boundaries of previous cases, including *Miller v. California* (1973) and *New York v. Ferber* (1982). In illustrating the overbreadth of the law, the court cited examples of legitimate materials that could be illegal under a loose interpretation of the law, such as photographs in a psychology textbook or a documentary film on child sexual abuse.[24]

Also in the mid-1990s, Congress began to address the problem of obscenity on the Internet with a series of three laws, two of which were declared unconstitutional by the Supreme Court. The first of the laws, the Communications Decency Act (CDA), was passed partly in response to a 1995 study by Carnegie-Mellon University that claimed that minors had access to "rampant pornography" on the Internet.[25] Those findings were later determined to be exaggerated, yet the study was taken seriously enough for Congress, led by Senator James Exon (D-Nebraska), to pass the CDA as part of the Telecommunications Act of 1996. The second law, the Child Online Protection Act (COPA), was similar to the CDA and was also ruled to be unconstitutional. The only one of the three laws still in effect is the Children's Internet Protection Act (CIPA), which requires libraries receiving public funding to install filters on their computers to prevent children from accessing sexually explicit material. All three laws are discussed in more detail in Chapter 10.

When President George W. Bush took office in 2001, new Attorney General John Ashcroft was planning to introduce a plan in early September of that year that would rededicate the resources of the Justice Department to obscenity prosecutions but with an emphasis on publications and videos rather than the Internet. The terrorist attacks of September 11, however, caused the Justice Department to de-emphasize the obscenity issue once again, this time in favor of homeland security and related issues. The changing priorities allowed the pornography industry to expand into a multi-billion dollar industry. *The Wall Street Journal* estimates the industry's impact on the American economy to be at least $10 billion annually, with $2 billion of that figure coming from online adult businesses. The *Journal* also estimates the latter figure to account for 5 to 10 percent of all the money spent online.[26]

In early 2006, under new Attorney General Alberto Gonzalez, the Justice Department announced the formation of an obscenity prosecution task force that would prioritize its work in areas such as child pornography and materials that involve violence and murder.

Regulating Indecency

In the latter half of the twentieth century, a number of cases were argued in the courts regarding indecency as heard on the radio, spoken over the telephone, or found in recorded music.

In *FCC v. Pacifica* (1978), discussed in more detail in Chapter 9, the Court ruled that profanity in a radio broadcast was indecency rather than obscenity and therefore the FCC could only regulate it; it could not ban it altogether.[27]

The court made a similar ruling in the case of *Sable Communications v. FCC* (1989), which began in the late 1980s when Congress attempted to ban "phone-sex" lines or the so-called "dial-a-porn" industry operating through 1-900 and 1-976 lines. When Congress first addressed the issue, its objective was to ban all types of telephone services for which users had to pay a per-minute charge.

Mainstream 1-900 companies lobbied against the proposed law because they were offering services such as weather reports, consumer advice, financial information, and medical referrals and objected to being put into the same category as the phone-sex companies. These companies were successful in influencing Congress to limit the legislation to just the dial-a-porn industry.

As a result, Congress passed the Telephone Decency Act of 1988 and put the Federal Communications Commission (FCC) in charge of enforcing it. The act was based on the Supreme Court definitions of obscenity and indecency; under the new law, "obscene" content would result in a fine of $500,000, but content labeled as "indecent" would carry a fine of only $50,000.

The law was quickly challenged by Sable Communications, one of the pioneers of the phone-sex business. The central question for the Supreme Court was whether phone sex should be considered obscenity or indecency. The Court decided that phone sex fit the category of indecency, meaning the FCC could establish time, place, and manner restrictions but could not eliminate it altogether. The Court then ruled that the law was too broad because Congress and the FCC had the right to ban obscenity but not indecency.

The Court ruled that regardless of its offensive content, phone sex was different from radio and television broadcasting because it was non-obtrusive. "Placing a phone call is not the same as turning on a radio and being taken by surprise by an indecent message," the majority opinion said. "Unlike an unexpected outburst on a radio broadcast, the message received by one who places a call to a dial-a-porn service is not so invasive or surprising that it prevents an unwilling listener from avoiding exposure to it."[28]

Because the material involved in the Sable case (and the majority of other phone-sex cases) was determined to be indecency rather than obscenity, the Court ruled in favor of Sable and suggested that Congress revise the law, which it did. The new law reinforced the FCC's authority to place "time, place, and manner" restrictions on indecency. Included in those restrictions is a requirement that callers be at least eighteen years old and establish an account in advance.

In the early 1990s, a pair of lawsuits against the sheriff of Broward County, Florida, limited his ability to stop record stores in the community from selling a

A record store clerk is arrested for selling the 2 Live Crew album, As Nasty as They Wanna Be, *in 1991.*

record album accused of being obscene. 2 Live Crew's album *As Nasty As They Wanna Be* was pulled from the shelves after some record store owners were visited by sheriff's deputies and threatened with arrest. Other retailers learned about the threats through the local media and removed the controversial album from the shelves voluntarily.

When the case of *Skywalker Records v. Navarro* (1990) was argued in Federal District Court, Sheriff Nick Navarro presented no evidence to support the obscenity charges against the group, other than a tape recording of the title track. The judge ruled the album was obscene but failed to consider the testimony of expert witnesses regarding the album's "artistic value" as defined by the Miller Test.[29] In the appeal of the case, *Luke Records v. Navarro* (1992), a higher court ruled that the sheriff's actions were an unconstitutional form of prior restraint and the lower court erred by declaring the album obscene based solely on listening to the tape. As a result, the album was categorized as indecent rather than obscene.[30]

The Supreme Court declined to hear the appeal of the *Luke Records* case, but several years later it heard the appeal of a case involving indecency in public displays of art. The conflict began in the late 1980s when artist Robert Mapplethorpe produced a display of indecent art using National Endowment for the Arts (NEA) grants. Outraged by the descriptions of the art and motivated by complaints from constituents, the NEA revised its funding process, requiring a higher standard of "artistic excellence and artistic merit" to be used in the distribution of future grants. Four artists, previously awarded NEA grants but denied funding under the new guidelines, sued the NEA for violation of their First Amendment rights.

Two lower courts ruled in their favor, judging the new rules to be unconstitutional. When the case reached the Supreme Court, however, those decisions were overturned. In *National Endowment for the Arts v. Finley* (1998), the Court ruled that the regulations were content neutral because they did not require the NEA to deny funding to indecent displays and instead suggested indecency as only one of several factors to be considered.[31]

The Movie Rating System

In an effort to prevent government regulation, the American film industry has made several attempts at regulating itself—not prohibiting controversial content but agreeing to a labeling system to help parents decide on the suitability of films for their children. In the late 1960s, the Motion Picture Association of America (MPAA) developed a rating system that placed films into four categories: G for general audiences, M for mature, R for restricted (children under the age of seventeen had to be accompanied by a parent or guardian), and X for adults only (no one under seventeen permitted).

In the 1970s, the M rating was changed to PG (parental guidance), and in the 1980s it was subdivided into PG and PG-13. PG meant that some material may not be suitable for children, while the PG-13 label meant that parents were strongly cautioned about bringing children under the age of thirteen to the theater. In the 1990s, the MPAA became annoyed at adult movie producers and theaters using the X label (and in some cases, XXX) for films that had never been rated, so the MPAA changed its X designation to NC-17 and registered it as a trademark in order to prevent its unauthorized use.[32]

In 1990, the producer of a Spanish film *Tie Me Up, Tie Me Down* sued the MPAA after the film received the X rating. The MPAA successfully defended itself in the case, but was admonished by the New York Supreme Court and told that its rating system was out-of-date. A group of Hollywood directors agreed and urged the association to update its system, which it did. In addition to changing X to NC-17, the association added more details to the descriptions of the other ratings.[33]

The ratings are given by committees of individuals—many of them parents—serving on jury-like panels.

Banning Books, Movies, and Videos

Just as they have with movies, communities have also attempted with varying degrees of success to ban controversial books and videos.

In a 1933 case, an effort to ban James Joyce's *Ulysses* from libraries and bookstores was struck down by a federal judge in New York. While not allowing that work to be banned, his decision provided that books could be banned if they were obscene, which the judge described as books written with the intent of "stirring lustful thoughts" in the minds of the reader.[34] In the late 1950s and early 1960s, similar efforts were undertaken to ban controversial books such as D. H. Lawrence's *Lady Chatterley's Lover,* Henry Miller's *Tropic of Cancer,* and *Memoirs of a Woman of Pleasure,* which was a re-titled version of John Cleland's *Fanny Hill,* which had been briefly banned in the city of Boston in the 1820s. In each case, however, lower courts ruled the books fell short of meeting the Roth Test.

In a mid-1960s case unrelated to the MPAA rating system described earlier, the city of Boston attempted to ban the film *I am Curious Yellow.* When the case reached the Supreme Court, the Court ruled against the city and cited the slippery slope argument: "I think the First Amendment bars all kinds of censorship," Justice William O. Douglas wrote in the majority opinion. "What can be done to literature under the banner of obscenity can be done to other parts of the spectrum of ideas when party or majoritarian demands mount and propagandists start declaiming the law."[35]

In the late 1990s, an anti-pornography group called Oklahomans for Children and Families attempted to have the award-winning film *The Tin Drum* banned from video rental stores and the public library in Oklahoma City, claiming that despite its artistic and historical value, it was child pornography. City police confiscated copies from store and library shelves, as well as from the homes of private citizens. The stores and individuals sued the city, claiming violation of their First Amendment right of freedom of expression and Fourth Amendment rights regarding unreasonable search and seizure. After two years of litigation, the city agreed to pay a judgment in excess of $500,000 to the companies and individuals involved. According to news reports, legal fees pushed the cost to the taxpayers to more than $1 million.[36]

Frequently Asked Questions about Pornography and Obscenity

1. *I often hear terms such as hard-core pornography and soft-core pornography. Are these terms the same as "obscenity" and "non-obscene sexual expression"?* No. "Hard-core" and "soft-core" are adjectives not applicable to a serious discussion of sexual expression, as the two terms—sometimes used to describe different levels of printed and visual material—have no legal foundation. "Non-obscene sexual expression" includes what some people may refer to as soft-core pornography, but it is actually a broader term because it also includes intangible forms of expression, such as exotic dancing.

2. *Why is nudity by itself not enough to make a movie obscene?* In a 1974 case, *Jenkins v. Georgia,* the Supreme Court ruled that nudity by itself is not obscene.

The determination was significant because without it, a claim could be made that photographs in medical journals or sex-education films shown in school were obscene merely because they included nudity.[37]

3. *Does the "X" or "NC-17" rating mean that a motion picture is obscene?* Most likely not. The rating system is a voluntary measure enacted by the motion picture industry, while obscenity is a legal standard that only a court can determine. Although the rating system establishes age limitations for certain films, the industry leaves it up to the theater operators to enforce them. There is little correlation between a film being rated NC-17 and being declared obscene. The MPAA may rate a film NC-17 because it is sexually explicit, but the film may not be offensive enough for a court to find it obscene. Conversely, many low-budget films would be declared obscene by a court but have never been submitted for an MPAA rating.

Point/Counterpoint: Punishing Pornography

Why Pornography Should be Outlawed

Pornography is immoral and corruptive. Because sex is an activity intended mainly for procreation, critics point out, its portrayal simply for gratification has little or no social value, especially when done out of wedlock. In their 1993 book, *Pornography,* sociologists Daniel Linz and Neil Malamuth describe the "conservative-moralist" view of pornography that states, "What was wrong yesterday is still wrong today and will be wrong tomorrow . . . Prohibitions against homosexuality, adultery, and promiscuity in the interest of preserving heterosexual fidelity, marriage, and the family reflect enduring and immutable values."[38]

The availability of pornography results in an increase in violence against women. Feminist scholar Catharine MacKinnon argues that consumption of pornography leads to the trivialization and glamorization of acts such as rape, child sexual abuse, and sexual harassment, and motivates immature men to act out their sexual fantasies in an unhealthy and often violent fashion.[39]

Even without the violent result, pornography is demeaning to women. The Reverend Jerry Falwell, a long-time critic of the pornography industry, wants to expand the scope of obscenity laws to outlaw forms of pornography that are now considered legal. "Gloria Steinem (feminist scholar) and I don't agree on much, but we do agree that pornography is a scourge on society," Falwell said in a 1996 interview. "It's demeaning to women and children. It affects your relationship with your spouse and children and your attitude toward life."[40]

Why Pornography Should Not be Outlawed

Pornography is a legitimate form of art, just like sculpture, painting, music, and dance. It's an unusual form of art and may not be for everyone, but it is art nonetheless.

Evaluating the value of sexually explicit material is a matter of taste, not law. Creating tougher laws against pornography is the government's way of punishing unpopular expression.

Pornography is a non-obtrusive form of speech. Adult video stores are easy to recognize from a distance and can be easily avoided. At newsstands and in bookstores, adult magazines are sealed in plastic and not sold to minors. Theaters showing explicit movies do not allow underage patrons.

Outlawing pornography is a slippery slope. If we decide to ban pornography, how should we define it? Will museums around the country be forced to remove from their exhibits the classic works of European art because they include nude figures? Will libraries be required to remove from the shelves any books that include photographs of that artwork?

Chapter Summary

There are three categories used by the Supreme Court to define various types of sexual expression—obscenity, non-obscene sexual expression, and indecency, and the Court and applies a number of rationale behind treating the categories differently. The terms *obscenity* and *pornography* are often confused, but they are substantially different concepts. *Obscenity* is a term used to describe sexually explicit material that is so offensive it is deemed to have no social or artistic value. *Pornography,* part of a broader category known as "non-obscene sexual expression," is a term used to describe material of a sexual nature that is not offensive enough to be categorized as obscene. The latter term is used to not only describe the material itself but also the industry that produces it—an industry that technology has helped to grow to a multi-billion dollar enterprise.

Whether material is obscene or merely non-obscene sexual expression is determined by the Miller Test, a standard established by a 1973 Supreme Court case. Despite the view of many scholars that technology has rendered it outdated, the Miller Test is still used today to evaluate cases involving material accused of being obscene.

CASE PROBLEM

A Miller Test for the Twenty-First Century

Considering the rapid growth of the Internet and the difficulty in regulating it, should the Miller Test be revised to deal with new forms of obscenity? If you had the power, which of the following actions would you take: (a) keep the Miller Test exactly as it is; (b) revise or update the Miller Test to reflect new technology; (c) throw out the Miller Test in its entirety and replace it with a new standard; or (d) throw out the Miller Test and not replace it?

SOCRATIC DIALOGUE QUESTIONS

1. Do you agree with the Miller Test? Should each community be allowed to set its own standards, or should the determination of what is "obscene" be made on the national level? Is there a Fourteenth Amendment conflict involved in this issue?

2. In numerous cases involving the advertising industry, the Supreme Court has determined that advertising, despite its economic motives, is worthy of some degree of First Amendment protection (but not as much as political speech). Because many forms of non-obscene sexual expression (such as pornography) are also produced more for profit than for more admirable motives, does that disqualify them from deserving the limited First Amendment protection it receives?

3. In several cases, the Supreme Court has ruled that the government has a legitimate interest in regulating citizens' access to indecent material. But in recent commercial speech cases, the Court has used the rationale of "First Amendment right to receive information" in protecting the rights of advertisers. Is this a contradiction or inconsistency? What are some of the similarities and differences in the two forms of communication?

4. Find at least one case in Chapter 4 with which you strongly disagree with the court ruling (in the final resolution of the case) and be prepared to share your opinion with the class.

GLOSSARY OF TERMS

Censorship The act of not allowing the publication or broadcast of specific communication, either in whole or in part. The formal legal term is *prior restraint* (explained in Chapter 3).

Comstock Act The first federal obscenity law in the United States, passed by Congress in 1873. Named for Anthony Comstock, a New York grocer and social activist appointed by the government to investigate the problem of obscenity sent through the mail.

Hicklin Rule A now-defunct rule in English law, established in 1868, that determined a work was obscene if it "had the tendency to deprave and corrupt those whose minds are open to such immoral influences."

Indecency A legal term used to describe offensive (but not obscene) material that includes profanity or references to sex or other bodily functions.

Miller Test A Supreme Court standard for evaluating obscenity cases. Instead creating a uniform national definition, the Miller Test allows individual communities to define obscenity according to their own standards.

Non-obscene sexual expression Material or activity of a sexual nature considered not offensive enough to be labeled "obscenity"; examples include nude dancing, topless dancing, some adult videos, and photographs in most adult magazines.

Obscenity Material or activity of a sexual nature considered so offensive as to not receive any constitutional protection.

Pornography Entertainment of a sexual nature in the form of literature, photography, audiotape, videotape, or motion picture film; generally an artistic term rather than a legal term.

Roth Test From the 1957 Supreme Court case of *Roth v. United States*, the standard for evaluating obscenity cases from 1957 through 1973; the forerunner of the Miller Test.

Variable obscenity A pricipal that allows individual communities to set different standards for different audiences when defining obscenity.

NOTES

1. *Miller v. California*, 413 U.S. 15 (1973).
2. *New York v. Ferber*, 458 U.S. 747 (1982).
3. *Osborne v. Ohio*, 495 U.S. 103 (1990).
4. *Barnes v. Glen Theatre*, 501 U.S. 560 (1991).
5. *Ginsberg v. New York*, 390 U.S. 629 (1968).
6. *Renton v. Playtime Theatres,*475 U.S. 41 (1986).
7. *Erznoznik v. City of Jacksonville*, 422 U.S. 205 (1975).
8. Andrea Dworkin and Catharine MacKinnon, *Only Words*. Cambridge, Mass.: Harvard University Press, 1993, p. 15.
9. Marianne Wesson, "Pornography as Speech and Product." *University of Chicago Law Review* 60 (1993): 845.
10. *Regina v. Hicklin*, L.R. 3QB 360 (1868).
11. *Mutual Film Corporation v. Industrial Commission of Ohio*, 216 U.S. 230 (1915).
12. *Joseph Burstyn Inc. v. Wilson*, 343 U.S. 495 (1952).
13. *Butler v. Michigan*, 352 U.S. 380 (1957).
14. *Roth v. United States*, 354 U.S. 476 (1957).
15. *Memoirs v. Massachusetts*, 383 U.S. 413 (1966).
16. *Osborne v. Ohio*, 495 U.S. 103 (1990).
17. *Stanley v. Georgia*, 394 U.S. 557 (1969).
18. *Miller v. California*, 413 U.S. 15 (1973).
19. *Pope v. Illinois*, 481 U.S. 497 (1987).
20. *Ginsberg v. New York*, 390 U.S. 629 (1968).
21. *Soundgarden v. Eikenberry*, (871 P.2d 1050 (1994).
22. *New York v. Ferber*, 458 U.S. 747 (1982).
23. *American Booksellers Association v. Hudnut*, 598 F. Supp. 1316 (1985).
24. *Ashcroft v. Free Speech Coalition*, 122 S.Ct. 1389 (2002).
25. Marty Rimm, "Marketing Pornography on the Information Superhighway." *Georgetown Law Journal* 83 (June 1995):1849–1934.
26. Frederick S. Lane. *Obscene Profits*. New York: Routledge, 2000, p. 17.
27. *FCC v. Pacifica*, 438 U.S. 726 (1978).
28. *Sable Communications v. FCC*, 492 U.S. 115 (1989).
29. *Skywalker Records v. Navarro*, 739 F. Supp. 578 (1990).
30. *Luke Records v. Navarro*, 960 F.2d (1992).
31. *National Endowment for the Arts v. Finley*, 524 U.S. 569 (1998).
32. "Everything You Wanted to Know About the Movie Rating System." Brochure published by the National Association of Theatre Owners, date unknown.
33. "The Obscenity Debate." *CQ Researcher* (December 20, 1991): 969–92.
34. *United States v. A Book Titled Ulysses*, 5 F. Supp. 182 (1933).
35. Harold H. Hart, *Censorship: For and Against* (New York: Hart Publishing, 1971), p. 63.
36. "City Council Approves 'Tin Drum' Settlement." Associated Press report, March 16, 1999.
37. *Jenkins v. Georgia*, 418 U.S. 153 (1974).
38. Daniel Linz and Neil Malamuth, *Pornography.* Newbury Park, Calif.: Sage Publications, 1993, p. 7.
39. Catharine MacKinnon. "Not a Moral Issue." *Yale Law and Policy Review* 2 (1984):321.
40. *Larry King Live*, December 14, 1996.

5 The First Amendment and Campus Issues

It can hardly be argued that either students or teachers shed their constitutional rights to freedom of speech or expression at the schoolhouse gate.

Justice Abe Fortas
*Tinker v. Des Moines Independent
Community School District,* 1969

The first rule of free speech on a college campus: For every action, there is an equal and opposite over-reaction.

Leonard M. Niehoff
Adjunct Professor, University
of Michigan Law School

LEARNING OBJECTIVES

As a result of reading this chapter, students should:

- Understand how the courts apply various free speech principles to the unique environments of K–12 and college campuses, and why those two venues are often treated differently in terms of First Amendment protection.
- Understand that while campus media remain the focus of court cases regarding the college campus, many other First Amendment conflicts take place there also, including conflicts over the allocation of student activity fees and the establishment of speech codes and free speech zones.

Deciding Factors in Campus Speech Cases

Despite court rulings that have established that the First Amendment applies to speech and press on high school and college campuses, administrators often attempt to limit speech and exercise editorial control over campus media. And because of the students' limited legal resources, many are either unwilling or unable to challenge those administrators in court.

In the rare cases that such conflicts do reach the legal system, the courts take many factors into consideration, including:

1. Speech that takes place on a high school campus can be controlled to a greater degree than speech that takes place on a college campus. The courts' rationale for this disparity is two-fold. First, college students are older and assumed to be more mature than high school students, rendering them more capable of processing complex or controversial information and making appropriate judgments regarding its validity. Second, the college campus is often a venue for debating conflicting political ideas and opinions, thus making many campus activities (including student media) the equivalent of public forums; the same cannot be said about the high school environment.

2. Sanctioned activities such as student newspapers, yearbooks, literary magazines, drama club productions, and half-time entertainment at athletic events can be controlled to a greater degree than non-sanctioned activities such as informal gatherings and extemporaneous speeches.

3. Communication involving a **captive audience,** such as a class activity or assembly for which attendance is required, can be controlled more than communication to a **non-captive audience,** such as a gathering on the school grounds for which attendance is voluntary. Because of the captive audience concept, the courts acknowledge school administrators' authority to regulate speech that may be disruptive to the educational process. Therefore, the courts typically side with school leaders and allow them to enforce dress codes and other regulations that would not apply to adults or children off school grounds.

4. Students at private schools are more subject to speech and press limitations than their counterparts at public schools. Administrators at private schools are given more leeway to censor campus media than their counterparts at public schools because public schools are considered agencies of the state government, and the courts seldom allow agencies of government to infringe upon speech. At private schools, however, the courts generally allow administrators to control campus media and are reluctant to interfere, especially at church-run schools, because of the doctrine of separation of church and state. If the catalog at a private university made a promise of free speech, however, a student who believes that right was violated might prevail in a breach of contract lawsuit.

The K–12 Campus

Student Expression in General

The first Supreme Court case involving the free speech rights of public school students was *Tinker v. Des Moines Independent Community School District* (1969). Students who wore black armbands to protest the Vietnam War were suspended because administrators claimed the armbands were disruptive to the educational process. The Supreme Court, however, ruled that students and teachers do not "shed their constitutional rights to freedom of speech or expression at the schoolhouse gate."

In siding with the students, the Court ruled that the armbands were a form of "passive" protest that did not interfere with the educational mission of the school. The court placed the burden of proof on school administrators to prove the armbands were disruptive, rather than on the students to prove that they were not.[1]

The concept of "captive audience" was the issue in *Bethel School District v. Fraser* (1986). Parents in Washington State sued the school district after their son, who had previously been suspended for using indecent language when speaking at a school assembly, was denied the opportunity to speak at commencement ceremonies, even though the student body had elected him to do so. A lower court ruled that the administration could not limit his speech and issued a court order requiring the administration to allow him to speak.

By the time the school board could appeal the case to the Supreme Court, the commencement, including the student's address, had already taken place. The school district continued the appeal in an attempt to establish the principle. The U.S. Supreme Court overturned the lower court ruling and said the school had the right to limit speech in such cases because of the "captive audience." In its ruling in the *Bethel* case, the Court backed down from the *Tinker* decision in which it said that students do not shed their constitutional rights when they walk onto the campus, stating instead that students' constitutional rights are not "co-existent" with the rights of adults in other settings and that a school "does not have to tolerate speech which is inconsistent with its educational mission."[2]

Today, many courts justify their support for allowing high school administrators to censor student papers by pointing to the administrators' responsibility in preventing the school from being sued for libel or invasion of privacy. Advocates of a robust student press are skeptical of that position, however, pointing to the Student Press Law Center's claim that "there has never been a published court decision reporting a successful libel claim against a high school publication."[3]

While courts tend to side with high school principals in the majority of cases involving student speech, that tendency is not an absolute. In the 2001 case of *Saxe v. State College Area School District*, for example, two Christian high school students were charged under the school district's speech code for stating publicly their belief that homosexuality was a sin. The trial court ruled in favor of the school, but the Circuit Court of Appeals reversed that decision, ruling that the school's code was unconstitutional because administrators failed to meet their burden of proving that the code was necessary to protect other students or to maintain order.[4]

Censorship of K–12 Student Media

Two years after the *Bethel* decision, the courts considered a case more specific to school media in *Hazelwood v. Kuhlmeier* (1988). A high school principal in suburban St. Louis censored the school newspaper, objecting to two stories—one about teen pregnancy and birth control and the other about the effect of divorce on

Court rulings give high school principals the authority to censor student newspapers, but many choose not to do so.

children when they were of high school age. The principal objected to the first story because of its sexual nature and objected to the second because he believed the privacy of specific families was at risk (even though none were specifically identified). Students on the newspaper staff sued the principal, and the case eventually reached the Supreme Court. The Court ruled in favor of the principal, determining that censorship was acceptable if it:

1. served the educational mission of the school;
2. was done in a reasonable manner;
3. was related to pedagogical concerns; and
4. served a valid purpose.

The Court determined that a high school newspaper, produced in a laboratory environment and under the supervision of a school employee, was not a public forum and was therefore not analogous to a daily newspaper with regard to First Amendment protections. "Educators do not offend the First Amendment by exercising editorial control over the style and content of student speech in school-sponsored expressive activities so long as their actions are reasonably related to pedagogical concerns," Justice Byron White wrote in the majority opinion.[5]

In the decade following the *Hazelwood* ruling, school administrators took advantage of the precedent. Some well-publicized cases include the following:

- A high school principal in Texas refused to allow the student newspaper to publicize students' plans to hold an "alternative prom," prompted by the school's warning that it planned to administer breathalyzer tests to those attending the official prom.
- In Alaska, administrators at a high school confiscated copies of a student newspaper that contained an editorial that criticized the school for recognizing cheerleading as an "official sport."
- In Chicago, a student was suspended after writing an editorial criticizing the school's decision not to allow students to wear shorts.

Each of the above cases either failed to make it to court or were dismissed early in the process, leaving the decisions of the principals in place and reinforcing the *Hazelwood* decision.

In the early 2000s, high school journalists across the country have seen their work subject to prior restraint after attempting to publish or broadcast stories dealing with sensitive issues such as teenage sex and pregnancy, sexually transmitted diseases, drug abuse, body piercing, youth violence, or race relations at the school. While many such examples would be found by the courts to fall within the guidelines of the *Hazelwood* decision, some other prior restraint decisions are harder to justify. For example, in 1997 a high school principal in Alabama permitted the student newspaper to publish a story about safe-sex practices but a few weeks later prohibited a story critical of cafeteria food.

Although six states—Colorado, Arkansas, Iowa, California, Massachusetts, and Kansas—have passed laws that give high school journalists the same level of rights as their counterparts on college campuses, the courts have not been consistent in supporting those rights. When seeking to have those rights verified in court, many students instead are frustrated to see the courts apply the *Hazelwood* standard.

Banning of Books from K–12 Libraries

The American Library Association and other free speech advocates estimate that nationwide, there are more than 300 instances each year of book-banning affecting libraries at high schools, middle schools, and elementary schools. The actions are most often taken by school boards in reaction to complaints from parents or other concerned adults. From the 1970s through the 1990s, the books most often

Under pressure from parents, many school libraries remove controversial books from their shelves.

criticized and removed from libraries included John Steinbeck's *Of Mice and Men,* J. D. Salinger's *Catcher in the Rye,* Maya Angelou's *I Know Why the Caged Bird Sings,* and Mark Twain's *Huckleberry Finn.* Those books are still being banned in the early 2000s but have now been joined by J. K. Rowling's series of *Harry Potter* titles.

These conflicts rarely reach the courtroom and are instead resolved by compromises, such as placing controversial books behind the library circulation counter and requiring students to obtain parents' written permission to access them.

In the few cases that have resulted in lawsuits, the courts have ruled that such actions are permissible as long as they are intended to eliminate material that is "educationally unsuitable," but are not allowed in cases in which school officials simply object to the political ideas expressed in a book. Opponents of book-banning, however, point out that the problem in those rulings is that they give principals the discretion to determine which books fall into which category, allowing for the slippery slope to work in favor of book-banning and against access to the materials.

Dress Codes

Limitations on student clothing have taken place at both ends of the political spectrum. Students have been sent home—or ordered to turn T-shirts and sweatshirts inside-out—for wearing items that display the confederate flag or anti-abortion messages, as well as slogans denouncing President George W. Bush and the war in Iraq.

The American Civil Liberties Union often provides legal support for students in such cases, but courts typically side with school principals and rule that dress codes are constitutional because of the potentially disruptive nature of some clothing.

The College Campus

Organizational Models for Student Newspapers

There are three organizational models commonly found among college newspapers. In the **laboratory model,** the paper is produced as part of one or more classes (usually in the journalism department). In the **advisor model,** there are no classes associated with the production of the paper, but a faculty member serves as the advisor. In both the laboratory and advisor models, the newspapers receive part of their funding from student activity fees.

In the **independent model,** there is no official relationship between the paper and the university, and in most cases the newspaper offices are located off-campus and receive no student activity fees.

While the laboratory model provides more structure and a wide pool of staff talent to produce the student newspapers, there are many disadvantages. Newspapers produced almost entirely by students in a journalism program become so strongly identified with that program that it generates the perception on campus that the newspaper "belongs" to that department. At some universities, administrators claim that the student newspaper is a vehicle for faculty members to grind personal axes against the leadership of the school by directing student journalists to pursue negative stories that fit the faculty members' agenda (despite the fact that assignments are usually made by other students rather than faculty).

While the perceptual problem is significant, the more troubling issue is legal liability. The more closely aligned a newspaper or other media outlet is to an academic department, the greater the level of liability is for the university.

Important Cases Involving College Media

Student media at colleges and universities have had a long and colorful history. One of the earliest cases was *Dickey v. Alabama State Board of Education* (1967), in which the president of Troy State University established a rule that prohibited the university newspaper from publishing editorials critical of the governor or state legislature but allowed editorials supporting the governor and legislature.

After one editorial was rejected by the president, the faculty advisor gave student editor Gary Dickey an article on an unrelated topic to run in its place. But instead, the editor left the space blank except for the word *censored*. That happened late in the spring semester, and over the summer Dickey was told he could not attend the school in the fall because of "willful and deliberate insubordination."

Dickey sued the university, and the district court cited *Tinker,* ruling that the students' free speech rights could not be limited unless the school could prove "disruption or substantial interference" to the educational process. In this case, the school could not.[6]

Three years later, in *Antonelli v. Hammond* (1970), a Federal District Court ruled that the president of Fitchburg State College in Massachusetts could not exercise prior restraint over the campus newspaper. The case began when President James J. Hammond, objecting to the student newspaper's publication of an article containing profane words, established a committee to review and approve future issues of the newspaper. Editor John Antonelli objected to the new policy and sued. Even though the district court ruled against the president, it left the door open to the possibility of censorship in the future if the material in question was "damaging to the educational process."[7]

The same year, a court made a similar decision in *Channing Club v. Texas Tech University*, ruling that the university administration could not stop a student organization from publishing its own newsletter because it objected to profanity contained in it. The court ruled that it was not enough for the university to claim the possibility of disruption; it had to prove that such disruption was imminent, which it could not. The court also pointed out that the language in the newsletter was no worse than language found in books at the campus library and bookstore.[8]

In *Joyner v. Whiting* (1973), a Circuit Court of Appeals ruled that a university president could not prove "disruption to the educational process" and could therefore not exercise editorial control over the student newspaper. The plaintiff was Johnnie Joyner, editor of the student newspaper at North Carolina Central University, a historically black institution in Durham, North Carolina. At issue was a front-page editorial that said white students were not welcome at the school, that white students could not serve on the student newspaper staff, and that the paper would not accept advertising from white-owned businesses. University President Albert Whiting, fearing that the university might be in violation of the Fourteenth Amendment's Equal Protection Clause, as well as the Civil Rights Act of 1964, withdrew funding for the paper until he could set up a process for approving the copy prior to publication.

A federal court agreed with the university president and ruled that because of the Fourteenth Amendment and the Civil Rights Act, state funds could not be used to support racial segregation, even indirectly. But the Circuit Court of Appeals reversed that decision, ruling that the president could not exercise prior restraint over the newspaper because the editorials did not disrupt the educational process and that just expressing a point of view in the student newspaper did not mean the university itself was in violation of the law. The court also stated that the university had no legal obligation to create a student newspaper, but once it did, it could not shut it down simply because it objected to its content.[9]

Two years later, in *Schiff v. Williams* (1975), the student press was victorious again. At Florida Atlantic University in Boca Raton, Florida, the university president fired the entire editorial staff of the newspaper—not because of content but because of poor grammar, incorrect spelling, and non-libelous factual errors. The president claimed a student publication supported by state funds had no right to "reflect discredit and embarrassment upon the university." The students sued the president in Federal District Court and won reinstatement to their positions. The university appealed to the Circuit Court of Appeals, claiming that the student editors were state employees and the president was within his rights to fire them, but the appeals court sided with the students and upheld their reinstatement.[10]

While advocates of a free and robust student press were no doubt pleased with the outcome of the *Antonelli, Channing Club, Joyner,* and *Schiff* cases, their long-term significance is debatable. Because none reached the U.S. Supreme Court and were instead decided at lower levels of the judicial system, they are not binding in all jurisdictions. In addition, the decisions were narrowly tailored to specific forms of speech—a student newspaper or literary magazine, for example—and failed to address the larger question of whether student journalists at public universities have the same First Amendment rights as their professional counterparts.

Two more recent cases raise an even more troubling question: Can the administration of a university use the Hazelwood ruling—a case involving a high school newspaper—as a rationale for exercising prior restraint over a college newspaper? In *Kincaid v. Gibson* (1999) and *Hosty v. Carter* (2003), administrators cited the "disruption of the educational process" principle from the Hazelwood case.

The *Kincaid* case was eventually decided in favor of the students but only after seven years of appeals. During that time, the lower courts' decision in favor of the university's right to confiscate copies of the student newspaper and yearbook was left in place, and the result was an atmosphere of uncertainty in college newsrooms across the country.

The conflict began in 1994 when the newspaper's faculty advisor was removed after refusing to censor articles, editorials, and cartoons that were critical of the university's administration. The university also confiscated copies of the yearbook, based on its title, *Destination Unknown,* and its purple cover, which did not match the university's colors of green and gold. Both the newspaper and yearbook were funded by student activity fees.

After filing a grievance with the university's judicial panel, the faculty advisor was reinstated but given a new job description that required her to censor the newspaper and remove materials considered "harmful to the university's image." The advisor and several students then sued the university in Federal District Court, claiming that both the advisor's new job duties and confiscation of the yearbook were illegal forms of prior restraint.

The advisor and students lost in the trial court and again in an appeals court. Both courts cited *Hazelwood,* determining that the administrators' actions were taken "in a reasonable manner." Early in 2001, the appeals court reviewed the case again and finally reversed it, ruling in favor of the students.[11]

In the *Hosty* case, student editors at Governors State University in Illinois sued the university after the dean of student affairs instructed the company that held the contract to print the student newspaper not to print any issue until it was approved by a university official. A trial court ruled in favor of the university, but a three-judge panel of the Circuit Court of Appeals reversed and ruled in favor of the students. In June 2005, an eleven-judge panel of the same Circuit Court of

Appeals reversed again, determining that the *Hazelwood* ruling that gave high school principals the authority to censor student newspapers also applied at the college level. In February 2006, the U. S. Supreme Court refused to hear the case, leaving the ruling of the Circuit Court in place.[12]

Although the Circuit Court decision in *Hosty v. Carter* applies only to states within that circuit (the Seventh, consisting of Indiana, Illinois, and Wisconsin), organizations such as the Student Press Law Center (SPLC) and College Media Advisors (CMA) fear it may be used in other states—opening the door to new attempts at regulating student media and creating a timid, less aggressive student press. "We believe the nation's colleges and universities should be havens for free expression, diverse viewpoints, and controversial opinions," said CMA President Lance Speer in a statement issued after the Supreme Court's decision not to hear the case. "And student journalists should be able to enjoy the same constitutional freedoms of the commercial and private press to question or criticize those in positions of power and influence without fear or reprisal or sanction. The *Hosty* decision certainly poses a threat to that ability."[13]

As many college newspapers began publishing online editions in the late 1990s, advisors became concerned with the level of control that administrators might attempt to exercise. Most institutions have an "acceptable use policy" that prohibits the use of university-owned computer networks to transmit pornography, indecency, and other objectionable material, and advisors worry that such policies might be used to limit speech in the online newspapers. While no such cases have yet reached the courts, the Student Press Law Center issued a report in 1998 that predicted that no "acceptable use policy" would be successful in attempting to circumvent rights guaranteed by the First Amendment.

While university administrators may have little control over student newspapers, that is not the case with student-run television and radio stations because of the licensing procedures of the Federal Communications Commission (FCC). In 1982, for example, the president of Indian River Community College in Florida instructed the staff of a campus radio station to cease broadcasting stories that were critical of area real estate developers, many of whom were also major financial supporters of the college. When the student radio station manager refused, he was fired by the president and then sued the college in Federal District Court. After seven years of litigation, a Circuit Court of Appeals ruled that the college's board of trustees held the power to regulate content on the station because the FCC license was issued to them—not to the students or their advisor—and they had the right to delegate control of the station to the university president. The court did not, however, allow the president to fire the station manager.[14]

Journalistic Privilege

Just as student journalists generally win the debate over the right to make content decisions, they are also successful, in most cases, when claiming the same level of reporter privilege as their professional counterparts. In *New Hampshire v. Seil* (1982), for example, a judge ruled that student reporters did not have to reveal their sources of information (see a more detailed discussion of shield laws in Chapter 8) for newspaper stories about campus crime. Even though New Hampshire did not have laws allowing journalists to protect their sources of information, the judge ruled that the students could do so in this case because the prosecutor had not exhausted all other possible sources of information prior to seeking it from the students.[15]

In 2000, a California judge ruled in favor of a student editor at California State University at Sacramento who challenged a subpoena to turn over unpublished photographs of a fight that took place at a football game. The attorney for an individual involved in the fight claimed her client was the victim of excessive force on the part of the arresting officers. The judge, however, ruled that the attorney knew the identities of more than a dozen witnesses to the incident and should have subpoenaed them first, and by not doing so, had not exhausted other sources of information.[16]

Access to Information

Student journalists often encounter challenges when attempting to gather statistics about crimes taking place on or near campus. In 1990, Congress passed the Campus Security Act, which required colleges and universities across the United States to disclose information about crimes committed on or near campus to prospective students, their parents, on-campus and off-campus media, and the general public. The law was expanded in 1998 and renamed the **Jeanne Clery Act** in memory of a nineteen-year-old student at Lehigh University who was raped and murdered in 1986. Her parents had lobbied for passage of the original law.

Despite the law, however, many universities are still reluctant to release crime statistics for fear of frightening current and potential students and their parents. A 2006 report from the Student Press Law Center claimed that only 37 percent of colleges and universities in the country are in compliance with the Jeanne Clery Act. As a result, student media outlets as well as professional journalists often file suit to obtain such information, using either the Jeanne Clery Act or the state's public records law.

In 2006, the Massachusetts Supreme Court ruled that Harvard University was exempt from state public records laws because it was a private institution. The Jeanne Clery Act applies to both public and private institutions but was not a factor in the Harvard case because the act deals primarily with more generalized statistical data, whereas the student newspaper at Harvard was interested in specific incident reports covered under the state law. The newspaper argued (unsuccessfully) that because the university police department had many of the same powers given to city and county law enforcement agencies in the state, it should be held to the same standards in terms of disclosure of information.

Some universities have been successful in limiting negative publicity regarding campus crime by dealing with cases internally. Rather than referring cases of alleged sexual assault, hazing, and gay-bashing to local prosecutors (and by doing so allowing news to leak into the off-campus press), many universities attempt to deal with such cases as student disciplinary actions—the results of which are protected by state and federal privacy laws.

Student Newspapers and Theft

One disturbing trend of the 1990s and early 2000s is that of student newspapers being the target of individuals or groups who object to negative coverage in the student newspaper and retaliate by stealing—and in many cases destroying—copies of the paper.

A number of such cases took place in 2006. At Westminster College in Pennsylvania, for example, two unidentified students were charged with "abridgement of freedom of speech" (but no criminal offenses) resulting from a 2006 incident in which the students allegedly stole more than 1,300 copies of the campus newspaper, which carried a negative story and editorial about one of them. The same year, a student facing drug charges was charged with the theft of more than 800 copies of the student newspaper, which carried a story about her arrest.[17] At Kansas State University, members of a campus fraternity allegedly stole more than 8,000 copies of the student newspaper, which published a story critical of the group after university officials accused it of hazing and substance abuse.[18] At Pasadena City College in California, members of a Hispanic student group were more brazen. Not only did they steal 5,000 copies of the campus newspaper, but they bragged about it publicly and even sent to the newspaper offices garbage bags full of the torn-up copies of the newspaper, along with a note claiming responsibility for the theft. Members of the group said they looked at the incident not as a crime but rather as a publicity stunt designed to draw attention to the newspaper's failure to cover the group's events.[19]

Because student newspapers are distributed free, few administrators or campus police departments consider such incidents a law enforcement priority. Some observers even believe that administrators condone such activity. "On most college campuses, administrators are well aware that they cannot directly censor the student newspaper without risking a lawsuit and a lot of bad publicity," attorney and professor Wayne Overbeck wrote in his textbook, *Major Principles of Media Law*. "But with a wink and a nod, they can certainly encourage someone else to do the dirty work for them by rounding up all the copies of an offending newspaper."[20]

Advertising in Student Newspapers

Editors of student newspapers face two issues related to advertising—(1) their right to deny space to advertisers promoting controversial products, services, or issues, and (2) the authority of administrators or state officials to make such decisions for them.

In the 1976 case of *Mississippi Gay Alliance v. Goudelock*, a Circuit Court of Appeals ruled that a university newspaper could not be compelled to accept advertising to which it objected.[21]

The courts make exceptions to this principle in cases in which decisions are made by administrators rather than students, however. In a 1969 case, a Federal District Court ruled against the University of Wisconsin—Whitewater when the institution was sued by a student group that was denied the opportunity to advertise in the student newspaper. The court ruled that because the decision to deny access was made by the university administration rather than student editors, it was censorship done "under the color of state law" and was therefore unconstitutional.[22]

Early in 2001, political activist David Horowitz attempted to place an ad in college newspapers across the country—the content of which many of the papers found objectionable but published nonetheless. The ad, titled "Ten Reasons Why Reparations for Blacks is a Bad Idea for Blacks—And Racist Too," outlined his view of the public debate over slavery reparations. Of the newspapers that received the ad, many rejected it outright. Other newspapers published the ad but elsewhere in the same issue denounced its message while explaining their First Amendment right to publish it. Other papers published the ad without explanation and later apologized to their readers.

About the same time, other student newspapers across the country were dealing with controversial ads dealing with political issues such as abortion and commercial issues such as alcoholic beverages. Student newspapers at other institutions began receiving complaints after accepting advertising from local exotic dancing establishments attempting to recruit students as performers.

In the 2004 case of *Pitt News v. Pappert,* a Circuit Court of Appeals in Pennsylvania struck down a state law that prohibited college newspapers from accepting advertising related to alcoholic beverages. Ironically, the law called for fines levied against the advertisers rather than the newspapers that accepted the ads, but the American Civil Liberties Union (ACLU) claimed that it was prior restraint nonetheless and argued the case on behalf of student journalists at the University of Pittsburgh. In ruling in favor of the students, a federal judge ruled that university administrators could only offer "speculation and conjecture" to support their claim that banning alcohol advertising would reduce the demand for alcohol by underage students.[23]

Speech Codes

A **speech code,** which is often incorporated into an educational institution's policies on student conduct, is a set of rules that limit or prohibit speech that may offend women or other constituent groups on campus. Opponents of speech codes criticize them as examples of "political correctness taken to an extreme" and as the universities' efforts to punish students not only for what they say but also for what they think.

The most significant conflict involving campus speech codes is the 1989 case of *Doe v. University of Michigan.* In the years leading up to the case, the university had been dealing with the problem of sexual and racial harassment among students, including sexist and racist graffiti, the display of swastikas and other offensive symbols in dormitory windows, and racist and sexist jokes on the campus radio station. The university attempted to curtail such activity by adopting a "speech code" that prohibited speech that "stigmatized or victimized" women, minorities, or gays.

When the speech code, formally titled "Policy on Discrimination and Discriminatory Harassment," was introduced, it appeared at first to serve the university's legitimate interest in providing what it called a "comfortable learning environment" for minority students. In defending the policy, the university president cited the Supreme Court's 1919 decision that the principle of free speech does not allow a man to "falsely shout 'fire' in a crowded theater" and said that the institution should not allow "discriminatory remarks which seriously offend many individuals beyond the immediate victim, and which, therefore detract from the necessary educational climate of a campus." But detractors objected when a follow-up document attempted to clarify the policy by providing examples such as "A male student makes a remark in class such as, 'Women just aren't as good in this field as men,' thus creating a hostile learning atmosphere for female classmates."

The case was filed by a graduate teaching assistant using the pseudonym John Doe. He claimed that the code would limit speech in a psychology class he taught because the subject matter called for the discussion of differences between the races and sexes and that he could not effectively teach the class because of his fear that offended students could file complaints against him or other students in his classes based on the policy.

A federal court judged in his favor, ruling that the code was vague and overbroad, based on its use of terms such as *victimize* and *stigmatize* that were too difficult to define. Further, the court ruled that the code was so broad that it "swept within its scope a significant amount of verbal conduct which is unquestionably protected under the First Amendment." The court also determined that while the university's motive of providing a "comfortable learning environment" was admirable, it feared that the code could also be misused in order to limit speech on other topics, such as comments critical of the university.[24]

Despite the court ruling, many observers claim the climate of "political correctness" still prevails at the University of Michigan. Just a few years after the *Doe* case, a University of Michigan student was threatened with sexual harassment charges after a female graduate teaching assistant claimed to be offended by an essay he wrote that included characters he named "Dave Stud" and "Joe Sixpack." The student dropped the class, and the teaching assistant dropped her complaint.[25]

In 1992, administrators at the University of California at Berkeley suspended students for wearing T-shirts showing a Hispanic man sitting on a beach and the caption, "It doesn't matter where you came from, as long as you know where you are going." The action was prompted by complaints from Mexican American students, but after the suspended students threatened to sue the university for violating their free speech rights, the suspensions were lifted.[26]

In January 1993, University of Pennsylvania student Eden Jacobowitz was accused of violating the institution's speech code when he shouted "Shut up, you water buffalos" to a group of African American women at an outdoor party outside of his campus apartment. The women complained to university administrators, who began a five-month investigation that attracted national media attention. Jacobowitz claimed the term *water buffalo* was slang for "fool" or "dummy" and was not racist, but he was nonetheless charged under the university's speech code. After a lengthy investigation and the threat of legal action by women's rights groups on one side and the ACLU on the other, the case was settled when the women dropped their complaint and the university elected not to pursue the case further. After several months of negative publicity, the university eliminated its speech code.

The ACLU applauded the move, saying that the university should "spend more time educating students and less time limiting their freedom of expression." Even after the code was abolished, the "water buffalo" case created a public relations nightmare for the university, as newspaper editorials and radio talk shows kept the story alive for nearly a year.[27]

Today, policies regulating hate speech exist on nearly every public college and university in the country, but the extent to which they are enforced varies. An outgrowth of diversity programs and other efforts to support multiculturalism on campus, the codes are designed to protect women, gays, African Americans, the disabled, and other minorities. Critics of speech codes, however, claim they constitute prior restraint and are examples of political correctness out of control.

The main criticism of speech codes is their tendency toward overbreadth and vagueness, a problem that would make most of them unconstitutional if challenged. Examples:

- The University of Maryland has a sexual harassment policy that bans "idle chatter of a sexual nature, sexual innuendoes, comments about a person's clothing, body, and/or sexual activities, comments of a sexual nature about weight, body shape, size, or figure, and comments or questions about the sensuality of a person."
- At Shippensburg State University in Pennsylvania, a clause in the Student Code of Conduct prohibits expression that is "inflammatory, demeaning, or harmful toward others."
- At Syracuse University, a speech code prohibits "offensive remarks" and provides examples such as "sexually suggestive staring, leering, sounds, or gestures."
- At the State University of New York, a speech code says that "All members of the college community should respect the rights and dignity of other individuals and avoid display of bias in public actions or utterances."
- The Stanford University speech code uses the Chaplinsky definition of fighting words (see Chapter 2) as "those that by their very utterance inflict injury or tend to incite an immediate breach of the peace."

New York University students take part in a protest against the war in Iraq on NYU's campus in lower Manhattan in March, 2003.

Free Speech Zones

A **free speech zone** is an area of campus, typically a common area such as a plaza or other gathering place, where students are allowed to hold rallies, distribute literature, or make extemporaneous speeches on controversial topics. Such a gathering place generally fits the description of a "traditional public forum" as discussed in Chapter 3. Students engaging in controversial speech outside of the free speech zone would be subject to the institution's disciplinary policies.

Institutions often defend their free speech zones as content neutral and as reasonable "time, place, and manner" restrictions that are necessary to minimize disruption of academic activities elsewhere on campus. Some claim a free speech zone is a "traditional public forum" while the remainder of the campus is a "limited public forum." Opponents, however, claim that such zones are unnecessary forms of prior restraint, arguing that the entire campus should be a free speech zone since university campuses are designed to be locations where controversial ideas are debated.

There are no Supreme Court cases involving free speech zones on college campuses, but lower courts typically rule that such policies violate the First Amendment. Before such conflicts can reach the courtroom, however, most policies regarding free speech zones are abandoned after student and faculty protests or under the threat of legal action. Other universities still have free speech zones but are reluctant to enforce those policies.

Allocation of Student Fees

Mandatory student activity fees are sometimes the basis of student claims of "compelled speech," but the courts typically reject those claims. In the 1983 case of *Stanley v. McGrath*, for example, a federal appeals court ruled that students at the University of Minnesota could not refuse to pay a portion of their student fees allocated to the student newspaper simply because they objected to content of the publication.[28]

In a more recent case, *Board of Regents of the University of Wisconsin System v. Southworth*, students were unsuccessful in challenging their university's fee system. The conflict began in 1996 when conservative students at the University of Wisconsin at Madison sued the university to protest the use of student fee money to fund student organizations that advocated abortion rights, gay rights, and other controversial causes. The plaintiffs claimed that the student fee system was a form of compelled speech because they were being forced, through payment of the fees, to participate in speech to which they objected.

A Federal District Court and Circuit Court of Appeals ruled in favor of the plaintiffs. But the Supreme Court overturned that ruling early in 2000, rejecting the students' "compelled speech" argument and ruling in favor of the university, which claimed that its mandatory fee system was "appropriate to further its educational mission." Writing the majority decision, Justice Anthony Kennedy stated, "The First Amendment permits a public university to charge its students an activity fee used to fund a program to facilitate extracurricular student speech if the program is viewpoint neutral."

The Court also ruled that universities had the option of providing students an "opt out" but were not legally obligated to do so. But Kennedy added a caution that allowing students to "opt out" of the fee system because it indirectly subsidizes speech with which they disagree would be "so disruptive and expensive that the program to support extracurricular speech would be ineffective."[29]

Frequently Asked Questions about Campus Speech

1. *What can students do when their free speech rights are being limited, but they cannot afford to hire a lawyer?* At both the high school and college level, students or teachers who find their free speech rights in danger have three advocacy groups to which they can turn to for help: the Student Press Law Center, the American Civil Liberties Union, and the Foundation for Individual Rights in Education.

The Student Press Law Center (SPLC) is an Arlington, Virginia–based nonprofit organization that advocates free speech rights for student journalists at high schools and colleges. It receives more than 2,000 requests for help each year from students and faculty advisors. Attempts at prior restraint by high school principals and university administrators are the most common cause for complaints. At the university level, the fastest-growing part of SPLC work is in the area of access to information, as student journalists often find it difficult to obtain information regarding university budgets and campus crime statistics, even though much of the information is required to be made public by state public records laws.

The **American Civil Liberties Union** (ACLU) is a national organization based in New York, with affiliates in all fifty states, that advocates adherence to the Constitution in all areas of American life, including the First Amendment. While the SPLC would be the primary organization involved in conflicts involving campus media, the ACLU would be more likely to get involved in free speech conflicts other than those involving media, such as dress codes.

The **Foundation for Individual Rights in Education** (FIRE) is a Philadelphia-based group that defends both students and faculty members charged with violating speech codes.

2. *If a university is funding the student newspaper or broadcasting facility, why can't it control the content?* In most cases, campus media are funded by a combination of student fees and advertising sales, meaning that the university itself is actually paying little (or perhaps none) of the cost for student media. Administrators often claim that because a student newspaper is housed on campus and uses the name of the institution, the content of the publication reflects on the school, but courts seldom find this a valid reason for administrative control.

Campus television and radio stations that are FCC-licensed are subject to more administrative control, however, because the license is issued to the university rather than the students.

Point/Counterpoint: Campus Speech Codes

Support for Speech Codes

Universities are obligated to provide all their students with a comfortable learning environment. In defending their school's speech code, University of Michigan administrators cited the Supreme Court's 1919 decision that the principle of free speech does not allow a man to "shout 'fire' in a crowded theater" and said that the institution should not allow "discriminatory remarks which seriously offend many individuals beyond the immediate victim, and which, therefore detract from the necessary educational climate of a campus."[30]

Dr. Amitai Etzioni, professor of sociology at George Washington University, says that hate speech should receive no protection, especially on a college campus where it may influence the audience to harm innocent persons. "When words take action, then we need to be concerned," Etzioni says. "Expressions of hate speech on campus should be seen as an indication that we haven't done our jobs as educators."[31]

Speech codes represent a reasonable balance of competing interests. In this case, administrators enforcing speech codes to protect minority students are placing their Fourteenth Amendment rights above the First Amendment rights of the speakers.

Criticisms of Speech Codes

Many university speech codes tend to be vague and overbroad. Many such codes would be found unconstitutional if challenged. Alan Charles Kors and Harvey A. Silverglate, authors of *The Shadow University: The Betrayal of Liberty America's Campuses,* claim that speech codes have the potential to "trap the innocent by making it impossible to know what was and was not prohibited."[32]

The college campus is a unique setting where controversial ideas are supposed to be debated and evaluated. University administrators should therefore encourage free speech rather than attempt to stifle it. In his 1993 book, *Speech Acts and the First Amendment,* author Franklyn Haiman opposes speech codes and instead recommends that universities respond to hate speech by challenging its accuracy and value rather than attempting to eliminate it. "The answer to offensive speech is more speech, not less speech," Haiman wrote.[33]

Speech codes take away an important safety valve for dissent. Like most forms of hate speech, expressions of dissatisfaction that take place on a college campus provide students and others with the opportunity to "blow off steam."

Speech codes create a slippery slope. Gwen Thomas, a black administrator at a university in Colorado, says that universities need to protect free speech in all of its forms, no matter how objectionable, because "if we infringe on the rights of any person, we may be next." Thomas adds that "Young people have to learn to grow up on college campuses. We have to teach them how to deal with adversarial situations. They have to learn how to survive offensive speech they find wounding and hurtful."[34]

Chapter Summary

The courts, including the U.S. Supreme Court, apply various free speech principles to the unique environments of K–12 and college campuses but do not always do so consistently. One generalization often asserted is that K–12 principals are given a great deal of leeway to restrict speech on their campuses, based on the relative maturity level of the students (compared to college students) and the fact that activities on a K–12 campus, including the student newspaper, do not function as "public forums." College administrators, however, have less ability to restrict speech, both because of the increased maturity level of the students and the fact that many activities that take place on a college campus, including student media, are indeed public forums.

While campus media remain the focus of court cases regarding the college campus, some of the more interesting cases involve issues other than student media, such as conflicts over the allocation of student activity fees and the establishment of speech codes and free speech zones.

CASE PROBLEMS

Big Problems in the Political Science Building

As part of a national anti-abortion campaign, a conservative student organization uses its bulletin board, in a common area of the political science building, to display graphic photographs of aborted fetuses. In the bottom corner of the bulletin board is a pocket containing brochures promoting the anti-abortion movement. If you were a university administrator, what action would you take? Which First Amendment principles (from Chapters 2 and 3) apply? What if the photographs were on a professor's office door?

You Won't Believe What I Heard on the Radio

You're the staff attorney for Enormous State University, and the faculty advisor and student manager of the campus radio station (funded by student activity fees) have asked you for help with the following matter.

Background: Bob Randall is a controversial radio talk show host who is known for his ultra-conservative and sometimes offensive comments about the state of American society. While he has many critics, he also has built a loyal following, including a surprising number of college-age listeners. A year ago, in order to serve this newly discovered segment of his audience, Randall began offering college and university radio stations around the country daily, pre-recorded three-minute radio commentaries in which he provides his opinions on topics of interest to students, including legal, political, and social phenomena.

A sample of his comments: women are inferior to men; sexual harassment is a myth and not a real problem; the majority of female students are in college only to meet husbands; colleges and universities should abolish "Women's Studies" programs; colleges and universities should not use student activity fees to fund "women's centers"; and other causes Randall refers to as "unnecessary and trivial."

Randall offers the daily commentaries to the campus radio stations for free, but he has two requirements: (1) the stations must accept the series in its entirety and must air every segment; they cannot "pick and choose" which topics they want to air; and (2) stations must air each commentary in its entirety; they cannot delete one word. The commentaries have become instant hits at universities across the country, and despite the unusual ground rules, the number of campuses accepting his offer has grown exponentially during the last year.

The campus radio station at your institution, WESU, has announced plans to begin airing the Randall commentaries early next month. Needless to say, there is much disagreement on campus and in the surrounding community about the radio station's plans.

The station's faculty advisor, student manager, and members of the Student Media Board are in a quandary as to what they should do. On one hand, they recognize the First Amendment "free speech" issues at stake and believe the university should be a forum for discussing controversial issues. But on the other hand, they're concerned about (1) protecting the feelings of the university's female students (and other offended groups); (2) protecting the image of the university by avoiding the public perception that the school endorses or agrees with Randall's ideas; and (3) the possibility of violence (other college stations subscribing to the Randall commentaries have been plagued by bomb threats and violent protests).

A recent meeting of the Student Media Board turned into an emotional debate on the issue. The professor who chairs the Student Media Board made the following comments: "We realized that many people would object to this series, but we're looking at this as a free speech issue. Many of us on the Student Media Board, including myself, disagree with some of Randall's commentaries, but we felt the purpose of campus media is to stimulate debate on current issues and provide a forum to get those views out in the open. We have to remember that the university campus is supposed to be the place for free speech and debate."

Chemistry professor Dr. I. C. Waterboyle, who is not on the Student Media Board but who spoke at the meeting, said, "I don't believe the university should allow this man access to our student body. I believe in the First Amendment and free speech as much as anyone else, but I object to the university providing this man a forum from which to spread his message. It provokes hatred. It also makes the university look bad to be associated with this man. I think the students will be outraged when they realize their student activity fees are being used in this way."

The Student Media Board will discuss the issue at a special meeting next week and make a final decision as to whether to enter the agreement. They've asked you not only for a recommendation but also an explanation of the legal principles involved and references to appropriate case law and/or common law. (*Note:* Your employer is making more of a policy decision than a legal determination, but you should base your recommendation on legal principles.)

SOCRATIC DIALOGUE QUESTIONS

1. If the principal of a high school issued a rule prohibiting students from wearing clothing known to be "gang colors," what are some of the legal principles (from Chapters 2 and 3) he or she could use to justify that rule? Which legal principles (from the same chapters) could students use in arguing against this rule?

2. Of the three organizational models commonly found among college newspapers, which model is followed at your school? If you transferred from another university, what model was followed there? If you were in charge of starting a student newspaper for a newly opened university, which model would you prefer?

3. Should student media at high schools enjoy the same legal protections (freedom from prior restraint, etc.) as professional media? What about student media at colleges and universities?

4. Based on examples provided in this chapter, should student newspapers have the right to refuse advertising related to controversial products and issues? Should there be different policies for advertisers associated with the university (such as student organizations) and off-campus groups such as bars and adult nightclubs?

5. Do you agree with the court's decision in *Doe v. Michigan*? What are some of the positive and negative effects of a college or university having a speech code? What about free speech zones?

6. Do you agree with the court's decision in *Board of Regents of the University of Wisconsin System v. Southworth*? Do you agree with the students' claim that this was a case of compelled speech? Why or why not? Should student activity fees be used to fund student organizations involved in controversial issues such as abortion, gay rights, and race relations? How is this different from the license plate case ("Live Free or Die") in Chapter 3? When students pay their student fees, should they be given the opportunity to specify which campus organizations the money can go to ("opt in") or which they cannot go to ("opt out")?

7. Find at least one case in Chapter 5 with which you strongly disagree with the court ruling (in the final resolution of the case) and be prepared to share your opinion with the class.

GLOSSARY OF TERMS

Advisor model   A method of structuring student media in a college setting; a faculty member serves as advisor to the media organization, but the production of content is not connected to academic classes.

Captive audience   A situation in a school setting in which attendance is mandatory, such as a class session or student assembly.

Free speech zone   A specific location on a college campus where the distribution of literature or other forms of speech are allowed; such activities are not allowed outside the zone.

Independent model   A method of structuring student media in a college setting; the media outlet serves the institution but is located off-campus and receives no financial support from the institution.

Jeanne Clery Act   Originally called the Campus Security Act, this federal law requires colleges and universities to disclose information about crimes committed on or near campus to prospective students, their parents, journalists, and the general public.

Laboratory model   A method of structuring student media in a college setting; content for student media is produced by specific classes in exchange for academic credit.

Non-captive audience   A situation in a school setting for which attendance is voluntary, such as a club meeting or athletic event.

Speech code   A set of rules or limitations on speech that may offend women or minority groups, often incorporated into a college's code of student conduct.

NOTES

1. *Tinker v. Des Moines Independent Community School District*, 393 U.S. 503 (1969).
2. *Bethel School District v. Fraser*, 478 U.S. 675 (1986).
3. *Law of the Student Press.* Arlington, Va.: Student Press Law Center, 1993, p. 104.
4. *Saxe v. State College Area School District*, 77 F. Supp. 621 (1999).
5. *Hazelwood v. Kuhlmeier*, 484 U.S. 260 (1988).
6. *Dickey v. Alabama State Board of Education*, 273 F. Supp. 613 (1967).

7. *Antonelli v. Hammond,* 308 F. Supp. 1329 (1970).

8. *Channing Club v. Texas Tech University,* 317 F. Supp. 688 (1970).

9. *Joyner v. Whiting,* 477 F.2d 456 (1973).

10. *Schiff v. Williams,* 519 F.2d 257 (1975).

11. *Kincaid v. Gibson,* 191 F.3d 719 (1999).

12. *Hosty v. Carter,* 412 F.3d 731 (2005).

13. College Media Advisors news release, February 21, 2006.

14. *Schneider v. Indian River Community College Foundation,* 875 F.2d 839 (1989).

15. *New Hampshire v. Seil,* 8 Med.L.Rptr. 1625 (1982).

16. Student Press Law Center Alert, March 21, 2001.

17. "'Hit List' Story Prompts Theft of Newspapers." *Student Press Law Center Report,* March 31, 2006.

18. "Stolen Papers Cost $6,500, Editor Says." *Student Press Law Center Report,* April 28, 2006.

19. "Student Journalist Still Waiting for Answers on Newspaper Theft." *Student Press Law Center Report,* June 7, 2006.

20. Wayne Overbeck, *Major Principles of Media Law.* Fort Worth, Texas: Harcourt Brace, 1999, p. 522.

21. *Mississippi Gay Alliance v. Goudelock,* 536 F.2d 1073 (1976).

22. *Law of the Student Press.* Arlington, Va.: Student Press Law Center, 1993, p. 208.

23. *Pitt News v. Pappert,* 379 F.3d 96 (2004).

24. *Doe v. University of Michigan,* 721 F. Supp. 852 (1989).

25. John J. Furedy, "Political Correctness: Dispatches from the Front Lines." *Gravitas: A Quarterly Journal of Current Affairs* 1, no. 3 (Fall 1994).

26. Richard Miniter, "Campus Speech Wars: Waving the Tacky Shirt." *Insight,* 10, no. 4 (June 1994): 18–21.

27. Alan Charles Kors and Harvey A. Silverglate, *The Shadow University: The Betrayal of Liberty on America's Campuses.* New York: Harper Collins, 1998, p. 9–33.

28. *Stanley v. McGrath,* 719 F.2d 279 (1983).

29. *Board of Regents of the University of Wisconsin System v. Southworth,* 120 S.Ct. 1346 (2000).

30. *Doe v. Michigan,* 721 F. Supp. 852 (1989).

31. "Yes or No." *First Amendment News* (February 1998): 7.

32. Alan Charles Kors and Harvey A. Silverglate, *The Shadow University,* p. 116.

33. Franklyn Haiman, *Speech Acts and the First Amendment.* Carbondale, Ill.: Southern Illinois University Press, 1993, p. 28.

34. "Group Takes Aim at Campus Speech." Associated Press report, April 30, 2003.

CHAPTER

6 Defamation

He who steals my purse steals trash, but he who filches me of my good name robs me of that which not enriches him, but makes me very poor indeed.

Shakespeare
Othello

A lie can travel half-way around the world while the truth is still putting on its shoes.

Mark Twain, 1905

Words, once they are printed, they've got a life of their own. Words, once spoken, have a life of their own.

Carol Burnett
Plaintiff, *Burnett v. National Enquirer, 1981*

LEARNING OBJECTIVES

As a result of reading this chapter, students should:

- Understand the factors that a plaintiff must establish to have a successful defamation claim as well as the defenses commonly used by defendants, including those associated with First Amendment freedoms.
- Understand the difference between public figures and private figures in terms of their status as potential defamation plaintiffs.
- Understand how court decisions have shaped defamation law throughout the history of journalism and how communication technology may affect defamation cases in the future.

Libel vs. Slander

Libel and slander are two categories of a broader legal area called **defamation,** a term that refers to damage to a person's or an organization's reputation or standing in the community or to exposing a person or organization to public shame, hatred, or ridicule.

What's the difference between libel and slander? You often hear people casually explain the difference by saying that libel is written and slander is spoken. But that's not a complete definition because defamation that occurs in a radio broadcast is spoken into a microphone, yet is considered libel because of the size of the audience and the fact that it is transmitted over the airwaves. A more accurate delineation is to say that libel is published or broadcast to a wide audience, while slander is communicated on a personal level and to a smaller audience.

Some state laws specify that defamation that takes place over the broadcast airwaves would be libel if it was read from a prepared script (because it was therefore "premeditated") but slander if it was ad-libbed. The distinction between libel and slander is not as dramatic as it once was. Many states make no such distinction in their laws and simply have one statute to cover both forms of defamation, allowing judges and juries to make the distinction in the size of their damage awards. West Virginia, for example, has no statutes referring to libel or slander but instead has an "insulting words" statute that provides a number of examples of defamation. Some other states use the blanket term **injurious falsehood** to cover both libel and slander.

Like most of American communication law, many of our laws dealing with defamation are based on those found in England. Both libel and slander are based on an old English principle that there is nothing more important to an individual than his or her reputation. Slander is a much older concept than libel, as it is found in the laws of England and other countries as far back as the 1400s. Libel became part of English law in the early 1700s and has been part of American law since the country was founded.

Common law defines slander as "words which tend to expose one to public hatred, shame, contempt, ridicule, aversion, or disgrace."

Only living persons can be slandered. Neither family members nor friends can claim slander on behalf of a dead relative. Organizations cannot sue for slander, as courts have ruled that damage to the reputation of an organization is not as serious as damage to the reputation of a person. A business owner can, however, sue for slander if the words in question refer to his or her competence, judgment, or integrity in operating the business.

In the early 1900s, the most common examples of slander involved either the false accusation of a crime or criticism of someone's personal character, business reputation, or sexual conduct. In 1940, for example, a hotel owner in Georgia sued a merchant for slander after learning that the merchant made unflattering comments about the inn when visitors to the town asked for a recommendation. The merchant repeatedly cautioned visitors to avoid that specific hotel because it was "not morally clean" and because the owner employed women there "for immoral purposes." Other cases from the early 1900s included that of a shoe store employee who sued the store owner for telling customers that he "spent too much time flirting with female customers" and a department store customer who sued the retailer after a clerk loudly accused her in front of other customers of having bad credit. In a 1990 case, a man living in a small town in Nebraska won a $25,000 slander judgment against a woman who spread rumors that he had AIDS, which later proved to be false. The court based the dollar amount on lost wages, injury to his reputation, and mental suffering.[1]

Today, one of the most common examples of slander is criticism of an individual's job performance or suitability for employment. Employers are therefore extremely cautious in the words they choose when describing an employee's job performance or explaining to a third party the reasons for one's termination. Human resources personnel are also cautious in giving and receiving information (either in writing or by telephone) about past or present employees, including letters of recommendation, the results of performance reviews, or other evaluative information. The potential cost of litigation has caused many employers to enforce policies about who can provide information about current and former employees and what kinds of evaluative information can be shared.

Because the cost of litigation affects the plaintiffs as well as the defendants, and because of the difficulty in proving damages, slander cases reaching the courtroom stage are rare in today's legal system. Instead, conflicts involving alleged slander are often resolved out of court and for minimal financial consideration.

A Brief History of Libel

The history of libel is divided into two time periods: Everything that happened prior to 1964, and everything that has happened since. That's because of the 1964 case that was the first of its kind to reach the U.S. Supreme Court. Prior to that, libel was a matter that was kept strictly within state court systems, and the cases seldom received much publicity outside of the communities in which they were tried.

But beginning with the 1964 case of *New York Times v. Sullivan* (see pp. 116–117 for detailed discussion), many cases have gone to the Supreme Court for appeal, and the results have helped change and better define exactly what libel is. Even though the cases reaching the U.S. Supreme Court garner a great deal of attention, the majority of cases are still resolved in state courts.

The Libel Defense Resource Center (LDRC) conducts annual studies of libel and privacy litigation nationwide and issues reports that track individual cases as well as overall trends. In recent years, those reports have contained both good news and bad for the news media. The good news is that the total number of cases has gradually decreased over the last twenty-five years, and the successful defense rate has gradually improved and now exceeds 50 percent (up from 40 percent in the early 1990s).[2]

But the bad news is that in cases won by the plaintiffs, damage awards are increasing exponentially. One example was the $220.72 million judgment for the plaintiffs in the 1997 case of *MMAR Group v. Dow Jones & Co*. Even though the award was overturned on appeal in 1999, the amount of the original trial court judgment is still a record.[3]

According to the LDRC, the average jury award in libel and privacy cases won by plaintiffs is more than $3 million. Many publishers and broadcasters have learned that it is often more practical to settle a libel claim out of court. Even though the dollar amount paid to the plaintiff is considerably lower, legal fees may still cost an additional $100,000 or more.

The potential cost of libel litigation, as well as the damage to a journalist's reputation and that of his or her employer, are serious concerns for the journalism profession. Some journalists and observers use the term **chilling effect** to refer to the reluctance of journalists and their employers to pursue aggressive or investigative journalism for fear that even the slightest reporting error may result in a multi-million dollar libel suit.

The majority of libel litigation is based on the content of news stories, but also vulnerable are photographs, captions, headlines, and advertisements. Even non-controversial news items such as notices of births, engagements, weddings, and obituaries are not exempt from libel suits. For example, newspapers that fail to authenticate such notices may find themselves victims of practical jokes, as individuals will submit a fictional engagement notice involving two people with strong dislike for each other or phony death notices involving someone very much alive. In addition to the embarrassment and loss of credibility suffered by the newspaper, such cases are also ripe for libel suits, although most are settled out of court and for minimal financial consideration.

Libel Per Se and Libel Per Quod

There are two types of libel: **libel per se** and **libel per quod.** Libel per se means that the words are directly harmful on their face. Libel per quod means that the words may seem harmless but may be interpreted as libelous. It's libel through innuendo.

Examples: If a newspaper reports that the director of a local charity has been stealing money out of the organization's bank account—and it turns out to be false—that is libel per se. But if the newspaper reports that the charity's director is driving a luxury car, lives in a fancy house, and takes extravagant vacations that reflect an income level far above his salary at a time when thousands of dollars are missing from the organization's bank account, that is libel per quod.

Categories of Libel

There are six major categories of libel:

1. *False accusation of a crime.* Because of the potential damage to a person's reputation based on errors, crime news is the most heavily edited and scrutinized material published in a newspaper or broadcast on radio or television. Editors require reporters to double-check and sometimes triple-check police reports and court records to ensure accuracy. Suspects are often identified as specifically as possible, including their middle names, ages, addresses, and occupations.

Journalists should be cautious when using verbs such as *arrested, arraigned, charged, accused,* and *questioned,* as well as terms used to classify crimes, such as *burglary, robbery, theft, larceny, rape, sexual assault, murder, homicide,* and *manslaughter.* Each of those terms has a specific legal meaning, and the terms should not be used casually or interchangeably. Another standard precaution that journalists take is to use only those terms found in law enforcement documents and court records and not to assume that a certain term applies when no official source has used it.

A good illustration of libel suits in this category took place in 1997, when the National Broadcasting Company and the Cable News Network (CNN) reached out-of-court settlements with Richard Jewell, a security guard at the 1996 Summer Olympics in Atlanta, who was erroneously described as a suspect in a bombing that took place at the event. Jewell was never formally charged and was eventually cleared by investigators, but he claimed that media coverage implied his guilt. NBC agreed to pay Jewell $500,000; the terms of the agreement with CNN were not disclosed.[4]

2. *False criticism of personal character, habits, or obligations.* Examples in this category include false claims of promiscuity, dishonesty, cruelty, mental illness, alcoholism, drug abuse, contagious diseases, gambling habits, or poor parenting skills.

False accusation of homosexuality was once considered libelous under common law, but as society becomes more tolerant of the gay lifestyle, legal scholars believe that libel suits resulting from false accusations of being gay will become less likely. In the late 1990s, actor Tom Selleck sued a newspaper over a story that suggested he was gay, but the case was settled out of court for an undisclosed amount and did not establish a precedent. A few years later, a bodyguard for singer Madonna was unsuccessful in his libel suit against a tabloid magazine that falsely identified him as gay. The court ruled that while the plaintiff may have been embarrassed by the error, homosexuality no longer carried the stigma that it once did.[5] In 2005, an Ohio court made a similar ruling in a case of a college student who sued classmates for defamation after they put up posters on campus accusing him of being gay. "Publicizing that someone is a homosexual is not libel per se because being a homosexual is not a crime, nor is it a disease," the court's decision stated. "Additionally, being a homosexual would not tend to injure a person in his trade or occupation."[6]

Reporters and editors should be cautious about the casual use of slang terms or other "red flag" words that may result in libel suits. These include terms such as *deadbeat dad, computer hacker, welfare mother, junkie, adulterer, addict, sex offender, sexual predator, terrorist, drug abuser, town drunk, gadfly, peeping Tom, slumlord, curmudgeon, floozie, compulsive gambler, slut,* or *ex-convict.* Adjectives requiring caution include *fraudulent, unethical, corrupt, bankrupt,* and *promiscuous.*

3. *False criticism of professional performance or competence.* For example, news stories about physicians accused of performing unnecessary surgeries or overbilling insurance companies are ripe for libel suits if the accusations turn out to be false. And, of course, the term *malpractice* should always be used with caution.

4. *False criticism of business performance or financial standing.* In the early 1980s, a small daily newspaper in New Jersey reported that a retired banker in the community received a questionable loan from his former bank in order to establish a horse-breeding farm. Because of a factual error, the subject of the story sued the newspaper for libel, claiming that it damaged not only his reputation as a banker but also that of his new business venture. In *Mayo Sisler v. The Courier News* (1983)[7], the plaintiff was awarded $1.05 million by a trial court. The New Jersey Supreme Court later reversed the judgment, claiming that the newspaper was simply carrying out its role as a reporter of public affairs and that as a public figure, the plaintiff failed to prove that the newspaper acted with malice. Even though the newspaper eventually won, the stress and expense of the six-year case serves as a reminder to journalists of the importance of fact-checking.

5. Product disparagement *or trade libel,* which involves false criticism of a product rather than an individual or company.

6. *False criticism of political or religious belief or affiliations,* such as incorrectly labeling someone as a communist or atheist. In contrast, the courts have ruled that racial or ethnic slurs do not damage a person's reputation and are therefore not grounds for a libel suit.

Components of Libel

In order to have a successful libel claim, a plaintiff must prove six factors:

1. *Defamation.* *The Restatement of Torts,* a legal reference book that summarizes common law, defines defamation as "communication which has the tendency to so harm the reputation of another as to lower him in the estimation of the community or to deter third persons from associating with him."[8] Name-calling by itself does not constitute libel nor does simply claiming embarrassment.

2. *Harm.* This element is sometimes included as part of the "defamation" factor and sometimes listed separately. Generally, "harm" or "damages" refers to injury to a person's reputation, financial condition, or emotional well-being.

3. *Identification.* In order to have a strong libel claim, a person must be identified directly rather than indirectly. A person mentioned by name can obviously make a successful claim of identification. But if a news story makes a reference to a "high-ranking city official" or "university administrator," that's not specific enough to constitute identification. **Group libel** refers to actions taken by individuals claiming they were defamed by criticisms of a group. The validity of a group libel claim depends on two factors: the size of the group (the larger the group, the less likely the courts will rule in favor of the plaintiff) and the likelihood that an individual would be harmed by libelous information concerning the group. Examples of stories with the potential of sparking group libel cases are that all lawyers working for a certain firm are incompetent or that all professors at a certain university are members of the Communist Party.

4. *Communication.* Three parties must be involved in a successful libel action: the publishing or broadcasting entity, the victim, and a third person who can identify the victim. Newspapers and magazines are considered to have "published" if one or more copies are circulated. Radio and television stations are considered to have "communicated" when they air a broadcast. In the case of alleged libel on the Internet, "communication" takes place when a third party has access to the information. In most states, libel laws provide a statute of limitations of one or two years, meaning that plaintiffs have that period of time to file their complaints with the appropriate court.

5. *Fault.* The two levels of fault are negligence (sometimes called "sloppy reporting") and **actual malice** (also called **reckless disregard for the truth**). Examples of negligence including relying on an untrustworthy source, failure to seek additional information from the person who is the subject of the story, failure to allow that person to respond, failure to check dubious facts, or failure to read (or the misreading of) pertinent documents.

The "reckless disregard" standard is used in cases in which the journalist knew something was false but reported it anyway. The distinction between the two levels of fault is significant and will be discussed in the section describing the difference between public and private figures.

6. *Falsity.* Generally, plaintiffs in libel cases bear the burden of proving the published information is false. Minor errors—such as incorrect dates or similar details—that do no damage cannot be the basis for a defamation suit.

Who Can Sue—and Who Cannot

Most libel plaintiffs fall into one of the following categories: (1) living persons and (2) organizations (businesses or nonprofit associations).

The issue of whether family members or other interested parties can sue for libel on behalf of a deceased person varies by state. Only a handful of state libel statutes allow family members of a deceased person to sue for libel under a concept known as "desecration of memory." Most others specify that when an individual dies, the right to sue for libel dies also. Other states do not permit family members to initiate a libel suit after the death of the defamed person but do allow them to continue to pursue a libel suit filed by the defamed individual before his or her death.

Common law provides two other general rules about the nature of libel plaintiffs:

1. *Government units and agencies cannot be plaintiffs in libel suits.* In a democratic society, courts have ruled, journalists and other citizens have the right to scrutinize their city, county, state, and federal government, and those government units and agencies cannot be defamed. Although most such criticism would otherwise be protected against libel action by the "fair comment" defense, common law has provided this protection as an additional defense. Individual government employees can sue, however, but only on their own behalf. *The Government Can't Sue anyone as a who for libel actions. They have to sue individuals.*

2. *Plaintiffs cannot claim "libel of omission."* Individuals who believe they should have been mentioned in a positive news story have the right to ask the newspaper or magazine to correct the omission but do not have grounds for a libel action. Common examples include the omission of a person from a newspaper story that lists students at the local high school who earned academic awards or from a story that lists all of the citizens of the community who earned awards for military service. While the omitted person might have a claim that he or she was offended by the omission, courts have ruled that such oversights are not libelous.

The person who's name was omitted out of a positive news story has the right to ask the newspaper / magazines to correct it but they cannot sue.

KAB

Private Figures, Public Figures, and Public Officials

As discussed previously, whether the plaintiff is a private figure or public figure determines the level of fault he or she is required to establish. Private figures have to prove only negligence or sloppy reporting, while public figures must show actual malice or "reckless disregard for the truth." About one-third of all libel cases are filed by public figures, mostly persons in elected or appointed government positions, professional sports, or the entertainment industry.

There are three types of public figures:

1. An **all-purpose public figure** is a "celebrity" whose name is a "household word." This includes public officials, well-known professional athletes, and entertainers. Generally, all aspects of such a person's life are public.

2. A **limited or "vortex" public figure** is one involved only in a specific event, issue, or controversy. The limited public figure label applies in cases in which (1) the issue or controversy in which the individual is involved began before publication of the allegedly libelous material, or (2) the individual is voluntarily participating in or attempting to resolve the issue or controversy.

3. An **involuntary public figure** is a person who does not seek the spotlight but instead is thrust into it, such as the witness to a crime or other individual involved in a news story by circumstance.

Whether an individual's status in the community makes him or her a public figure often depends on the size of the community in which the publication or broadcast of defamatory information took place. In a large city, police officers and other low-level local government employees are rather anonymous in their work, and it is unlikely they would be considered public figures for libel purposes. But in a small town, where nearly every citizen would know local law enforcement officers by name, that might not be the case. In a small town in West Virginia, for example, two police officers were accused in a 1992 newspaper story of providing a bar owner with advanced warning of a vice raid. The story proved to be false, and the officers won their libel suit at the trial court level. The West Virginia Supreme Court reversed the decision, however, ruling that because the officers were well-known in the small town, they were public figures and could not prove malice on the part of the newspaper.[9]

Major corporations and nonprofit organizations are often considered the equivalent of public figures for libel purposes. When making that determination, the courts take a number of factors into consideration, including size, name recognition, pervasiveness of advertising, and involvement in political and social issues.

Defenses against Libel Claims

There are three defenses commonly used in libel cases; defendants need to establish only one in order to successfully defend their stories.

1. *Truth.* If a journalist can prove his or her story is true, the libel suit is often thrown out altogether, regardless of other conditions. Terms such as *truth* or *falsity* refer to the details that form the core of the story. In extreme cases, truthful information can be libelous if the court determines there was no justifiable reason for publishing it. In most such cases, however, a plaintiff would likely have more success pursuing a private facts claim (see Chapter 7) than a libel claim.

2. *Fair comment and criticism,* also known simply as "opinion." The courts have defined an "opinion" as an expression that is not provably false. The Supreme Court has ruled in numerous cases that there is no such thing as a false opinion.

The fair comment defense exists to allow journalists, commentators, or the general public the opportunity to fairly criticize (1) public officials for their performance in office, (2) businesses for the quality of their products and services or the performance of their employees, and (3) entertainment products such as restaurants, books, television programs, movies, and concerts for their quality.

In order to be protected under the fair comment defense, editorials, personal commentaries, and other forms of opinion writing must be supported by evidence and may not include factual errors (this exception is discussed later in this chapter). Editors of newspaper opinion pages report that many of the original versions of letters to the editor they receive might be determined by a court to be libelous because of factual errors. Before publishing the letters, editors will either correct or omit the errors or offer the writers the opportunity to revise their submissions.

The fair comment defense came out of the 1930 case of *Hoeppner v. Dunkirk,* in which a New York state court ruled that "everyone has a right to comment on matters of public interest and concern, provided they do so fairly and with an honest purpose . . . such comments or criticisms are not libelous, however severe in their terms."[10]

3. Privilege. Under most circumstances, speakers taking part in governmental meetings or legal proceedings cannot be guilty of libel, nor can a reporter quoting them. At the national level, members of Congress enjoy absolute privilege provided the comments in question are made as part of their legislative duties. In *Hutchinson v. Proxmire (1979)*, however, the Supreme Court ruled that this protection does not extend to a public official's non-legislative duties, such as his or her communication with constituents (this case is discussed in more detail in Chapter 13).[11]

Many state laws extend similar protections to **public officials** and participants in legal proceedings. In some states, however, the protection is referred to as qualified privilege because it is more limited than the scope of similar laws at the federal level. At the federal level and in many states, the privilege defense also applies to information gleaned from transcripts and other public documents related to the proceedings.

The rationale for the privilege defense is that both public officials and private citizens speaking at public meetings should be able to do so without fear of being sued, and that journalists should be able to report on what was said. Despite this common-law protection, libel suits are filed based on comments made, but the courts typically side with the defendants unless there is overwhelming evidence that the journalist intentionally misquoted or exaggerated the individuals' comments.

There are a variety of other defenses employed in defamation cases, but they are not recognized by all courts.

Neutral reportage, an extension of the privilege defense, refers to the rights of journalists to report information gathered in situations other than governmental and legal proceedings, such as interviews, even if the journalist suspects the comments might be false. Most courts that recognize this defense have established three qualifications: (1) the matter must be one of public interest, (2) the information must be from a credible source, and (3) the journalist must allow the criticized party the opportunity to respond.

The neutral reportage defense was not successful in two cases argued in the late 1990s.

The case of *Khawar v. Globe International* (1998) began when a Pakistani immigrant seen in published photographs to be nearby when presidential candidate Robert F. Kennedy was assassinated in 1968 learned that a tabloid newspaper, *The Globe,* implied that he was the assassin. The newspaper's defense was that it was merely repeating charges that had been made in Robert Morrow's 1988 book about the assassination, *The Senator Must Die.* A trial court, as well as the California Supreme Court, ruled against the newspaper in its neutral reportage claim because the original book was not a credible source and the newspaper made no effort to contact the subject of the story for his response.[12]

In *Troy Publishing v. Norton* (2005), the Pennsylvania Supreme Court upheld a lower court ruling that a newspaper could be sued for libel when it reported a political candidate's false charges against a rival. The case began when William T. Glenn, a city councilman in West Chester, Pennsylvania, claimed in a newspaper interview that Mayor Alan Wolfe and fellow councilman James Norton were "liars" and "draft dodgers." Attorneys for the newspaper claimed that politicians "have been hurling false and damaging charges at their rivals throughout American history" and that the media should be allowed to accurately report what charges are being made, regardless of whether they were true or not. But the court ruled that the press has never "enjoyed a blanket immunity" from being sued over stories that print falsehoods that damage a person's reputation.[13]

The **wire service defense** provides limited protection for newspapers or other media outlets that publish or broadcast defamatory information derived from wire service reports. In order to successfully use this defense, four conditions must be met: (1) the wire service is a reputable one, (2) the defendant did not know the story was false, (3) there were no indicators (i.e., "red flags") in the story to raise suspicions of possible falsity, and (4) the defendant did not alter the material to a substantial degree.

Rhetorical hyperbole is a defense in which a defendant claims that a statement is so clearly an exaggeration that no reasonable member of the audience would believe it. Examples are statements such as "your mother's so fat that . . . . "

In the 1988 case of *Hustler v. Falwell* (discussed in more detail in Chapter 7), for example, a trial court ruled that an ad parody involving a well-known evangelist was not libelous because the accusations in it were "so outrageous that no reasonable person would have believed them."[14]

Another example is found in the case of *Seelig v. Infinity Broadcasting Corporation* (2002), in which a California court dismissed a libel suit against a radio station that called a local woman a "chicken butt" because she refused to participate in an interview following her appearance on a nationally broadcast reality television program.[15]

Libel Cases of National Significance

Public Officials, Public Figures, and the Actual Malice Rule

The most famous libel case in the history of American journalism is *New York Times v. Sullivan* (1964). It is significant for several reasons, the most important of which was the creation of the actual malice rule that drew a distinction between public officials and private figures and required **public figures** to meet a higher burden of proof in libel cases.

The plaintiff in the case was L. B. Sullivan, the police commissioner of Montgomery, Alabama, in the late 1950s and early 1960s. At the height of the civil rights movement, the *New York Times* published an advertisement, paid for by a civil rights group, which accused the Montgomery police department of brutality and of violating the civil rights of some of the people involved in the movement. Sullivan was not identified in the ad, but his department was.

A lower court in Alabama awarded Sullivan $500,000, but the U.S. Supreme Court overturned the judgment, determining that in order to prove libel, public officials must show "actual malice," meaning that the journalist or media organization in question knew (or should have known) that the information was false but chose to publish or broadcast it anyway. Private persons, by contrast, would simply be required to prove "negligence" or "sloppy reporting" on the part of the defendant.

In its 9-0 decision, the Court determined that to allow public officials to prevail in defamation cases would create a chilling effect and violate the media's First Amendment rights to scrutinize the performance of public officials. The Court did not define what a public official was in the Sullivan case, but in a later case, it defined a public official as anyone who is "elected to a public office or who participates in policy development."

In addition to creating the actual malice rule, the Court determined in the *Sullivan* decision that in many cases, alleged libel was a natural by-product of free speech and should be tolerated as something that results from the "heated exchange of public debate." As a result, the burden of proof in libel cases was shifted from the defendant to the plaintiff.[16]

Some legal scholars believe the objective of the Supreme Court was to scrutinize state libel laws and provide more First Amendment protection for the press by requiring public officials—and in some cases public figures—to meet the actual malice standard. In cases subsequent to *Sullivan*, the Supreme Court (and lower courts) has ruled that because of the traditional First Amendment protections given the press, public figures are obligated to accept public scrutiny and criticism as part of their positions and should be successful in their libel claims only in extreme cases—i.e., actual malice. The Sullivan case is also interesting in that the alleged libel took the form of an advertisement; prior to this case, libel was typically thought of as something that occurred only within the context of a news story.

In a series of cases that followed *Sullivan*, the courts expanded the actual malice rule to cover not only public officials but also public figures—a category that would include entertainers, athletes, and individuals campaigning for public office or speaking on controversial public issues.

The first such cases—*Associated Press v. Walker* and *Curtis Publishing v. Butts*—reached the Supreme Court on the same day in 1967.

The Walker case involved former U.S. Army General Edwin Walker, who left military service and became involved in numerous conservative political causes. In the early 1960s, he was a critic of the civil rights movement and proposals to integrate public schools and universities. When an Associated Press report accused him of instigating a riot at the University of Mississippi as a black student attempted to enroll, Walker sued the wire service for libel. He won at the trial court level, but the Supreme Court reversed the judgment and ruled in favor of the Associated Press, determining that Walker's role in national politics made him analogous to being a "public official" as the term pertains to the negligence-malice determination. In addition, the Court ruled, the story was produced under deadline pressure and therefore some errors were inevitable.[17]

That same day, however, the Supreme Court determined that a public figure could still win a libel suit if he or she was able to prove a publication failed to verify the facts of a story. At issue in *Curtis Publishing v. Butts* was a 1963 *Saturday Evening Post* article that accused University of Georgia Athletic Director Wally Butts of conspiring with University of Alabama Coach Bear Bryant to fix the outcome of the 1962 football game between the two schools.

The first step the Supreme Court took was to label Butts as a "public figure." But that designation was not enough to prevent Butts from winning his case, as the Supreme Court also looked at the other circumstances of the case before ruling in the plaintiff's favor. The story, based on an anonymous source, contained numerous factual errors and several inconsistencies that the magazine did not check out. The Court observed that the story was not produced in a deadline situation (as in the Walker case) in which the magazine could claim that the errors resulted from negligence or a simple mistake. The fact that the story was published several months after the game meant the magazine had adequate time and could have (and should have) made more of an effort to verify the details of the story.

Even though Butts was a public figure, the court ruled that the magazine's failure to better check the facts of the story constituted "malice" or "reckless disregard for the truth." The court upheld Butts's $460,000 jury verdict granted him by a lower court. In its majority decision, the Court ruled that the Butts story "was in no sense 'hot news' and the editors of the magazine should have recognized the need for a thorough investigation of the serious charges . . . elementary precautions were ignored." A concurring opinion referred to the publication's "slipshod and sketchy investigative techniques employed to check the veracity of the source."[18]

In *Rosenbloom v. Metromedia* (1971), the Supreme Court established the category of "limited public figures" to describe those persons who are private figures in most respects but become public figures when they are involved in or comment on a public issue. In this case, it overturned a lower court libel judgment award to George Rosenbloom, a Philadelphia magazine dealer who was arrested and charged with selling obscenity.

A local radio station had referred to Rosenbloom as a "smut peddler" and continued to do so even after he was found not guilty of the obscenity charge. A lower court sided with Rosenbloom and ruled that he was libeled, but the Supreme Court overturned the ruling, creating the "limited public figure" concept. Because Rosenbloom was involved in a public issue, in this case obscenity, he was therefore a public figure and was required to prove actual malice, which he could not.[19]

The "limited public figure" rule also applied in the case of *Gertz v. Robert Welch* (1974). The plaintiff was Elmer Gertz, a Chicago lawyer who represented the family of a man killed by police. During the trial of the police officers, Gertz was criticized by the John Birch Society in its magazine, *American Opinion*, which accused him of plotting to discredit local police. Much of the article was proven to be false. Even though Gertz had never been in trouble with the law, for example, the article claimed that he had a criminal record that was "so thick it took a fat Irish cop to lift it."

Gertz lost the libel suit against the magazine in trial court after he was determined to be a limited public figure, but the Supreme Court overturned the decision and ruled in his favor, determining that the "public figure" defense was not absolute and that Gertz's limited role in public affairs was overshadowed by the outrageousness of the libelous news stories.[20]

Despite the history of public figures losing libel cases because of being unable to prove actual malice, such cases are not impossible to win. The cases of *Goldwater v. Ginzburg* (1969), *Harte-Hanks Communications v. Connaughton* (1989), and *Turner v. KTRK* (1996) established that public officials and candidates for public office—once thought to be almost "libel-proof"—could indeed be successful in libel actions if their evidence was strong enough to prove actual malice.

The plaintiff in the *Goldwater* case was Barry Goldwater, an Arizona senator and 1964 presidential candidate. A magazine with the ironic title of *Fact* published a story during the campaign based on a survey it had mailed to hundreds of psychiatrists around the country asking them to assess Goldwater's mental condition and his suitability to be president.

The magazine received answers such as "mentally ill," "paranoid," "anti-Semitic," and "uncertain about his masculinity," and used those terms in its story. A candidate for president is as much of a public figure as a person can possibly be, but Goldwater won his suit because he was able to prove actual malice and reckless disregard for the truth—that the magazine knew the criticisms were false but published them anyway.[21]

Twenty years later, the Supreme Court made a similar ruling in the case of *Harte-Hanks Communications v. Connaughton* (1989). Daniel Connaughton was a candidate for a municipal judgeship in Ohio who sued a daily newspaper, claiming he was libeled by a story that falsely accused him of disparaging his opponent. Even though he was a public official, he was able to meet the "actual malice" standard by proving that the newspaper ignored other potential sources who attempted to provide information that could have cleared Connaughton of the charges. The Court ruled that the paper's refusal to consider those sources was evidence of "reckless disregard for the truth."[22]

In the *Turner* case, a candidate for the mayor of Houston sued a local television station over an investigative report that implied the candidate had been involved in a case of insurance fraud in his role as a probate attorney many years earlier. The television station defended its story by claiming that it never accused the candidate of criminal conduct; it merely questioned his qualifications to be mayor. After alleging the television station showed "reckless disregard for the truth" by declining to include interviews with court officials defending his conduct in the insurance case, the candidate was awarded $5.5 million, an amount that was later reduced on appeal.[23]

Limitations and Clarifications Regarding the "Fair Comment" Defense

There are two common misconceptions about the fair comment defense.

The first misconception is that in order for material to be protected, it must appear on the editorial page or, in the case or broadcasting, somehow labeled as opinion. While placement on the editorial page or overtly identifying material as "opinion" is legally advantageous, it is not absolutely necessary. Opinion writing in the form of political columns, movie reviews, book reviews, and restaurant reviews are generally protected, even if they appear in other sections of the newspaper.

The second misconception is that fair comment protection is absolute. That is also not the case. Generally, fair comment protection applies to any expression of an opinion that is based on facts. Once a writer or commentator provides a series of facts, whatever opinion he or she then presents to the audience is protected. But if he or she presents information that later proves to be false, and the error invalidates the opinion, the writer or commentator has lost fair comment protection.

The best illustration of the loss of fair comment protection is the 1990 case of *Milkovich v. Lorain Journal*. The plaintiff was Mike Milkovich, a high school wrestling coach near Cleveland, who was at a match when a fight broke out in the stands involving members of his team. When Milkovich was called in front of an investigative proceeding to give his account of what happened, he claimed he did not instigate the brawl. A sportswriter for a local newspaper wrote in his column that the coach lied under oath during investigation. Milkovich sued for libel, but a trial court ruled in the favor of the newspaper because it judged that the column represented the opinion of the writer.

The newspaper column was written in 1975, but the case did not reach the Supreme Court until 1990. The Court overturned the trial court's finding and ruled in favor of Milkovich, determining that the accusation of "lying under oath" was considered "provably false." The court awarded Milkovich $116,000, but in fifteen years of litigation, both sides spent far more than that in legal fees.[24]

Because they fall into the category of opinion writing, reviews of restaurants, books, films, plays, and concerts are customarily protected under the concept of fair comment because they are based largely on the opinion of the person writing the review. In reviews, there may not be facts at issue, but if a review is highly negative, the reviewer should substantiate his or her opinion by providing examples. In the 1994 case of *Moldea v. New York Times*, for example, a Circuit Court of Appeals ruled in favor of a newspaper book reviewer who was sued over a negative review. The author claimed that the review, which labeled his book as "sloppy journalism," damaged his reputation as an author. The court disagreed, however, ruling that the review was protected from libel action under the fair comment principle because it provided examples from the book to support the "sloppy journalism" charge and did not simply make the criticism in a casual manner.[25]

Libel in Non-Journalistic Products

Libel is not limited to journalistic products. It can also take place in non-journalistic materials such as correspondence, newsletters, and news releases.

In the 1985 case of *McDonald v. Smith*, a presidential nominee to be U.S. Attorney in North Carolina sued a private citizen for libel because of a letter sent to President Reagan criticizing the nominee for his past performance as a state court judge. The letter accused the nominee of violating the civil rights of persons appearing in his court, as well as fraud and violations of professional ethics. After the nominee proved the accusations were false, a federal court ruled in his favor in the defamation claim.[26]

Cases involving public relations materials such as newsletters and news releases are discussed in Chapter 13. Cases involving libel on the Internet are covered in Chapter 10.

SLAPP Suits

A SLAPP suit (Strategic Litigation Against Public Participation) is one in which a party seeks to discourage an individual or group from criticizing it publicly by suing for libel, or threatening to. Examples include suits filed against environmental advocacy groups by developers attempting to stifle the groups' public criticisms and suits filed by police departments attempting to intimidate witnesses from speaking to journalists about alleged incidents of police misconduct or brutality. When such threats are carried out, the resulting lawsuits are seldom successful, usually because defendants are successful in claiming a "fair comment" defense. In addition, judges and juries are often sympathetic to defendants because such cases are often cast in a "David and Goliath" context—the large corporation acting like a neighborhood bully by attempting to intimidate a concerned and well-meaning private citizen or nonprofit group. Knowing the potential costs of providing a defense, however, many targets of such suits are intimidated enough to change their behavior before cases get too far along.

Because they are considered threats to free speech, some state governments have attempted to discourage SLAPP suits by applying the actual malice rule. Other states have passed statutes that allow defendants to recover court costs and attorneys' fees when prevailing in court, and in extreme cases, defendants can collect compensatory damages if the actions of the plaintiffs are found to be excessive.

Recent Cases

Three recent libel cases illustrate a positive trend—an increase in successful defenses against libel suits. Interestingly, all three cases involved suits brought by organizations rather than individuals.

In *MMAR Group v. Dow Jones* (1997), a Houston stock brokerage firm won an initial judgment of $220.72 million against *The Wall Street Journal* following a story alleging that the firm overcharged for its services and engaged in deceptive business practices. Of the many details included in the story, some were proven to be true, some were proven to be false, and some could not be proven either way. The firm claimed the story caused it to lose nearly all of its customers and pushed it to the edge of bankruptcy. A trial court agreed and issued the financial award, but after two years of appeals, the U.S. Supreme Court overturned the judgment by determining that the company was the equivalent of a public figure and could not prove "actual malice."[27]

In *Texas Cattlemen's Association v. Winfrey* (1998), a trade association was unable to win its product disparagement case against talk show host Oprah Winfrey. Earlier in the year, an episode of Winfrey's syndicated program focused on beef contamination in England, where "mad cow disease" had killed more than twenty people. Guests on the program warned of the dangers of a similar outbreak in the United States, after which beef sales plummeted and stayed low for several weeks. The Texas Cattlemen's Association (TCA) filed a libel suit against Winfrey under the state's product disparagement laws, claiming that the program endangered the entire beef cattle industry in Texas and the economy of the state as a whole. A trial court sided with Winfrey, however, ruling that no false statements were made on the program and the discussion was protected as "fair comment" because it was based on the opinions of the guests.[28] The Winfrey case illustrated the high degree of risk involved in bringing such cases to trial. Not only did the TCA lose the case, but the publicity surrounding its lawsuit drew more negative attention to its product than the original television program.

A similar case occurred in 2002, when the electronics manufacturer Sharper Image sued *Consumer Reports* over a negative review of one of its products. The company not only lost the case, but after two years of litigation it was also forced to pay the legal fees the magazine incurred in defending itself. Product disparagement law in California, where the suit was litigated, includes a provision that requires unsuccessful plaintiffs to pay the legal fees of the defending party. The rationale for the law—which is similar to those of about half the states—is to encourage plaintiffs and defendants to seek out-of-court settlements to such disputes and pursue formal trials only when absolutely necessary.[29]

Frequently Asked Questions about Libel and Slander

1. *Why don't celebrities sue the tabloids for libel?* Some do, but those cases often result in out-of-court settlements and the financial terms are not disclosed. Many celebrities decline to sue tabloids because they know such litigation is a no-win situation. Even if they win a financial judgment against the publication, the damage to their reputations is already done, and suing for libel draws more negative attention to the original news story. Also, as public figures, celebrities know they will be unable to meet the "malice" standard required by modern libel law. When asked about their reaction to outrageous tabloid stories written about them, many celebrities acknowledge that such negative attention is part of the celebrity lifestyle.

One of best-known cases of celebrity libel suits going to trial was the 1981 case of *Burnett v. National Enquirer*. Actress and comedienne Carol Burnett sued the tabloid over a brief gossip item that described her as getting drunk in a Washington,

D.C., restaurant and arguing loudly and publicly with Secretary of State Henry Kissinger. Despite her status as a public figure, Burnett was able to prove the tabloid showed reckless disregard for the truth by basing the story largely on the account of one of its paid tipsters, even though the editors had doubts about his credibility. A trial court awarded Burnett $800,000.[30]

2. *Why is there a different standard of fault for public figures (actual malice) as opposed to private figures (negligence) in libel cases?* The differing standards are based mostly on the fact that public figures voluntarily enter public life by choosing politics, show business, or sports as a career. Courts have typically ruled that public criticism in the form of news stories (including those found in tabloids)—even those that are exaggerated or simply wrong—is part of the celebrity lifestyle. In addition, most public figures have opportunities to respond to criticism—such as news conferences or op-ed pieces—that private citizens do not.

Point/Counterpoint: Libel Reform and the Chilling Effect

Why (and How) America's Libel Laws Should be Overhauled

In recent decades, legal scholars and professional organizations have developed a variety of proposals to reform libel law in the United States, based on their belief that the current process of extended litigation is not beneficial for either plaintiffs or the journalism industry.

At the national level, the Annenberg Washington Program, a journalism think tank located at Northwestern University, conducted a study of the libel litigation process in the mid-1980s and produced a model for states to consider in reforming their libel laws. The model included a provision that would require libel action to proceed through three stages. In the first stage, potential plaintiffs would be required to contact the offending media outlet within 30 days of publication or broadcast of the libelous content and ask for a retraction. If the media outlet retracted the story within thirty days of being contacted, the plaintiff would not be allowed to pursue the matter further.

If the media outlet failed to respond to the request or refused to retract the story, the case would move into the second stage, at which either the plaintiff or defendant could then ask the court for declaratory judgment—a decision as to guilt or innocence without the complexity of a trial—based solely on the truth or falsity of the communication in question. Another provision of this stage would be a "loser pays" clause that would require the losing party to pay the winning party's legal fees. If neither side seeks a declaratory judgment, the action would move to the third stage, which resembles a more traditional libel trial, with each side responsible for its own legal fees.[31]

In the early 1990s, many state legislatures considered Uniform Correction Acts,[32] which were essentially variations of the Annenberg-Washington model.

Neither the Annenberg Libel Reform Project nor the Uniform Correction Acts resulted in any significant changes in libel litigation, but they did at least generate some discussion that may eventually lead to progress in this area. As of 2007, libel litigation remains a lengthy process that both plaintiffs and defendants find emotionally and financially draining, but state and federal court dockets are nonetheless backed up with libel litigation at the trial court and appellate levels.

Why Libel Law Should Not Be Overhauled

Opponents of proposed changes to libel law—most of them trial lawyers and media watchdog groups—believe that despite the lengthy backlog of cases in state and federal courts, lawsuits are often the only recourse that defamed individuals have to pursue compensation for their losses. They claim that the "chilling effect" performs an important function, as the fear of losing multi-million dollar lawsuits causes reporters, editors, publishers, and their broadcasting counterparts to be more careful in their work.

At worst, they claim, the length of time it takes a court to consider a libel case serves as an incentive for both sides to seek an out-of-court settlement.

Chapter Summary

Defamation is a complex area of communication law but an important one for journalists to understand. The defamation laws apply to other types of professional communicators as well, including those working in advertising and public relations, as they too are potential defamation defendants.

When evaluating defamation cases, courts require plaintiffs to meet a high burden of proof, including establishing, among other factors, that he or she was identified in the communication in question, that the information presented was both false and defamatory, and that he or she suffered as a result. While private figures are required to prove negligence on the part of the journalist or media organization, public figures must prove actual malice—a substantially higher standard.

There are a number of defenses that journalists and media organizations can use in defamation litigation. Included among these are truth, fair comment, and privilege. All three are related to the preservation of the media's First Amendment rights to gather and report news and comment on public issues.

Throughout the history of journalism and broadcasting, court decisions have helped to shape defamation law, and today it remains a constantly changing part of the legal system. Many of those changes are related to new technology.

CASE PROBLEM

Something Fishy

You're the attorney for the *Mudville Daily Tribune*. One of your star reporters, Sally Workhard, has recently completed a series of stories about working conditions in the local seafood processing facilities. The stories, based mostly on interviews with employees and their union representatives, include their claims of unsafe working conditions and the companies' repeated violations of federal and state labor laws. Several companies were mentioned in the series, and collectively they are your community's largest employers. When offered the opportunity to respond to the allegations, however, most of them refused to comment.

The largest of those companies is Mudville Seafood, Inc. Its owner, Mr. Fisher Cuttbate, has contacted your office requesting a retraction. None of the stories mentioned him by name, but they did refer to his company and quoted a union leader as saying that "the owner of Mudville Seafood was the worst of the worst when it comes to exploiting workers."

As owner of the largest seafood company in town, is Mr. Cuttbate a public figure or private figure? Are the union leader's comments about Mr. Cuttbate protected against libel action? As the attorney, what other information do you need before responding to Mr. Cuttbate's request for a retraction?

Unhappy Campers at Mudville Technical College

You're an administrator at Mudville Technical College (MTC), a two-year institution that offers courses and degree programs in medical technology, dental hygiene, automobile repair, and computer drafting. A few months ago you were forced to fire two admissions counselors for poor job performance, including frequent absenteeism, falsifying travel expenses, and returning from lunch breaks intoxicated.

You're now starting to hear from dozens of current and prospective students who bring to your office copies of electronic mail messages from the former employees. The messages encourage prospective students to choose another school instead and encourage current students to consider transferring. "What MTC isn't telling you," the messages read, "is that your degree is worthless. MTC lost its accreditation last year and has no chance of regaining it. Every employer in town knows that a degree from MTC is a joke."

At first, you dismiss the emails as just the immature actions of some disgruntled former employees and that a defamation lawsuit may be more trouble and expense than it is worth. You write to each of the individuals who received the emails to explain the situation, and as a pre-emptive measure, you also write letters to all prospective students warning them that they may also be contacted.

• Another month goes by, and a student brings to your attention a website with the name MTC-sucks.com. The two former employees are at it again, repeating their claims about the school having lost its accreditation (true, but the school is in the process of applying to be re-accredited) and the quality of MTC degrees (mostly their opinion).

As an administrator at MTC, consider the following questions: (a) In hindsight, were you correct to dismiss the first round of emails rather than file a defamation suit? If you had filed a lawsuit, would you have accused the two former employees of slander or libel? (b) Now that the former employees have expanded their attacks from simple email messages to their own website, does that change the nature of your potential lawsuit?

Possible Libel at Enormous State University

You're the faculty advisor for the student newspaper at Enormous State University. The paper has recently published a controversial article about faculty members who some students say have stayed in the teaching profession too long. The article generated a number of letters to the editor on both sides of the issue. One student-written letter mentioned a specific faculty member (not identified in the original story) and referred to him as a "senile old man." Could that be libelous? What if the student agreed to re-write the letter and changed that phrase to read, "too old to be an effective teacher"?

SOCRATIC DIALOGUE QUESTIONS

1. Why is libel more damaging to a person's reputation than slander?

2. One common analogy used to describe libel law is the concept of "journalistic malpractice"—just as a medical malpractice suit is sometimes a patient's best recourse against an incompetent or unethical physician, a libel suit is sometimes a news subject's best recourse against an incompetent or unethical journalist. Some critics of the journalism profession say that analogy of "journalistic malpractice" is appropriate because it causes journalists to be more careful in their work, and therefore the "chilling effect" is beneficial. Agree or disagree?

3. Do you agree with the differing levels of fault required for public figures as opposed to private figures? Should those different standards be modified or should they continue?

4. Find at least one case in Chapter 6 with which you strongly disagree with the court ruling (in the final resolution of the case) and be prepared to share your opinion with the class.

GLOSSARY OF TERMS

All-purpose public figure   For libel purposes, a public official or celebrity whose name is a "household word."

Chilling effect   The reluctance of journalists to pursue controversial topics for fear of libel suits.

Communication   As a factor in libel cases, communication refers to the fact that a newspaper story has been published, a broadcast story has gone out over the airwaves, or material on the Internet has been exposed to the public.

Defamation   A general term, found in some state laws, used to refer to both libel and slander. Known in some states as **injurious falsehood.**

Fair comment and criticism   A defense in libel cases that applies to forms of opinion writing such as editorials, columns, and entertainment reviews.

Group libel   Legal actions taken by individuals claiming they were defamed by criticisms of the group.

Injurious falsehood   A general term, found in some state laws, used to refer to both libel and slander. Also known as **defamation.**

Involuntary public figure   A person who does not seek the spotlight but is thrust into it by circumstance, such as being the witness to a well-publicized crime.

Libel per se   A form of falsehood stated directly.

Libel per quod   A form of falsehood that is implied rather than directly stated.

Limited public figure   An otherwise private person who is considered a public figure (for libel purposes) only in connection to a specific news story or issue. Sometimes referred to as a **vortex public figure.**

Malice   The intent of a communicator to disseminate information known to be false. Also known as **actual malice** or **reckless disregard for the truth.**

Neutral reportage   An extension of the privilege defense; applied to news sources other than legal or governmental proceedings, such as interviews. Not recognized by all courts.

Privilege   A libel defense in which information cannot be subject of libel action if it is announced at a government meeting or during a legal proceeding.

Product disparagement   A form of libel in which the subject is a company's product rather than the company as a whole.

Public figure   For libel purposes, an individual such as a public official, entertainment celebrity, or well-known professional or amateur athlete. Courts have ruled that businesses and nonprofit organizations with a high degree of name recognition are the equivalent of public figures for libel purposes.

Public official   Based on court rulings, a public figure is an individual who serves in public office, campaigns for public office, or participates in policy development.

Rhetorical hyperbole   A clear exaggeration or falsehood that is not intended to be taken seriously by the audience. Sometimes used as a defense in libel cases, but it is not recognized by all courts.

Wire service defense   Provides limited protection for newspapers or other media outlets that publish or broadcast defamatory information derived from wire service reports.

NOTES

1. William Robbins, "A Rumor of AIDS, a Slander Award." *New York Times,* July 23, 1990, p. A-8.
2. Libel Defense Resource Center news releases, 2005 and 2006.
3. *MMAR Group v. Dow Jones & Co.,* 187 F.R.D. 282 (1999).
4. John M. Touhy and Jeffrey W. Sarles, "Defamation Law." *National Law Journal,* September 8, 1997, p. B-6.
5. "Judge: 'Homosexual' Label Not Libel." Associated Press Report, May 30, 2004.
6. "Ohio Court Finds No Libel in Falsely Labeling Student as Gay." SPLC Legal Alert, December 2005.
7. Jonathan Friendly, "Does a Public Figure Have a Right to Privacy?" *New York Times,* June 12, 1983, Section 4, p. 8.

8. *The Restatement of Torts,* second edition. St. Paul, Minn.: American Law Institute, 1979.

9. *Dixon v. Ogden Newspapers,* 187 W.Va. 120 (1992).

10. *Hoeppner v. Dunkirk,* 172 N.E. 139 (1930).

11. *Hutchinson v. Proxmire.* 443 U.S. 111 (1979).

12. *Khawar v. Globe International,* 19 Cal. 4th 254 (1998).

13. *Troy Publishing v. Norton,* 125 S.Ct. 1700 (2005).

14. *Hustler v. Falwell,* 108 S.Ct. 876 (1988).

15. *Seelig v. Infinity Broadcasting Corporation,* 119 Cal. 2d 108 (2002).

16. *New York Times v. Sullivan,* 376 U.S. 254 (1964).

17. *Associated Press v. Walker,* 388 U.S. 130 (1967).

18. *Curtis Publishing v. Butts,* 1 Media L. Rep. 1568 (1967).

19. *Rosenbloom v. Metromedia,* 403 U.S. 29 (1971).

20. *Gertz v. Robert Welch,* 418 U.S. 323 (1974).

21. *Goldwater v. Ginzburg,* 414 F.2d 324 (1969).

22. *Harte-Hanks Communications v. Connaughton,* 491 U.S. 657 (1989).

23. *Turner v. KTRK,* 38 S.W. 2d 103 (2000).

24. *Milkovich v. Lorain Journal,* 497 U.S. 1 (1990).

25. *Moldea v. New York Times,* 22 F.3d 310 (1994).

26. *McDonald v. Smith,* 472 U.S. 479 (1985).

27. *MMAR Group v. Dow Jones & Co.,* 187 F.R.D. 282 (1999).

28. *Texas Cattlemen's Association v. Winfrey,* 212 F.3d 598 (1998).

29. "Sharper Image Slapped by Consumers Union." *Crisis Counselor,* December 1, 2004; David Kravets, "Judge Tosses Sharper Image Lawsuit Against Consumer Reports." Associated Press report, November 10, 2004.

30. *Burnett v. National Enquirer,* 144 Cal. App. 3d 991 (1983).

31. *Proposal for the Reform of Libel Law.* Chicago, Ill.: Washington-Annenberg Program, Northwestern University, 1988.

32. Richard N. Winfield, "Uniform Correction Act Moves Closer to Reality," *Editor & Publisher,* September 25, 1993, p. 3; Barbara W. Wall and Richard N. Winfield, "Uniform Correction Act Goes to States for Passage," *Editor & Publisher,* January 28, 1995, pp. 20–21; Debra Hersh Hernandez, "Uniform Correction Act Introduced," *Editor & Publisher,* July 22, 1995, p. 16.

7 Privacy

Instantaneous photographs and newspaper enterprise have invaded the sacred precincts of private and domestic life . . . Numerous mechanical devices threaten to make good the prediction that what was once only whispered in the closet can now be proclaimed from the rooftops.

> Samuel Warren
> and Louis Brandeis
> *Harvard Law Review* 1890

When the media use their strength to uncover government corruption or lay bare a public lie, they serve as the country's watchdog. But when the watchdog roams into our cherished private sphere, it seems to turn dangerous and predatory. Then we Americans turn on the press. We want a free press, we say, but not that free.

> Ellen Alderman and
> Caroline Kennedy
> *The Right to Privacy* 1995

LEARNING OBJECTIVES

As a result of reading this chapter, students should:

- Understand the four major areas of privacy law as they relate to mass communications: false light, private facts, intrusion, and appropriation.
- Understand how false light and private facts differ from the offense of defamation as described in the previous chapter, both in terms of the burden of proof required of the plaintiff and the common defenses available to those accused.
- Understand how the development of new technologies, as well as changing public attitudes toward the aggressive nature of the press, have affected how we look at the concept of intrusion.
- Understand the nature of appropriation and the conditions under which someone's image or likeness can and cannot be used for promotional purposes (or for entertainment purposes, as is the case with parodies).

The Origins of Privacy Law and Theory

Privacy is a broad legal term that covers a variety of issues, some of them governed by federal law and others by state law. At the federal level, the term is applied to issues such as (1) workplace privacy (such as an employer's right to administer drug tests to its employees, record their telephone conversations, or examine their electronic mail); (2) personal privacy (such as a school's right to administer drug tests to its athletes); and (3) electronic privacy (such as law enforcement agencies' right to wiretap the telephones of criminal suspects).

This chapter deals mainly with media privacy, however. Except for the Privacy Protection Act of 1980 (discussed in Chapter 8), which limits the government's ability to search newsrooms for work product materials, media privacy is largely a matter of state law.

Most communication law textbooks, including this one, place their chapters on media privacy immediately following the chapters on libel. And for good reason: There are some similarities between libel law and privacy law, and a few of the same terms apply—including the difference between private and public people.

There are three commonly accepted sources of privacy law and theory.

1. *Constitutional origins.* The term *privacy* cannot be found in the Constitution or in any of its amendments. The Fourth Amendment, however, is sometimes referred to as the "privacy amendment" and is applied to issues such as a woman's right to an abortion (under the concept of personal liberty), the drug-testing of government employees, and privacy within the home (under the concept of search and seizure). In the abortion example, Justice William O. Douglas used the term *privacy* in writing the majority opinion in *Griswold v. Connecticut*, a 1965 Supreme Court case dealing with abortion rights.[1]

The Fourth Amendment states that, "The right of the people to be secure in their persons, houses, papers, and effects, against unreasonable searches and seizures, shall not be violated." Scholars who study the Constitution have interpreted the phrase "to be secure" as including a person's physical health and safety as well as his or her emotional well-being, and therefore the right of personal privacy can be inferred. Even though the amendment deals specifically with government violation of individual rights, a broad interpretation of the amendment could extend to media violations.

2. *Warren and Brandeis article.* In 1890, legal scholars Samuel Warren and Louis Brandeis (later a Supreme Court justice) published a now-famous article in the *Harvard Law Review* in which they claimed that "advances in technology" and "voyeurism of the press" meant that some regulations were required to protect individual privacy. One important principle to come out of the Warren and Brandeis article was that "people have the right to be left alone."[2] Despite its age, the article is still quoted in privacy cases today.

3. *Prosser article and book.* Prior to 1960, there was little consistency in state privacy laws across the United States. But in 1960, law school professor William L. Prosser authored a groundbreaking journal article concerning media privacy, and in 1964 he incorporated that information into a book on tort law.[3] The main feature of the article was the establishment of four categories of privacy law—false light, private facts, intrusion, and appropriation. Over the next decade, many states updated their privacy statutes and included those four terms, which helped create the consistency in state privacy laws that we see today.

False Light

False light is the presentation of information about a person in a news story or other medium in a manner that may not be inaccurate per se but which is exaggerated or misleading. False light is different from libel because instead of claiming financial loss or serious damage to reputation, plaintiffs instead base their claims on embarrassment or humiliation—damage that is less tangible but, in the eyes of plaintiffs, is easier to claim. Major cases setting precedents in the area of false light were *Spahn v. Messner* (1964), *Time v. Hill* (1967), and *Cantrell v. Forest City Publishing* (1974).

The Spahn case was unusual in that it involved descriptions that were flattering rather than disparaging. Warren Spahn was a pitcher for the Atlanta Braves when freelance writer Julian Messner wrote an unauthorized biography of him based on newspaper clippings and other secondary sources. The book exaggerated Spahn's accomplishments, not only as an athlete, but also as a soldier in World War II. Spahn claimed he was not the war hero that Messner described in his book and that his battlefield injuries were not as serious as Messner described them.

Justice Louis Brandeis was the co-author of an 1890 article in the Harvard Law Review *that laid the groundwork for much of privacy law and theory that is applied today.*

The book also included fictionalized dialogue between Spahn and his team-mates, coming not from actual interviews but from Messner's imagination. Spahn sued for false light, claiming that he was embarrassed by the exaggerated descriptions in the book. A New York trial court ruled in Spahn's favor, awarding him financial damages and enjoining Messner from further publication of the book. The court clarified that minor inaccuracies in a biography or similar historical work were protected by the First Amendment but not if those inaccuracies were intentional.[4]

The *Time v. Hill* case began with a 1952 home invasion involving a family in Philadelphia. A group of escaped convicts broke into the home and held the family hostage, but not in the violent manner that was portrayed in a Broadway play and in a *Life* magazine article based on the incident. The magazine story included photos of the actors from the play and made the incident seem more violent than it actually was. The Hill family sued the magazine (owned by *Time*), claiming that the inaccuracies invaded their privacy. The Supreme Court ruled that even though the Hill family had not become public figures per se, their story was newsworthy and so they would have to prove more than just falsity—they would have to prove actual malice. The ruling in *Time v. Hill* was believed to be the first application of the actual malice rule, borrowed from libel law, to a false light case. Because the family could not prove actual malice, the court ruled in favor of the magazine.[5]

Cantrell v. Forest City Publishing (1974) involved another family drama, this one in Pomeroy, Ohio, just across the Ohio river from Point Pleasant, West Virginia. Following the collapse of a bridge spanning the two cities, *Cleveland Plain Dealer* reporter Joseph Eszterhas attempted to interview the wife of a man killed in the tragedy. The widow was unavailable, but Eszterhas got quotes from other sources and wrote a story that depicted the family as impoverished. It was later discovered that many elements of the story were either false or exaggerated. The family sued the *Plain Dealer* and won. The ruling was different from that in the *Time* case because the reporter knew the information in his story was false but wrote it anyway—an example of "actual malice" or "reckless disregard for the truth."[6]

Private Facts

The Restatement of Torts, a reference book that summarizes common law, describes **private facts** as the details of one's life that (a) would be highly offensive to a reasonable person, and (b) are not of legitimate interest to the public.

Private facts cases are distinguishable from libel in three respects:

1. While libel cases deal with falsehoods, private facts cases deal with information that is truthful.
2. Unlike a libel plaintiff, who must prove loss to financial standing or reputation, a private facts plaintiff sues for shame, humiliation, and mental anguish. In

other words, libel claims are based on how others view the plaintiffs, but private facts cases deal with how the plaintiffs view themselves.

3. Unlike libel defendants, a defendant in a private facts case cannot use truth as a defense.

According to common law, private facts are those concerning one or more of the following aspects of a person's life:

1. Mental and emotional condition, including grief.
2. Physical health.
3. Love and sexual relationships, including sexual orientation.
4. Decisions regarding procreation and contraception.
5. Family relationships.
6. Victimization of a violent or sexual crime.
7. Associational memberships and affiliations.
8. Religious beliefs or church membership.
9. Financial matters.
10. Academic records.

Among the factors not considered to be private facts violations—although many people believe they should be—are (1) "strange or unusual" lifestyle (examples are provided later in this chapter), and (2) accurate identification of criminal suspects. If someone is mentioned in a newspaper article or television broadcast as a criminal suspect or someone who has been arrested, that's not a violation of private facts law, even if the person is later found not guilty. That is why journalists are always careful to attribute criminal charges to the police. They do not report that "Joe Schmoe robbed First National Bank." They report that "Police have charged Joe Schmoe with robbing First National Bank." That way if it turns out later that it's a case of mistaken identify and it was not Joe Schmoe, they are sharing the responsibility for the incorrect identification with the law enforcement officials who provided the information, and in most cases neither party would be guilty of defaming the individual or of violating the suspect's privacy, provided the error was unintentional.

Private Facts Defenses

There are four common defenses that journalists use in private facts cases:

1. *Newsworthiness.* The newsworthiness defense includes two assumptions: (a) when a person leaves his or her home, he or she forfeits the expectation of privacy; and (b) in most cases, once a person becomes newsworthy, he or she remains newsworthy for life. The latter principle applies mainly to persons falling into the category of "all purpose public figures" (as found in libel law), such as former presidents of the United States and famous professional athletes. Therefore, stories

related to the health and financial standing of such individuals are generally immune from private facts suits. Because the notion of newsworthiness is subjective and varies from one media outlet to the next, the courts are fairly generous in allowing the media to determine for their own purposes what is newsworthy and what is not.

2. *Public domain.* News in the **public domain** includes that which has been previously published, broadcast, or is generally known, takes place at a public event, is contained in a government document, or is released at a government meeting. In order to be considered in the "public domain," the information must also be accurate and legally obtained.

3. *The information is not considered highly offensive.* Certain aspects of a person's life may fall into one of the ten aspects of a person's life listed on page 133, but not to the degree that they are embarrassing.

4. *Consent.* Information disclosed during an interview or otherwise revealed voluntarily cannot later be the subject of a private facts case. Once given, consent cannot be withdrawn. For example, in 2001 a woman in North Carolina agreed to be interviewed and photographed for a newspaper story about conditions in a city-run housing project. Before the story was published, she called the newspaper and asked that her photograph not be used, fearing retaliation by city officials or her neighbors. The newspaper declined her request.[7] Another example of a news source attempting to withdraw consent is the case of *Virgil v. Sports Illustrated* (discussed later in this section).

Significant Private Facts Cases

The newsworthiness provision that "once a person becomes newsworthy, he or she remains newsworthy for life" was a factor in two cases in the previous century, but the cases had different outcomes.

In the 1931 case of *Melvin v. Reid,* Gabrielle Darley, former prostitute who was tried and found not guilty of murder in 1918, found herself the subject of the movie *The Red Kimono* a decade later. By the time of the movie's release, Darley had changed her lifestyle dramatically, moved to another state, and married. When her background was revealed in the movie, she sued the producer and won in a California trial court.[8]

In *Sidis v. F-R Publishing* (1940), however, the U.S. Supreme Court made a different ruling. The plaintiff was William Sidis, a child prodigy in the early 1900s who defeated older students to win spelling bees and other academic competitions and who could solve math problems faster than a mathematician. When Sidis was in his forties, the *New Yorker* magazine published a story about people who had been famous earlier in the century, using a "Where Are They Now?" approach. Reporters found Sidis living in poverty and described his home, living conditions, and financial standing. He sued the magazine, but the court ruled that because he was famous earlier in life, public interest in him continued.[9]

These two rulings illustrate the danger in the "Where Are They Now?" approach to feature reporting (even though the *New Yorker* successfully defended itself in the *Sidis* case, the protracted conflict resulted in considerable legal expenses).

Neither Darley nor Sidis were all-purpose public figures, so at first glance it might appear that the two cases might have similar outcomes. Legal scholars believe that one of the factors behind the contrasting rulings was the degree to which each was newsworthy (Darley was not nearly as famous as Sidis) and the prevailing cultural and legal attitudes toward privacy. In the 1920s and 1930s, as Darley pursued her case through the lower courts and eventually through the U.S. Supreme Court, society and the legal system favored the protection of privacy; whereas in the 1940s, the media were given more leeway in pursuing news, often at the expense of individual's privacy. By the time of the Sidis case, the prevailing attitude of the media had become "that which was once public cannot later become private"—a concept that eventually led to the common-law principle that once a person becomes newsworthy, he or she remains newsworthy for life.

Two years after the *Sidis* case, a magazine was unable to use the newsworthiness defense in the private facts case of *Barber v. Time* (1942). Plaintiff Dorothy Barber was a hospital patient being treated for an eating disorder. *Time* magazine used her name in its story and illustrated it using a photograph that showed her head and arms. The caption underneath the photo referred to her as the "starving glutton."

Barber sued the magazine for invasion of privacy, even though at that time, the concept was not clearly addressed by state law. With no specific statute to cite, Barber based her suit on common-law references to the private nature of the doctor–patient relationship. The Missouri Supreme Court rejected the magazine's newsworthiness defense and ruled that it was not necessary to use the photograph to tell the story. The court contrasted the incident with the accounts of similar disorders as described in medical journals, which often featured photographs but were careful to protect the privacy of the patients.[10]

Newsworthiness was also a factor in *Virgil v. Sports Illustrated* (1967). In this case, surfer Mike Virgil sued *Sports Illustrated*, claiming he was embarrassed by its article, which the magazine was able to defend by claiming that "newsworthiness" included a person's "strange and unusual" lifestyle. According to the article, Virgil put out lit cigarettes inside his mouth, ate live insects, dove headfirst off staircases in order to impress women, and faked work-related injuries so he could collect worker's compensation and spend more time surfing. Virgil originally consented to the interview but later called the reporter and asked him to leave out some of the embarrassing details. The magazine refused to alter the story, and after its publication, Virgil filed a private facts lawsuit. *Sports Illustrated* claimed it was only trying to make a connection between Virgil's unusual lifestyle and his surfing style, but Virgil claimed the article ridiculed him.

The magazine asked a federal court for a summary judgment, meaning a decision by the judge based on written arguments rather than a decision by a jury based on a trial. The court refused, as did a Federal Appeals Court. The U.S.

Supreme Court refused to hear the case, so it returned to the district court level. A Federal District Court in California finally issued the summary judgment the defendant requested and ruled in favor of the magazine because it agreed with the newsworthiness defense and because Virgil had consented to the interview.[11]

Newsworthiness was also a successful defense in *Howard v. Des Moines Register* (1979). The case began three years earlier when the *Des Moines Register* published a story about deaths and mistreatment of clients at a home for retarded children and adults. Robin Howard, a woman identified in the story as being sterilized against her will, filed a private facts suit against the newspaper. Howard won at the trial court level, but the Iowa Supreme Court overturned the lower court's decision and ruled in favor of the newspaper because of the newsworthiness of the story, judging that the story was "sharing public information" and "was not morbid, sensational, or prying." The higher court concurred with the newspaper's claim that if it had published the story without Howard's name, it would not have been as credible.[12]

A newspaper's attempt to use the newsworthiness defense failed in the case of *Diaz v. Oakland Tribune* (1983). The plaintiff was Toni Diaz, a man who underwent a sex change operation to become a woman. Several years after the operation, Diaz became the first female student body president at a local community college and was involved in several campus controversies that were covered by the local news media. A story in the *Oakland Tribune* mentioned her sex change, leading to a private facts lawsuit. The trial court ruled in her favor, and the California appeals court denied the newspaper's appeal. Both courts ruled that her sex change was not related to her role in campus politics.[13]

The following year, sexual orientation was an issue in *Sipple v. Chronicle Publishing* (1984). The plaintiff was Oliver Sipple, who in the summer of 1975 was in the crowd at an outdoor event when a woman attempted to assassinate President Gerald Ford. Sipple grabbed the woman's arm and kept the gun pointed up in the air until the Secret Service agents were able to take the weapon away. Sipple was portrayed in the media as a hero who saved the president's life, but when the *San Francisco Chronicle* published a profile of him, it reported that he was gay, and other newspapers across the country included that detail in their stories about the incident. Sipple sued for invasion of privacy, claiming that his family, previously unaware of his sexual orientation, learned of it by reading the article. On a larger scale, Sipple claimed, the publicity exposed him to "contempt and ridicule" and caused him "mental anguish, embarrassment, and humiliation."

The *Chronicle* claimed two defenses: newsworthiness and public domain. The newspaper claimed its newsworthiness defense was based on (1) its belief that Sipple's heroics went against the stereotype of gay men being cowardly, and (2) Ford's reluctance to recognize Sipple as a hero. If Sipple had not been gay, the newspaper contended, he probably would have been invited to the White House and awarded a medal. But the *Chronicle* story implied that Ford downplayed the Sipple incident only because Sipple was gay.

In its public domain defense, the *Chronicle* claimed that Sipple's sexual orientation was already known because Sipple had been considered a leader in the gay community, had marched in Gay Pride parades, and had been interviewed for television and newspaper stories about gay issues long before saving the president's life.

The court ruled in favor of the newspaper. It rejected the newsworthiness defense but supported the public domain defense, ruling that Sipple's sexual orientation was already known and that he had voluntarily given up his right of privacy by consenting to media interviews on gay issues.[14]

The Public Domain Defense and the Cox Doctrine

Many private facts cases involve the "public domain" defense as applied to the naming of crime victims, including the 1975 case of *Cox Broadcasting v. Cohn*, which resulted in the Supreme Court invalidating state laws that prohibited identifying victims of rape and other sex crimes.

The case began in 1971 when a teenage girl in Georgia was raped and murdered. The name of the victim was not given during the coverage of the criminal investigation but was mentioned by an Atlanta television station during the trial of the suspects, which violated a Georgia law that made it a misdemeanor to identify rape victims by name.

The victim's parents sued the television station, basing their case on both the Georgia law and the private facts provision of common law. The state courts ruled in their favor, but the U.S. Supreme Court reversed in an 8–1 decision, ruling that it was permissible for the press to report such information if it was (1) truthful, (2) part of the public record, and (3) legally obtained. In the majority opinion, the Court said that certain types of private information should not be published, but that the means to that end was for the courts to limit the disclosure of such information, rather than for those courts to punish the media after the fact.[15] The three-part test that resulted from the *Cox* case became known as the **Cox Doctrine** and is still in effect today. It is seldom used, however, as many media outlets have a policy of not identifying rape victims by name—an ethical decision rather than a legal issue.

The Cox Doctrine was a factor in *Florida Star v. B.J.F.* (1989), which began when the newspaper published the identity of a rape victim whose name was disclosed by mistake. The victim claimed that publication of her name caused her emotional distress and prompted harassing phone calls. She later sought psychiatric counseling. A trial court found the newspaper negligent and awarded the woman $100,000 in damages. The court found two factors that differentiated the case from Cox. First, unlike the teenager whose rape and murder prompted the Cox case, the victim in this case, B.J.F., was very much alive, and her attacker was still at large. Second, the court noted, the disclosure of the name to the media was by mistake, not part of the official information available to the press. The U.S. Supreme Court reversed the lower court's decision, however, ruling that the newspaper could not be punished for publishing truthful information—even information obtained by mistake—and that the victim's claims of psychological distress and fear for her safety were not enough to outweigh the newspaper's First Amendment rights to gather and publish newsworthy information.[16]

The main exception to the Cox Doctrine is that the media can be restricted from publishing the names of victims or witnesses if their personal safety is at risk because of their identification of criminal suspects.

When it was first established by the Supreme Court, the Cox Doctrine applied only to rape victims, but in the 1980s it was expanded to include other individuals in the news.

Many newspapers and television stations have an ethical policy of not identifying minors accused of crimes, even though they could legally do so if they chose to. Many media outlets vary from this policy, however, in cases generating considerable public interest and media attention, such as those involving school shootings and similar crimes.

While law enforcement agencies may stick to their policies of not releasing the names of suspects, the media may learn the names from witnesses. Some media outlets justify their use of suspects' names by claiming that because such information has already been published or broadcast by their competitors, they are no longer ethically bound to withhold it themselves.

The U.S. Supreme Court cited the "public domain" defense when it ruled in favor of the defendant in *Briscoe v. Readers' Digest* (1971). The plaintiff was Marvin Briscoe, who was convicted of a 1959 hijacking of a truck in Kentucky. Several years after he was released from prison, *Readers' Digest* published a story about truck hijacking and mentioned Briscoe, who had by that time started a family but had not told his wife about his prison record.

The California Supreme Court ruled that *Readers' Digest* had violated Briscoe's privacy, but that decision was overturned by the U.S. Supreme Court, which ruled that his criminal record was in the public domain. The case was decided four years prior to establishment of the Cox Doctrine, but the court applied the same three-part test—ruling in the magazine's favor because the information was truthful, was part of the public record, and was legally obtained.[17]

The U.S. Supreme Court made a similar ruling in the 1977 case of *Oklahoma Publishing Co. v. District Court*. The case began with the highly publicized juvenile court trial of a teenager accused of murder. Media seldom use the names of juveniles as a matter of policy, but a local newspaper announced its intention to do so in this case because of the severity of the crime. The trial court judge ordered the newspaper not to publish the name or photo of the suspect, so the newspaper sued, claiming "prior restraint." The Supreme Court ruled that the printing of the name was permitted because of the same three-part test.[18]

Two years later, the Court made a similar ruling in *Smith v. Daily Mail Publishing*. The case centered on the trial of a fourteen-year-old West Virginia boy accused of killing a fifteen-year-old classmate. The *Charleston Daily Mail* obtained the suspect's name from witness interviews and included it in its stories because of the severity of the crime. The state attempted to punish the newspaper under a West Virginia law that prohibited media from publishing or broadcasting the names of juvenile suspects. On appeal, the Supreme Court ruled in favor of the newspaper, based on the three-part test.[19]

In another Supreme Court case, the Cox Doctrine was applied to subjects of government investigations in *Landmark Communications v. Virginia* (1978). The *Virginia Pilot* reported the name of a judge being investigated by a judicial review board, which violated a state law prohibiting the media from reporting details of judicial investigations until the issue of a final report. The newspaper was found guilty and fined $500. Despite the nominal amount of the fine, the newspaper appealed because of the principle involved. The Virginia Supreme Court upheld the conviction, so the newspaper appealed to the U.S. Supreme Court, which reversed and ruled in favor of the newspaper because the information was truthful, part of the public record, and legally obtained.[20]

Intrusion

Intrusion is the unauthorized invasion of a person's privacy by physical, photographic, or electronic means. Examples include trespassing, hidden cameras, misrepresentation, media ride-alongs, and harassment.

Trespassing, Hidden Cameras, and Misrepresentation

Intrusion in the form of trespassing includes misrepresentation, meaning that journalists cannot misrepresent themselves or conduct "hidden camera" interviews in a person's home. Intrusion does not require publication of information or photographs; the act of trespassing itself is enough to be "intrusion."

The landmark case of misrepresentation was *Dietemann v. Time* (1971), in which the court ruled in favor of Dr. A. A. Dietemann in his complaint that magazine reporters misrepresented themselves as patients when they visited his office, located inside his home, and used a hidden camera and tape recorder to document the visit. The reporters were researching a story on alternative medicine, which Dietemann practiced, and claimed the deception was justified in order to investigate the alleged unethical medical practices of which Dietemann was suspected.

The court, however, sided with Dietemann and awarded him $1,000. It ruled that even though the doctor's home served as the equivalent of his office, it was still his home, and reporters could not use hidden cameras in a home as they could in an office or place of business.[21] Despite the minimal amount of the award, the case served as a warning to journalists considering the use of modern photographic, taping, or surveillance equipment.

A more recent intrusion case is that of *Food Lion v. Capital Cities/ABC* (1997). The case began with a 1992 segment of ABC's *Prime Time Live* in which hidden cameras were used to document unsanitary conditions in Food Lion grocery stores. After the story aired, Food Lion took an unusual strategy in responding to it: instead of suing for libel, the company sued for trespassing and fraud. The

Even though Food Lion was successful in its 1997 fraud and trespassing case against ABC, an appeals court later reduced the damage award to $2.

alleged trespassing took place in backrooms, food processing areas, and other parts of the store that the public did not have access to. By doing so, the company avoided having to address the accusations or prove they were false.

Experts who deal in media law are afraid this might become a common plaintiff strategy in the future; instead of suing for libel—which is often difficult to prove—plaintiffs may find some other grounds for legal action that would provide an easier path. In libel cases, defendants often find support through the First Amendment defense, but such a defense would not be effective in a trespassing case. Plaintiffs may also find that juries are likely to be more sympathetic in cases of trespassing than in cases of libel, as trespassing is an easier concept to understand.

A North Carolina jury initially awarded Food Lion $5.5 million. ABC claims that at least part of the loss was due to the jury's anti-media bias. ABC appealed the judgment, and while the decision was not reversed at first, the network was successful in having the damages reduced. ABC continued the appeal, and in October 1999, the judgment was reduced to $2.[22]

Even before the Food Lion case, many newspapers and television news departments established internal policies regarding when the use of hidden cameras or misrepresentation is appropriate. Although policies differ from one media outlet to the next, a typical policy establishes three conditions under which such tactics are allowed:

1. The news story being pursued must be a substantial one for which the reporter has determined the need for further investigation (the search for the so-called "smoking gun"). The policy does not allow for "fishing expeditions."
2. The journalist must have exhausted all other reporting methods to collect the desired information before resorting to hidden cameras and/or misrepresentation.
3. The journalist must have approval in advance from either an editor (in the case of a newspaper or magazine) or news director (in the case of television or radio).

If journalists follow those guidelines and are sued under a state privacy law, most newspaper publishers and television station managers will assist them in their defense. Furthermore, judges and juries often consider adherence to the policy as evidence of responsible journalism. If journalists fail to adhere to the policy, however, their employers will likely not stand behind them in court, and judges and juries will be less sympathetic.

Closely related to the issue of hidden cameras is the matter of recording telephone conversations with news sources without their knowledge. In addition to applying the ethical policy explained above, journalists should also be aware of state laws regarding telephone privacy. Some state laws allow telephone conversations to be recorded as long as one party is aware of it, but some state laws require both parties (or all parties) to be aware of the recording.

Media Ride-Alongs

The popularity of "reality" shows on television has drawn attention to a new and controversial method of news-gathering known as the "ride-along," in which journalists accompany law enforcement officials and emergency medical personnel and record their work. There is little dispute over privacy rights when such work is done in public, but in numerous cases in the 1980s and 1990s, courts ruled that that in a person's home, such intrusions violated the Fourth Amendment right to privacy.

One of the earliest known cases involving the news-gathering tactic was *Miller v. NBC*, which began on October 30, 1979, when fifty-nine-year-old Dave Miller suffered a heart attack and his wife, Brownie, called 911. Paramedics arrived quickly, accompanied by a camera crew from a local television station, KNBC. While Brownie Miller waited downstairs, the camera crew recorded the drama as the paramedics worked desperately but unsuccessfully to save her husband's life.

When the Millers' daughter and son-in-law saw numerous replays of the incident on the television news and commercials promoting the station's series on the training and competency of paramedics, they persuaded Brownie Miller to complain to the management of the station, and—when that didn't work—to sue the station for invasion of privacy. During the protracted legal battle, station management and attorneys repeated their defense that "no one told us to leave." The family's response was that "no one invited you in."

At the trial court level, the station defended itself by claiming a First Amendment right to pursue a story about a legitimate public issue—the quality of emergency medical care in the community. It also claimed that having the approval of the paramedics provided additional legal protection. The Miller family, however, based its claim largely on common-law principles concerning privacy within the home.

But common law also provided that an invasion of privacy claim can be brought only by the person directly affected, and in this case, the central figure was deceased. The Miller family therefore added a claim of "intentional infliction of emotional distress" based on the repeated broadcast of the video. After nearly five years of litigation, the California trial court sided with KNBC on both the privacy and emotional distress claims, ruling in 1985 that the family had suffered no "actual harm."

In late 1986, an appeals court reviewed the case and while upholding the lower court's ruling on the privacy claim, it reversed the decision on the emotional distress claim. Not wanting to set a precedent for itself and other television news outlets by letting the split decision stand, KNBC appealed to the California Supreme Court. Before the case could get on the docket, however, the two sides reached an undisclosed out-of-court financial settlement.[23]

There were no major cases involving media ride-alongs for several years after the Miller case, but the issue surfaced again in the 1990s.

One such case was *Ayeni v. CBS*, which began in March 1992 when armed Secret Service agents raided the home of a credit-card fraud suspect in Brooklyn, New York. The agents invited a CBS camera crew to join them and videotape the raid. One of the agents wore a wireless microphone and provided a running commentary of the proceedings. When the agents arrived at the home, they found that suspect Babatunde Ayeni was not home, but his wife, clad only in a nightgown, and their five-year old son were. Both were visibly shaken by the raid and the presence of the CBS personnel and equipment. During the search, the CBS camera crew videotaped Mrs. Ayeni and her son repeatedly, in spite of her objections, and took close-up shots of the proceedings. No evidence of fraud was found.

The family then sued both CBS and the Secret Service. They sought civil damages for violation of their Fourth Amendment rights regarding "unreasonable search and seizure" as well as trespassing and infliction of emotional distress. In its defense, CBS asserted that its acts were protected because they were undertaken with the permission of the government. A U.S. District Court disagreed, based on its determination that the Fourth Amendment protects citizens against unreasonable governmental intrusions into areas where they have a reasonable expectation of privacy, particularly the home.

When CBS appealed the ruling, a Circuit Court of Appeals held that the video and sound recordings were "seizures" under the Fourth Amendment, and rendered the search far more intrusive than it needed to be.[24]

The Supreme Court ruled in two 1999 cases—*Hanlon v. Berger* and *Wilson v. Layne*—that a dividing line could be found at the doorstep of private homes. Outside that line, in areas that are visible or accessible to the public, the Court ruling implied that the media could continue to observe police activity and pursue news. But inside the home, the Court ruling said, it was not appropriate for police to bring anyone along who was not necessary for the police to do what they went to the home to do—whether to make an arrest or to conduct a search.

Hanlon v. Berger was based on a suit filed by a Montana couple against federal agents and a prosecutor who allowed a CNN reporter and camera crew to accompany them during a raid on the couple's ranch. Paul and Erma Berger sued after about twenty U.S. Fish and Wildlife Service agents rushed onto their sheep and cattle ranch searching for evidence of eagle poisoning.

The Bergers were acquitted of all charges except improper use of a pesticide. CNN eventually used video of the raid as part of its coverage of government efforts to protect endangered species. A U.S. Circuit Court of Appeals ruled that the Bergers could sue the government officials involved in the raid, as well as CNN.[25]

Wilson v. Layne involved the execution of an arrest warrant by federal and state law enforcement officials at a Maryland residence in 1992. A reporter and photographer from the *Washington Post* accompanied the officials during the execution of the warrant. The residents sued, alleging the officials violated their Fourth Amendment rights by allowing the media to watch and photograph the execution of the warrant.

After several years of litigation and appeals, the cases reached the U.S. Supreme Court, which ruled in favor of the plaintiffs. "It is a violation of the Fourth Amendment for police to bring members of the media or other third parties into a home during the execution of a warrant when the presence of the third parties in the home was not in aid of the execution of the warrant," Chief Justice William H. Rehnquist wrote in the majority opinion.[26]

Harassment

Intrusion can also include harassment, which was the determining factor in the case of *Galella v. Onassis* (1972). Freelance photographer Ron Galella had followed and photographed former First Lady Jackie Onassis and her children for several years. Onassis sued Galella for intrusion and won a restraining order that required Galella to stay at least twenty-five feet away from her and thirty feet away from her children.[27]

Following the death of Princess Diana of Wales while being chased by photographers in Paris in 1997, worldwide attention focused on the conflict between journalists' right to photograph newsworthy celebrities in public and those celebrities' claims that even when in public, they desire a certain level of privacy. Representative Sonny Bono of California—himself a celebrity often pursued by tabloid photographers—introduced in Congress a bill to make harassment by news photographers a federal crime. Bono's proposal, as well as similar bills introduced by other national lawmakers, was never passed, however.

In 1999, California became the first state to incorporate an "anti-paparazzi" clause into its privacy law. As of 2006, the law has not yet been tested in court. For a more detailed discussion of this, see FAQ number 4 on page 149.

Appropriation

Appropriation refers to the use of a person's name, image, or likeness for commercial purposes without permission and/or compensation. Although not considered as damaging to a person's reputation as libel or false light, plaintiffs nonetheless claim that being a victim of appropriation results in two forms of harm. First, a celebrity's fans or a politician's supporters may think less of him or her if they erroneously believe he or she has endorsed a controversial company or product. Second, a celebrity who generates income from product endorsements could claim financial loss in that one company is getting for free the benefit of an association that other companies are paying for.

Truth is not a defense in appropriation cases. A photograph can be taken and used for news purposes without the subject's permission, but the same photograph cannot be used for advertising or promotion.

The first appropriation case debated in the United States is believed to have been *Roberson v. Rochester Folding Box Co.* (1902). A flour company used the picture of teenager Abigail Roberson, without her permission, to advertise its product. A New York court ruled against Roberson, citing the lack of pertinent laws to support her claim.[28] But because of public disapproval of the verdict, the state of New York established its first law of appropriation soon thereafter.

Many other states followed, establishing laws that prohibited the unauthorized use of photographs and likenesses for promotional purposes but providing no restrictions on photographs used in news coverage of an event or issue.

In *Booth v. Curtis Publishing* (1962), the Supreme Court established an exception that allowed newspapers and magazines to use photographs to promote themselves but not to promote other products or services. The case originated when actress Shirley Booth was on vacation in the West Indies and a photographer from *Holiday* magazine took her photograph. The photograph was first used in a news context but was later used in an advertisement for the magazine itself. Booth sued, claiming that the second usage of the photograph was promotional in nature and not news. With its ruling in favor of the magazine, however, the Court created the **Booth Rule,** which allows newspapers and magazines to use their own news photos for self-promotional reasons—as long as the photos were newsworthy in their original context.[29]

In *Midler v. Young & Rubicam* (1992), a Federal District Court expanded the "image and likeness" concept to include a person's voice. Recording artist Bette Midler sued the Ford Motor Co. and its advertising agency, Young & Rubicam, after they produced a commercial using another singer imitating Midler's voice in performing one of her songs. Because it was a song with which Midler was widely associated, and because the impersonation was so similar to Midler's voice, the court ruled in Midler's favor, finding that appropriating a person's voice is the equivalent to using his or her photograph, image, or other likeness.[30]

Rights of the Deceased

Appropriation is different from libel in one important respect: in most states, survivors of a deceased person cannot sue for libel on his or her behalf, but in the majority of states, appropriation rights can be passed to heirs. Surviving family members often control how the names and likenesses of deceased entertainers are used for commercial or promotional purposes.

But in *Dr. Martin Luther King Jr. Center for Non-Violent Social Change v. American Heritage Products* (1981), the Supreme Court ruled that the estate of a deceased person cannot collect damages for the unauthorized usage of a person's photograph or likeness if the person in question did not benefit financially from his or her likeness while alive.

The King Center, a nonprofit museum and library in Atlanta that holds the copyrights to all of Dr. Martin Luther King, Jr's., writings and audio tapes, collects royalties when allowing them to be commercialized. But when the King Center attempted to stop American Heritage Products from selling plastic busts of King's likeness, the Court ruled that because King never made money off his image or likeness while he was alive (such as in the case of athletes or entertainers), there was no yardstick by which to measure how much money the rights were worth, and therefore the King Center could not make a claim based on financial loss.[31]

Entertainment vs. News

In *Zacchini v. Scripps-Howard* (1977), the Supreme Court ruled that entertainers can restrict the use of photographs and video taken during their performances. The case began when circus performer, Hugo Zacchini, objected to a local television station's videotaping of his act—being shot out of a cannon at a county fair in Ohio—and airing it on the evening news. Zacchini sued the station for unlawful appropriation, claiming that it had recorded his act without his permission, and because he was going to be shot out of the cannon two nights in a row, the station's airing of the video diminished public interest in coming to the second night's performance.

A trial court ruled in his favor, but an appeals court reversed on the grounds of press freedom and because the TV station did not gain financially from airing the story. The Supreme Court reversed again, claiming that his act was entertainment rather than news and was therefore subject to Zacchini's control.[32] Today, the legal principle of entertainers controlling the usage of their names and images is known as the **right of publicity.**

Today, the Zacchini ruling, combined with the rulings in similar cases (as well as copyright law), have provided the groundwork for professional sports organizations such as the National Football League, the National Basketball Association, the National Hockey League, and Major League Baseball to control the conditions under which highlights of their events can be used by television networks and local stations. Unless a network pays a licensing fee, such as in the case of ESPN's Sunday night program, *NFL Prime Time*, networks and stations can show only a limited number of minutes (the time limit varies by sport) of game highlights.

Matters of Taste and Judgment (Or the Lack of It)

While celebrities often file appropriation lawsuits based on economic loss, other public figures complain—sometimes in court and sometimes by other means—over matters of taste.

New York Mayor Rudolph Giuliani was involved in two such cases in the late 1990s. The first occurred when *New York Magazine* sponsored advertising on the sides of New York City buses that read, "*New York Magazine*—possibly the only good thing in New York that Rudy hasn't taken credit for." Using his authority as mayor, Giuliani ordered the advertisements removed. The magazine filed suit against the city, claiming the removal of the ad was a form of prior restraint. In its claim, the magazine claimed its use of the mayor's name was a parody because he

Former New York City Mayor Rudolph Giuliani was involved in two cases involving the unauthorized use of his name and photograph in advertising.

was the city's leading public official and the ad was based on his reputation for self-aggrandizement. The court ruled in favor of the magazine and ordered the city's transit authority to accept the advertisement.[33]

A few years later, Giuliani was the target of a more questionable ad, this time on a billboard sponsored by the People for the Ethical Treatment of Animals (PETA). As part of its advertising campaign claiming that milk contributes to prostate cancer, PETA used a photograph of the mayor with a "milk mustache" that parodied the dairy industry's more famous "Got Milk?" campaign. Next to the photograph was the question, "Got Prostate Cancer?" Giuliani, who had recently dropped out of the race for the U.S. Senate after being diagnosed with prostate cancer, threatened to sue, but PETA withdrew the ad and issued a formal apology.[34]

In late 1999, civil rights pioneer Rosa Parks filed an appropriation suit against the music group Outkast for using her name in the title (but not in the lyrics) of a hip-hop song she considered vulgar. In early 2005, the case was settled out of court without the terms being disclosed.[35]

Infliction of Emotional Distress

Although it is not part of privacy law per se, a tort known as **infliction of emotional distress** is occasionally included as part of a libel or privacy claim. It is sometimes subdivided into either "negligent" or "intentional" cases. A notable example is *Hustler v. Falwell* (1988), in which the Supreme Court ruled against evangelist Jerry Falwell in the appeal of his suit against *Hustler* publisher Larry Flynt over a parody that appeared in the adult magazine. At first glance, the full-page item appeared to be part of a series of advertisements in which celebrities talked about their first time drinking Campari Liqueur. But the Falwell piece was actually a parody that suggested that the reverend had sex (i.e., his "first time") with his mother and addressed his congregation while drunk. At the bottom of the page, in tiny print, was a disclaimer that read, "ad parody—not to be taken seriously."

Falwell sued Flynt for both libel and intentional infliction of emotional distress. A lower court ruled against Falwell on his libel complaint because it determined that the ad was "so outrageous that no reasonable person would have believed it," but it awarded him $200,000 on his emotional distress claim. The Supreme Court voted 9–0 to overturn that award, however, ruling that the parody was protected speech because it was a parody of a public figure and was analogous to a political cartoon or caricature. Many media organizations had filed amicus curie ("friends of the court") briefs on Flynt's behalf, concerned about the detrimental effects of a ruling in Falwell's favor. If Falwell was successful in his emotional distress claim, they feared, the result would be a chilling effect on forms of satire and public criticism such as opinion columns and editorial cartoons. "At the heart of the First Amendment is the recognition of the fundamental importance of the free flow of ideas and opinions on matters of public interest and concern," Chief Justice William Rehnquist wrote in the majority opinion. "In the world of debate about

Hustler *publisher Larry Flynt was sued by the Reverend Jerry Falwell for libel and intentional infliction of emotional distress. An appeals court overturned the trial court's libel award, and in 1988 the U.S. Supreme Court overturned the emotional distress claim.*

public affairs, many things done with motives that are less than admirable are nevertheless protected by the First Amendment."[36]

Frequently Asked Questions about Privacy

1. *Common law says that "victimization of a violent or sexual crime" is a private matter, yet the Cox Doctrine says that it is legal for the media to publish or broadcast the names of rape victims. Isn't that a contradiction?* No. The common-law rules about privacy assume that no aspect of newsworthiness exists, as newsworthiness is the most often-used defense in privacy litigation. The Cox Doctrine, while not mentioning newsworthiness, is based on the assumption that some aspect of newsworthiness exists and that the facts are legally gathered.

2. *Why is my university so strict about the privacy of student records?* In addition to common-law principles regarding privacy, students at colleges and universities have additional privacy rights under the Family Educational Rights and Privacy Act (FERPA), which limits the types of information an educational institution can release about them without their permission. When a student is the victim or alleged perpetrator of a well-publicized crime or a university athlete has been suspended from competition, for example, journalists often ask university officials for information regarding that student's mental or physical health, academic performance, or disciplinary history. Under FERPA, as well as a university's own student records policy, most of that information cannot be released to the media and is available to other university officials only on a need-to-know basis.

3. *If a journalist accompanies police or paramedics when they enter a home, does that override the privacy rights of the people inside the home?* It varies by court. In a 1976 case, *Florida Publishing Co. v. Fletcher*, the Supreme Court established a "custom and usage" principle, meaning that reporters are permitted on crime scenes or other private property if they are accompanying government officials. The plaintiff in this case was the mother of a young girl killed in a fire; the defendant was a newspaper whose photographer was allowed on the property by the Fire Department and took photographs of the outline of the body on the floor. The mother won at the trial court level, but the Supreme Court overturned the decision, ruling that it was customary to take photographs at crime and fire scenes and that the "custom and usage" principle applied.[37]

Today, however, the courts do not consistently recognize this precedent in similar cases. In two cases in 1999, for example, the Supreme Court backed away from the "customs and usage" principle when it ruled against the media in two cases involving media ride-alongs (discussed earlier in this chapter).

4. *Why can't tabloid photographers—the so-called paparazzi—be prevented from harassing celebrities?* Helping shield celebrities from tabloid photographers is seldom a priority for local law enforcement, and celebrities who hire private bodyguards often find that confrontations between the bodyguards and tabloid photographers can lead to larger publicity problems.

The term **paparazzi** has been around for several decades but was not widely used before the 1997 death of Princess Diana. While some believe the term to be an Italian word for "freelance photographer" or "photographic stalker," the term was actually derived from Paparazzo, a character in the 1960 film *La Dolce Vita*, who reminded director Federico Fellini of "a buzzing insect, hovering, darting, stinging."

As discussed earlier in this chapter, anti-paparazzi laws are often discussed (and sometimes passed) at the state and federal levels, but are difficult to enforce because of the media's First Amendment right to gather news.

5. Saturday Night Live *and other television comedy programs frequently include parodies of public officials such as Presidents Clinton and Bush and television personalities such as Larry King, Tom Brokaw, Dan Rather, and Barbara Walters. In addition, commercials for car dealers often feature Elvis Presley impersonators. Why isn't that a violation of appropriation law?* Parodies of public figures in venues such as this are not cases of appropriation because they are not used to promote a company or product. Instead, the motivation behind the parody is to entertain the audience, and there is seldom the intention to deceive the audience. In contrast, the Midler case (discussed earlier in this chapter) was decided in favor of the singer because the court ruled that the advertiser attempted to deceive the audience into believing that it was actually Midler performing the song.

Point/Counterpoint: Identifying Rape Victims

The 1975 case of *Cox v. Cohn*[38] began a national debate on the appropriateness of identifying rape victims by name, and that debate is still active more than thirty years later. While the Cox Doctrine allows the media to legally publish or broadcast names, most decline to do so as a matter of policy.

Why the Media Should Name Names

Observers who believe that the media should publish the names of rape victims make the following points:

As a general principle, the media should not be punished for publishing truthful information. Many news stories are embarrassing to persons identified in them, but there should not be exceptions for rape victims.

Victims of sex crimes should not be treated any differently than victims of other crimes. In panel discussions and op-ed pieces on the issue, publishers of newspapers that publish the names of rape victims say that victims of muggings, purse-snatchings, carjackings, and home invasions often ask that their names not be published, but that the editors and publishers see no difference among the categories of crime.

Publishing and broadcasting the names of victims will prevent people from making false accusations of rape. Because the defendants in rape cases are typically named, their accusers should also be named.

Withholding the names of rape victims perpetuates misconceptions about rape, including the perception that victims are partly to blame.

Why the Media Should Not Identify Rape Victims

Rape is different from other crimes in that it's more personal and traumatic than a carjacking or purse-snatching, and the media should recognize it as such. Some observers say that publishing the names of rape victims traumatizes the victims twice—the first time by the crime and the second time by the embarrassment of being publicly identified. Jerry Nachman, former editor of the *New York Post*, describes this as the "Bloomingdale Scenario" and illustrates it with the example of the victim in a well-publicized rape case receiving unwanted attention several years later when store clerks recognized her name on her credit card.[39]

Rape is different from other crimes in that the victim is often considered to be partly responsible. "There are no other crimes in which the character, behavior, and past of the complainant are seen as central elements in determining whether a crime has occurred," wrote columnist Katha Pollitt in a 1991 op-ed piece in *The Nation*. "When my father was burglarized after forgetting to lock the cellar door, the police did not tell him that he was asking for it."[40]

Publishing and broadcasting the names of victims will discourage victims from reporting the crime. Criminologists estimate that fewer than 10 percent of all rapes are reported to law enforcement, and more frequent publishing and broadcasting of the names of victims would reduce that percentage even more.

Withholding the name of the victim does not detract from the newsworthiness of the story. If one of the objectives of a news story is to warn the audience of a trend in crimes in a certain part of town, identifying a victim as "a twenty-nine-year-old woman walking alone downtown" is sufficient for readers to get the message. They don't need to know the woman's name.

Chapter Summary

There are four major areas of privacy law that relate to mass communications: false light, private facts, intrusion, and appropriation. On the surface, false light and private facts share some elements with defamation, specifically the difference between public and private persons in their role as potential plaintiffs. However, false light is different in that, unlike defamation, the communication need not be false per se in order to be considered false light; it need only be misleading or exaggerated. Private facts differs from defamation in that it deals with embarrassment and humiliation (how the person feels about himself or herself), while defamation deals with harm to reputation or financial standing (based on how others view that person). Defamation, false light, and private facts also differ greatly in the types of defenses available to those accused.

The development of new technologies (including photographic and recording equipment and the Internet), as well as changing public attitudes toward the aggressive nature of the press, have affected how we look at the concept of intrusion and will continue to raise new questions in the future.

CASE PROBLEM

Blast from the Past

You're the presiding judge in a court case in which a woman is suing the tabloid *National Inquisitor* for both libel and invasion of privacy/private facts.

Background: Throughout the 1970s, Ima Goodsinger was a popular recording artist with numerous gold records and sold-out concerts. By the early 1980s, however, her career had bottomed out. Few people came to her concerts and her CDs weren't selling. She dropped out of sight for more than twenty years, much of that time spent in drug and alcohol rehabilitation clinics.

It's now 2007, and Ima is attempting to make a comeback, having changed her musical style to fit the times. A national concert tour is planned, and a Hollywood studio has invited her to perform the soundtrack in an upcoming big-budget movie. She's also been offered, but has not yet signed, a recording contract with a major label. A return to the top of the music business now appears to be within her reach.

But just as her career comeback appears to be gaining momentum, the *National Inquisitor* publishes a story that recalls Goodsinger's downward spiral and details of the years during which she had dropped out of sight, including two failed marriages and giving up a newborn child for adoption. The story is based on interviews with a former manager and employees at two rehab clinics where the singer was treated. The emphasis of the article is that Goodsinger's career setbacks were directly connected to her drug and alcohol problems and not, as Goodsinger insists, because of the country's changing musical tastes.

Within a week of the article's publication, the movie studio informed Goodsinger that it had chosen another artist to perform the soundtrack, and the record label withdrew its contract offer. Numerous promoters have called to cancel concert dates. Goodsinger and her lawyer blame the sudden problems on the *Inquisitor* article and estimate the singer's financial loss at $20 million.

As the presiding judge, you have to decide whether Goodsinger's case against the *Inquisitor* should include (a) only the libel complaint, (b) only the private facts complaint, (c) both complaints, or (d) neither complaint (i.e., dismissing the case altogether).

Which of the four courses of action do you take, and why?

SOCRATIC DIALOGUE QUESTIONS

1. In 1890, Warren and Brandeis worried that "advances in technology" and "voyeurism of the press" meant that some regulations were needed to protect individual privacy. More than one hundred years later, does this concern still apply? Why or why not?

2. Look at the cases of *Barber v. Time* and *Howard v. Des Moines Register*. On the surface, the cases have many elements in common; yet courts reached different decisions, ruling in one case for the plaintiff and in another case for the defendant. Do you agree or disagree with how the courts made different rulings in the two cases? Considering the different times in which the cases were argued (1942 vs. 1979), how might have changing public attitudes toward privacy entered into the differing court decisions?

3. Look at the cases of *Diaz v. Oakland Tribune* and *Sipple v. Chronicle Publishing*. On the surface, the cases have many elements in common; yet the courts reached different decisions, ruling in one case for the plaintiff and in another case for the defendant. Do you agree or disagree with how the courts made different rulings in the two cases?

4. Do you think the Booth Rule is a good idea or bad idea? Why?

5. How does the case of *Hustler v. Falwell* differ from the conflicts involving New York Mayor Rudolph Giuliani (discussed earlier in this chapter)? What precedents might have been set if Giuliani had been successful in his suits?

6. Find at least one case in Chapter 7 with which you strongly disagree with the court ruling (in the final resolution of the case) and be prepared to share your opinion with the class.

GLOSSARY OF TERMS

Appropriation The unauthorized use of a person's name, image, likeness, or voice for commercial purposes. Sometimes called **misappropriation.**

Booth Rule A ruling by the Supreme Court that newspapers and magazines may use their own news photos for self-promotion, provided the photos were newsworthy in their original context.

Cox Doctrine A common-law principle that permits journalists to publish or broadcast the names of crime victims, juvenile suspects, or subjects of governmental investigations provided the information is truthful, part of the public record, and is legally obtained. Originally applied in the 1975 Supreme Court case, *Cox v. Cohn.*[41]

False light The presentation of information about an individual that is not false per se but which is misleading or embarrassing.

Intentional infliction of emotional distress A tort in which one party accuses another of intentionally inflicting emotional distress.

Intrusion The unauthorized invasion of a person's privacy by physical, photographic, or electronic means.

Paparazzi A slang term for freelance photographers who pursue and sometimes harass celebrities. The term was derived from a character in the 1960 film *La Dolce Vita* but became more widely used following the 1997 death of Princess Diana.

Private facts An area of privacy law pertaining to the details of one's life that (a) would be highly offensive to a reasonable person, and (b) are not of legitimate interest to the public.

Public domain A defense commonly used in private facts cases; it refers to information that has been previously published, broadcast, or is generally known; takes place at a public event; is contained in a government document; or is released at a government meeting.

Right of publicity The right of entertainers and celebrities to control the use of their names and images for promotional purposes.

NOTES

1. *Griswold v. Connecticut*, 381 U.S. 479 (1965).
2. Samuel Warren and Louis Brandeis, "The Right to Privacy." *Harvard Law Review*, Vol. 4 (1890), p. 193.
3. William L. Prosser, "Privacy." *California Law Review*, Vol. 48 (1960), p. 383; William L. Prosser, *The Law of Torts*. St. Paul, Minn.: West Publishing, 1964.
4. *Spahn v. Messner*, 221 N.E. 2d 543 (1964).
5. *Time v. Hill*, 385 U.S. 374 (1967).
6. *Cantrell v. Forest City Publishing*, 419 U.S. 245 (1974).
7. Parsons, Allen. "Withdrawn Consent a Difficult Issue." *Wilmington Star-News* (N.C.), August 4, 2001, p. 1-B.
8. *Melvin v. Reid*, 297 P. 91 (1931).
9. *Sidis v. F-R Publishing*, 113 F.2d 806 (1940).
10. *Barber v. Time*, 1 Med. L. Rep. 1779 (1942).
11. *Virgil v. Sports Illustrated*, 527 F.2d 112 (1975).
12. *Howard v. Des Moines Register*, 283 N.W. 2d 289 (1979).
13. *Diaz v. Oakland Tribune*, 139 C.A. 3d 118 (1983).
14. *Sipple v. Chronicle Publishing*, 10 Med.L.Rep. 1690 (1984).
15. *Cox Broadcasting v. Cohn*, 420 U.S. 469 (1975).
16. *Florida Star v. B.J.F.*, 491 U.S. 524 (1989).
17. *Briscoe v. Readers' Digest*, 4 Cal.3d 529(1971).
18. *Oklahoma Publishing Co. v. District Court*, 430 U.S. 377 (1977).
19. *Smith v. Daily Mail Publishing*, 443 U.S. 97 (1979).
20. *Landmark Communications v. Virginia*, 435 U.S. 829 (1978).
21. *Dietemann v. Time*, 449 F.2d 245 (1971).
22. *Food Lion v. Capital Cities/ABC*, 877 F. Supp. 811 (1997).
23. *Miller v. NBC*, 232 Cal.Rep. 668 (1986).
24. *Ayeni v. CBS*, 35 F.3d 680 (1994).
25. *Hanlon v. Berger*, 27 Med.L.Rep. 1716 (1999).
26. *Wilson v. Layne*, 119 S.Ct. 1692 (1999).
27. *Galella v. Onassis*, 487 F.2d 986 (1972).
28. *Roberson v. Rochester Folding Box Co.*, 64 N.E. 442 (1902).

29. *Booth v. Curtis Publishing*, 1 Med.L.Rep. 1784 (1962).

30. *Midler v. Young & Rubicam*, 849 F.2d 460 (1992).

31. *Dr. Martin Luther King Jr. Center for Non-Violent Social Change v. American Heritage Products*, 508 F. Supp. 854 (1981).

32. *Zacchini v. Scripps-Howard*, 433 U.S. 562 (1977).

33. Fred Siegel, *The Prince of the City: New York and the Genius of American Life*. San Francisco, Calif.: Encounter Publishing, 2005.

34. Ibid.

35. Richard Willing, "Rosa Parks at the Center of a Legal Storm." *USA Today*, December 28, 2004, p. 3-A.

36. *Hustler v. Falwell*, 485 U.S. 46 (1988).

37. *Florida Publishing Co. v. Fletcher*, 340 So.2d 914 (1976).

38. *Cox v. Cohn*, 420 U.S. 469 (1975).

39. "Chronicle of a Rape Trial." Video teleconference, The Learning Channel, 1989.

40. Katha Pollitt, "Naming and Blaming: Media Goes Wilding in Palm Beach." *The Nation*, June 24, 1991, pp. 833–838.

41. *Cox Broadcasting v. Cohn*, 420 U.S. 469 (1975).

8 Problems in News-Gathering

The jury system puts a ban upon intelligence and honesty and a premium upon ignorance, stupidity, and perjury. It is a shame that we must continue to use a worthless system because it was good a thousand years ago. In this age, when a gentleman of high social standing, intelligence, and probity swears that testimony given under solemn oath will outweigh street talk and newspaper reports based on hearsay, he is worth a hundred jurymen who will swear to their own ignorance and stupidity, and justice will be far safer in his hands than theirs.

Mark Twain
Roughing It, 1891

The Constitution gives every defendant the right to a public trial. It does not give him the right to prime time. If the public wants to see how the justice system works, they should turn off their TVs, get off their butts, and catch a bus to the courthouse.

Christopher Darden
Criminal prosecutor in the
O.J. Simpson trial, 1995

There must be no secrecy around government decisions or acts which can be made public without injury to the national interest.

Tom Johnson
President, CNN News Group

What makes our country unique is its commitment to being open, to making its leaders accountable.

Janet Reno
U.S. Attorney General, 1996

The main function of government secrecy is to protect politicians and officials from the consequences of their own cowardice, incompetence, duplicity, and dishonesty.

Editorial, *Wilmington Star-News*
(North Carolina) March 20, 2005

The problem with secrecy for security's sake is that it doesn't protect us. It simply spares the government from any accountability to the public.

Myriam Marquez
Columnist, *Orlando Sentinel*

LEARNING OBJECTIVES

As a result of reading this chapter, students should:

- Understanding the potential conflicts between a criminal defendant's right to trial by an impartial jury (the Sixth Amendment actually uses the term *public trial*) and the media's rights in covering the judicial process.

- Understand the complex issues involving confidentiality and privilege, including the rules regarding the circumstances under which journalists may or may not protect their information, sources, and news materials.

- Understand the issues that journalists often face in obtaining access to news events and locations (including meetings of governmental bodies), as well as public records.

The Media and the Courts

The Sixth Amendment to the Constitution requires that criminal defendants be tried in proceedings that are open to the public, and while qualities such as "fairness" and "impartiality" are not specified in the amendment, those factors are nevertheless mentioned in any discussion involving the rights of the accused. But the quest for an impartial jury became substantially more difficult in the latter half of the twentieth century, due to the growth of the mass media into a twenty-four-hour industry and the public's increasing interest for news about criminal trials involving celebrities from the fields of sports and entertainment.

But it is not only celebrity trials in which the conflict between free press and fair trial is found. Even in trials involving non-celebrities, potential jurors arrive at the courthouse on the first day of the trial with extensive knowledge about the crime, the victim, and the defendant, often including inaccurate information that may never be introduced during the course of the trial.

Judges are responsible for balancing the defendant's Sixth Amendment right to a fair trial against the media's First Amendment right to cover criminal proceedings such as trials and pre-trial hearings. The most common problems for journalists covering legal proceedings are those associated with pre-trial publicity, cameras in the courtroom, and the naming of juvenile defendants and other news subjects.

Pre-Trial Publicity

The main concern associated with excessive pre-trial publicity is that it may contaminate the pool of potential jurors. A trial judge may sequester jurors during a trial to protect them from newspaper and television accounts, but one cannot sequester a jury during the lengthy period of time that it takes to run the course of pre-trial proceedings, because the jury has not yet been selected. In most high-profile cases, media coverage begins long before or during those pre-trial proceedings.

The first of the major cases in which pre-trial publicity became an issue was *Irvin v. Dowd* (1961), which began with the April 8, 1955, arrest of Leslie Irvin on suspicion of burglary and fraud. A few days later, Indiana police issued press releases saying Irvin had confessed to six murders, even though the confession was later determined to have been coerced. The press releases identified him by his nickname, "Mad Dog Irvin," and that nickname was repeated in the newspaper stories.

During the process of screening prospective jurors, 430 individuals were questioned, and 370 said they had already determined that Irvin was guilty based on what they had read and heard in the media. Of the twelve jurors finally seated, eight said before the trial started that they had already decided on Irvin's guilt, but they were seated on the jury nonetheless. Irvin was found guilty, and his appeal reached the Supreme Court in 1961. His lawyers provided a sampling of newspaper headlines and editorials from the pre-trial publicity, which included details of Irvin's prior convictions for arson and burglary and reports that he had been court-martialed from the Army. His lawyers produced circulation reports to prove that those newspapers reached 95 percent of the population of the town from which the jury was selected.

The Supreme Court ruled that Irvin did not get a fair trial because of the excessive pre-trial publicity, so it sent the case back to the lower court to be re-tried. The second trial was moved about one hundred miles away, where Irvin was convicted again.[1]

A few years later, pre-trial publicity and an inappropriate courtroom atmosphere during a trial were the issues in *Sheppard v. Maxwell* (1966). The case began with the July 4, 1954, murder of Marilyn Sheppard in her family's home in the Cleveland suburb of Bay Village. Her husband, a well-known physician in the community, quickly became the primary suspect.

The local media implied Sam Sheppard's guilt long before the trial began, reporting all of the details of the investigation, including rumors that he had had numerous affairs with female patients, the fact that Sheppard had refused to take a lie detector test, and alleged evidence that was later determined not to exist. Editorials in the local newspapers claimed that Sheppard must have been guilty because he hired one of the most expensive criminal attorneys in the Cleveland area. The jury was selected from the community in which that media coverage had taken place.

Sheppard was convicted in his criminal trial. For his appeal Shepphard hired F. Lee Bailey, who at the time was a little-known criminal lawyer. Bailey eventually took the appeal to the U.S. Supreme Court, arguing that Sheppard did not get a fair trial based on the level of pre-trial publicity and because the media caused a "carnival-like" atmosphere in the courtroom.

Included in the evidence of the disruptive courtroom atmosphere were accounts of local television reporters interviewing the judge as he entered and exited the courthouse and Sheppard being brought in the courtroom ten minutes before the proceedings each day and forced to pose for newspaper photographs. Local newspapers and television reporters also interviewed witnesses before and after their testimony and asked them to expand on it, with no attempt made to sequester the jurors or to admonish them not to read newspapers or watch television coverage of the trial.

In overturning Sheppard's conviction and ordering a new trial, the Supreme Court ruled that "a murder trial is not like an election that can be won or lost through the use of the newspaper, the radio, or the town meeting hall." The Court also determined that "trial courts must take strong measures to ensure that the balance is never weighted against the defendant."[2]

Two determinations came out of the *Sheppard* case that are still applied today. The first was that it is the judge's responsibility to ensure a fair trial, and therefore judges have the authority and responsibility to prevent trials from getting out of hand. The second was that it is unlikely to find jurors with no knowledge of a case, so the emphasis should be on finding jurors who may know something about the case but have yet not decided guilt or innocence.

The combination of the *Irvin v. Dowd* and *Sheppard v. Maxwell* rulings led many states to establish their own voluntary guidelines for press coverage of criminal trials. State bar associations worked with state press associations to develop guidelines about what should and should not be part of pre-trial publicity. In the guidelines are examples of information that is customarily not allowed to be discussed in court and which should therefore be treated cautiously by the media. Those elements include:

1. Confessions.
2. Prior criminal records of the defendant.
3. Results of polygraph tests, blood tests, or other scientific tests; or refusal to take such tests.
4. Character flaws or lifestyle of the defendant.
5. Potential witnesses, evidence, or testimony.
6. Speculation by officials.
7. Sensational or inflammatory statements or information, including nicknames (such as in the case of "Mad Dog Irvin").

From their inception, the guidelines were of only marginal value because enforcement was left up to individual trial judges, and many were reluctant to enforce the guidelines for fear they would be overturned on the grounds of prior restraint. Their value became lessened even more in the 1990s with the media's increased interest in reporting crime news and their tendency to publicize information without confirming it. Today, judges, prosecutors, and defense attorneys know that the best way to keep potentially harmful information out of the media is to not allow the information to be discussed in open court, because once it is revealed, it is difficult to restrain the media from reporting it.

Another pre-trial publicity case was that of *Murphy v. Florida* (1975). Jack Roland Murphy was a jewel thief who became famous by being part of a plot to steal a sapphire called the "Star of India" from a museum in New York. Later, he turned up in Florida and made a career out of conning his way into the homes of wealthy people and stealing their art and jewelry. Murphy was in and out of prison several times and earned the nickname "Murph the Surf." In 1968, he was tried and convicted in Florida on charges of assault and robbery, and his prior criminal record had been reported in the media and was known to jurors.

The U.S. Supreme Court upheld his conviction, however, ruling that mere knowledge of a case does not cause a jury to be prejudicial, and that in this case, the media coverage did not imply guilt as it did in the Sheppard case. The Court's ruling in this case was considered an invalidation of the notion that any knowledge of a case obtained through the media automatically prejudices the jury against the defendant. "The Constitution requires that the defendant have a panel of impartial, indifferent jurors," the Court's majority opinion read. "They need not, however, be totally ignorant of the facts and issues involved."[3]

The following year, gag orders were at issue in *Nebraska Press Association v. Stuart* (1976). The case began with a grisly murder on October 18, 1975, in the small town of Sutherland, Nebraska, in which thirty-year-old Erwin Simants raped and killed an eleven-year-old neighbor, then killed five other members of the family who had witnessed the crime. Before his trial started, Simants had already been tried and convicted by the media and in the court of public opinion.

The trial judge had a reputation for being a "renegade judge" who often placed gag orders on lawyers arguing cases in his court. In this case, he issued a gag order on the lawyers not to talk about the case outside of the courtroom and also on the media covering the trial. He allowed media to attend the pre-trial hearings, but ruled that they could not report details until after the trial was over. The judge based his actions on the voluntary guidelines developed after the *Sheppard* case; in effect, he took voluntary guidelines and made them mandatory for his courtroom.

The Nebraska Press Association (NPA), representing the media covering the trial, appealed the gag order to the Nebraska Supreme Court. The court issued an order overturning the trial judge's gag order, but it left in place the restrictions on information implying guilt or a confession.[4] After the trial, the media that covered the trial asked the NPA to continue the appeal to the U.S. Supreme Court to prevent similar judicial actions in the future. The Court sided with the media, ruling that gag orders applied to the media were an unconstitutional form of prior restraint.

In rare cases, judges have taken the additional step of forbidding journalists to identify jurors by name, claiming that jurors needed to be free of influence by friends and co-workers. Journalists sometimes claim that such rulings violate the First Amendment, but higher courts typically rule in favor of the judges.

In the 1996 trial of Timothy McVeigh, the man accused of blowing up a federal building in Oklahoma City two years earlier, the judge ordered a temporary wall constructed in the courtroom to protect the identity of jurors from the media. The American Society of Newspaper Editors (ASNE) unsuccessfully argued that watching the jurors' facial expressions in reaction to trial testimony was an important part of the news-gathering process and that the judge's action violated the spirit of the public-trial concept.[5]

Judicial Remedies for Excessive Pre-Trial Publicity

If a judge believes that excessive pre-trial publicity may interfere with a defendant's Sixth Amendment right to a fair trial, he or she may take one or more of the following steps.

Closing of pre-trial proceedings: Judges often exclude the public (including the media) from pre-trial proceedings. State laws vary; in some cases one or both parties in the case must agree. Only in extreme cases will the trial itself be closed to the public.

Change of venue: Usually done at the request of defense attorneys in criminal cases, a "change of venue" means the relocation of a trial to another city in an attempt to find jurors who have not been exposed to as much pre-trial publicity. Because of the travel and hotel costs for jurors, witnesses, attorneys, and court employees, it is an expensive and inconvenient measure that is used only when other remedies have been exhausted. In addition to the costs, some legal authorities contend that a change of venue is inappropriate because of the constitutional provision that trials be conducted with "a jury of one's peers."

Change of venire: In a change of venire, which is the opposite of a change of venue, the trial remains in the same courtroom but the jury is brought in from another community. It is less expensive and more practical than a change of venue but may still create a "jury of one's peers" problem.

Voir dire: From the French term meaning "to speak the truth," this is also known as "jury screening." Judges, prosecutors, and defense attorneys question potential jurors about their prior knowledge of a case (specifically about knowledge obtained through the media) to determine their suitability for the jury.

Sequestering: A "sequestered" jury stays in a hotel near the courthouse for the duration of the trial and is not allowed to have any contact with family members or access to any media. This is also expensive and inconvenient and is chosen only in extreme cases.

Admonition: An alternative to sequestering, a judge issuing an "admonition" may allow the members of the jury to go home every day but he or she instructs them not to discuss the trial with family members (or anyone else) and not to read or listen to any media coverage of the trial.

Gag orders: Although judges are reluctant to place **gag orders** on journalists covering a trial (which would allow journalists to attend the proceedings but not report on them until the conclusion of the trial), they often apply gag orders to prosecutors, attorneys, and witnesses by ordering them not to speak to the media between court sessions.

Cameras in the Courtroom

The issue of cameras in the courtroom began in 1935 when Bruno Hauptmann was on trial for kidnapping and murdering the son of aviator Charles Lindbergh. More than 800 reporters covered the trial, and photographers defied the judge's order banning photography during the proceedings.

Even though there was not as much concern for the concept of "fair trial" as there is today, the American Bar Association (ABA) was concerned about the formality of the courtroom setting and claimed that cameras were disruptive and undignified. Shortly after the trial, the ABA amended its Code of Ethics to include Canon 35, which prohibited cameras in and around courtrooms. In 1963, the ABA added a provision barring television cameras as well as still cameras.

In 1965, the ABA relaxed its rules, but that same year, the presence of cameras in a courtroom created controversy again. In *Estes v. Texas* (1965), Billy Sol Estes, a Texas banker and friend of President Lyndon Johnson, was on trial for theft, fraud, and embezzling money from his own bank. Both still cameras and television cameras were allowed in the courtroom. Estes was convicted, but he appealed, claiming the cameras disrupted his trial and violated his Sixth Amendment rights. The Supreme Court ruled that cameras had been intrusive in this case and had resulted in an unfair trial. The Court ordered the case to be re-tried in the state court without cameras. Estes was convicted again,[6] but as a result of the earlier ruling, the use of cameras declined briefly.

In issuing its ruling in the *Estes* case, the Supreme Court pointed out several problems caused by cameras in courtroom. The first was the problem of multiple trials of a single defendant; when a defendant faces more than one trial, the jurors in one trial may have seen still photographs or television coverage of an earlier trial. The *Estes* ruling was long before Court TV and news coverage of trials in their entirety (such as in the 1995 O. J. Simpson case), but there was still concern that even highlights of a trial on the evening news might prejudice future juries.

Second, the Supreme Court noted that close-up shots of court officers might affect their job performance and that close-up shots of defendants would make them self-conscious and inhibit their ability to assist in their defense.

A third point the Court made was that "a defendant on trial deserves his day in court, not in a stadium or nationwide arena." The Court reiterated the role of the trial judge in controlling trial coverage and ruled that judges have the authority to make reasonable "time, place, and manner" restrictions on the media.

By the mid-1970s, cameras were smaller, quieter, and less intrusive in that they did not need supplemental lighting like they once did, so the ABA dropped its objections. Vilification of cameras in the courtroom continues to this day, however, with critics claiming that cameras affect the way court officers and witnesses act and imply the guilt of those on trial to the audience. But the Supreme Court disagrees, ruling that cameras are intrusive only in extreme cases and that, in general, they do not harm the judicial process and do not interfere with the defendant's Sixth Amendment right to a fair trial. The Supreme Court has not ruled that courts must allow cameras; it has only given states the discretion to make that decision.

Today, all fifty states allow cameras in the state courts to some degree. In some states, the laws relating to cameras apply to all courts; in others, they apply only to certain levels of the judicial system. Additionally, in some states, the decision on cameras in the courtroom is left entirely up to the trial judge, while other states allow individual participants to decline to be photographed.

Generally, cameras and other video or audio recording devices are not permitted in Federal District Courts, except for cases in which cameras are used for closed-circuit broadcasts. One recent example was the McVeigh trial (discussed earlier in this chapter). That trial took place in Denver, and the television signal was available only to a limited audience of media and family members watching in Oklahoma City. Cameras are also allowed in federal courts for ceremonial occasions such as the installation of new judges or the naturalization of new citizens.

While the U.S. Supreme Court has ruled in numerous cases that still or video cameras do not disrupt the judicial process in other courtrooms, it ironically does not allow cameras of any kind in its own sessions. As a result, television networks covering Supreme Court proceedings use artists' sketches instead of photographs. The justices seldom comment publicly on their objectives to cameras, but when they do they cite concern for the solemnity and dignity of the proceedings. Prior to his death in 2005, for example, Chief Justice William Rehnquist said the cameras would "lessen the court's mystique and moral authority."[7] In 1996, Justice David Souter told a congressional committee that "the day you see a camera in the courtroom, it will have rolled over my dead body."[8] During his first year on the Court (2005–06), Chief Justice John Roberts reiterated the court's anti-camera policy.

Television networks asked for an exception to the no-cameras rule late in 2000, hoping they could televise the Supreme Court proceedings in *Bush v. Gore,* the case dealing with the controversial presidential election of that year. The Court denied the networks' request, but did agree for the first time to allow the oral arguments to be broadcast on radio. Subsequent suggestions that cameras be allowed into Supreme Court sessions have been met with continued resistance, but journalists who cover the Court predict that may soon change as older judges are replaced by younger, more technologically savvy ones.

Of the state courts that allow cameras, most have rules that prohibit narration, artificial lighting, and the photography of jurors. In instances in which space in the courtroom is limited, judges may require the formation of **media pools** in order to keep the actual number of cameras and technical personnel in the courtroom to a minimum. In a typical pool arrangement, three reporters are allowed—one each representing newspapers, television, and radio. Each of the three would be required to share information with their counterparts waiting outside the courtroom. A similar arrangement is made for sharing still photographs and video.

Support for pool cameras resulted from the Supreme Court decision in *Chandler v. Florida* (1981). The defendants were Miami Beach police officers Noel Chandler and Robert Granger, who were charged with robbing a restaurant while off duty. When jurors in their criminal trial were asked if a camera in the courtroom would be disruptive, they replied that it would not, so one pool camera was allowed.

Chandler appealed his conviction, claiming that the pool camera affected the outcome of the trial, but the Supreme Court ruled that it did not. Chandler's lawyer cited the *Estes* decision, in which the Supreme Court said that cameras were disruptive, but the Supreme Court said that the circumstances in the Chandler case were different because there was only one camera and it was not in a position to be as intrusive as the multiple cameras in the Estes trial. The Supreme Court also put the burden of proof on the defendants to prove that the pool camera was unfair, which they could not.[9]

Today, critics of courtroom cameras often cite the 1991 rape trial of William Kennedy Smith and the 1995 murder trial of O. J. Simpson as evidence that television cameras create a circus-like atmosphere in the courtroom, cause trials to be longer than necessary, and offer lawyers the opportunity to become celebrities themselves.

Identification of Crime Victims and Suspects

Some states have laws aimed at protecting the identity of juvenile suspects, sexual assault victims, mental health patients, and subjects of governmental investigations. In addition, most media organizations have voluntarily adopted policies that prohibit such identification. But regardless of whether it is law or simply policy, unusual circumstances, such as the serious nature of a crime, often lead the media to publish or broadcast names. In some cases, the result is an invasion of privacy suit filed by the person named; in other cases the media's identification of victims or suspects leads to prior restraint, a contempt citation issued by a court, or a fine imposed after the publication (these cases are discussed in the "Private Facts" section of Chapter 7). In many of those cases, the Supreme Court has cited the three-part test of the "Cox Doctrine" and ruled that information that is truthful, part of a public record, and legally obtained can be published or broadcast without punishment.

The Supreme Court applied the Cox Doctrine to the naming of juvenile suspects in *Oklahoma Publishing Co. v. District Court* (1977) and *Smith v. Daily Mail Publishing* (1978). It also applied the doctrine to subjects of governmental investigations in *Landmark Communications v. Virginia* (1978). All three cases are discussed in Chapter 7.

Confidentiality and Privilege

Journalists have an obligation to maintain confidentiality in regard to the identity of their sources, the information they gather, and the materials with which they work, such as notes, photographs, and video and audio recordings. Their obligation is to their employers, their sources, and to the profession of journalism. Several legal areas, including shield laws, reporter privilege, and protection of news materials, govern confidentiality and privilege.

Shield Laws and Reporter Privilege

A **shield law** is a state statute that allows journalists to protect sources and not reveal their identity, even when called upon by the court to do so. As of early 2006, thirty-one states and the District of Columbia have media shield laws. A federal shield law has been proposed in the past but was rejected, most recently in 2005.

State shield laws vary greatly in their scope and language. Some are **limited shield laws** that protect only the sources of information and not the information itself; others are **comprehensive shield laws** that protect both the information and the sources.

Regardless of whether a shield law is limited or comprehensive, most state laws establish three conditions that must exist to override the law. These conditions make up what is commonly referred to as the **qualified privilege test.** The three conditions are:

1. *The journalist must have information relevant to a specific crime.* The "specific crime" requirement prevents prosecutors or other government investigators from going on "fishing expeditions" and demanding help from journalists. As an example, a journalist preparing or having produced a story about food stamps cannot be required to reveal information to a prosecutor who believes *some* of the people interviewed *might be* involved in food stamp abuse. In such a case, the prosecutor would have to prove that a crime had already been committed or was about to be committed.

2. *The information must be unavailable from other sources.* Investigators, prosecutors, or defense attorneys who want the information must convince the judge that they have exhausted all other possible sources for the information. In that way, attempting to get information from a journalist is a last resort, not a first resort.

3. *The need to obtain the information must be greater than the journalist's need to keep it confidential.* Therefore, the crime in the first qualification must be a serious offense, such as murder, drug trafficking, or serious misconduct by government officials. In the example provided in the first condition, it is unlikely that the abuse of food stamps would be considered serious enough to override a shield law unless the government officials themselves were suspected of being involved in the fraud.

When journalists believe that one or more of these rules do not apply, they can challenge the orders. They can also challenge such orders if they have evidence they are being harassed. A fourth qualification that applies only in some states is that there was no understanding of confidentiality. If the reporter says, "I promised the source I would keep his name confidential," that's enough to protect the information in most cases.

There are three exceptions mentioned in many state shield laws. The first is that a shield law would not apply if the reporter in question witnessed a crime taking place. Many states refer to this as the **Branzburg Rule** (discussed later in this section) as a result of the ruling in *Branzburg v. Hayes* (1972).

The second exception is that few state shield laws would protect journalists defending themselves in libel suits. A reporter being sued for libel would therefore not have as much protection as in cases in which the reporter is a third-party observer.

The third exception is that a shield law does not protect a journalist in non-news situations. For example, if a reporter witnesses a traffic accident or other event not related to any story he or she is working on, he or she cannot claim "reporter privilege" and refuse to testify in court about the event. In that case, the reporter is like any other citizen and is obligated to testify to what he or she witnessed.

Even in states without shield laws, journalists are not completely without protection, as reporters called upon to provide information in legal proceedings can ask the judge to respect the concept of "confidentiality." So instead of referring only to shield laws, a broader and more appropriate term is **reporter privilege,** because even in states without shield laws, reporters attempting to protect information and sources often receive support from judges.

Cases Involving Shield Laws and Reporter Privilege

The first important Supreme Court case dealing with reporter privilege was *Branzburg v. Hayes* (1972), which was a combination of three cases from three different states that reached the Supreme Court at the same time. Because all three cases were all in the area of reporter privilege, the Court consolidated them and made a single ruling.

One of the cases involved Paul Branzburg, a reporter for the *Louisville Courier-Journal*, who wrote a story about drug use based on his observations and was called before a grand jury and asked to provide names of the persons involved. The Supreme Court ruled the Kentucky shield law did not apply because the journalist witnessed a crime being committed, and like any other citizen who witnessed a crime, he could not defy a subpoena to testify.

The two other cases involved newspaper reporters in California and Massachusetts who wrote stories about the Black Panthers after attending meetings of the militant group. Both reporters had promised their sources they would not reveal their identity, but grand juries in both states were investigating death threats against federal judges and other suspected crimes and demanded access to the notes and recordings the two reporters had made.

The Supreme Court decided 5–4 against privilege in all three cases, ruling that the needs of law enforcement outweighed the needs of journalists. The justices voting in the majority rejected the First Amendment claims, ruling that these cases did not involve prior restraint or punishment after the fact. The justices also focused on the distinction between these cases, in which the journalists actually *witnessed a crime*, and other cases, in which journalists would not be required to testify based solely on *their knowledge of a crime*. That distinction gave birth to what would eventually become known as the **Branzburg Rule.**[10]

Journalists did, however, receive support from the dissenting opinions in which other justices stated that confidentiality was necessary for effective news-gathering. In his dissent, Justice Potter Stewart expressed concern over the potential for future scenarios in which government investigators and prosecutors could take shortcuts and depend too much on journalists for help. Stewart wrote that if shield laws were not available to protect journalists, or if those laws were routinely undermined by the courts, the effect would be to "undermine the historic independence of the press by attempting to annex the journalistic profession as an investigative arm of the government."[11]

Eight years after the *Branzburg* case, in *United States v. Criden* (1980), the Supreme Court refused to hear the appeal of *Philadelphia Inquirer* reporter Jan Schaffer, who was ordered by a prosecutor to testify in a government corruption trial. Schaffer had conducted an off-the-record interview with the prosecutor in the case, and the defense attorneys wanted Schaffer to testify about what the prosecutor had told her in order to prove that the prosecutor was violating judicial procedures. Both the trial court and appeals court ruled that Schaffer was required to testify, the latter applying the three-part "qualified privilege" test, which failed to give Schaffer the privilege she sought. After the U.S. Supreme Court refused to hear her appeal, she testified as ordered.[12]

The three-part qualified privilege test was also applied in the case of *United States v. Blanton* (1981), during which a Federal District Court ruled that a reporter could not be required to provide information to law enforcement officials because they had not yet exhausted alternative sources for the information. Dr. Fred Blanton was a Ft. Lauderdale ophthalmic surgeon on trial in Miami, accused of distributing narcotics through his medical practice. *Miami Herald* reporter Patrick Malone was assigned to cover the trial. Prosecutors who read his stories asked him to voluntarily cooperate and provide additional information that was not in his stories, but he declined, claiming protection under Florida's shield law. When he received a subpoena to appear in court and provide the information, a *Miami Herald* attorney was able to have the subpoena quashed (invalidated).[13]

In 2001, English teacher and freelance journalist Vanessa Leggett was held for 168 days in a Texas prison after she refused to turn over her notes from jailhouse interviews she conducted with a murder suspect. Leggett was released after the term of the grand jury investigating the case expired.[14]

Two more high-profile privilege cases were argued in 2004. One involved Rhode Island television reporter Jim Taricani, whose television station aired a videotape showing an undercover FBI agent bribing a city official in Providence. Taricani broke no laws in airing the tape but was cited for contempt of court for refusing to reveal the tape's source. A federal judge believed the tape had been leaked to the media in order to disrupt the investigation or influence the jury, and ordered Taricani to identify the source. Within a week of Taricani's conviction, a defense attorney admitted that he was responsible for leaking the tape to the television station, but that did not alleviate Taricani of the contempt charge. Under Rhode Island law he could have been sentenced to six months in prison but instead was sentenced to six months of home confinement because of his health problems. Despite the lenient sentence, however, the case still caused concern for journalists because it served to weaken state shield laws across the country.[15]

New York Times *reporter Judith Miller arrives at a federal courthouse on July 6, 2005.*

The second case involved two reporters who were held in contempt for refusing to testify in a federal investigation. The government wanted to know who leaked the identity of Central Intelligence Agency operative Valerie Plame to syndicated columnist Robert Novak, an act that violated federal law. Judith Miller of the *New York Times* and Matthew Cooper of *Time* magazine reported on the leak but refused to identify the source of the leak when questioned by federal authorities. Early in 2005, a Circuit Court of Appeals ruled against the journalists, as did the U.S. Supreme Court. Cooper testified before the grand jury after his sources released him from his promise of confidentiality. Miller refused to appear, and in July 2005 she was jailed for contempt of court. She remained in jail for eighty-five days and released after she, too, testified in the case, having also been released of her promise of confidentiality by her source. One of the ironies of the latter case is that Miller never wrote a story based on her research and was jailed for what her newspaper's publisher said was simply "routine news-gathering on an important public issue."[16]

Protecting News Materials

In addition to court testimony, law enforcement officials and defense attorneys often ask reporters to turn over notes, photographs, videotapes, audiotapes, or computer disks. If the journalist resists, the person wanting the information or materials has two recourses. The first is a **subpoena**—a written order from a judge or other court official requesting the materials. The second is a **search warrant**—a court order allowing investigators to search a newspaper office or radio or television station and confiscate materials. In very rare circumstances, officials may search reporters' homes.

The Reporters Committee for Freedom of the Press (RCFP) advises journalists that they should not move too quickly to comply with orders to produce news materials and should instead immediately consult the newspaper's or television station's attorney. In cases in which a newspaper or television station suggests that the reporter cooperate but he or she is still reluctant, the RCFP suggests that reporters consider hiring their own attorneys. The RCFP clarifies that while journalists may not wish to comply with the requests to turn over news materials, they may not ignore subpoenas and must at least appear in court to explain their refusal to cooperate. If a reporter chooses not to comply with a request for information, his or her attorney may ask the court to quash it.

One of the more famous cases of asking reporters to voluntarily turn over notes is referred to as *The Matter of Farber* (1978). *New York Times* reporter Myron Farber was researching a story about a hospital in neighboring New Jersey at which patients were dying at an unusual rate. As is the case with most news stories, Farber used only a small portion of his written notes for the story.

When Mario Jascalevich, a doctor at the hospital, was indicted on five murder charges, his attorneys wanted access to Farber's notes, believing they might be helpful with the doctor's defense. After Farber refused to turn them over voluntarily, the lawyers asked the judge to order Farber to cooperate. The judge issued the order, but Farber refused to comply and was cited for contempt and jailed. In addition, the *New York Times* was fined $100,000, plus $5,000 a day for each day Farber refused to comply. Farber spent the course of the forty-day trial in jail, and the newspaper's fines totaled more than $300,000.

On the same day Jascalevich was acquitted, Farber was released from jail. He later wrote an account of his case in a book, *Somebody is Lying*. In 1982, New Jersey Governor Brendan Byrne pardoned Farber and ordered the fine refunded to the newspaper.[17]

Another legal challenge facing the media—the vulnerability of newspapers to search and seizure—was at issue in *Zurcher v. Stanford Daily* (1978). During a campus disturbance at Stanford University in which demonstrators occupied part of the university's hospital, police officers were injured in a scuffle with the demonstrators. Police could not identify the attackers but believed that the *Stanford Daily,* the university's student newspaper, was holding unpublished pictures in which the suspects could be identified. The prosecutor obtained a search warrant to go into the newspaper office and look for them, but the search did not reveal any photos other than those already published. The newspaper then sued under the Fourth Amendment, claiming "unreasonable search and seizure." One of the points in the newspaper's argument was that search warrants were intended to be a method by which law enforcement personnel could search the property of a suspect, while in this case, the newspaper was not suspected of any wrongdoing; it was a neutral third party. A lower court ruled in favor of the students, but on appeal, the Supreme Court overturned the decision, ruling 5–3 that law enforcement officers may obtain search warrants and make surprise searches of newsrooms to confiscate notes, audiotapes, and videotapes, even though no one in the newsroom was accused of a crime. Much like the *Branzburg* case, it was an example of the needs of law enforcement taking priority over reporter privilege.[18]

A similar situation occurred at Southern Illinois University in 1994, in which the student newspaper had pictures of an off-campus disturbance that happened at a city-wide Halloween party. The party ended in violence, including rock and bottle throwing and the overturning of cars. The city police chief asked all local media to turn over photographs and videotapes so that the police could look through them in order to identify suspects. All three local TV stations and the daily newspaper did so voluntarily. But the campus newspaper refused, and under threat of a subpoena, it reached a compromise with the police: the police would use the pictures and video from the other newspaper and the TV stations to put together a list of incidents, and the student newspaper staff could go through its photographs and pick out only those that were connected with those specific incidents.

The difference between these two situations is that in the Stanford case, the university police used a search warrant and confiscated what they wanted. In the Southern Illinois case, a legal confrontation was avoided by cooperation and compromise.

Two years after the *Stanford Daily* newsroom was searched, Congress passed the Privacy Protection Act of 1980, which now restricts the government's and law enforcement's ability to search newsrooms. Since that law was passed, there have been few newsroom searches, for two reasons: first, because judges know they will likely be overruled by higher courts; and second, because police and prosecutors are reluctant to ask for searches because, by doing so, they are admitting that they need help.

The Privacy Protection Act drew a distinction between **work product materials** and **documentary materials.** Work product materials include handwritten notes, audiotapes, videotapes, computer disks, and drafts of stories; they have the most protected status because they are produced by the journalist and are therefore his or her property.

In order to search for work product materials, law enforcement must establish one of the following conditions:

1. The journalist has committed a crime.
2. The taking of material may prevent injury or death.
3. The material may be classified or pertains to national defense.

Documentary materials include wire service copy, photocopies of records gathered, or other materials not produced by the journalist. Such materials are easier for law enforcement to request by subpoena, using the same three criteria as applied in the case of work product materials but involving a lower burden of proof.

One of the common justifications government officials and the courts use in ordering reporters to testify in criminal trials or surrender news materials is to clarify inconsistencies between what witnesses say in media interviews and what they say in police interrogations, depositions, or court testimony. One such example was the 1996 case that resulted in a *Miami Herald* reporter serving a seventy-day sentence for contempt when he refused to testify in the trial of a man accused of murdering his stepdaughter. When prosecutors found discrepancies between what the defendant told police at the time of his arrest and what he later told the reporter in a jailhouse interview, they issued a subpoena that would have required the reporter to testify and provide additional, unpublished information. Florida's limited shield law did not apply because it protected only the source and not the information, and the source was already known. The reporter refused and, despite being urged to cooperate by the newspaper's attorney, chose to go to jail instead.[19]

In the late 1990s, two cases involving NBC's *Dateline* program illustrated the ability of parties involved in litigation to subpoena a media outlet's work product materials to support their cases.

The first case took place in 1995, when the Graco Corporation was defending itself in a product liability suit filed by parents who charged that the company's defective product caused the death of their children. But when parents were interviewed on *Dateline*, Graco officials found inconsistencies between what the parents said in the television interview and what they previously said under oath in pre-trial depositions. Graco attorneys asked NBC to turn over the portion of the interviews that were not aired, but the network refused and claimed protection under the New York shield law. Eventually, however, NBC turned over the tapes after being ordered to do so by a federal judge.[20]

The second case, *Gonzales v. NBC* (1998), began when a Hispanic couple accused a sheriff's deputy of stopping and detaining them without cause as they drove across Louisiana on Interstate 10. A few months later, *Dateline* journalists posing as out-of-state travelers were stopped and detained in a similar fashion and used a hidden camera and microphone to record the incident. After the program aired, the Gonzales's obtained a subpoena for the complete tape of the incident, hoping it would be helpful in their civil suit against the deputy who detained them, even though it was not the same one who detained the *Dateline* employees. Shortly thereafter, the deputy involved in the second incident also requested a subpoena for the same tape. NBC refused to comply with the subpoenas and was cited for contempt by a Federal District Court. The Circuit Court of Appeals ruled that both the Gonzales couple and the deputy involved in the second incident had met all three conditions of the qualified privilege test, and the court ordered NBC to comply with the subpoenas.[21]

One of the newest and most comprehensive state shield laws was passed by the North Carolina General Assembly in 1999. The genesis of the law was two 1995 cases, including one involving the investigation into the murder of basketball star Michael Jordan's father. The new law, which the legislature enacted at the urging of the North Carolina Press Association and North Carolina Association of Broadcasters, is similar to the shield laws of other states in most respects, but includes three significant differences. The first difference is that the North Carolina law covers both confidential and non-confidential contact between reporters and sources, while most other state shield laws cover only those conversations in which there was an understanding of confidentiality. The second difference is that it applies in actions in which the journalist or media company is a defendant in a libel suit (this is not the case in most other states). The most significant difference, however, is who is covered by the law. Unlike most other state shield laws, which use the definition "full-time, professional journalists," the North Carolina statute uses the broader description of "anyone engaged in gathering, compiling, writing, editing, photographing, recording, or processing information that is disseminated as news." In theory, that means it would protect part-timer writers, freelancers, and student journalists, as well as producers of "underground" or "fringe" publications (on paper or on the Internet), although it will take one or more test cases to determine how broad the coverage of the law will actually be.

While North Carolina's law would include Internet products such as web logs or "blogs," the rights of Internet journalists in other states is a matter just now being debated. A test case emerged early in 2006 when Apple Computer asked a California court to require bloggers to reveal the source of their information and graphics related to Apple's new product titled "Asteroid." Before the product's release, bloggers had used their Internet sites to distribute technical information and schematic drawings related to the product, which the company claimed were protected under trade secret laws. Apple argued that the bloggers were not eligible for protection under California's shield law and that the company's interest in protecting its trade secrets outweighed the bloggers' journalistic rights.[22] The District Court ruled in favor of the bloggers, determining that they were protected under the state law and that in the eyes of the law, there was little distinction between online journalists and traditional journalists.

Promising Confidentiality

In *Cohen v. Cowles Media* (1991), the Supreme Court ruled that media outlets could be held liable for violating confidentiality agreements in circumstances other than those required by subpoena or court order. The court also gave each state the authority to decide whether its law would permit such lawsuits.

The Cohen case began during the 1982 election for governor of Minnesota. Dan Cohen was an advertising agency executive who worked on one of the candidate's campaigns. He leaked negative information on an opposing candidate to reporters for local newspapers and, in doing so, was promised confidentiality.

Editors at one of the papers overruled the promise, however, and added Cohen's name to the stories as the source of the negative information. Cohen was fired from the advertising agency and sued the newspaper for breaking the promise of confidentiality. He was awarded $200,000 in compensatory damages for the loss of his job and $500,000 in punitive damages.

The jury handed down its $700,000 judgment on a Saturday afternoon, and by coincidence the newspaper had just printed a story for its Sunday edition in which it identified a source that had originally been promised confidentiality in a case unrelated to the Cohen case. It then took 640,000 copies of the Sunday edition off its circulation trucks and destroyed them, just before they were about to be put on the newsstands.

The Minnesota Supreme Court reversed the judgment and sided with the newspaper, invalidating both the compensatory and punitive damages. The U.S. Supreme Court reversed that and ruled in favor of Cohen, but gave him back only the compensatory damages. The Court based its ruling partially on its determination that the First Amendment did not permit the newspaper's editors to override a good-faith promise made by its employees.[23]

Access to Information

"Access to Information" refers to journalists' right to be at the location of news events, to attend meetings of governmental bodies, and to examine government records.

At the federal level, Congress makes laws pertaining to access to federal meetings and records, while state legislatures make laws concerning such access at the state, county, and city levels. At all levels of government, some amount of secrecy is legitimate, but some cases provide obvious examples of abuse.

There are two general rules governing media access to records and meetings:

1. At a minimum, the press is guaranteed as much access as the general public.
2. Governments and governmental agencies cannot discriminate against specific persons or organizations or play favorites among media.

These rules come with two important clarifications:

a. Requiring reporting or photographic pools is not considered "playing favorites" because the media themselves, not the news sources, choose the pool representatives.
b. Specific reporters can have their press privileges revoked if they have a history of disrupting meetings or damaging or attempting to steal records. But such punishment would have to be content neutral, meaning that the government would bear the burden of proof to establish that the action was taken because of the reporter's behavior and not because of anything that the reporter wrote or broadcast.

Access to News Events and Locations

For more than a century, the legal system has struggled to balance the rights of journalists to gather news with the needs of government agencies, the courts, the military, and law enforcement to conduct their work without interference. The most contentious examples of this conflict are courtrooms, military installations, prisons, and crime and accident scenes. Even though the first three are examples of government property, they are not in the same category as other federal buildings.

Courtrooms. In most courtrooms, judges have broad authority to regulate the number and position of courtroom cameras and can require the media to use a pool system. In some cases, judges may close the courtroom for pre-trial proceedings to protect the privacy of witnesses or victims or to avoid damaging pre-trial publicity. In the 1979 case of *Gannett Newspapers v. DePasquale,* the Supreme Court upheld a judge's right to close a pre-trial hearing in which the parties debated whether to admit the confessions of two defendants.[24] In several subsequent cases, courts have upheld the judges' authority to close pre-trial proceedings for similar reasons.

But once a trial begins, judges are less willing to close the proceedings to the public or the media, and higher courts typically overturn their attempts to do so. In the 1982 case of *Globe Newspaper Co. v. Superior Court,* for example, the Supreme Court rejected the idea of closing court proceedings to protect minors involved as either defendants or witnesses.[25]

A murder suspect is brought into the courtroom in Elmira, New York in 2006. The Constitution requires that trials be open to the public, and that right of access also applies, with some limitations, to journalists reporting on legal proceedings.

Military Installations.   When visiting military installations, journalists are customarily accompanied by public affairs officers, and photographers are limited in how they may photograph aircraft, ships, weapons complexes, and electronic devices.

In *J.B. Pictures v. Department of Defense* (1996), a Federal District Court ruled that reporters did not have guaranteed access to Dover Air Force Base in Delaware, where bodies of deceased American soldiers were brought for processing, because the base was neither a traditional nor a limited public forum, meaning that the rules of access did not apply.[26]

As discussed in Chapter 3, the military can also restrict media access to war zones.

Prisons and Execution Chambers.   Reporters visiting a prison are often assigned escorts and must abide by the warden's rules about where they can go and to whom they may speak.

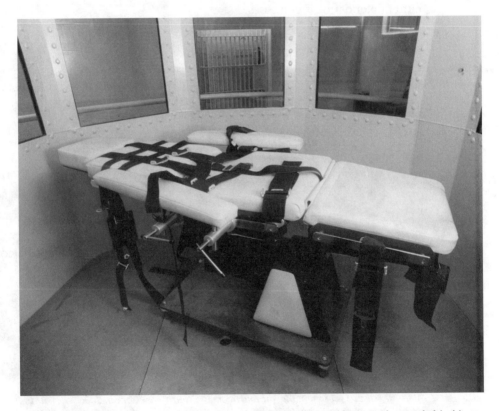

The death chamber at a state prison in California. Observation windows can be seen behind in the background. Although journalists are allowed to witness executions as part of the reporting process, they are not allowed to take photographs or video of the proceedings.

The 1974 case of *Procunier v. Pell*, one of the first important cases related to access to news locations, dealt with the rights of journalists to interview prison inmates. The conflict began with a California prison riot and the escape of dozens of inmates. After most were re-captured, newspaper reporters were allowed into the prison to interview some of those involved. Prison officials later complained that the news stories made the prisoners into celebrities, so the officials created a new rule that when the media came to the prison in the future to do interviews, they could interview only those prisoners the officials designated, rather than choosing who they wanted.

The rule was appealed to the Supreme Court, which decided in favor of the prison officials—saying that the prison setting was a unique one and that the journalists did not have the right to go anywhere they chose. Furthermore, prison officials could make reasonable "time, place, and manner" restrictions on the interviews.[27] The same day, the Court made the same ruling in a similar case, *Saxbe v. Washington Post*.[28] Three years later, the Court made a similar ruling against a television station in *Houchins v. KQED*, rejecting the station's First Amendment claims and stating that journalists did not have the right to go any place where the general public could not go.[29]

In the 2002 case of *California First Amendment Coalition v. Woodford*, a Circuit Court of Appeals ruled that the media have a First Amendment right of access to attend executions.[30] The traditional ban against photographing executions remains in place, however, even though it is periodically challenged. Talk-show host Phil Donahue made two such challenges in the 1990s. In 1994, Donahue sought government permission to televise the execution of a convicted murderer in North Carolina, and in 1997 he sought permission to televise the execution of Timothy McVeigh, convicted in the 1995 Oklahoma City bombing. Both requests were denied.

Crime and Accident Scenes.   The courts typically side with law enforcement personnel in their attempt to restrict media access to crime scenes, based on the importance of preserving evidence and protecting the privacy of victims. In the case of hostage situations that are broadcast on live television, reporters and camera operators are admonished not to announce or show the location of SWAT teams or other law enforcement personnel in case the hostage-taker has access to a television set.

Two cases decided in separate state supreme courts ten years apart established that a journalist's access to certain news locations such as accident scenes—even those on public property—can be limited in the interest of public safety and the privacy rights of injured persons.

The 1979 case of *State v. Lashinsky* began with an automobile accident on a New Jersey highway. A photographer from a local newspaper was the first to arrive at the scene, and instead of trying to help the victims trapped inside the vehicles, he began taking photographs. When law enforcement and emergency medical teams arrived, they noticed that one of the vehicles was leaking gasoline and ordered the photographer and other bystanders to leave the area. The photographer refused to leave, claiming "freedom of the press." He was arrested and convicted of violating a New Jersey law that made it illegal to "obstruct or interfere with a matter involving law enforcement or public safety." He appealed to the New Jersey Supreme Court, but the court ruled against him, rejecting his "First Amendment right of access" claim.[31]

The 1989 case of *City of Oak Creek v. King* began when a commuter airplane took off from Milwaukee County Airport and crashed into the nearby suburb of Oak Creek, Wisconsin. City police declared the crash site off-limits to everyone except emergency medical personnel, including the print and broadcast journalists attempting to get closer to the crash site. A television news van penetrated the roadblock by following a fire truck, and its driver, Peter King, was arrested and convicted of trespassing and disorderly conduct.

King appealed, claiming "First Amendment right of access," but the Wisconsin Supreme Court upheld the conviction and ruled that "the rights of the injured and the dying should be recognized as having preference over the newly created rights of the news-gatherer, who is simply trying to beat his competitor or meet his employer's deadline."[32]

Even though the rulings in the above cases came from state supreme courts and are therefore binding only in those states, they have since been cited in numerous similar cases in other states.

While law enforcement officials have the right to limit media access to such scenes, many agencies will cooperate with journalists and photographers by establishing an "outer perimeter" and "inner perimeter" at the scenes of crimes or accidents. While the public would be required to remain beyond the outer perimeter, journalists and photographers may be allowed to approach the inner perimeter with the understanding that they must not interfere with the investigation and must respect the privacy rights of the injured.

Access to Public Meetings

The Government in the Sunshine Act, passed by Congress in 1976, requires approximately fifty federal agencies, commissions, and boards to meet in public. Most states have similar laws that apply to meetings of state, county, and city governmental bodies within those states. Collectively, such laws are known as **sunshine laws,** although most states have specific titles for their laws, such as the North Carolina Open Meetings Law, the Florida Government in the Sunshine Law, or the West Virginia Open Governmental Proceedings Act.

Generally, a journalist can attend any meeting that is open to the general public. Most governmental bodies can apply exemptions, however, such as meetings during which the discussion of certain topics may impede law enforcement investigations, affect labor negotiations, or be harmful to the privacy of individuals involved, such as health matters and hiring/firing decisions. In most states, open meetings laws would not apply to jury deliberations or meetings of grand juries and parole boards.

When only a portion of a meeting is closed, it is referred to as **executive session.** During a school board meeting, for example, the board may go into

A city council meeting in Austin, Texas. Traditionally, meetings of governmental bodies are open to both the press and the public.

executive session numerous times to debate personnel disciplinary matters, discuss security matters (such as the type of alarm system to purchase for a school building), or negotiate real estate transactions or labor agreements with teachers' unions.

State medical boards declare "executive session" when disciplining a physician or other medical professional. In such instances, the media and members of the public are required to leave the room, with only the officials, subjects of the investigations, participants providing information, and their attorneys remaining in the room.

Most states have open meetings laws that allow such discussions to be held in private, but require that the final votes be taken in public. Alleged violations of open meetings laws frequently result in legal action, but in many states, penalties for violations are weak or non-existent. In some states, there is no punishment at all; the only result of a court decision in favor of the plaintiff is that the body is required to meet again, this time in public, to discuss the same issues. In some cases, media organizations that are successful in gaining access by winning their cases against governmental bodies receive as part of the judgment the reimbursement of the legal costs they incurred in filing their complaints.

Access to Public Records

At the federal level, most government documents are open for review by the media and general public under a 1967 law called the Freedom of Information Act (FOIA). Journalists or other persons denied access to documents subject to the FOIA (i.e., materials not included in its exemptions) file their complaints with the nearest Federal District Court. If the court agrees with the request, it issues a **writ of mandamus,** which is a legal document ordering the appropriate agency or government employee to comply with the FOIA request.

One of the rationales for the FOIA is that it helps journalists fulfill their role as watchdogs on government as they uncover waste, fraud, and corruption. A recent example occurred in 2004, when reporters at the *Fort Lauderdale Sun-Sentinel* used the FOIA to uncover problems with the Federal Emergency Management Agency (FEMA). After four hurricanes crossed the state of Florida, FEMA was called in to assist with the disaster recovery claims, most of which were legitimate. But the agency was oblivious to the millions of dollars paid to families who fraudulently claimed hurricane damage and used their FEMA checks to purchase luxury items. That fraud would have not been exposed if journalists had not uncovered it using the FOIA.[33]

Many states have public records statutes that provide public and media access to documents maintained by the state as well as county and city governments and agencies. At those levels, the state attorney general is the public official in charge of enforcement, so journalists denied access must appeal to that office. If successful, the attorney general will issue a writ of mandamus.

At the state and local level, the most contentious areas for dispute involves records gathered and maintained by law enforcement agencies. Most agencies organize their records into three categories—(1) incident and arrest reports, (2) records of ongoing investigations, and (3) criminal histories or "rap sheets." Incident and arrest reports are typically available for inspection by journalists and the general public. In fact, part of the training for new reporters is to visit the police headquarters once each day to peruse the police blotter. These reports typically list the nature, time, and location of reported crimes; the name, age, and address of the accused; and a description of charges filed. Records of ongoing investigations reports are protected by federal and state laws because their disclosure may interfere with those investigations and lead to prejudicial pretrial publicity. Criminal histories are protected for the same reasons, even though they consist of information previously listed in arrest reports.

At all levels of government, agencies are allowed to charge "reasonable fees" for making photocopies. When legal action is required for journalists to gain access to records, plaintiffs can often recover legal fees in the same manner they would following open meetings conflicts.

In many cases, the government officials and agencies know they will likely lose their cases, but they attempt to stall as long as they can, hoping that either the journalist will lose interest in the story he or she is working on, or by the time the case is settled, the release of the information would not have as much effect as it might have had earlier.

The Freedom of Information Act
and Its Exemptions

The FOIA includes the following exemptions, and many state public records laws include similar provisions:

1. *National security.* This exemption, often abused, prevents many documents from being disclosed.

2. *Agency rules and practices.* This exemption allows government agencies to protect information on procedures such as long-term planning, purchasing, and employee hiring and training. The rationale for the exemption is that the disclosure of such rules might assist outsiders in circumventing those rules. A hypothetical example is the reporter who requests information on official FBI policy in negotiating with hostage-takers or the agency's policy in dealing with reporters covering hostage situations. Even though this example illustrates the need for such an exemption, the provision also covers trivial matters, such as how a government agency makes its employees' parking lot assignments and schedules their coffee breaks and vacation days.

3. *Statutory exemptions.* This exemption covers materials that have been declared secret by acts of Congress.

4. *Confidential business information.* Government agencies customarily protect sensitive business information in order to prevent competitors from using the FOIA to obtain access to confidential information.

5. *Agency memoranda.* This exemption protects internal documents such as working drafts, policy statements, proposals, and investigative reports. This exemption is also known as "executive privilege." The rationale for the exemption is that government employees need to communicate with each other and share ideas and suggestions that go into the decision-making process without concern that those documents might one day become public. Government agencies claim that potential disclosure of such documents would limit the "robust discussion" necessary for effective policy development. Federal courts that have evaluated FOIA cases dealing with this exemption have ruled that the public has a right to know what policies a government agency has adopted, but not the details of the behind-the-scenes discussions that helped shape the policy.

6. *Personnel and medical files.* The federal FOIA protects all personnel files of federal government employees, but state laws vary. In the case of public officials, only their salaries are public information.

7. *Law enforcement investigative records.* These materials are protected while the investigation is in progress, but are often released after the cases are closed. The justification for this exemption is the avoidance of excessive pre-trial publicity.

8. *Information about banks.* This exemption prevents the release of communication between banks and the government agencies that regulate them.

9. *Information about geological test sites, such as wells.* This exemption, seldom challenged, is to prevent land speculators and other persons from learning about the success or failure of drilling experiments and what valuable natural resources may have been discovered.

10. *Critical infrastructure.* This exemption, the most recent addition to the FOIA, allows the government to protect documents related to electricity, communications, water supplies, transportation networks, and other matters that, if released, might provide useful information to terrorists. When first proposed, this exemption was criticized by the Society of Professional Journalists and the American Civil Liberties Union as "vague and overbroad" because of the potential for abuse by government officials who may use it to protect non-sensitive information. Over their objections, however, the exemption was passed into law as part of the Homeland Security Act of 2002.

A notable case in which the courts upheld an FOIA exemption was *New York Times v. National Aeronautics and Space Administration* (1990). The *New York Times* learned of the existence of an audiotape containing cockpit conversations aboard the space shuttle Challenger in the minutes before it exploded on January 28, 1986, killing the seven astronauts aboard. Because NASA is a government agency, the tape was considered a government record. The *Times* filed an FOIA request for the tape, but NASA declined it based on the privacy exemption, claiming that it did not want to subject the families to the trauma of hearing the tape.

The trial court ruled the privacy exemption did not apply because it was not contained within a personnel file or medical file. NASA appealed to a Circuit Court, which ruled that NASA could exempt the tapes under the privacy clause because of the emotional distress it would cause the astronauts' families.[34]

Another notable case followed the 2001 death of race car driver Dale Earnhardt during the Daytona 500, as newspapers in Florida clashed with members of the Earnhardt family over access to photographs taken during the driver's autopsy. The prevailing law in Florida at the time required that autopsy records be public, but it did not specifically address the issue of accompanying photographs. Florida newspapers sought access to the photographs as part of their investigation into the safety equipment available to race car drivers. While the Earnhardt family obtained an injunction prohibiting release of the photographs, the Florida Legislature passed the Dale Earnhardt Family Relief Act, which would prohibit such access permanently on the basis of preserving family privacy. While the law applies only within the state of Florida, the rationale behind it is likely to be cited in similar cases in other states in the future.

Soon after the law was passed, lawyers for the *Orlando Sentinel* and the *Independent Florida Alligator,* the student newspaper at the University of Florida, challenged it on First Amendment grounds, but a state appeals court determined that the law was constitutional. When the Florida Supreme Court refused to hear the case on further appeal, the ruling of the appeals court stood.

The newspapers announced their intentions to appeal to the U. S. Supreme Court, but decided to drop the case after the Court ruled in an unrelated case that death-scene photographs of Vince Foster, a member of President Clinton's White House staff who committed suicide in 1993, were exempt under the Freedom of Information Act's law enforcement exemption. The rationale for the ruling was that the family's privacy interests outweighed the public interest in seeing the photographs.

Government Attempts to Limit Access

In an attempt to discourage journalists and citizens' groups from filing Freedom of Information Act requests and complaints regarding access to public meetings, some government agencies threaten to file countersuits against those requesting information and access. One recent case took place in Burlington, North Carolina, in 2005, when the city government attempted to sue a local newspaper in order to deter numerous public records and public meetings complaints. In response, the North Carolina Legislature considered a new law to allow government agencies to file "pre-emptive" lawsuits against companies, journalists, and private citizens who file complaints.[35]

The North Carolina League of Municipalities, in supporting the proposed legislation, claimed that its purpose was not to punish journalists or citizens, but instead was to allow government agencies to seek "declaratory judgments" that would clarify the issues involved in access cases. But opponents claimed that the purpose was to frustrate and intimidate inquisitive parties and that such a law would be inconsistent with the spirit of open government and would punish parties for merely asserting their constitutional rights. The North Carolina Supreme Court eventually ruled that the City of Burlington did not have the authority to pursue such suits, and the proposed legislation was not passed.

Another recent trend that frustrates journalists and other parties seeking access to public information is the privatization of government functions. Rather than expand already cumbersome and bureaucratic systems, many state governments find it efficient to hire private management firms to operate their hospitals, prisons, lotteries, and other departments. As a result, the actions of these agencies are often not subject to the state's public meetings and public records laws. Likewise, state universities wishing to hire new presidents are able to circumvent state laws by using executive recruiting firms to conduct the searches.

Frequently Asked Questions about the News-Gathering Process

1. *Why is it important for the media (and the public) to have access to criminal trials and other legal proceedings?* Media access to the judicial process is important for three reasons. First, media coverage of trials is an expansion of the "public trial" concept. While the framers of the Constitution were mostly concerned about the rights of defendants to have the public attend their trials in person, the concept of "public trial" has been expanded to include coverage by the print and electronic media. Therefore, public access has been interpreted to include media access. In the 1980 case of *Richmond Newspapers v. Virginia*, the Supreme Court ruled that criminal trials are "presumptively open" to both the public and the media and may be closed only in those cases in which the court's interest in protecting a witness or victim outweighs the media's interest in access.[36] Two years later, in *Globe Newspapers v. Superior Court*, the Supreme Court ruled that the right of access applies even in cases of sex-abuse trials in which victims or witnesses are minors.[37]

The second reason is that the media perform a watchdog function. Observers of the legal process claim that when journalists are present in the courtroom, judges and lawyers will be more likely to follow correct procedures, and witnesses will be more likely to provide truthful testimony.

The third reason is that media coverage of trials maintains public confidence in the judicial process. Some legal scholars believe that public trials, especially those on television networks such as Court TV, help the public understand the judicial system and help maintain confidence in the legal process.

2. *Why is it important for the media (and the public) to have access to public meetings and public records?* Put simply, when a governmental body—Congress, the state legislature, the city council, or a county school board—meets, it is often to decide how to spend taxpayer money. The taxpayers therefore have a right to hear the discussion, and the media have the right to report on the results for those people not able to attend the meeting.

In the cases of public records, taxpayer money is used to gather, organize, and maintain the records, so the same principle that applies to public meetings also applies to public records.

Point/Counterpoint: Cameras in the Courtroom

Support for Courtroom Cameras

Courtroom cameras represent an expansion of the "public trial" concept. As Supreme Court Justice Louis Brandeis once wrote in a journal article, media access to the court system was important because "sunshine is the best disinfectant."[38] In another case, the Court stated that "public scrutiny of a criminal trial enhances the quality and safeguards the integrity of the fact-finding process, with benefits to both the defendant and society as a whole."[39]

Courtroom cameras help the public to better understand the judicial system. Wall Street Journal editor Stephen J. Adler, quoted in a 1996 article in *Editor & Publisher*, said, "When you put a camera inside the courtroom and watch the events, you might disapprove of some of them, you might like others; you learn a lot about how the process works . . . but more to the point, the circus tends to take place outside the courtroom."[40] In the same interview, Adler disputed the idea of cameras creating the circus atmosphere.

Courtroom cameras are a check on judicial power. Some legal experts argue that because judges are given so much authority to regulate courtroom procedure, broadcasting trials is necessary to ensure that such power is not abused.

Criticism of Courtroom Cameras

Courtroom cameras increase the workload for judges. The introduction of cameras to the courtroom adds to the administrative workload of judges, who must make decisions regarding the number and location of cameras and whether or not a pool system will be required.

Courtroom cameras may have a harmful effect on future trials. If a re-trial is necessary, or if multiple defendants are involved in separate trials for the same crime, potential jurors for subsequent trials will be exposed to an increased level of media coverage of previous trials.

Courtroom cameras have the potential to intimidate and distract. Cameras may intimidate or distract witnesses, jurors, and inexperienced lawyers, and create the opportunity for "showboating" by flamboyant lawyers.

Courtroom cameras give viewers an inaccurate view of the judicial system. By showing only highlights of a trial on the evening news, television coverage of a trial may present an inaccurate picture of the legal process and mislead the public into believing that criminal trials are more dramatic than they really are.

Point/Counterpoint: Shield Laws

Support for Shield Laws

Shield laws and journalistic privilege are controversial topics for discussion in journalism classes and the profession as a whole.

Supporters of shield laws make the following points:

Shield laws can be justified within the scope of the First Amendment's "press freedom" clause. The right to protect sources is not mentioned specifically in the First Amendment, but advocates claim the ban on "abridging the freedom of the press" should be interpreted as supporting the concept.

Shield laws are necessary because of the importance of anonymous sources in investigative journalism. Advocates claim that many sources would not come forward if they could not receive a promise of confidentiality, and as a result, investigative journalism would be more difficult.

Shield laws limit the potential for "annexation" of the journalism profession. Some advocates worry that if reporters were customarily put on the witness stand to testify at criminal trials or otherwise required to provide information, they would become part of the law enforcement process. In a dissenting opinion filed in a Supreme Court case in which the court did not support a reporter's right to protect his sources, Justice Potter Stewart wrote that if shield laws were not available to protect journalists, the effect would be to "undermine the historic independence of the press by attempting to annex the journalistic profession as an investigative arm of the government."[41]

Criticism of Shield Laws

Opponents of shield laws counter with the following criticisms:

Shield laws provide unethical journalists with the opportunity to fictionalize stories. Opponents of shield laws claim that unconditional journalistic privilege might result in unethical reporters making up fictional confidential sources and then using a state shield law to cover up the absence of real ones.

Shield laws limit the defendant's right to challenge trial evidence. One of the principles of the American judicial system is that the defendant has a right to know the identity of his or her accuser and to challenge the evidence presented in court. Because limited shield laws protect the source of the information without protecting the information itself, it often leads to situations in which a reporter might provide information to the court without citing its source, making it difficult for the defendant to challenge that information.

Shield laws provide privileges that are not available to everyone else. If the average citizen is required to testify in court, he or she cannot say "that's confidential." Some critics therefore believe it is unfair for journalists to have such a confidentiality privilege.

Shield laws are problematic because of the difficulty of determining who qualifies as a journalist. Journalism is not a well-defined profession like law or medicine—fields in which there are educational requirements and licensing procedures that help define those professions. Journalism is very loosely defined, and most state shield laws choose to draw the line as narrowly as they can—usually with terms such as "full-time" and "professional." Because of the growth of underground or "fringe" publications, including those on the Internet ("blogs"), the determination of who is a "journalist" becomes more difficult.

Shield laws are inconsistent from state to state. In addition to the differences between limited and comprehensive shield laws, there are other factors that vary greatly from one state to the next. Some states protect newspapers but not magazines, while others protect print journalists but not broadcast journalists. Some use the terms *full-time* and *professional*, while others use broader definitions. In cases in which a reporter's employer is based in one state, but he or she is reporting on a matter in an adjoining state, there is often confusion as to which state shield law should apply.

Chapter Summary

The professional news-gatherer faces a number of challenges in his or her work, including those related to covering the judicial system (such as pre-trial publicity and the role of cameras in the courtroom), the extent to which he or she can protect the identify of his or her sources and news materials, and the issue of obtaining access to news events and locations (including meetings of governmental bodies) as well as public records. Of primary importance to the journalist covering national issues is an understanding of the Freedom of Information Act (FOIA), a law governing media access (and public access) to records maintained by the federal government. The majority of FOIA conflicts involve the various exemptions used to protect sensitive information, although these exemptions are occasionally abused. Journalists covering state and local issues will find that most states have public records laws that parallel the FOIA, and many of the exemptions are also the same.

CASE PROBLEMS

The People v. Joe Loozer

You've been assigned as the presiding judge for the upcoming trial of Joe Loozer, also known as the "Southside Rapist," the only suspect in a string of well-publicized rapes in your community. The pre-trial proceedings were open to the public and press, and you were pleased with the responsibility and good judgment that the media from the immediate community showed in their coverage. But now that the trial itself is about to start, media from around the state are expected to come, and you're concerned that they may not show the same responsibility and judgment. You've decided to issue a one-page memorandum outlining the rules of procedure and decorum for the media covering the trial.

Your memorandum should address issues such as cameras in the courtroom, whether or not the name of the victims should be used, and voluntary press association/bar association guidelines (usually associated with pre-trial publicity, but in this case, consider those for the trial itself). You must balance the rights of the victims, the rights of the defendant, and the rights of the press covering the trial.

Hint: Do not make any rules that would likely be found unconstitutional (prior restraint, etc.) if appealed. Be careful with your time, place, and manner decisions.

Sally's Simultaneous Subpoenas

You're the attorney for the *Mudville Daily Tribune,* and one of your paper's star reporters, Sally Workhard, faces a dilemma. For the last two years, Ms. Workhard has written numerous stories about scandals involving the county school system. Her latest series of stories focuses on the school superintendent, who has been accused of embezzling thousands of dollars from the school system's budget. Like most reporters, Workhard used only a small portion of her handwritten notes in her stories.

During the first week of the superintendent's trial, Workhard is one of several reporters asked to participate in a roundtable discussion of public affairs on a local television program. The superintendent's trial is one of several topics discussed. During the program, Workhard offers her opinion that the superintendent is being framed by other county officials as part of a widespread cover-up of even bigger corruption taking place in county government.

It is obvious that Workhard knows more about the case than the other guests on the show. When the moderator presses her to provide more detail, she replies, "You'll just have to buy my paper next week."

Both the superintendent's attorney and the prosecutor assigned to the case see the TV program, but neither wants to wait until next week. Workhard is at her desk the next morning when she receives two subpoenas—one from each side in the court case. Both want her to report to the courthouse that afternoon to testify about what she knows about the superintendent's case and to bring with her all of her notes, computer disks, and drafts of stories not yet published.

Workhard comes to your office and shows you the subpoenas, which require her to be at the courthouse at 2 p.m. You spend a few moments explaining to Workhard your state's limited shield law, then look at your watch and see that it's 10 a.m. How do you spend the next four hours?

Sex, Lies, and Audiotape

You're an attorney who has been approached by both sides in a case. Both sides want to hire you, so you're in the unusual position of being able to choose which side you would rather represent.

Background: The controversial mayor of Mudville is a known philanderer with at least one mistress in each key voting district. Last night, his wife and two children came home and found that the mayor had been the victim of a grisly murder. His wife called 911 to report the crime, and she is heard on the audiotape screaming that she saw one of his many mistresses (who she identifies by name) running from the house with a gun in her hand. The children, both minors, are heard screaming in the background. Word of the existence of the 911 tape circulates quickly among the local media.

The Mudville Press Association (MPA) wants to hire you and suggests that you file a request under your state's public records law to give the media access to copies of the tape for airing on television and radio. Because the 911 service is administered by the city government and funded by taxpayers, the media believe the tapes should be considered public records. If you take this side, the MPA suggests that you include in your brief the following factors:

a. An implied First Amendment right of access
b. Public records laws (assume your state's law is consistent with those described in this chapter)
c. Private facts common law (including defenses)

But at the same time, the city manager (now the acting mayor) for the city of Mudville wants to hire you to represent the city and argue the other side. If you take this side, he suggests that you immediately file an objection to the MPA's request and suggests that you include in your argument:

a. The lack of specific First Amendment right of access
b. Exemptions to public records laws
c. Private facts common law (countering the defenses used above)

In addition, the city manager reminds you that as a former criminal attorney, you should be concerned with the murder suspect's Sixth Amendment right to a fair trial, which might be damaged if the name on the tape is heard.

Decisions, decisions. You have to choose which side you would prefer to represent, and what points you would make in your legal brief, points that would either (a) support the MPA's action to obtain and broadcast the 911 tapes, or (b) support the city's objections to the tapes being released.

SOCRATIC DIALOGUE QUESTIONS

1. If you have served on a jury, please share your experience with the class, including explanation of any steps the judge took to deal with excessive pre-trial publicity.

2. Are cameras in the courtroom a good idea or a bad idea? Why? Do you agree or disagree with the judicial view that rules limiting the location of courtroom cameras represent a reasonable "time, place, and manner" restriction?

3. Do you think the Branzburg Rule is a good idea or a bad idea? Why?

4. What can be done to address Justice Stewart's concerns about the possible "annexation of the press as an investigative arm of government"?

5. Suppose you were the governor of a state that had no shield law, but the state assembly sent one to your desk for your signature. Would you sign it and establish a shield law for your state? Or would you veto it? Why?

6. Do you agree with journalists' claims that they should have "First Amendment right of access" to accident scenes such as airplane crashes and automobile accidents?

7. Find at least one case in Chapter 8 with which you strongly disagree with the court ruling (in the final resolution of the case) and be prepared to share your opinion with the class.

GLOSSARY OF TERMS

Branzburg Rule A principle that a state shield law does not apply in cases in which a journalist has witnessed a crime. From the 1972 Supreme Court case, *Branzburg v. Hayes*.[42]

Documentary materials Materials used by journalists in their research, such as photocopies or microfilm printouts of government documents or court records. These materials are subject to less protection than work product materials.

Executive session A portion of a governmental meeting that is closed to the public and the media; usually invoked to protect the privacy of individuals or the confidentiality of information.

Gag orders   A judge's order to participants in a legal proceeding not to discuss the case outside of the courtroom. When applied to the media, it restricts their ability to publish or broadcast details of the case.

Media pool   An arrangement, usually mandated by a judge, in which access to a courtroom or similar location is limited to a small number of journalists, photographers, and videographers, who then share information, still photographs and video with other media outlets.

Qualified privilege test   A three-part standard for overruling a state shield law: the journalist has knowledge of a specific crime; the information is unavailable from other sources; and the court's need to obtain the information is more important than the journalist's need to keep it secret.

Reporter privilege   A common-law principle that allows journalists to protect their information and sources; often applied in states without shield laws.

Search warrant   A court order allowing law enforcement officers to search a resident or place of business.

Shield law   A state statute that allows reporters to protect information and sources. A **comprehensive shield law** protects both the information and the identity of the sources; a **limited shield law** protects the sources but not the information.

Subpoena   A court order requiring the appearance in court of an individual or the production of documents.

Sunshine laws   A collective term for state laws that require governmental bodies to meet in public.

Work product materials   Materials produced by a journalist in the course of his or her work, including handwritten notes, audiotapes, videotapes, computer disks, and drafts of stories not yet published. Work product materials are subject to a greater degree of protection than documentary materials.

Writ of mandamus   A document issued by a court or government official instructing a government agency to comply with a request; often used in cases involving requests filed under the Freedom of Information Act or state public records laws.

NOTES

1. *Irvin v. Dowd*, 366 U.S. 717 (1961).
2. *Sheppard v. Maxwell*, 384 U.S. 333 (1966).
3. *Murphy v. Florida*, 421 U.S. 794 (1975).
4. *Nebraska Press Association v. Stuart*, 424 U.S. 539 (1976).
5. *U.S. v. McVeigh*, 918 F. Supp. 1467 (1996).
6. *Estes v. Texas*, 381 U.S. 532 (1965).
7. Grady, Sandy. "Time for Supreme Court Reality TV." *USA Today*, September 13, 2005. p. 13-A.
8. "Supreme Court: No TV Cameras." *NewsMax*, September 2006, p. 32.
9. *Chandler v. Florida*, 366 So.2d 64 (1981).
10. *Branzburg v. Hayes*, 408 U.S. 665 (1972).
11. Ibid.
12. *United States v. Criden*, 634 F.2d 346 (1980).
13. *United States v. Blanton*, 534 F. Supp. 295 (1981).
14. James C. Goodale, "Why Vanessa Leggett Went to Jail." *New York Law Journal*, June 7, 2002, p. 3; Vanessa Leggett, "My Principles Have Landed Me in Jail." *Newsweek*, September 3, 2001, p. 12.
15. Michael Mello, "Journalist Guilty of Contempt." Associated Press report, November 19, 2004; Brooke McDonald, "Reporter Freed After Four Months of Confinement." Associated Press report, April 10, 2005.
16. Pete Yost, "Times Reporter Jailed for Not Revealing Source." Associated Press report, July 7, 2005; Nancy Benac, "Players Big and Small Caught Up in Probe of the 'Outing' of CIA Agent." Associated Press report, October 24, 2005.
17. *The Matter of Farber*, 394 A.2d 330 (1978).
18. *Zurcher v. Stanford Daily*, 436 U.S. 547 (1978).
19. Dorothy Giobbe, "Reporter Jailed for Contempt." *Editor & Publisher*, October 19, 1996, p. 17.
20. *Krause v. Graco Children's Products*, 24 Media L. Rep. 1607 (1995).
21. *Gonzales v. NBC*, 194 F.3d 29 (1998).
22. Howard Mintz, "Bloggers Want Journalists' Rights." Knight-Ridder report, April 19, 2006.
23. *Cohen v. Cowles Media*, 501 U.S. 663 (1991).
24. *Gannett Newspapers v. DePasquale*, 443 U.S. 368 (1979).

25. *Globe Newspaper Co. v. Superior Court*, 457 U.S. 596 (1982).
26. *J.B. Pictures v. Department of Defense*, 86 F. 3d 236 (1996).
27. *Procunier v. Pell*, 417 U.S. 817 (1974).
28. *Saxbe v. Washington Post*, 417 U.S. 843 (1974).
29. *Houchins v. KQED*, 438 U.S. 1 (1978).
30. *California First Amendment Coalition v. Woodford*, 299 F.3d 868 (2002).
31. *State v. Lashinsky*, 81 N.J. 1 (1979).
32. *City of Oak Creek v. King*, 436 N.W. 2d 285 (1989).
33. Mark Tapscott, "Boondoggles Need Exposure." Syndicated column, December 8, 2004.
34. *New York Times v. National Aeronautics and Space Administration*, 782 F. Supp. 628 (1990).
35. "They Want You in the Dark." Editorial, *Wilmington Star-News* (North Carolina), May 10, 2005, p. 8-A.
36. *Richmond Newspapers v. Virginia*, 448 U.S. 555 (1980).
37. *Globe Newspapers v. Superior Court*, 457 U.S. 596 (1982).
38. Louis Brandeis, "What Publicity Can Do." *Harper's Weekly*, December 20, 1913, p. 92.
39. *Globe Newspapers v. Superior Court*, 457 U.S. 596 (1982).
40. Debra Gersh Hernandez, "Courtroom Cameras Debated." *Editor & Publisher*, February 17, 1996, pp. 11–13.
41. *Branzburg v. Hayes*, 408 U.S. 665 (1972).
42. Ibid.

Broadcasting and Cable

*Regulation of emerging video technologies requires a delicate balance of
competing interests.*

Judge Learned Hand
Quincy Cable Television v. FCC 1985

LEARNING OBJECTIVES

As a result of reading this chapter, students should:

- Understand the differences between the regulatory processes for the broadcast media and the print media.
- Understand the differences between the regulatory processes for broadcast television and cable television.
- Understand the role of the Federal Communications Commission in regulating the broadcasting industry.

Technology and the First Amendment

As discussed in Chapter 2, James Madison was not looking very far into the future when he wrote the First Amendment a little more than two centuries ago. Anxious for citizens of the new country to have more freedoms than they had under British rule, Madison and other Founding Fathers saw the First Amendment as an instrument that would protect one's rights to criticize the government either orally or through the nation's early attempts at newspaper journalism.

The First Amendment seemed to work well for more than a hundred years. But beginning in the early 1900s, advances in technology, along with two World Wars and the growth of communism in other countries, provided a number of challenges to the notions of free speech and free press.

Many of those challenges have come from technology that is growing rapidly and changing constantly. The first challenge of the early 1900s was motion picture film, which was followed quickly by radio in the 1920s, broadcast television in the 1950s, and cable television in the 1960s. Politicians and other concerned individuals struggled for decades with questions of how—and sometimes if—such technologies required regulation, as those technologies changed how we look at issues such as political speech, hate speech, indecency, and sexual expression.

Philosophy Behind Broadcast Regulation

It does not take a legal expert to recognize the substantial difference between how the government regulates the print and broadcast media. While newspapers and magazines are subject to little regulation other than what results from the occasional defamation or invasion or privacy suit, television and radio stations and networks are heavily regulated by the Federal Communications Commission (FCC). When challenged, those FCC regulations are usually upheld by the courts as reasonable limitations that do not violate the broadcasters' First Amendment rights.

The justification for the different levels of regulation is based on three factors:

1. *Public ownership of the airwaves.* Broadcasters do not own the frequencies on which they broadcast—the airwaves are owned by the public, and broadcasters are allowed to use them as a privilege, with the FCC as the custodian.
2. *Scarcity.* Because of the limited number of frequencies on which broadcasters can operate, the Supreme Court has determined that government regulation of those frequencies—specifically through its licensing procedure—is justifiable. As far back as 1943, the Court addressed the issue of radio station licensing in the case of *National Broadcasting Co. v. United States.* "Unlike other modes of expression, radio inherently is not available to all," the Court ruled. "That is its unique characteristic, and that is why, unlike other modes of expression, it is subject to governmental regulation. Because it cannot be used by all, some who wish to use it must be denied."[1] In the 1969 case of *Red Lion Broadcasting v. FCC,* the Court added that "a license permits broadcasting, but the licensee has no constitutional right to be the one who holds the license or to monopolize a radio frequency to the exclusion of his fellow citizens."[2]
3. *Pervasiveness.* Radio and television are not always obtrusive, but they have the potential to be so. If an individual is offended by something in the print media, he or she can simply choose not to look at it. That is not the case with broadcasting.

Role of the FCC

The Federal Communications Commission (FCC) is an independent United States government agency, directly responsible to Congress. The FCC was established by the Communications Act of 1934 and is charged with regulating communications by radio, television, wire, satellite, and cable. The FCC's jurisdiction covers the fifty states, the District of Columbia, and U.S. possessions.

The FCC is directed by five commissioners who are appointed by the president and confirmed by the Senate for five-year terms, except when filling an unexpired term. The president designates one of the commissioners to serve as chairperson. Only three commissioners may be members of the same political party, and none of them can have a financial interest in any commission-related business.

The FCC's responsibilities fall into the following areas:

1. **Licensing** of television and radio broadcasters.
2. **Regulating** television and radio broadcasters. This responsibility includes:
   a. *Political advertising.* Section 312 of the FCC code requires that broadcasters provide "reasonable access" to political candidates and organizations. Section 315 of the FCC code requires that candidates seeking political office must be given "equal time" to present their campaign messages. There are exemptions for coverage of news events such as news conferences and debates. Political advertising is also subject to rules of the Federal Elections Commission (FEC) as well as state election laws.
   b. *Obscenity and indecency.* Generally, the FCC can ban obscenity in its entirety and regulate (but not ban) content deemed to be indecent.
   c. *Children's television.* The Children's Television Act of 1990, enforced by the FCC, requires that stations provide educational programs for children and limit the number of commercials to 10.5 minutes per hour for weekends and 12 minutes per hour for weekdays. The CTA also prohibits the advertising of a product during a program based on that product. The most common examples involve action figures such as the Teenage Mutant Ninja Turtles, which are also characters found in children's programming.
   d. *Ownership issues* (discussed later in this chapter).
3. **Investigating consumer complaints** regarding content and policies of television and radio broadcasters.
4. **Educating and informing consumers** about telecommunications products and services.
5. **Regulating the use of cellular telephones**, pagers, two-way radios, remote control toys, garage door openers, and similar devices.
6. **Establishing and enforcing rules** regarding fair competition among providers of wireless communication services.

History of Broadcast Regulation

The history of broadcast regulation began with two laws that dealt with radio.

The first was the Wireless Ship Act of 1910, the first law of any type to affect broadcasting. It required passenger ships to have wireless equipment on board, capable of broadcasting at least one hundred miles, and a skilled operator. There were serious shortcomings in the 1910 law, however, and two things happened that caused Congress to reconsider the Wireless Ship Act and strengthen it.

The first was the sinking of the Titanic in 1912, a tragedy that was blamed partly on the lack of effective radio communication. The other factor was the realization by the Army and Navy of the potential military applications of radio technology. The armed forces were concerned that there were so many amateurs and hackers using the airwaves that it would be difficult to fight through the clutter if those radio frequencies were needed in a national emergency.

Based on these concerns, Congress passed the Radio Act of 1912. It strengthened standards for emergency communications on ships (in response to the Titanic sinking) and gave the Secretary of Commerce the power to issue licenses to radio operators and assign frequencies (in response to the concerns of the Army and Navy).

When Herbert Hoover became Secretary of Commerce in the early 1920s, he organized a national conference to discuss problems facing the radio industry. As a result of the conference, Congress enacted the Radio Act of 1927.

The act had four provisions:

1. It created the Federal Radio Commission (FRC, later to become the FCC) and gave it the authority to control operating conditions, hours, power, frequencies, and logging procedures.
2. It required broadcasters to act in the "public interest, convenience, and necessity."
3. It established a licensing procedure.
4. It gave radio limited First Amendment protection.

The Radio Act of 1927 is still in effect, but in 1934, it was revised and re-named the Communications Act of 1934, which changed the FRC into the FCC.

The first cases to test the government's authority to regulate broadcasting came in the 1932 cases of *KFKB v. FRC* and *Trinity Methodist Church vs. FRC.*

The KFKB case involved a radio station in Kansas and one of its on-air personalities, John Brinkley, an unlicensed doctor who offered medical advice on a call-in show. Other physicians heard his program and notified the FRC that his advice was not based on proper medical procedures, and upon investigating further, the FRC learned that Brinkley was recommending a specific pharmacy in the community without disclosing that he was its owner.

The FRC advised the station to cancel Brinkley's program under the threat of losing its license, but the station owner refused, claiming the FRC's proposed action was a form of prior restraint that violated the First Amendment. When the station's license was up for renewal, its application was denied based on the FRC's determination that the station was not acting in the public interest. KFKB appealed the case to the Supreme Court, which ruled in the FRC's favor, determining that refusing to renew a license was within the FRC's authority and did not violate the First Amendment.[3]

The same year, in the case of *Trinity Methodist Church vs. FRC,* the Supreme Court reaffirmed the FRC's authority to reject a radio station's license renewal application. The applicant was Trinity Methodist Church of the South, the licensee of a radio station in Los Angeles. One of its on-air personalities was the Reverend

Robert Shuler, who routinely spoke out against gambling, drinking, prostitution, and other vices. Shuler also attacked local judges, accusing them of taking bribes; and other state and federal government officials, claiming they were guilty of corruption and election fraud. He also attacked other religions, including making disparaging remarks about Jews and Catholics.

As it did in the KFKB case, the FRC advised the station to drop its controversial speaker or risk losing its license. The station refused, and when its license was up for renewal, the application was denied. The FRC claimed the station was not acting in the public interest, and the Supreme Court ruled in the agency's favor, denying the station's First Amendment claim.[4]

In 1969, the FCC's authority was tested again in *Red Lion Broadcasting v. FCC.* The Supreme Court upheld the FCC's authority to regulate broadcasting, ruling that its authority did not violate the First Amendment.[5]

The case began when controversial author Fred Cook was attacked on a radio station and asked for time to respond under an FCC regulation known as the **Fairness Doctrine,** which required broadcasters to provide such opportunities. When the station denied him that opportunity, the FCC stepped in to enforce its rule. When the case reached the Supreme Court, it ruled that the Fairness Doctrine was valid and that the station must allow Cook time to reply. In its majority opinion, the Court stated that the rights of the viewers and listeners are more important than the rights of the broadcasters. Even though the Fairness Doctrine was repealed in 1987, this case solidified the regulatory differences between print journalism and electronic journalism and reinforced the FCC's authority to regulate broadcasting based in part on the "scarcity" principle.

Broadcasting and Indecency

Section 29 of the Radio Act of 1927 gave the Federal Radio Commission—later to become the Federal Communications Commission—the authority to regulate obscene, indecent, or profane language on the radio. When the 1927 law was revised into the Communications Act of 1934, the provision was re-numbered to become Section 326. But that section also included an anti-censorship clause that stated that the FCC could not censor broadcasts. At first the clause that banned obscenity and indecency and the clause that prohibited censorship appeared to contradict each other, but later court rulings clarified that the non-censorship clause applied solely to speech other than that found to be obscene or indecent.

In 1948, the ban was rewritten and became Title 18, Section 1464, of the United State Code. It was not until the 1970s, however, that the FCC attempted to enforce the rule to any great degree. The most noteworthy case was *FCC v. Pacifica*, which began when a radio station aired a twelve-minute skit by comedian George Carlin titled, "Filthy Words." Although the station provided a warning prior at the beginning of the skit, a listener complained to the FCC, prompting the investigation.

Instead of fining the station, the FCC simply documented the incident and withheld judgment while it waited to see if other complaints would follow. No other complaints were received, but the FCC nonetheless decided to take action, based on its belief that (1) radio was accessible by unsupervised children, (2) listeners might not hear warnings such as the one provided before the airing of the Carlin skit, and (3) the scarcity of the broadcast spectrum required the Commission to exercise its regulatory authority.

As a result of the incident, the FCC established a rule that radio stations could air indecent material only between the hours of 10 p.m. and 6 a.m., during what it called the "later evening day parts." Pacifica challenged the rule, and a lower court ruled in its favor, calling the FCC rule a form of censorship and determining that a broad interpretation of the rule would mean that parts of the Bible might be declared indecent if read over the airwaves. In a 5–4 decision, the U. S. Supreme Court overturned the lower court ruling, agreeing with the FCC's view that broadcast airwaves were intrusive because they came into the home uninvited and often reached unsupervised children. In his majority opinion, Justice John Paul Stevens wrote that because of radio's potential to be obtrusive, "the individual's right to be left alone plainly outweighs the First Amendment rights of the intruder." Two other justices concurred with Stevens, claiming that the radio audience is much different from one that might attend one of Carlin's live performances or purchase one of his recordings. The former might be unprepared for the coarse language, whereas the latter would be prepared because they attended the performance or listened to the recording voluntarily.

In their dissenting opinions, four justices lamented the majority decision for a number of reasons. Primary among them was their view that much like those persons exposed to the "Fuck the Draft" message on the back of a person's jacket (the incident that led to the *Cohen v. California* case discussed in Chapter 2), the exposure was brief and could easily be terminated. They were also concerned that based on the majority opinion, future incidents involving political speech deemed to be indecent might lead to court rulings limiting that form of speech.

The court compared its "time, place, and manner" ruling to finding "a pig in a parlor instead of a barnyard . . . we simply hold that when the (FCC) finds a pig has entered the parlor, the exercise of its regulatory power does not depend on proof that the pig is obscene." Another interesting quote that came out of the Supreme Court decision in the Pacifica case was that "sexual and vulgar speech was a 'poor stepchild' of the First Amendment because few of us would march our sons and daughters off to war to protect sexual expression."[6]

In 1987, the FCC created the **safe harbor rule** that limited indecent programming to the hours of midnight to 6 a.m. It was a variation of the "later evening day parts" concept that came out of the Pacifica case. Even during these hours, broadcasters were required to provide a warning that offensive material might be included in a program.

Two years later, the FCC announced its intention to eliminate the safe harbor rule and enforce the ban twenty-four hours a day. The only television station to be fined under the twenty-four hour rule was a Kansas City station that aired the soft-core pornographic movie *Private Lessons* during prime time. Radio stations were a more frequent target of FCC action. In 1989, for example, a Detroit radio station was fined $2,000 for airing "Walk With an Erection," a parody of the Bangles hit, "Walk Like an Egyptian."[7]

The broadcasting lobby objected to the twenty-four hour ban, and a Circuit Court of Appeals eventually struck it down.[8] The court did, however, allow the FCC to once again apply the safe harbor rule and expanded it to the hours of 10 p.m. and 6 a.m. In the Pacifica case, the FCC had defined indecency as "language that describes in terms patently offensive, as measured by contemporary community standards for the broadcast medium, sexual or excretory activities and organs, at times of day when there is a reasonable risk that children may be in the audience,"[9] and the FCC now wanted to enforce that provision.

In the late 1990s and early 2000s, the era of "shock jocks" such as Howard Stern created a new culture of crude and offensive material on the radio airwaves, and more public pressure on the FCC to limit or punish the broadcasters. The FCC fined several national radio conglomerates for allowing indecent speech by their on-air personalities, but the minimal amounts of the fines (considering the profits produced by the programs) made the fine system ineffective, so in 2004 Congress authorized the FCC to dramatically increase the financial penalties for indecency. Under this new threat, in early 2006 Stern moved his program to a satellite radio company, where it would be out of reach of FCC regulators.

Under the leadership of Chairman Michael Powell, the FCC became more aggressive in its crackdown of broadcast indecency following an incident shown on worldwide television during the halftime show of Super Bowl XXXVIII in January 2004. The game was broadcast by CBS, which also planned the halftime show. The main performers were pop stars Janet Jackson and Justin Timberlake, and at one point in the performance, Timberlake pulled away part of Jackson's costume, briefly revealing one of her breasts. He later described it as a "wardrobe malfunction" and claimed there was supposed to be another garment underneath. The FCC received numerous complaints about the incident, and in September of that year it fined Viacom, the network's parent company, $550,000. The size of the fine created a "chilling effect" that prompted networks and local stations from airing controversial programming. Two months after the FCC announced the fine, for example, numerous ABC affiliates declined to air the movie *Saving Private Ryan* for fear its graphic violence and course language might result in fines.

Ownership and Concentration Issues

As part of the Telecommunications Act of 1996, discussed in more detail later in this chapter, restrictions on the number of radio and television stations that may be owned by one company or individual were loosened, which allowed media companies to acquire more networks and local stations, including many that served the same markets. In the early 2000s, the FCC used the changes in the law to revise its own ownership rules. The FCC wanted to further relax the ownership rules that it labeled as "outdated."

Consumer advocates worried that such changes would result in less diversity of opinions in news and public affairs programming and the potential for media companies to exert more political influence without having that influence challenged by competitors. They pointed to the example of one radio network that in 2003 ordered its affiliates not to play songs by The Dixie Chicks in response to negative political comments attributed to the group.

In June 2004, a Circuit Court of Appeals in Philadelphia ruled against the FCC and in favor of the plaintiffs, the Consumers Union and the Media Access Project, a Washington, D.C.–based public interest legal advocacy group. The court agreed with the plaintiffs' concerns that conglomeration of media ownership "might allow one or two media giants to dominate the most important sources of local news and information in almost every community in America." The court did, however, allow the FCC to repeal its rule that once prohibited a company from owning both a television station and newspaper in the same city.[10]

Regulation of Cable and Satellite Television

The FCC has some authority over cable television, but not nearly as much as it does over traditional broadcasting. The rationale for this distinction is that (1) cable television is technically not "broadcasting" because its signals are transmitted over wires rather than the airwaves, and (2) the audience pays for the service and invites it into the home; it therefore is not as pervasive as traditional broadcasting.

When the cable industry began to flourish in the 1960s, however, the FCC was concerned with the welfare of smaller, locally owned broadcast stations that might find themselves unable to compete with larger, out-of-state cable companies. Based on its philosophy that broadcasters must "serve the public interest," the FCC established a "must-carry" rule that required cable companies to include local stations in its offerings. Cable companies challenged the "must carry" rule, claiming it infringed on their First Amendment rights, but the U.S. Supreme Court upheld the rule in the 1972 case of *U.S. v. Midwest Video*. The FCC maintained its regulatory rule over cable television but stopped short of proposing a licensing procedure.[11]

In 1984, as cable television became a dominant form of home entertainment, Congress passed the Cable Communications Policy Act of 1984, today referred to as "The Cable Act." It amended the Communications Act of 1934 and divided the authority to regulate cable service between the FCC and local governments, which the act referred to as "local franchising authorities," or LFAs. While such authorities were able to choose which companies could serve a community, they had little or no ability to control prices or programming policies.

In 1985 and 1987, federal appeals courts ruled in separate cases that the "must carry" rules violated the First Amendment and that the "scarcity" rationale that applied to broadcasting could not be applied to cable. In 1992, however, Congress revisited the idea of a "must carry" rule when it passed the Cable Television Protection and Consumer Act of 1992. But instead of having only the "must carry" rule, the law allowed local stations to choose one of two ways to work with cable companies—"must carry" or "may carry." If the broadcaster chose a "must carry" format, the cable company would be required to carry that broadcast station but would not be required to compensate the station. Under the "may carry" option (sometimes called "retransmission consent"), the station negotiates with the cable company the fee it charges to carry that station's programming.

The "must carry" provision within the Cable Act of 1992 was challenged by Turner Broadcasting in the 1994 case of *Turner Broadcasting v. FCC*. The cable company argued that the "must carry" rules violated its First Amendment rights. On appeal, the Supreme Court ruled 5–4 to send the case back to the District Court, where it was determined that must-carry provisions do not violate the First Amendment. The court agreed with the FCC's claim that the "must carry" provision was necessary because of the monopolistic status of most cable television providers and that the provisions promoted competition and protected local broadcast stations from being "shut out" in specific communities and that without the "must carry" protection, some local cable companies might go out of business.[12]

A slightly different rule is in effect for providers of satellite television service. The "carry one, carry all" rule states that if a satellite provider chooses to carry one local channel, it must also carry all other local channels in that community that request to be carried. But similar to the case involving cable companies, the local channels can choose either the "must carry" or "may carry" (retransmission consent) arrangements.

For much of the history of cable television, the FCC and other regulatory bodies have been concerned mainly with the business practices of cable companies and have paid little attention to content issues. One of the FCC's rare attempts at content regulation took place in 1975 when it established an anti-siphoning rule that prohibited cable companies from providing pay movie channels with feature films less than three years old. The rationale behind the rule was that showing films on pay channels delayed their release to broadcast channels and thus limited the audiences' right to access the content via "free TV." When Home Box Office challenged the rule, a Circuit Court of Appeals ruled against the FCC, determining that neither the broadcasters nor their audiences were being harmed by "siphoning" and that the FCC was trying to solve a problem that did not exist.[13]

In another case dealing with the regulation of cable television content, the U.S. Supreme Court ruled that cable channels operate as limited public forums, and therefore cable companies should not be allowed to censor content they find objectionable. That ruling, in the case of *Denver Area Educational Telecommunications Consortium v. FCC*, invalidated a section of the 1992 Cable Act, as well as the Telecommunications Act of 1996, that allowed cable operators to refuse to carry programming it viewed as obscene or indecent, or which promoted unlawful conduct. While the Court's decision meant that cable operators would not be allowed to censor specific content, they could still make fundamental business decisions regarding which channels to carry or not carry.[14]

In later cases, the Court struck down another part of 1992 Cable Act that dealt with indecency on pay-per-view channels. That provision on the law required cable operators who offered sexually explicit material to group all such programming onto one channel and limit access to subscribers who had to request access thirty days in advance. In overturning that part of the Cable Act, the Court ruled that subscribers had a right to access the material on short notice and that the thirty-day rule would create a "chilling effect"—that viewers would fear appearing on a list of people who like to watched "dirty movies."

Telecommunications Act of 1996

In 1996, Congress passed a sweeping package of new laws to deal with changes in the telecommunications industry. It was the first major revision of telecommunications law since passage of the Communications Act of 1934. The new bill, called the Telecommunications Act of 1996, had four major components, each affecting a segment of the industry.

In telephone services, the bill created more competition among long-distance providers and allowed telephone companies to compete with cable television providers by offering "video on demand" service. It also allowed telephone companies to expand their services and become Internet service providers.

As discussed earlier in this chapter, the broadcasting section of the act relaxed rules regarding television station and radio station ownership. This part of the act eliminated the rule that prohibited licensees from owning stations reaching more than 25 percent of the national audience and eliminated the rule prohibiting a network from owning more than one station per market. The broadcasting portion of the act also required newly manufactured television sets to include a "V-chip" that allows parents to program the set to exclude certain types of objectionable programming.

In cable television, the bill lifted price controls on cable service, thus allowing local cable providers to raise their monthly fees.

The bill's most controversial component dealt with regulation of the Internet. Titled the Communications Decency Act, the law provided punishment for transmitting obscene or indecent material over the Internet. This portion of the bill was declared unconstitutional in the case of *Reno v. American Civil Liberties Union*, which is discussed in Chapter 10.

Frequently Asked Questions about Broadcast and Cable Regulation

1. *Why are there different regulatory standards for traditional broadcast television and cable television?* Cable television is not subject to the same level of FCC regulation as traditional broadcast television because, unlike the traditional networks, cable networks are using privately owned technology rather than the publicly owned airwaves. Also, broadcast television is free and therefore reaches a wider audience and has more potential to be obtrusive. Cable signals—which subscribers pay for—are less likely to be considered intrusive.

2. *Why does the FCC have rules regarding the number of television stations and radio stations an individual or company can own?* In most other industries, the government generally encourages competition in hopes that consumers will benefit from greater choice and lower prices. In broadcasting, however, price is not an issue; yet the government as well as consumer advocates believe that audiences are better served when they can choose from a variety of information and entertainment sources. From time to time, however, that diversity is threatened by media mergers and consolidations. The ownership of multiple radio or television stations in the same market—as well as the cross-ownership of television stations, radio stations, and newspapers by individuals and companies—creates the potential for media monopolies that provide a narrower view of the world for their audiences.

Point Counterpoint: Regulation of Cable Television

Why Cable Television Should Be Regulated the Same as Broadcast Television

Because of the growth of the cable television industry in the last three decades, cable signals now reach an audience comparable to those of broadcast networks and stations. And because cable broadcasts are often seen in locations where parental supervision is lacking, those signals should be subject to some form of regulation. The Federal Communications Commission should therefore be authorized to apply the same rules regarding indecency and other objectionable material that it applies to broadcast signals.

Why Cable Television Should Not Be Regulated

As a form of entertainment, cable television is significantly different from broadcast television and therefore deserves to operate with far fewer restrictions—and perhaps none. To begin with, cable networks are using privately owned technology rather than the publicly owned airwaves (as in the case or broadcasting). Also, broadcast television is free and therefore reaches a wider audience and has more potential to be obtrusive. Cable signals—which subscribers pay for—may reach large audiences, but parents have more control over their children's access. Therefore, cable programming is much less likely to be intrusive.

Chapter Summary

The broadcast media are subject to far more regulation than print media, based on the fact that the airwaves are said to be owned by the public, the scarcity of available frequencies on which broadcasters can operate, and the potential for pervasiveness of broadcast content. In contrast, cable television is subject to little regulation. The rationale for not regulating cable television is based on the three factors above not being applicable, and also because the audience invites the medium into their home by payment of a subscription fee.

The government agency responsible for regulating the broadcasting industry is the Federal Communications Commission. Its primary concerns are issues such as the licensing and regulation of television and radio broadcasters, political advertising, obscenity and indecency, children's television, ownership issues, consumer complaints, educating and informing consumers about telecommunications products and services, regulating the use of personal electronic devices, and establishing and enforcing rules regarding fair competition among providers of wireless communication services.

Today, regulating the broadcasting and cable industries—while not regulating the Internet—raises a number of legal and philosophical questions and causes us to reexamine issues such as political speech, hate speech, indecency, sexual expression, and privacy.

CASE PROBLEM

A Problem with Time Zones

The Federal Elections Commission is a federal agency in charge of establishing rules and procedures for electing public officials such as the president and congressional representatives. Recently the commission has been studying the problems related to media coverage of the recent presidential election campaign and is recommending a number of changes to be made to federal election law. One of the controversial ideas it has proposed is to prohibit the television networks (including cable) from projecting winners of the presidential race before 10 p.m. EST, as that would coincide with the 7 p.m. PST closing time of polling places on the West Coast. Local election officials and candidates for city and state offices in California, Washington, and Oregon complained that their voter turnout in the previous presidential election was poor because the networks had already projected the results of the presidential race, thus decreasing the number of people voting in those three states during the last few hours before the polls closed.

If approved by both houses of Congress, the new law will take effect with the next presidential election. The National Association of Broadcasters has already threatened to file suit if the law is passed.

While you're not a practicing lawyer, you did take numerous courses in constitutional law and media law while in college, and you remember almost everything you learned. You're now a staff aide to Senator Noah Vale, who has asked for your opinion as to whether or not the FEC's proposed law would be constitutional. If you were to write a brief memo to the senator, what points would you make?

SOCRATIC DIALOGUE QUESTIONS

1. Do you agree with the rationale for regulating broadcast media differently from print media? Should that be changed, and if so, how?

2. The Radio Act of 1927 established the principle that broadcast licensees are required to act in the "public interest, convenience, and necessity"—a principle that is still in effect today. What are some examples of how broadcasters act in the public interest or perform public service?

3. Do you agree with the rationale behind the varying degrees of regulation regarding broadcast and cable television?

4. Do you agree with the Supreme Court's decision to overturn the 1992 rule (part of the Cable Act) regarding access to indecent material? Or could limiting access to indecent material be justified as a time, place, and manner restriction?

5. Find at least one case in Chapter 9 with which you strongly disagree with the court ruling (in the final resolution of the case) and be prepared to share your opinion with the class.

GLOSSARY OF TERMS

Fairness Doctrine   An FCC rule that required broadcasters to air a diversity of views in their coverage of political and social issues. The rule was repealed in 1987.

Safe harbor rule   An FCC rule that requires broadcasters to limit indecent programming to the hours of 10 p.m. to 6 a.m.

NOTES

1. *National Broadcasting Co. v. United States*, 319 U.S. 190 (1943).
2. *Red Lion Broadcasting v. FCC*, 395 U.S. 369 (1969).
3. *KFKB v. FRC*, 47 F.2d 670 (1931).
4. *Trinity Methodist Church vs. FRC*, 62 F.2d 850 (1932).
5. *Red Lion Broadcasting v. FCC*, 395 U.S. 369 (1969).
6. *FCC v. Pacifica*, 438 U.S. 726 (1978).
7. John R. Bittner, *Broadcast Law and Regulation.* Englewood Cliffs, N.J.: Prentice-Hall, 1992, p. 120.
8. Roger L. Sadler, *Electronic Media Law.* Thousand Oaks, Calif.: Sage Publications, 2005, p. 260.
9. *FCC v. Pacifica*, 438 U.S. 726 (1978).
10. *Prometheus Radio Project v. FCC*, 373 F.3d 372 (2004).
11. *U.S. v. Midwest Video*, 406 U.S. 649 (1972).
12. *Turner Broadcasting v. FCC*, 512 U.S. 622 (1994).
13. *Home Box Office v. FCC*, 567 F.2d 9 (1978).
14. *Denver Area Educational Telecommunications Consortium v. FCC*, 116 S.Ct. 2374 (1996).

10 Cyberspace Issues

The Internet has changed the way the law is broken, but it has not changed the law.

Andrew Oosterbaan
U.S. Department of Justice

LEARNING OBJECTIVES

As a result of reading this chapter, students should:

- Understand the unique challenges presented by the Internet and other new technologies and be prepared to discuss the role of the government in regulating (or not regulating) such technologies.
- Be prepared to discuss in class their opinions regarding the legal and ethical issues raised by personal web pages and social networking sites such as MySpace.com.

Attempts at Internet Regulation

While the courts have generally upheld the government's authority to regulate traditional forms of broadcasting such as television and radio, that is not the case with the Internet. Advocates of cyberspace regulation claim that the Internet is similar to traditional forms of broadcasting because it involves transmission through an electronic forum. Opponents of Internet regulation, however, point out that the three factors that justify the regulation of traditional broadcast media—public ownership, scarcity, and pervasiveness—are absent in the case of cyberspace. There is also a bigger matter—practicality. With millions of websites accessible via the Internet—and many of them originating in other countries—politicians realized long ago that any attempts to regulate the content of the Internet would be futile. Whether to apply standards—such as those spelling out the differences between hate speech and fighting words, between obscenity and nonobscene sexual expression, and between libelous and nonlibelous content—is a subject of continued debate.

In terms of both obscenity and nonobscene sexual expression, Congress has made three attempts to regulate sexual content on the Internet. The first attempt to regulate the Internet—the Communications Decency Act (CDA)—was part of the Telecommunications Act of 1996. The controversy surrounding the CDA reached the Supreme Court in 1997 in the case of *Reno v. American Civil Liberties Union*. The ACLU filed suit against Attorney General Janet Reno, challenging the Justice Department's authority to enforce the CDA. The Court ruled in favor of the ACLU and declared parts of the CDA unconstitutional and unenforceable.[1]

The court found two problems with the CDA. First, it failed to take into account established definitions for obscenity and indecency. Because of the well-established precedents in which the Court had ruled that obscenity can be prohibited but indecency cannot, the Court ruled that the CDA was unconstitutional as it was written.

The second problem was that the law was deemed to be vague and overbroad. In addition to failing to draw a distinction between obscenity and indecency, the law also used terms such as *lewd, lascivious,* and *annoying*—terms the Court found to be too open-ended. In its majority opinion, the Court referred to the Internet as an "electronic town crier" and that it would be difficult to separate the political speech from sexual expression. Further, the Court ruled, it would be impractical to hold the providers responsible for indecent or obscene traffic.

In writing their dissenting opinions, two justices suggested that Congress make another attempt at regulating objectionable content on the Internet. It did so in 1998, adopting the Child Online Protection Act (COPA), which prohibited commercial website operators from making sexually explicit material available to minors. COPA was signed into law by President Clinton in 1998 and endorsed by the Bush administration that followed. COPA was challenged by the ACLU, which claimed it represented the interests of online booksellers, artists, and operators of websites offering how-to sex advice or health information. A Federal District Court in Pennsylvania ruled in *American Civil Liberties Union v. Reno* that COPA was also unconstitutional because it did not rectify the CDA's shortcomings. That ruling was upheld by the Supreme Court in the 2004 case of *Ashcroft v. ACLU.*[2]

Even before the Supreme Court's ruling on COPA, Congress made a third attempt at Internet regulation. In 2000, it passed the Children's Internet Protection Act (CIPA), which required schools receiving government funding to install filtering devices in libraries and computer labs to prevent students from accessing sexually explicit materials. In early 2003, a Federal Appeals Court ruled that CIPA was also unconstitutional.[3] The Supreme Court reversed that decision and determined that the filtering devices were reasonable "time, place, and manner" restrictions that did not violate the First Amendment. As a result, CIPA is still in effect.[4]

Just as the federal government has limited ability to regulate content on the Internet, many school administrators have attempted to punish students for comments attributed to them on their personal websites and on social networking services such as MySpace.com—only to be forced into reversing those actions under the threat of legal action. In 2003, for example, a New Jersey student was

Children's access to sexually explicit material on the Internet has been the subject of several attempts at federal legislation, but the Supreme Court has found most of those laws unconstitutional because they also limit access to the same material by adults.

suspended for a week and banned from his high school baseball team for stating on his personal web page that his school was the "worst on the planet." The American Civil Liberties Union successfully sued the school on the students' behalf, forcing the school to issue a letter of apology and pay his legal fees. In 2006, a high school student in Colorado was suspended for fifteen days for comments he made on MySpace about the physical condition of his school building. His suspension was overturned after the ACLU threatened legal action.[5]

Defamation on the Internet

In addition to presenting new challenges for the concept of free speech as a whole, the Internet has created controversy over the issue of defamation.

In most cases, the courts have ruled that the legal liability of Internet Service Providers [ISP] for libelous content depends heavily on the amount of editorial control the ISP exercises. Because most ISPs do not regulate the content of material disseminated on their networks (and often post disclaimers to that effect), they are largely immune from libel suits.

One of the first such cases took place in 1991. In *Cubby v. CompuServe,* one ISP sued another, claiming it was libeled by a third party on the latter's bulletin board, appropriately called "Rumorville." A Federal District Court in New York ruled that because the defendant exercised no editorial control over the content, it could not be liable.[6]

In 1997, Sidney Blumenthal, a senior staff member in the Clinton Administration, filed a $30 million libel suit against Internet columnist Matt Drudge over a story that accused Blumenthal of abusing his wife. The two agreed to an undisclosed out-of-court settlement in 2001.[7]

In 2003, a Federal District Court made a similar ruling in a case involving non-commercial sites known as web logs or "blogs." In those cases, the liability for defamatory content was determined to apply to the individuals who posted the content and not to the individual or company hosting the site. The defendant in the case claimed that as the manager of a politically oriented blog, she could not be responsible for the accuracy of the more than 200 messages posted each day, nearly all of which would be protected speech under the "fair comment" defense.[8]

The New York State Supreme Court made the opposite ruling in the 1995 case of *Stratton Oakmont v. Prodigy Services Co.* A securities investment firm won a financial settlement from an Internet service provider that allowed libelous comments to be posted on a message board. The court ruled that because the company claimed in its literature to have editorial control over the content posted on message boards, it was liable as a publisher.[9] In the late 1990s and early 2000s, individuals who could prove they were libeled on commercially hosted websites in which the ISPs claimed to monitor content were successful in winning libel suits—or settling out of court for undisclosed financial compensation.

Internet consultant Reid Goldsborough says the threat of libel suits resulting from commentary on the Internet is largely overstated. "Anybody who has participated in online discussions for any period of time has undoubtedly seen libel accusations bandied about," he wrote in a 2001 article. "Little of this ever goes anywhere . . . . this, however, doesn't stop people from hiring lawyers to try to intimidate others into offering online apologies. Your best bet is to stick to the issues and avoid personal attacks. Your mother's advice still holds: Think before you speak."[10]

As for commercially hosted sites, however, traditional libel law still applies because the information is staff-produced and presented in the context of news rather than opinion.

Employer Regulation of Internet Traffic

While the government is unwilling or unable to regulate communication over the Internet, that is not the case with private industry. Employers often monitor incoming and outgoing email traffic on company-owned computer networks. Not only are they trying to prevent the unauthorized release of company information, but they are also attempting to limit other forms of communication that may result in lawsuits involving libel, privacy, or sexual or racial harassment.

Experts in the fields of both law and technology point out that when individuals use their employer's computer equipment and Internet access to vent in cyberspace, their bulletin board postings and electronic mail postings are not as private as they might believe. In an effort to prevent employees from engaging in libelous speech or otherwise exposing the company to legal liability, many large employers monitor employee email traffic and hire outside consultants to develop systems for determining the origin of anonymous postings to industry bulletin boards. "If you work at a Fortune 500 company, chances are good your email has been reviewed at least once," says Joan Feldman, founder of the Seattle-based Computer Forensics Inc., which helps companies track their employees' illegal or unethical use of company-owned technology.[11]

While some free speech and privacy advocates claim that employer monitoring of email violates the rights of employees, recent news stories provide the best evidence of the dangers that companies face by not doing so. When investigators looking into allegations of financial wrongdoing at Enron in 2003 gained access to archived computer files, for example, they found pornography, racial comments, offensive jokes, and other material in employee email that would have exposed the company to lawsuits if it had been detected before it went bankrupt.

Regulating Unwanted Commercial Messages

Shortly after the Internet experienced its initial growth spurt in the mid-1990s, marketers began sending unsolicited messages via electronic mail on a mass scale. The gathering and selling of individual email addresses became an underground industry, and the resulting inbox clutter became known as **spam.** Many of the incoming messages are disguised to appear to be personal in nature, a tactic known as **spoofing.**

Beyond the simple annoyance of spam, the vulnerability of electronic mail to intrusion by unwanted parties leads to more serious consequences. Some criminals send users phony email messages that attempt to deceive the recipients into thinking the communication is coming from their bank or credit union. The messages often use logos and graphics that are difficult to differentiate from the authentic ones and ask the recipient to provide personal identification numbers such as birthdates or social security numbers. The result is **identify theft,** a crime in which the person's information is used to open bank accounts and credit card accounts to be used for fraudulent activities. Many criminals send out phony solicitations in mass quantity, knowing that even if only a small number of recipients are duped into providing personal information, the resulting information will make the endeavor worthwhile. The tactic of sending out mass emailings for this purpose is known as **phishing.** While the Federal Trade Commission and Justice Department have been able to prosecute some offenders for the more serious crime of fraud, the financial institutions whose logos have been re-created on phony websites have had little success in suing the offending parties for trade-mark infringement.

Companies that depend heavily on employee email networks have responded to problems such as spamming and spoofing by purchasing filtering devices that block incoming email that appears to be of a commercial nature. Without such filters, many companies claim their email servers would be so cluttered with spam that they would be unable to function smoothly for legitimate business purposes. For their individual customers, Internet service providers offer filters to use on their home computers. To combat identify theft, banks and credit card companies provide some degree of fraud protection, but also admonish their customers to be wary of incoming unsolicited email.

Although many states have established laws restricting unsolicited email, the laws are difficult to enforce for two reasons. The anonymous nature of the Internet allows senders to disguise their locations, making prosecutions difficult. There are also jurisdictional problems; if the message originates in one state but is received in another, there is often confusion as to which state law should apply.

In order to address this second problem, in 2003 Congress passed the Can-Spam Act, a law that requires mass emailers to label unsolicited email as "advertising" or "sexually explicit" and to offer recipients the right to "opt out" of receiving future messages. Spammers are also prohibited from using artificial return addresses and from harvesting email addresses from other Internet sites.

Government prosecutions under state and federal laws are still rare, but in some cases Internet service providers have taken matters in their own hands and sued marketers for using their networks to send unwanted commercial messages. One significant case in this area was *Cyber Promotions v. America Online* (1996), in which a federal court ruled in favor of an Internet service provider that attempted to block a marketing company's usage of its network to send unsolicited commercial messages. The court ruled that commercial interests do not have a First Amendment right to use an ISP as a conduit to reach its subscribers.[12]

Frequently Asked Questions
about the Internet

1. *How did the Internet get started, and who decided that it should not be regulated?* The history of the Internet can be traced back to the mid-1950s, when the Department of Defense needed a communication system that could withstand a worldwide nuclear war. Prompted by the Soviet Union's 1957 launch of the first artificial satellite, Sputnik, the U.S. government created the Advanced Research Projects Agency (ARPA) to conduct the necessary research and construct the infrastructure for such a network. The result was **ArpaNet,** a system of military-controlled computers—similar to modern-day electronic mail servers—that would allow government officials and military leaders to communicate with each other in a national emergency. Few people outside of government and the military knew of the system is existence. The main feature of the system was that it was decentralized, meaning that no one nuclear strike would cause the system to fail. In the 1980s, a similar system called **BizNet** was created to connect businesses, research centers, and universities. In the 1990s, software developers created programs such as Gopher, Mosaic, and the World Wide Web, which expanded the use of computer networks far beyond simple electronic mail and created the Internet that we see today.

There was no conscious decision that the Internet should not be regulated, but the primary reason that any such attempt would be impractical is the same characteristic that made the old ArpaNet network appealing—its decentralized structure.

2. *Is defamation that occurs on the Internet considered libel or slander?* When websites became popular forums for political and social commentary in the mid-1990s, it was several years before the courts were able to decide on a consistent basis whether defamation that occurs on an Internet bulletin board or in a chat room would be considered libel or slander. Eventually, courts decided that because the Internet was more analogous to broadcasting than to casual conversation, laws dealing with libel were more applicable than those dealing with slander.

In the case of a simple electronic mail message from one individual to another individual or group, however, most courts would rule that such communication is subject to slander law rather than libel law and courts would therefore be reluctant to award significant damages due to the limited scope of the communication and the likely inability of the plaintiff to prove harm.

Point/Counterpoint: Regulation of the Internet

The rapid growth of the Internet as a forum for the transmission of hate speech and sexually explicit materials has prompted many politicians to suggest that the federal government exercise a greater degree of prior restraint on communication in cyberspace.

The movement in that direction began in the mid-1990s with the passage of the Communications Decency Act, which has since been found by the Supreme Court to be unconstitutional.

Why the Government Should Regulate Cyberspace

Regulating the Internet will protect children from obscenity, while allowing adults to view milder forms of pornography. Regulation could distinguish between obscenity and simple pornography, prohibiting the former and allowing the latter. "Some of the stuff online makes *Playboy* and *Hustler* look like Sunday-school stuff," said Senator James Exon, who proposed the original Communications Decency Act. "Just as we have laws against dumping garbage on the interstate, we ought to have similar laws for the information superhighway."[13]

Regulating the Internet will protect children from pedophiles and other criminals trying to lure them into meetings in the real world. One of the most alarming crime trends in the country involves the abduction, rape, and murder of children by adults they met online.

Regulating the Internet will reduce incidents of hate speech. According to hate-speech watchdog groups such as the Simon Wiesenthal Center and the Southern Poverty Law Center, the Internet has provided a new tool for hate groups to spread their message to new audiences.

Children's Internet usage habits cannot be as easily monitored as their television viewing habits. The CDA and other attempts to regulate cyberspace are necessary because parental controls are only of marginal value. Parental controls at one home cannot stop a child from accessing objectionable material at someone else's home.

Why the Government Should Not Regulate Cyberspace

Any attempt to regulate the Internet would be hopelessly overbroad. Even before the CDA reached the courts, many members in Congress objected to the CDA on both First Amendment and common-sense grounds. "(The CDA) might make us feel good," said Senator Patrick Leahy at a panel discussion held shortly after passage of the bill. "But it can toss an awful lot of valuable political, artistic, scientific, and health-related speech off the Internet."[14]

An attorney participating in the panel added that any benefit seen by the law would be "outweighed by the burden it imposes on protected speech and the First Amendment." Other experts pointed out that the CDA's use of terms such as *indecent* was "hopelessly vague" and that the law "created for parents the unrealistic belief that their children will be protected from objectionable online material."[15]

Protecting children from pornography and pedophiles is the responsibility of parents—not the government. "There are more serious problems—the homeless, crime. The government should let parents handle their kids," said one interviewee in a 1995 *Newsweek* article.[16]

The Internet is not as obtrusive as broadcasting, and the same rules should not apply. In order to access objectionable material on the Internet, an individual must seek it out, so any regulation that takes place should be at the receiver, not at the source.

Regulation of the Internet would be of little help in protecting kids from pedophiles. Ernie Allen, director of the National Center for Missing and Exploited Children, says the concern over children being abducted by online pedophiles has been "fueled by ten or twelve well-publicized cases."[17] Kids are also at risk when not online and can be as easily abducted walking home from school or visiting a public playground.

Regulation of the Internet would be of little help in fighting hate speech. "It is not possible to make anti-Semitism or (other forms of hate) go away by censoring them," says Mike Godwin of the Electronic Frontier Foundation.[18]

Chapter Summary

Much like the communications technologies that preceded it—radio and television—the Internet is a rapidly growing and changing phenomenon that presents unique challenges to those who seek to regulate it. Specific concepts such as political speech, commercial speech, hate speech, fighting words, defamation, sexual expression, and journalist privilege are just now beginning to be examined in the context of cyberspace, meaning that no significant accumulation of case law exists to help courts and legal scholars make critical legal determinations.

Because of its decentralized and open-ended nature, however, the Internet defies most regulatory schemes that are easily applicable to television and radio. Despite the impracticality (and eventual failure) of some early attempts at regulation, politicians and other concerned parties nevertheless continue to advocate government control of emerging technologies.

CASE PROBLEM

The Internet Communications Commission

After many years of discussion about regulation of the Internet (or the lack thereof), Congress is considering legislation that would create a new government agency to be called the Internet Communications Commission (ICC). The new agency would regulate the Internet just as the Federal Communications Commission (FCC) regulates the broadcasting industry, and the two agencies would be similar to each other in many ways. Much like the FCC, for example, the ICC would be run by a panel of five commissioners who would be appointed by the president and confirmed by Congress.

The scope of the ICC's authority would fall into four areas:

1. licensing and regulating Internet service providers in the same way that the FCC licenses and regulates television networks.
2. regulating sexual content by applying the Miller Test and Supreme Court definitions for obscenity, non-obscene sexual expression, and indecency.
3. prohibiting spam and other unwanted email and investigating Internet scams (taking over these responsibilities from the Federal Trade Commission).
4. regulating commercial sites such as Ebay and social networking sites such as MySpace and YouTube, including supervising the development of new sites.

You're a legislative aide to Senator Battson D. Belfry, and the senator is undecided about which way to vote on the proposed legislation. He's asked you for your opinion—not just an off-the-cuff "yes" or "no," but a well-thought-out analysis of the situation that explores the appropriateness of the ICC-FCC analogy. Consider the philosophy and rationale behind the FCC's authority to regulate the airwaves (from Chapter 9) and whether or not the same conditions apply to regulating cyberspace.

SOCRATIC DIALOGUE QUESTIONS

1. Suppose you use your home computer to produce a World Wide Web newsletter about city and county politics. Your newsletter includes complaints about local tax policies, the quality of local schools, and other issues such as garbage pick-up, street maintenance, and dangerous intersections in need of traffic lights. The city manager finds your website and believes that you have access to information not available to most other citizens, and he demands to know which city employees have been leaking information to you. He sends you a subpoena to appear in municipal court and reveal your sources of information. Are you protected by a state shield law? (Review the basics of shield laws in Chapter 8.)

2. Should personal web pages such as blogs, as well as social networking sights such as MySpace.com, be subject to defamation law? (Re-read the basics of defamation law in Chapter 6.)

3. To what degree should school administrators have the ability to punish students who criticize the school on their blogs and on social networking sites such as MySpace? What about threats? (Base your answer on the free speech principles discussed in Chapters 2 and 3.)

GLOSSARY OF TERMS

ArpaNet   A network of military computers developed in the 1950s in order to allow communication among government agencies and military installations in the event of nuclear war or other national emergency; ArpaNet is the forerunner of today's Internet.

BizNet   Another forerunner of today's Internet, this network was created in the 1980s to connect businesses, research centers, and universities.

Identify theft   A crime in which the person's information is used to open bank accounts and credit card accounts to be used for fraudulent activities.

Phishing   A method of sending out commercial messages in order to induce recipients to provide personal information that may later be used fraudulently.

Spam   Unwanted commercial messages received by electronic mail, many of which are sexually explicit in nature and/or associated with potentially fraudulent enterprises.

Spoofing   The method of disguising commercial electronic mail messages to appear to be personal in nature.

NOTES

1. *Reno v. American Civil Liberties Union*, 117 S.Ct. 2329 (1997).
2. *Ashcroft v. ACLU*, 535 U.S. 564 (2004).
3. *American Library Association v. United States*, 2002 U.S. Dist. Lexis 9537 (2002).
4. *United States v. American Library Association*, 539 U.S. 194 (2003).
5. "Dot-Commentary's Lessons." *USA Today*, June 6, 2006, p. 8-A.
6. *Cubby v. CompuServe*, 776 F. Supp. 135 (1991).
7. *Blumenthal v. Drudge*, 186 F.R.D. 236 (1999).
8. Juliana Barbassa, "Federal Court Protects Blogs From Libel Suits." Associated Press report, July 3, 2003.
9. *Stratton Oakmont v. Prodigy Services Co.*, 23 Media L. Rep. 1794 (1995).
10. Reid Goldsborough, "Warding Off Internet Legal Woes." *Public Relations Tactics*, July 2001, p. 6.

11. "More Companies Monitor Employee E-Mail." Associated Press report, March 11, 2002.

12. *Cyber Promotions v. America Online*, 948 F. Supp. 436 (1996).

13. Jim Exon, "Keep Porno Out of Children's Hands on the Internet." Scripps Howard News Service, April 16, 1995.

14. "Saving Children or Sacrificing Rights?" *The Freedom Forum News*, April 8, 1996, p. 1.

15. Ibid.

16. Steve Levy, "No Place for Kids." *Newsweek*, July 3, 1995, pp. 47–50.

17. Philip Elmer-DeWitt, "On a Screen Near You: Cyberporn." *Time*, July 3, 1995, pp. 38–45.

18. Tony Mauro, "Long Arm of the Law Reaches Into Cyberspace." *First Amendment News*, February 1998, p. 6.

11   Intellectual Property

> With the click of a mouse, copies can be made and distributed around the
> world. The original copyright owner may never know about the copies, much
> less be paid for them.
>
> Jonathan Newcomb
> President, Simon and Schuster

> The results of this case (MGM v. Grokster) upheld a very simple thought: Thou
> shalt not steal, even on the Internet.
>
> Andrew Lack
> Chief Executive Officer
> BMG Music Entertainment

LEARNING OBJECTIVES

As a result of reading this chapter, students should:

- Understand the basics of intellectual property law, with an emphasis on copyright law.
- Understand (and be prepared to discuss in class) how technology presents new challenges in determining ownership rights related to creative work and to what extent individuals and organizations can protect their creative work.

History of Intellectual Property Law

Much of American intellectual property law is grounded in Article I, Section 8, Clause 8, of the United States Constitution, which seeks to "promote the progress of science and the useful arts, by securing for limited times to authors and inventors the exclusive right to their respective writings and discoveries."

Protecting individual ownership of inventions through patents and protecting ownership of literary works through copyrights was not new to the United States, however; many of the same principles had been practiced for several centuries in Europe. In 1474, for example, the city of Venice, Italy, adopted a law giving legal ownership to inventors. Italian astronomer and inventor Galileo reportedly received such a "patent" for his 1594 invention of a water pump.

In England, the concept of "letters patent," later shortened to "patent," referred to the granting by the king or queen to a party the monopoly power over the commercial exploitation of an invention for a limited time. The laws were expressed in detail in the Statute of Monopolies, enacted in 1623. The Statute was the culmination of a lengthy conflict between the English Parliament and the crown to place limitations on royal power. The Statute was basically a method of formalizing the existing common law, which for centuries had already given inventors and authors the rights to their works.

Prior to the Revolutionary War, inventors and authors living in the American colonies were subject to the Statute of Monopolies. After the war, the governing bodies of the individual states assumed this authority. Prior to the drafting of the U.S. Constitution, nearly every state had enacted some form of copyright statute, but there was a great deal of inconsistency among them and few included provisions for enforcement. The government offices granting such privileges were not busy, however. In many of the colonies, the economies were based on agricultural production rather than manufacturing and publishing, and therefore patents and copyrights were not issued in large numbers.

In response to this problem of inconsistency and lack of enforcement power in the state statutes, the delegates to the second Continental Congress were prepared to revise the Articles of Confederation to include a provision granting power to the Congress to provide for patents and copyrights when they assembled in Philadelphia for the Constitutional Convention in the summer of 1787. During the proceedings, the need for intellectual property law was advocated by some of the nation's most influential individuals, including publisher Noah Webster and steamboat inventor John Fitch. In drafting the intellectual property clause, the designers of the Constitution were influenced by the Articles of Confederation as well as by English, colonial, and state practices regarding patents and copyrights. The main concerns of the founding fathers were protection for literature and maps, as those two materials were subject to the most piracy in England and the colonies at the time.

Areas of Intellectual Property Law

The four areas of intellectual property law recognized at the federal level are:

1. **Copyrights**—protection for creative works such as art, music, literature, still photographs, motion picture film, and video.
2. **Patents**—protection for tangible inventions or developments such as electronic and mechanical devices and chemical formulas.
3. **Trademarks**—protection for an organization's name or logo, or the name or logo of a product or service.
4. **Trade secrets**—protection for information or processes such as those used in manufacturing.

Copyrights and patents are covered by federal law only. Trademarks and trade secrets are covered by both federal and state law.

Copyrights

American copyright law has been expanded over the years to cover art prints, music, photographs, and paintings. In addition to being revised to cover different forms of expression, copyright laws have also been expanded to include all of the various recording methods that have been developed, including phonograph records, motion picture film, audiotape and videotape, computer disks, compact disks, and digital video disks.

The first specific copyright law was enacted by Congress in 1790. Major revisions were enacted in 1909, 1976, and 1998, and elements of all three revisions are still in effect today. The most important component of the 1909 revision is the works for hire doctrine, which deals with copyright conflicts between an organization and its employees. In short, the doctrine states that products created as part of an employee's assigned work duties belong to the employer and not to the individual employee. (The works for hire doctrine is discussed in more detail later in this chapter.)

The 1976 revisions dealt with the extension of limited copyright protection to unregistered works (sometimes called "common law copyright") and fair use— a set of exceptions that allow copyrighted material to be used for nonprofit or educational purposes without permission or compensation. The 1998 revisions dealt mostly with issues raised by the Internet and other technological developments.

Copyright Basics

Copyright Eligibility.   Ideas cannot be copyrighted, but a fixed or tangible expression of an idea, such as that expressed in a film, video, drawing, photograph, or piece of fiction or non-fiction writing, can be. Although it may not be in a fixed form to the same degree as material printed on paper or recorded on tape or film, much of the content found on the Internet is eligible for copyright protection (and in most cases is protected).

A copyright deals only with ownership; it has nothing to do with truth, quality, or social value. One could publish a magazine with content consisting entirely of falsehoods, and it would still be eligible for a copyright (the libel action would be a separate problem). The same rule applies to quality and taste; the copyright office makes no judgments about how good or how bad the product is. A poorly written movie script or pornographic film is nonetheless eligible for copyright protection.

One criterion the courts use to determine eligibility for copyright protection is the amount of originality or creativity that was involved in the development of the work. The **originality and creativity principle** was the deciding factor in several major Supreme Court cases involving conflicts between intellectual property law and the First Amendment. The basic principle is that the more originality and creativity involved in the creation of a work, the greater amount of copyright protection it receives. The courts generally rule that facts are not "created" but are only "discovered," and therefore a simple presentation of facts, without any creative arrangement or interpretation, is not deserving of copyright protection.

Example: If a history professor writes a book about the Civil War that is only a chronological presentation of known facts—without interpretation or commentary on those facts—it does not deserve much copyright protection. But if the author adds some interpretation, opinion, or commentary, that increases the amount of copyright protection because the author has expended more effort. If the author uses the Civil War as the backdrop for a historical novel—starting with known historical facts and adding fictional characters and dialogue—it receives even more protection because of the greater degree of creativity and effort involved.

Generally, fiction gets more protection than non-fiction. Collections of facts have very little protection, so companies that compile mailing lists, telephone directories, and computer databases find it difficult to protect them because of court rulings that no special effort, creativity, or skill is involved in compiling them.

One of the earliest conflicts involving application of the "originality and creativity" principle was the 1918 case of *International News Service v. Associated Press*. The Supreme Court ruling in this case established the principle that facts cannot be copyrighted, but an original presentation of facts can be. A newspaper can copyright a story it has published based on facts, but it cannot copyright the facts themselves.

International News Service (INS) was a worldwide news-gathering agency that was in competition with the Associated Press (AP), but it borrowed generously from AP wire stories and disseminated the information as its own. When AP filed suit, the INS tried to claim that AP was just reporting the facts, and because facts could not be copyrighted, it could take whatever it wanted off the AP wire. The Supreme Court ruled in favor of AP, however. The Court acknowledged the principle that facts cannot be copyrighted but ruled that, in this case, a certain arrangement of facts, such as that in a news story, is eligible for copyright protection. The court ruled that competing news agencies could use each other's wires for news tips, but could not copy the text itself.[1]

In the 1981 case of *Miller v. University City Studios*, a federal appeals court ruled that a fact does not belong to the person who discovered it. The court used that justification in ruling against a newspaper reporter who sued a studio that produced a motion picture based loosely on a book he had written about a widely publicized kidnapping. While the film included many details that had been reported only in the book—including errors—the court determined that the studio had a right to use the facts the author had discovered and arrange them in a different form of expression. The author therefore failed to meet the "substantial similarity" test (explained later in this chapter).[2]

Prior to 1991, the courts often considered both "originality and creativity" as well as "effort" when determining the level of copyright protection a work deserved. Considering the level of effort expended was sometimes referred to as the **sweat of the brow rule;** the more effort expended by the creator, the higher degree of copyright protection the work deserved. The 1991 case of *Feist Publications v. Rural Telephone Co.*, however, drew a distinction between "originality" and "effort" and established the rule that originality and creativity were more important.

The conflict began when competing telephone companies were in a dispute over a list of names and telephone numbers. Rural Telephone Company (RTC) published a local telephone directory but declined to sell its directory listings to Feist, a larger publisher attempting to publish a regional directory. When Feist appropriated the listings over the objections of Rural Telephone Company (the smaller company was able to prove infringement by including four fictitious names among the 1,300 names in the directory), RTC filed a copyright infringement complaint.

On the surface, this case appeared to be a clear example of copyright infringement, but after many years of litigation and appeals, the U.S. Supreme Court sided with the larger company. It applied the originality and creativity principle and ruled that assembling a list of names and telephone numbers required no special creativity, and therefore that list was not eligible for copyright protection. In its majority opinion, the Court stated that all the larger company had done was to "take the data provided by its subscribers and list it alphabetically by surname" and the resulting book was "a garden variety white pages directory, devoid of even the slightest trace of creativity."[3]

In a similar case in 1997, a Federal Appeals Court ruled in the case of *Warren Publishing Co. v. Microdos Data Corp.* that copyright protection did not apply to an industry directory because it was merely a collection of factual information.[4]

Copyright Notice.   The copyright notice consists of three parts: the copyright symbol (or the word "copyright"), the year, and identification of the copyright holder. Examples:

> © 2008 Allyn and Bacon
> copyright 2008 Allyn and Bacon

In order for a work to receive full copyright protection, the holder must submit a form to the government and pay a small fee. For most items, two copies of the work must be submitted—one for the copyright office to keep on file, and the other to be on file at the Library of Congress. Although a work is copyrighted once it is in a fixed form and registration is not required, such action is still recommended and is legally advantageous (the concept of an "unregistered" or "common law copyright" is discussed later in this chapter).

Length of Copyright Protection.   Under current law, copyright protection for work created by an individual lasts for seventy years past the life of the creator. For work created by an organization, copyright protection lasts for 120 years after its creation or ninety-five years after its first usage, whichever comes first. Prior to passage of the Sonny Bono Copyright Term Extension Act of 1998, each of those time periods was twenty years shorter. The new terms now apply retroactively to works created prior to 1998.

Public Domain. Works said to be in the **public domain** can be used by others without permission or compensation. Public domain applies to four categories of work:

1. Works that hold special social, cultural, or scientific significance, such as The Bible, the Constitution, The Declaration of Independence, the music and lyrics to "The Star-Spangled Banner," the design for the American flag, or the Periodic Table of the Elements, which appears in most chemistry textbooks.
2. Works that are so basic as to have no significant value, such as calendars or height/weight charts.
3. Documents produced by the federal government. Research reports or other works created by private parties using government funding may be copyrighted, but not government documents such as census reports or similar materials.
4. Works for which the copyright has expired, including songs such as "Here Comes the Bride," "Pomp and Circumstance," patriotic marches, and church hymns. A common misconception is that the song "Happy Birthday to You" is in the public domain, but it is not. Warner Communications holds the copyright, which expires in 2030. (For more detail, see Frequently Asked Questions, no. 6, later in this chapter.)

Rights of the Copyright Holder. Holding a copyright gives the owner the right to control four aspects of the work:

1. Derivatives (making books into movies, television shows, etc.).
2. Distribution (how a product is bought and sold).
3. Performance and display.
4. Copying.

Proving Infringement. **Infringement** is the term used to describe violation of an individual's or company's copyright. In order to have a successful claim, the plaintiff must prove (1) access (the fact that the defendant had the opportunity to copy the material), and (2) substantial similarity between the two items in question. "Access" is important to prove because it helps to negate one of the common defenses—coincidence. It is often easy for a defendant to claim that the similarity is a coincidence, and difficult for the plaintiff to prove that it was not.

Both the entertainment industry and the court system acknowledge the fact that nearly every possible story line for motion pictures and television programs has been exhausted, and therefore the difficulty of finding completely new ideas means that the threshold of "substantial similarity" gets harder to meet. In his 2005 book, *The Movie Business*, entertainment lawyer Kelly Crabb explains this using a parable about a screenwriter developing a story about a young couple and worrying about its similarity to *Romeo and Juliet*. "Even if *Romeo and Juliet* was under copyright protection (which it isn't), that protection would not prevent you from doing a story about two young lovers caught in a tragic enmity between their respective families," Crabb wrote. "The mere fact that your story plot has two young lovers, involves their families who hate each other, and has an unhappy ending is not enough to stop you."[5]

Works for Hire

The **works for hire doctrine,** first introduced into copyright law with the 1909 revision, deals with the legal differences that exist between the relationships that companies have with their regular employees and the relationships between companies and independent contractors.

The basic difference is that materials created by regular employees belong to the employer, not the employee. In the case of freelancers or independent contractors, however, whatever they create belongs to them after the first usage unless a written agreement or contract with a "works for hire" clause has been signed by both parties.

The works for hire principle was the key issue in the 1989 case of *Community for Creative Non-Violence v. Reid.* The Community for Creative Non-Violence (CCNV) was a nonprofit organization dedicated to drawing attention to and reducing the problem of homelessness. In the fall of 1985, the organization hired sculptor James Earl Reid to design a display that combined a biblical manger scene with a modern-day portrayal of a homeless family. The parties did not sign any written agreements, and neither mentioned copyright.

After the finished product was displayed at a month-long CCNV event in Washington, D.C., the organization announced plans to take it on a nationwide tour. Reid objected, fearing it would be damaged in the process. He requested that it be returned to him, and that started a four-year dispute that began in Federal District Court and ended in the U.S. Supreme Court.

The lower court ruled in favor of Reid, claiming that because Reid was not an employee and no "works for hire" agreement was executed, the artwork belonged to him. The U.S. Court of Appeals for the District of Columbia and the U.S. Supreme Court agreed[6], and the case set the standard for how organizations would deal with freelance writers, photographers, and other independent contractors for the next two decades (and likely beyond).

Public Performance and Display of Copyrighted Work

Copyright law prohibits protected material from being performed or displayed without compensation of the copyright holder. In order to streamline the compensation process, music publishers register their work with one of three organizations—the American Society of Composers, Artists, and Performers (ASCAP), Broadcast Music, Inc. (BMI), or Sound Exchange. The organizations collect fees from parties wishing to use copyrighted music and then distribute those proceeds to the copyright holders.

The rights purchased through a licensing fee are called "blanket rights" because they apply to all of the work under control of the licensing organization, sparing the purchaser from having to specify which work they want to use.

Blanket rights fall into two categories. "Performance rights" allow radio stations, bars, restaurants, and other public venues to play copyrighted music; the annual fee is based primarily on the size of the potential audience. Schools and churches are exempt from the licensing procedure provided they do not charge admission to the events at which the music is played. "Synchronization rights" are purchased by television and motion picture producers that wish to use a piece of music as background for a video production, thus creating a new product.

For many years, the three licensing organizations did not require small retail stores, restaurants, and bars to pay licensing fees provided they use home-style radios and speakers rather than commercial-quality equipment. This exception was codified by the Fairness in Music Licensing Act of 1998, which applied to "small" retail stores of less than 2,000 square feet and bars and restaurants of less than 3,750 square feet.

The licensing process just described applies only to the *playing* of a recorded version of a work. When artists *perform* someone else's copyrighted music in a nightclub or at a live concert, it is the responsibility of the venue or event organizer to arrange for licensing. If an artist wishes to perform another's work in public, or plans to re-record or "cover" another artist's work, he or she must pay a fee to the original copyright holder. Even incorporating a few notes or lyrics from someone else's copyrighted song into a new song, known in the music industry as "sampling," requires the permission of the copyright holder.

Copyright Revision Act of 1976

The 1976 revision of copyright law introduced two concepts that had not been addressed in previous copyright laws: (1) unregistered copyright, sometimes called a **common law copyright** and (2) **fair use.** Both concepts are at the heart of many copyright cases debated today.

Unregistered or "Common Law" Copyright.   Prior to 1976, authors and publishers making a claim of copyright infringement had to have formally registered their work with the U.S. Copyright Office. While registration is still recommended and is legally advantageous, it is no longer absolutely required to make a copyright claim, due to a clause in the 1976 revision that recognizes that an author's work is legally protected as soon as it is completed, even if never registered. A common law copyright gives the copyright holder the right to prevent unauthorized use of his or her work, but not the right to recover financial damages, for which the copyright must be formally registered.

The most common examples of the common law copyright principle being applied are in the cases of photographs taken for a model's portfolio or an actor's press packet, works of fiction or poetry submitted in amateur writing competitions, and proposals for creative projects such as movie screenplays or television pilots.

A California state court made a ruling based on a similar principle, even though the case was decided seven years before the idea of an unregistered copyright was codified by the Copyright Act Revision of 1976. In *Williams v. Weisser* (1969), a court ruled that a university professor's lectures were protected by copyright law, even though they were not registered with the copyright office.

The plaintiff at the trial court level (the defendant on appeal) was J. Edwin Weisser, owner of a company called Class Notes, Inc., which hired students at the University of California at Los Angeles to take notes in their classes. The students would then type and organize the notes in order for the company to reproduce and sell them to other students in those classes. The university had been aware of the company's practice, but in a 1964 policy memo announced it was up to individual professors to determine whether or not to allow it. None objected until 1965, when anthropology professor B. J. Williams sued the company for violating his copyright interests and for invasion of privacy.

Courts have ruled that a professor's lecture notes are protected by copyright law, even though they are not formally registered with the U.S. Copyright Office.

Williams based his privacy claim on the fact that his name was used to promote the sale of the notes without his permission, a violation of appropriation law (discussed in Chapter 7). Weisser claimed that the university, as Williams's employer, should be the only party to have standing to file the suit, but a Los Angeles County Superior Court ruled that Williams was the true copyright holder and therefore did have such standing. Ruling that Williams could protect his work even without a formal copyright, it awarded him $1,000 in compensatory damages and $500 in punitive damages, both of which were upheld on appeal by the California Supreme Court.[7]

Today, courts continue to rule that college professors' lecture notes and similar materials are protected by the "unregistered copyright" principle.

Fair Use. **Fair use** is a set of exemptions in the copyright law that allow for the usage of copyrighted materials for certain nonprofit purposes. The concept was officially recognized in Section 107 of the Copyright Revision Act of 1976. Examples include (1) news reporting and criticism and (2) classroom teaching and academic research. The main limitations of fair use are that copies are reasonable in number, are not sold for profit, and are used for a brief period of time. The law does not define terms such as *reasonable in number* and *brief periods of time*, meaning that plaintiffs must either pursue copyright infringement cases against or negotiate agreements with alleged copyright infringers. A third category of fair use application is that of **parody**—a concept also found in privacy/appropriation law. The "brief period of time" rule would not apply to parodies, however, and potential plaintiffs would have little or no basis in claiming financial loss.

When evaluating fair use cases, courts take a number of factors into consideration:

1. Purpose and character of the use, including whether such use is for some nonprofit or educational purpose or for commercial purposes.
2. The nature of the copyrighted work. The greater degree of originality and creativity involved in the production of a work, the greater degree of copyright protection it receives. As an example, a work of fiction deserves more protection than business directories and similar works of nonfiction.
3. The amount of substantiality of the portion used in relation to the copyrighted work as a whole. In "fair use" cases involving educators, court decisions often turn on factors such as "brevity" and "spontaneity." For published works such as articles or book chapters, "brevity" is defined as a work of 2,500 words or less, reprinted in its entirety; or for longer works, a maximum of either 10 percent of the work or 1,000 words, whichever is less. But these definitions are guidelines rather than hard-and-fast rules, and in some cases even brief excerpts can result in a copyright infringement complaint if such borrowing harms the market value of the original work. "Spontaneity" means that the copying is done on such short notice that requesting the copyright holder's permission could not be done in a timely manner. Brevity and spontaneity are less relevant in commercial

cases, as the courts allow commercial parties less leeway than they provide to educators.

4. The effect of the use on the value of or potential market for the copyrighted work. Plaintiffs in copyright cases bear the burden of proving if, and to what degree, the copyright infringement resulted in financial harm.

The "news reporting and criticism" provision means that journalists may use brief or reasonable excerpts from copyrighted works in published or broadcast news stories without permission. Book reviewers, television critics, and movie critics may also do so. There is no definition for what constitutes "brief" and "reasonable," but since most news stories and reviews are beneficial to the work rather than harmful, this element of "fair use" is seldom challenged.

One example of the "fair use" doctrine applied to news reporting is the 1990 case of *New Kids on the Block v. News America Publishing*. At the heart of the case was a newspaper survey that asked, "Who is your favorite member of New Kids on the Block?" The musical group's agent filed a copyright complaint, claiming that the group did not authorize the newspaper to use its name. But the newspaper successfully argued that its survey was part of its news-gathering function and it did not need permission to use the group's name.[8]

The category of "classroom teaching and academic research" raises issues for educators at all levels, from kindergarten through graduate school. Soon after the 1976 revision was adopted, a series of court rulings and congressional actions clarified that educators may copy portions of books and periodicals for distribution to students provided the proportion is "reasonable" and the copies are not sold. In 1981, this allowance was expanded to include broadcast television programs (except those shown on a pay-per-view basis) for classroom usage. Computer software may not be copied, however.

Even though it was decided a year before the Copyright Revision Act of 1976, the case of *Williams & Wilkins Co. v. United States* (1975) is significant, as it dealt with government photocopying in locations such as government offices, libraries, and archives. The case originated when a publisher of various medical journals sued the federal government because agencies such as the National Institutes of Health and the National Library of Medicine frequently made photocopies of articles, upon request, for physicians and researchers.

The court determined that the practice was acceptable, ruling that government agencies could make copies of copyrighted works for internal distribution provided that the agencies established reasonable limitations on the number of copies made and did not charge a fee to the recipients of the copies. When the case was appealed, the Supreme Court was deadlocked at 4–4 with one justice abstaining, so the ruling of the lower court remained in effect.[9]

Another significant fair use case was *Basic Books v. Kinko's Graphics Corporation*, argued in a New York District Court in 1991. Basic Books, representing ten major textbook publishers, had filed suit against Kinko's Graphics Corporation, parent company of a nationwide chain of photocopying shops, for copyright infringement. The publishers charged that the copy shops, most of which were located near college campuses, copied excerpts from textbooks, compiled them into course packets, and sold them to students for profit. Kinko's called the practice "Professor Publishing" and promoted it as one of its primary services to educational institutions.

The plaintiffs claimed that Kinko's actions were beyond the provision of "fair use" and harmed the potential market for the source material from which the copies were made.

While the court acknowledged that educational use of copied material does constitute a nonprofit enterprise and is therefore worthy of fair use consideration, the fact that Kinko's made a profit from the copying constituted a commercial use and so that copying was not entitled to fair use protection. Kinko's admitted during the proceedings that the selling of course packets was done at a profit and that its "Professor Publishing" was one of its most profitable services. The court drew a distinction between the *Williams* case, in which there were a limited number of copies being made with no substantial effect on the market for the original products, and the Kinko's case, in which copy shops engaged in mass copying— both in terms of the proportion of the original work copied as well as the total number of copies generated—and harmed the potential market for the original works. The court therefore ruled that commercial copying, such as that in the Kinko's case, is not entitled to fair use protection, but "library" and "nonprofit" copying, such as in the case of *Williams & Wilkins Co. v. United States*, does fall within fair use guidelines.

In the Kinko's case, in order to bolster their claim that the amount and proportion of the works copied were too excessive to be considered fair use, the plaintiffs provided five examples of Kinko's course packets, which involved twelve works they considered instances of copyright infringement. The twelve items ranged in length from fourteen to 110 pages and constituted 8 to 25 percent of the original works from which they were taken. Many were book chapters taken as individual units and "anthologized" with chapters from other texts to create customized texts.

In responding to the plaintiffs' claim that the copying "unfavorably impacts upon plaintiffs' sales of their books and collections of permissions fees," Kinko's pointed out that many of the books it copied were out of print, and therefore it was not possible to harm the potential sale of books that were no longer for sale. The plaintiffs, however, claimed that harm to out-of-print books was even greater because permissions fees were the only source of income for the authors and copyright owners involved. The court agreed.

The court found considerable merit to the plaintiffs' claim that Kinko's had gone into the publishing business and was competing against them. The court also drew a distinction between Kinko's profit-making copying activities and other cases in which profit was not a factor, such as *Sony Corp. v. Universal City Studios* (1984). (In that case, a court ruled that simply copying a television program on a home videocassette recorder to view it later was within fair use.)[10]

In the Kinko's case, the court awarded Basic Books and the co-plaintiffs injunctive relief and statutory damages in the amount of $510,000, and ordered the defendant to pay legal fees and court costs.[11]

A year after the Kinko's decision, in *Princeton University Press v. Michigan Document Services* (1992), three publishers won a judgment against Michigan Document Services in Federal District Court. The court ruled, and a Circuit Court of Appeals later agreed, that the copying and for-profit sales of copyrighted materials did not constitute "fair use," regardless of the educational connection.[12]

Following the *Kinko's* and *Princeton* cases, many copy shops began to offer "copyright clearance" services to faculty; the copy shops would contact copyright holders and negotiate royalties to be incorporated into the purchase price of the coursepacks and passed on to the copyright holder. The services have met with moderate success, but for many professors they are impractical because of the lengthy lead time necessary to obtain permission. Some copy shops still print copyrighted material without permission, and at least nineteen such cases resulted in copyright suits filed between 2002 and 2006. Most were settled out of court and in favor of the publishers, with copy shops paying the plaintiffs' legal fees and agreeing to seek copyright clearance in the future.

One of the important provisions of the "fair use" principle is that copying is done on a not-for-profit basis. That principle was tested in the mid-1990s when a consortium of authors, led by Jack O'Dwyer, publisher of two public relations industry newsletters, accused the Public Relations Society of America (PRSA) of copyright infringement. For many years, PRSA had operated an Information Center that archived articles from national news publications, professional journals, and industry newsletters. Upon request, PRSA employees organized articles into packets based on subject headings and shipped them, for a fee, to both members and non-members. PRSA claimed that it was not selling the packets, merely "loaning" them for three-week periods. O'Dwyer claimed, however, that PRSA had no realistic plan for retrieving the packets or preventing recipients from making their own photocopies before returning them.

For more than three years, PRSA insisted that the Information Center was a service that fell within the guidelines of fair use, even though O'Dwyer claimed that recipients were charged fees that far exceeded the cost of staff time, photocopying, and postage incurred. No lawsuit was filed and PRSA offered no compensation to the authors, but PRSA apologized to the authors, renamed the service "The Professional Resource Center," and agreed to refrain from copying articles other than those found in PRSA publications.[13]

The concept of "parody" is applied in fair use cases in which one work may resemble another but is different enough to avoid confusion among the audience. Examples include entertainers who write and perform songs that are similar to better-known works but in which the lyrics have been changed for the purposes of humor, such as 2 Live Crew's 1980 parody of Roy Orbison's song, "Pretty Woman" (*Campbell v. Acuff-Rose Music Co.*[14]) and numerous parodies by "Weird Al" Yankovich. Courts have ruled that such parodies are not copyright infringement, partly because there is no financial loss suffered by the copyright holder and because there is no impact on the potential market for the performer's original material. In addition, parodies are generally protected against copyright infringement cases because many take the form of commentary or criticism and therefore have First Amendment value.

While musicians have a great deal of leeway in applying the parody principle, book authors have not been as successful.

In 2001, the estate of *Gone With the Wind* author Margaret Mitchell reached an out-of-court settlement with Houghton Mifflin over the publication of a book titled *The Wind Done Gone,* which author Alice Randall claimed was a parody of the better-known Civil War novel but which told the story from a slave's point of view. A trial court had issued an injunction to stop publication of the book, agreeing with the Mitchell estate that it borrowed too many settings, characters, and other plot elements from the original and went beyond the provisions of parody and fair use. A Circuit Court of Appeals reversed the ruling and claimed the trial court's decision was a form of prior restraint that violated the First Amendment. Before the case could be appealed to the U.S. Supreme Court, the two parties reached a settlement that allowed the book to be published, with a portion of the proceeds being donated to Morehouse College, a historically black institution in Atlanta. The agreement also allowed Randall to retain the movie rights to her book.[15]

A few years earlier, a similar case involved a novel titled *Lo's Diary.* The authors claimed their book was a parody of Vladimir Nabokov's *Lolita* but was told through the eyes of a different character. After a lengthy legal battle, the two sides agreed to simply split the royalties from the second book.[16]

Digital Millennium Copyright Act of 1998

In 1998, Congress passed the Digital Millennium Copyright Act (DMCA), the first major revision of copyright law since 1976. The DMCA had two main purposes: (1) to address cyberspace issues and (2) to bring U.S. copyright laws into closer alignment with those of other countries. Advocates of the law included lobbyists representing movie producers, television producers, music publishers, and Internet service providers.

The DMCA has two main components:

1. Punishment for circumvention—making it illegal to manufacture or sell software that breaks the encryption codes used in computerized communication. The advocates said that this provision was needed not because of technology that existed at the time but because of technology that might be developed in the future.
2. Limited liability for online service providers for copyright infringement that takes place on their networks, meaning that Internet Service Providers (ISPs) are not required to be the "copyright police." This component includes, however, a **notification clause** that requires ISPs to remove copyrighted material upon request of the copyright holder. It also provides ISPs with immunity from liability when they remove copyrighted material.

In the same session in which it passed the DMCA, Congress also lengthened the term of copyright extension by twenty years (see details previously in this chapter). The law was named the Sonny Bono Copyright Term Extension Act to honor the late musician-turned-congressman who advocated the legislation.

Recent and Ongoing Issues in Copyright Law

Challenges to Copyright Extension.   The Sonny Bono Copyright Term Extension Act (CTEA) was challenged in 2003 by Internet service providers, librarians, and other parties seeking access to copyrighted materials that were originally sched-uled to move into the public domain in the near future. In *Eldred v. Ashcroft*, plain-tiffs pointed to the example of Mickey Mouse, a copyrighted character of the Disney Corporation, which first appeared in Disney's "Steamboat Willie" in 1928. That copyright was set to expire in 2003, but as a result of the CTEA, that date was pushed back to 2023. Plaintiffs also used examples of classical music of the early 1900s that they felt did not deserve further copyright protection. They claimed that in adding twenty years to the length of copyright protection, the CTEA was inconsistent with the language of the constitutional origins of copyright law, which used the phrase "limited times." The Supreme Court, however, ruled that the law was valid and that the new copyright terms were constitutional. Although two dissenting justices argued that the new law would "inhibit new forms of dis-semination," the majority ruled that it was not the role of the Court to "second-guess congressional determination and policy judgments of this order" and that the CTEA was not an "impermissible exercise of congressional power." It also determined that the "fair use" provision of copyright law provided the public with sufficient access to protected materials.[17]

Freelance Journalists and Electronic Databases.   In 1993, a group of freelance writers, led by Jonathan Tasini, president of the National Writers Union, filed a lawsuit against *The New York Times* and several other publications, claiming the publications should be required to compensate freelance writers under the "sub-sequent usage" principle when their work is re-published in electronic databases such as LexisNexis, which compensates the publications but not the authors. A trial court ruled in favor of the publishers in 1997, agreeing with their claim that the electronic versions were simply "revisions" and not subsequent uses of the material. In 1999, a Circuit Court of Appeals reversed the decision and ruled in favor of the freelancers, and in 2001, the U.S. Supreme Court upheld that decision in *New York Times Co. v. Tasini*.[18] Many of the publications involved in the suit had been selling the database rights for more than twenty years and realized that attempting to retroactively compensate the writers would be problematic, so instead they agreed to withdraw the materials from the databases. In addition, the publishers began requiring freelance journalists to sign "works for hire" agree-ments that assigned all rights to the publications.

Customization of Content.   One of the newer issues in copyright law is the prolif-eration of companies that alter movies to delete offensive dialogue and images

The cartoon character Mickey Mouse is one of the most famous copyrighted characters in American culture. In 2003, the U.S. Supreme Court ruled that the character could continue to be protected because of the Sonny Bono Copyright Extension Law.

and sell the "cleaned up" versions on digital video disks. Movie studios claim that such actions violate the artistic integrity of the work and compare it to a museum curator who covers up parts of nude paintings or statues.

Another variation of the issue involves companies that sell equipment that will filter out objectionable material without altering the original material. In 2005, the U.S. House of Representatives passed the Family Movie Act, which allows such products to be manufactured and sold. Those companies claim that the technology does not violate copyright law because the original work is not affected, as the alterations to the content are made not on the DVD but on the hard drive of the machine being used.

As of 2005, no cases involving either of these two scenarios have reached the federal court system.

Contributory Infringement. **Contributory infringement** is a concept that was first applied in trademark law, such as in cases in which a retail store is found to be selling products that violate someone else's trademark rights. The producer of the product in question is responsible for the plaintiff's economic loss, the store owner shares the liability only if he or she was aware of the violation. A store owner not aware of the violation would not be liable for the plaintiff's economic loss but can be enjoined from further contributory activity.

The concept of contributory infringement has recently been applied to copyright law as well. In this case, a contributory infringer is analogous to a criminal accomplice in that he or she does not directly participate in the copyright infringement but contributes to the violation by providing the method or opportunity.

The first significant conflict involving the concept of contributory infringement was the 1984 case of *Sony Corp. v. Universal City Studios.* The plaintiffs included Universal City Studios, the Walt Disney Company, and numerous other film studios concerned about the potential for copyright infringement by persons using home video recorders to record television programs.

When the case eventually reached the Supreme Court, the Court ruled that simply copying a television program on a home videocassette recorder to view it later was within "fair use" because there was no profit involved. This case gave birth to the phrase "time-shifting." Another factor in the decision was the Court's reluctance to allow for the banning of a device that has numerous legal uses simply because it can also be used for illegal purposes. In his written opinion, Justice John Paul Stevens wrote that Congress "should take a fresh look at this new technology just as it so often has examined other innovations in the past . . . but it is not our job to apply laws that have not yet been written."[19] The presumption in such cases is that the copies are not sold, their availability is not advertised, and no admission is charged when the tapes are shown.

Today, the concept of contributory infringement (sometimes called "inducement") is at the heart of conflicts between the entertainment industry and companies that provide the technology to download music and video files through the Internet. In the 2001 cases of *A&M Records v. Napster* and *Recording Industry Association of America v. Napster,* a Federal District Court ruled that Napster's file-sharing technology violated the copyrights of music publishers. In essence, the court ruled that getting something of value for free was the equivalent of profiting from copyright infringement and harming the market, thus negating Napster's "fair use" claim. The court ruling did not require Napster to prohibit all exchanges of the record companies' copyrighted works, but instead placed the burden on the record companies to inform Napster of each copyright infringement.[20] Faced with this daunting task, Napster went out of business.

The Napster case was not the end of the file-sharing issue, but rather the beginning of an even larger conflict that would involve not only recorded music but also feature films. Companies such as Kazaa, Soulseek, Bittorrent, and Grokster developed software programs that allowed users to exchange copyrighted material without going through a central computer (as in the *Napster* case). Without a centralized computer at the center of the exchange, the "peer-to-peer" exchange meant that identifying the violators would be problematic.

That didn't stop the copyright holders from suing the companies manufacturing the software, however. In the 2004 case of *MGM v. Grokster,* a Federal Appeals Court ruled that a company that made computer file-sharing software programs

Napster founder Shawn Fanning held a news conference following the 2001 case in which a court rules that the company was guilty of contributory infringement.

could not be held liable for contributory infringement in cases in which customers used the software to illegally trade movies online. Part of the rationale behind the decision was that the equipment in question could also be used for non-infringing activities, and therefore an outright ban was impractical and raised serious First Amendment issues. The Supreme Court reversed that decision in 2005, ruling in favor of the movie producers and differentiating the case from *Sony v. Universal City Studios* because the activity it promoted went beyond time-shifting, circumvented copyright protection, and was simply a profit-generating enterprise for the companies that provided the technology. The Motion Picture Association of America subsequently announced plans to pursue copyright infringement cases against individuals and companies that use computer file-sharing technology to traffic in pirated copies of motion pictures and other copyrighted video productions.[21]

In response to the concerns of the music and motion picture industries, Congress debated in the fall of 2004 a proposed Inducing Infringement of Copyrights Act (IICA), which would have make third parties liable for inducing others to violate copyright laws, such as by providing the technology. The legislation failed, but is likely to be re-introduced in different forms in the near future.

Patents

A **patent** is legal protection for tangible inventions or developments such as electronic and mechanical devices and chemical formulas. Much like the originality and creativity rule that applies to copyright law, patent law provides that the more work or skill involved in the development of an invention, the higher degree of patent protection it deserves. Federal law states that an invention is not eligible for patent protection if it "would have been obvious at the time the invention was made to a person having ordinary skill."

The principle of employers owning the creative work of their employees is often enforced in manufacturing industries in which scientific and technological developments carry with them a substantial market value. Much like the "works for hire" doctrine found in copyright law, common law as applied to patent cases generally favors the rights of employers over those of employees. In higher education, however, colleges and universities could apply the works-for-hire principle and claim ownership of work created by faculty members, but most choose not to exercise that right—for two reasons. First, while faculty-produced research may be of great intellectual value, much of it lacks market value outside of academia, meaning that the financial stakes are so small as to not be worth arguing over. Second, both universities and faculty members agree that the ability of professors to control their creative work is one of the benefits of working in academia.

There are two significant exceptions to this general principle, however. The first involves faculty members in biotechnology, engineering, computer science, or other technical fields, in which work products have significant market value. The second involves faculty members who produce courses offered via the Internet (the newly created term is "distance learning"). In both of these cases, details regarding the ownership of work products and how royalties will be divided are established in contracts signed before the work begins.

Trademarks

A **trademark** is a legal protection for an organization's name or logo, or that of a product or service. Federal trademark law was established by the Lanham Act. The purposes of a trademark are to (1) allow the trademark holder to protect itself against imitators trying to benefit from the name recognition of the better-known company, and (2) protect consumers from being confused by similar company names, product names, characters, or logos.

After an initial registration period of five years, a trademark must be renewed every ten years. Unlike copyrights, which have a finite term, trademarks can be renewed in perpetuity provided they are still used.

A trademark can be lost if its owner fails to use it for a period of two years or longer, or if the trademark becomes commonly used for similar products. Many companies are therefore vigilant in protecting their trademarks and often scold journalists for using trademarked terms generically. Companies such as Xerox, Coca-Cola, and Kleenex, for example, bristle when those terms are used to refer to photocopiers, soft drinks, or facial tissues in a general sense. One specific measure companies take is to remind journalists and other parties that the names of their products should always be capitalized rather than lowercased. While their defensiveness appears silly to some, they are simply trying to avoid losing their trademarks in the same way that trademark owners have lost the rights to terms such as *aspirin, band-aids, cornflakes, cellophane, yo-yo,* and *linoleum.* The popularity of consumer electronic devices will likely represent the next challenge to companies attempting to protect their trademarks, as brand names such as Blackberry, iPod, Bluetooth, TiVo, and OnStar may soon become generic terms for similar devices offered by competing companies.

The most recognized corporate trademarks include the McDonald's arches, the Nike swoosh, the Macintosh apple, and the Olympic rings. In addition to logos, companies also seek trademark protection for fictional characters that appear on their packaging and in their advertising, such as Ronald McDonald, Tony the Tiger, the Jolly Green Giant, Uncle Ben, Aunt Jemima, the Keebler Elves, Mr. Clean, and Betty Crocker.

Organizers of major sporting events trademark the official names of those events to prevent companies from selling unauthorized souvenirs. Examples include the Super Bowl and Pro Bowl (trademarked by the National Football League), the World Series (trademarked by Major League Baseball), and The Final Four (trademarked by the National Collegiate Athletic Association), as well as events such as The Olympics, Rose Bowl, Kentucky Derby, Indianapolis 500, and Master's Golf Tournament.

Similarly, most colleges and universities trademark their names to prevent unauthorized usage. An unusual extension of that practice occurred in 2006 when Texas A & M University obtained a court order preventing the Seattle Seahawks from selling merchandise bearing the phrase "The 12th Man," a term the university used to refer to its fan base. The university had used the term for decades but did not obtain the trademark until 1990. After months of controversy, the two parties reached an agreement under which the Seahawks could continue to use the term but would acknowledge the university's ownership of the phrase and pay the university an undisclosed licensing fee.[22]

Although seldom referred to as "fair use," trademark law includes a common law provision that limits its application strictly to commercial usage and not to journalistic products. Therefore, while vendors may not legally produce T-shirts or other items bearing the name of a company, university, sporting event, or sports organization, print and broadcast journalists may still freely use such names in their stories. This distinction has been clarified in cases in which *Playboy* magazine produced pictorials titled "Girls of the Southeastern Conference" or "The Women of Wal-Mart" over the objections of those trademark holders.

Included in trademark law is the concept of a **service mark,** which allows a company or nonprofit organization to protect the name of an intangible concept. A bank, for example, may offer senior customers a special bank-account option and call it a "Golden Age" account. The service mark would prevent a competing bank from using the name "Golden Age" to describe its program, but it would not prohibit another bank from offering a similar program under a different name.

Two common complaints in trademark cases are "likelihood of confusion" and "trademark dilution."

The term **likelihood of confusion** is applied in cases in which the intentional or unintentional similarity between the product names or logos of two different companies creates the false impression that there is an affiliation or endorsement between the two parties.

One example of such a conflict was the 1952 case of *Conde Nast Publications v. Vogue School of Fashion Modeling.* Conde Nast Publications was the parent company of the fashion magazine, *Vogue.* In the late 1940s and early 1950s, the Vogue School of Fashion Modeling (not associated with the magazine) developed a logo similar to that of the magazine's nameplate and used replicas of magazine covers in illustrating some of its promotional brochures.

The magazine obtained an injunction against the modeling school, claiming that by using a similar logo to that on the magazine covers, the modeling school was implying that it was either associated with or endorsed by the magazine, which it was not.[23]

The production of specialty items such as T-shirts and hats has also prompted a number of "likelihood of confusion" cases, but many trademark holders are unable to stop vendors from producing and selling merchandise with logos or slogans that parody those of better-known organizations. For many years, the New York State Department of Economic Development, which holds the trademark to the "I Love New York" logo (the capital letter I, followed by a red heart, followed by the initials NY) has been unable to stop their counterparts in other states from producing T-shirts and other products with similar logos such as "I Love KC" (Kansas City) or "I Love NC" (North Carolina).

The term **trademark dilution** is applied in cases in which an older, more established company claims that its reputation is harmed by another party's intentional use of a similar name, logo, or other image—usually producing a negative result.

Because of the high burden of proof, many trademark holders, however, take legal action only in extreme cases. For example, lingerie retailer Victoria's Secret recently litigated a trademark dilution case against a small retail store selling lingerie, pornography, and sex toys under the name Victor's Little Secrets. The larger company lost, however, as the U.S. Supreme Court ruled that few consumers would be confused by the similar names and that the alleged damage to its reputation would be difficult to quantify.[24]

In a similar conflict, the movie studio Warner Brothers has been unable to stop vendors from producing and selling T-shirts bearing a logo similar to that of the movie studio and the slogan, "If You See the Police, Warn a Brother."[25]

In both likelihood of confusion and trademark dilution cases, many other potential plaintiffs are reluctant to take action against non-controversial parties and in other situations in which there is no potential harm to their reputations. For example, the International Olympic Committee holds a trademark on its logo and the word *Olympics,* but does not enforce it against organizations holding events such as the "Special Olympics" and "Senior Olympics." Likewise, in the 1990s the *Wall Street Journal* declined to take action against a community business organization that titled its newsletter "The Small Street Journal" and used a nameplate similar to that of the national newspaper.

Lingerie retailer Victoria's Secret sued a pornography retailer for calling his store "Victor's Little Secrets," but a court ruled that a "reasonable consumer" would not be confused by the similar names.

Trade Secrets

Trade secret law is most often applied in high-technology industries such as computer software, electronics, and biotechnology. Trade secrets are often lost when an employee leaves a company to work for a competitor or to establish his or her own competing enterprise. Like most other categories of intellectual property law, courts often require plaintiffs in trade-secret cases to meet a high burden of proof.

In addition to protection offered by state and federal laws, trade secret protection is also incorporated into the Freedom of Information Act, which includes an exemption that allows companies to protect company secrets from disclosure to competitors or the general public.

Proponents of the free market system often find trade secret laws problematic because they have the potential to discourage individual enterprise and stifle competition. The courts generally agree, and because of the high burden of proof required, few companies attempt to punish former employees for alleged trade secret violations. Repeated loss of trade secrets, however, has caused many firms to include confidentiality or "no compete" clauses in employment contracts, the enforcement of which is easier to pursue than a case involving trade secret law.

Intellectual Property in the International Marketplace

In the late 1800s, as European book publishers began realizing the potential for international sales, government officials from around the world met to discuss international copyright issues. The result was the Berne Convention for the Protection of Literary and Artistic Works, a set of rules that requires member countries to respect the copyright laws of other countries without requiring copyright holders to file copyright applications in every country in which a work was distributed. The rules were expanded in 1908 and 1971. The United States did not join the convention at first, and throughout much of the 1900s, American book publishers blatantly republished the work of European authors without compensation to the copyright holders.

In the 1980s, the role of the United States in the international copyright arena shifted from major perpetrator to major victim. Frustrated at not being able to stop piracy of their works and apparently not recognizing the double standard, American publishers, movie producers, and music industry leaders persuaded the U.S. Congress to join the Berne Convention in 1989.

In 1996, a worldwide agreement known as the General Agreement on Tariffs and Trade (GATT) included intellectual property rules that were similar to those in the Berne Convention, but applied to a greater number of countries. The rules also applied to trademarks, which are slightly different from copyrights but not covered by the Berne Convention.

Today, enforcement of intellectual property law in the international marketplace is a constant challenge for American companies and is part of nearly every trade negotiation. Specific problem areas include music, movies, and computer software, protected by copyright law; clothing, jewelry, and handbags, protected by trademark law; and prescription drugs and sports equipment, covered by patent law. The worst offenders are found in China, Russia, and countries in Eastern Europe and Latin America. Governments in those countries attempt to enforce the rules, but large black markets continue to flourish around the world.

Frequently Asked Questions about Copyright Law

1. *Is it legal for me to copy a song from one CD to another and then give the CD to a friend as a gift?* Common law provides a concept known as **incidental** or **de minimis copying,** which is technically a violation of copyright law but is unlikely to result in criminal prosecution. Examples include copying a song from one compact disc to another or photocopying a cartoon or article from a newspaper or magazine to show to a friend, to retain for reference, or to post on a bulletin board at school or work. The reluctance of copyright holders to pursue legal action in such cases is based on the following factors: (1) the difficulty of tracking down such violations,

(2) the minimal nature of the financial loss, and (3) the fact that some cases of copying are actually beneficial to the copyright holder because it exposes the work to a broader audience. The tendency of the copyright holders to "look the other way" is based on the following assumptions, however: the number of copies made is limited, the products are not sold, and their availability is not advertised. Some music publishers and movie producers have sued individual computer users for sharing music files because the copying was done on a large scale and went far beyond the spirit of incidental copying as described above.

2. *I have an idea for a television series and have written a pilot episode. Should I have it copyrighted before I send it to the networks?* Absolutely. It's the best way to protect your creative work. But here are a few things to keep in mind: Most networks prefer only a plot summary (described as a "treatment") rather than a complete script. Many television and motion picture studios will look only at treatments and will return thicker envelopes unopened. Unless you've already had some success in the screenwriting business, it's better to work through an agent. An attorney who specializes in entertainment or contract law can help you find one.

One of the few drawbacks to copyrighting a treatment is that such documents, once processed by the U.S. Copyright Office, become public record and may tip off a competing screenwriter to your idea, which he or she may alter slightly and submit to producers. Because of this danger, some screenwriters prefer to register their work instead with the Writers Guild of America (WGA). The WGA lacks the enforcement power of the U.S. Copyright Office but can at least document the date on which your work was submitted.

3. *I've always heard that if I write something and then mail it to myself by certified mail and don't open it, the process of doing so gives me copyright protection. True or false?* This is not spelled out in copyright law, but doing so documents the date on which you completed the work and would help you pursue a copyright case under the "unregistered" or "common-law" copyright principle. Serious writers and artists, however, take the additional step of formally registering their work with the U.S. Copyright Office. It requires little time or effort to complete the paperwork, is relatively inexpensive, and provides considerably more legal protection than depending on the common-law principle.

4. *What about cartoon characters used in television advertising? Isn't that copyright infringement?* It is copyright infringement if it is done without permission. Many copyright holders simply refuse to allow their characters to be used in commercial advertising because they don't want to appear to be endorsing products, no matter how uncontroversial they may be. In the few cases in which copyright holders give such permission, such as for MetLife's use of the Peanuts characters or Office Depot's use of characters from the Dilbert comic strip, the fee is quite high. Some copyright holders are more generous when it comes to supporting charities, however. United Media, which holds the copyright to the Peanuts comic strip and its characters, allows a charity in North Carolina to use the name Project Linus (and the Linus character). The charity provides blankets for injured and seriously ill children.[26]

A related question deals with why some cartoon characters (and other fictional characters) are copyrighted, while others are trademarked. Some are even protected by both. Generally, if a character is used for entertainment purposes, it is protected by copyright. If the character is used in a company's advertising, packaging, or for other promotional purposes (such as Betty Crocker or Mr. Clean), it is protected by trademark. In rare cases a character could be protected by both copyright and trademark, as in the case of Mickey Mouse.

5. *What's the difference between copyright infringement and plagiarism?* The term *copyright infringement* (a legal term) is often confused with plagiarism (an ethical term), but the terms are not interchangeable. If a newspaper reporter takes a wire service story, changes only a few words, and then submits it to his newspaper under his byline, he has committed both the legal offense of copyright infringement (for which the wire service could sue the newspaper), and the ethical offense of plagiarism, for which he could be reprimanded by his newspaper. If a student borrows generously from a book in the public domain, without proper citation, he or she has not violated copyright law but is still guilty of plagiarism. But even if a student (or any other individual) acknowledges the source of the work, he or she may still be guilty of copyright infringement if the amount of the material borrowed from the copyrighted work exceeds the provision of fair use (explained earlier in this chapter). In other words, attribution or citation is not a defense in copyright infringement cases.

6. *What's the deal with "Happy Birthday"? Arguing over that seems to be rather silly to me.* But the copyright holder takes it very seriously. Technically, employees of a restaurant violate the company's copyright when they sing the song (without paying the licensing fee) to celebrate the birthday of a customer, but pursuing such a claim through the court system would be impractical. That premise was tested, however, in 1996 as the American Society of Composers, Artists, and Performers (ASCAP), a copyright clearinghouse representing the interests of copyright holders, attempted to collect licensing fees from Girl Scouts based on their singing of "Happy Birthday to You," "God Bless America," and other copyrighted songs at meetings and campouts. Following months of negative publicity, ASCAP backed down.

Point/Counterpoint: Computer File-Sharing

Why Sharing Music and Movies through Computer File-Sharing Should be Illegal

An individual's creative work should be protected to the same degree as his or her tangible property. "It's the same as me going into a store and saying 'I really love that shirt' and walking out with it," said songwriter Dianne Warren in a 2003 interview. "I can't do that. I don't own the shirt and I didn't pay for it. When you take someone's music off the Internet, you're stealing."[27]

Downloading music and movies violates the spirit of the constitutional origins of copyright law. "Every time someone downloads a commercial book, song, film, or software program that they ought to pay for, they're not just committing a crime, they're spitting on our Constitution and devaluing the American way of life," wrote Andrew Burt, a computer science professor and science fiction author, in 2003.

Illegal trafficking in copyrighted material is harmful to the creative community and society as a whole. If musicians, film producers, and authors lose control over their work and the financial rewards for producing it, their motivation to create new products lessens, and society as a whole loses. "Victims include wealthy stars but also poor artists who haven't yet broken through," claimed a 2005 editorial in the *Tampa Tribune.* "Everyone associated with the legal sale and distribution of music has suffered."[28]

Why Music Publishers and Movie Producers Should Not Attempt to Stop File-Sharing

Losing control of one's creative work is one of the risks of being in the entertainment business. Any time an individual produces a song or motion picture, he or she offers it to the public and should accept the risk of not being compensated for it.

Artists don't make money off music sales anyway. The artists' income comes from concerts and merchandise sales. The money from music sales goes to the publishers, not the artists, so the artists' claim that they are losing money is phony.

File-sharing is beneficial to some musical artists. File-sharing provides exposure for artists who are unlikely to find an audience otherwise.

Trying to stop file-sharing of music and movies is impractical. Each time a technology is developed to prevent such copying, those determined to do so will simply find other ways to circumvent whatever safeguards are put in place.

Chapter Summary

Intellectual property is an area of law that deals with the protection of the creative work belonging to an individual or organization. Copyright—protection for creative works that are mostly intangible—is the most complex and most often discussed part of intellectual property law. Other areas of intellectual property law include patents (protection for tangible inventions or developments such as electronic and mechanical devices and chemical formulas), trademarks (protection for an organization's name or logo, or that of a product or service) and trade secrets (protection for information or processes such as those used in manufacturing).

The origins of American copyright law can be found in the Constitution; the first specific copyright was enacted by Congress in 1790. The major concern at the time was the protection of literature and maps, as those were the materials subject to the most piracy in Europe at the time.

Major revisions to copyright law took place in 1909, 1976, and 1998, and elements of all three revisions are still in effect today. Those revisions expanded the law to cover forms of expression such as art prints, music, photographs, and paintings. In addition to being revised to cover different forms of expression, copyright laws have also been expanded to include all of the various recording methods that have been developed, including phonograph records, motion picture film, audiotape and videotape, computer disks, compact disks, and digital video disks.

Today, technology presents new challenges in determining ownership rights related to creative work and in determining to what extent individuals and organizations can protect their creative work.

CASE PROBLEM

WeHatePhilippeSanTrappe.com

Philippe San Trappe is a young, dark-skinned professional golfer who was born and raised in France. He has created controversy in the sports world because of his negative comments toward American culture, despite the fact that he lives in the United States and is successful on the American golf tour. Despite the controversy, however, he also has a large number of fans both in the United States and around the world.

WeHatePhilippeSanTrappe.com is a website at which golf fans (or anyone else) can express their opinions about the controversial athlete. Part of the site includes a video clip (about thirty seconds) of San Trappe's golf swing, which the site's creator captured by sneaking a video camera into a recent tournament. While most of the comments posted to the site are hostile, they include no specific threats. The comments do, however, include some racial slurs and suggestions that San Trappe "quit the pro golf tour and give the game back to white golfers, where it belongs."

Although the name of the site indicates negativity, about 10 percent of the comments posted to the site are actually defending San Trappe and praising his golf ability.

San Trappe, however, is not pleased with the site, and has filed a lawsuit in an attempt to shut it down. His suit is based on (a) the fact that he did not give his permission for the video to be used in such a way and (b) his concern that someone visiting the site may be incited to harm him. This case problem involves elements of intellectual property (this chapter), appropriation (Chapter 7), and hate speech (Chapter 2).

Because of San Trappe's fame and the volatile nature of the conflict, the case has received a great deal of national publicity. You're a nationally known First Amendment and intellectual property lawyer, and National Public Radio has contacted you to set up a telephone interview on the topic. To prepare for the interview, sketch out the legal points you would make during the interview.

SOCRATIC DIALOGUE QUESTIONS

1. What violations of copyright law do you see on a regular basis, in your personal life, experiences in college, and experiences at work? Based on the criteria the courts use to evaluate copyright cases, which of these violations should be investigated? In which cases should the party whose copyright is being violated simply shrug it off?

2. What is your opinion of the *Napster* and *Grokster* cases? Are the defendants in these cases guilty of "contributory infringement"? How do those cases differ from *Sony v. Universal City Studios?* In retrospect, officials in the movie industry now say that the industry has benefited from VCRs and similar technology because of additional royalties from movie rentals. Might the same thing happen in the *Napster* and *Grokster* cases? Are there any practical solutions to this problem?

3. Find at least one case in Chapter 11 with which you strongly disagree with the court ruling (in the final resolution of the case) and be prepared to share your opinion with the class.

GLOSSARY OF TERMS

Common law copyright   A provision in the Copyright Revision Act of 1976 that allows creators to protect their work upon completion, even if not registered with the Copyright Office.

Contributory infringement   The act of condoning an act of copyright or trademark infringement by providing the technology or opportunity.

Copyright   Legal protection for creative works that are mostly intangible.

De minimis copying   The act of making a limited number of copies of copyrighted material; technically a violation of copyright law but unlikely to be prosecuted. Also called **incidental copying.**

Fair use   A provision in the Copyright Revision Act of 1976 that allows for the use of copyrighted materials for certain nonprofit purposes, such as news reporting and criticism, classroom teaching, and academic research. The fair use doctrine is applicable to parodies under most circumstances.

Incidental copying   The act of making a limited number of copies of copyrighted material; technically a violation of copyright law but unlikely to be prosecuted. Also called **de minimis copying.**

Infringement   The act of using another party's copyrighted materials without permission and/or compensation.

Likelihood of confusion   A term used in trademark law to refer to the degree to which consumers may be confused by the similarity between the names of competing companies or products.

Notification clause   A clause in the Digital Millennium Copyright Act of 1998 that requires ISPs to remove copyrighted material upon request of the copyright holder and provides ISPs with immunity from liability when they remove copyrighted material.

Originality and creativity principle   The principle that the more originality and creativity involved in the creation of a work, the greater the amount of copyright protection it receives.

Patent   Legal protection for tangible inventions or developments such as electronic and mechanical devices and chemical formulas.

Parody   The imitation of a copyrighted work done for purposes of entertainment or humor.

Public domain   The status of material that has either never been copyrighted or for which the copyright has expired.

Service mark   Similar to a trademark; it applies to a service rather than a product.

Sweat of the brow rule   A common-law principle applied to copyright and patent law; the amount of effort expended in the creation of a work determines the level of copyright protection given. This rule is seldom applied today, as courts give more weight to "originality" than "effort."

Trademark   Legal protection for an organization's name or logo, or that of a product or service.

Trademark dilution   The intentional or unintentional similarity between company names, product names, or logos that incorrectly states or implies an association or endorsement between the two parties.

Trade secret   Legal protection for information or processes such as those used in manufacturing.

Works for hire doctrine   A principle introduced into copyright law in 1909 that makes a legal distinction between the relationships that companies have with their regular employees and those that companies have with independent contractors.

NOTES

1. *International News Service v. Associated Press,* 248 U.S. 215 (1918).
2. *Miller v. University City Studios,* 650 F.2d 1365 (1981).
3. *Feist Publications v. Rural Telephone Co.,* 499 U.S. 340 (1991).
4. *Warren Publishing Co. v. Microdos Data Corp.,* 115 F.3d 1509 (1997).
5. Kelly Crabbe, *The Movie Business.* New York: Simon & Schuster, 2005, p. 27.
6. *Community for Creative Nonviolence v. Reid,* 490 U.S. 730 (1989).
7. *Williams v. Weisser,* 273 Cal. App. 2d 726 (1969).
8. *New Kids on the Block v. News America Publishing,* 745 F. Supp. 1540 (1990).
9. *Williams & Wilkins Co. v. United States,* 487 F.2d 1345 (1975).
10. *Sony Corp. v. Universal City Studios,* 464 U.S. 417 (1984).
11. *Basic Books v. Kinko's Graphics Corporation,* 758 F. Supp. 1522 (1991).
12. *Princeton University Press v. Michigan Document Services,* 74 F.3d 1528 (1992).
13. "Public Relations Protest." *Editor & Publisher,* October 28, 1995, p. 12.
14. *Campbell v. Acuff-Rose Music Co.,* 510 U.S. 569 (1994).
15. William Safire, "Gone With the Copyright?" Syndicated column, May 15, 2001.
16. Michael Kakutani, "Humbert Would Swear This Isn't the Same Lolita." *New York Times,* October 29, 1999, p. 28-A.
17. *Eldred v. Ashcroft,* 537 U.S. 186 (2003); Daniel Gross, "Of Mice and Men." *Attache,* February 2002, p. 13–15; Joan Biskupic, "Copyright Case to Determine Use of Classic Culture." *USA Today,* October 9, 2002, p. 5-A.
18. *New York Times Co. v. Tasini,* 533 U.S. 483 (2001).
19. *Sony Corp. v. Universal City Studios,* 464 U.S. 417 (1984).
20. *A&M Records v. Napster,* 239 F.3d 1004 (2001) and *Recording Industry Association of America v. Napster,* 284 F.3d 1091 (2001).
21. *MGM v. Grokster,* 380 F.3d 1154 (2004).
22. "Seahawks Ordered to Stop '12th Man' Merchandise." Associated Press report, February 1, 2006; "Seahawks, A&M Reach Deal." Associated Press report, May 9, 2006.
23. *Conde Nast Publications v. Vogue School of Fashion Modeling,* 105 F. Supp. 325 (1952).
24. *Moseley v. Victoria's Secret,* 537 U.S. 418 (2003).
25. Maria Castro, "Popular T-Shirt Raises Concerns Over Copyright." Columbia News Service report, January 14, 2006.
26. Marty Minchin, "Security Blankets Bring Solace." *Charlotte Observer,* August 13, 2005, p. 1-E.
27. Dianne Warren, interviewed on CBS "Sunday Morning," April 23, 2003.
28. "Internet's Greedy Tune-Traders Must Not Be Licensed to Steal." *Tampa Tribune,* May 27, 2005, p. 10-A.

12 Advertising

The Federal Trade Commission sometimes acts as if the First Amendment is merely a rumor.

Richard C. Christian
Advertising Executive

LEARNING OBJECTIVES

As a result of reading this chapter, students should:

- Understand the difference between commercial and political advertising and why those two forms of communication are treated differently in terms of First Amendment protection.

- Understand the role of the Federal Trade Commission in regulating advertising and protecting consumers from illegal or unethical advertising practices.

Commercial vs. Political Advertising

Advertising typically takes one of two forms. Commercial advertising (sometimes referred to as "commercial speech") deals with products and services, while political advertising deals with the candidates for public office and issues being debated in society. Based on seven decades of Supreme Court decisions, commercial advertising is considered to be of less value than political advertising and is subject to considerably more regulation. Political advertising, considered a form of political speech, receives a high degree of First Amendment protection and is subject to much less regulation.

One of the earliest known cases involving the difference between commercial and political advertising was *Valentine v. Chrestensen* (1941). F. J. Chrestensen was a millionaire and eccentric living in New York who bought a decommissioned Navy submarine for $2 million, positioned it in the East River, and opened it for public tours. In order to promote it, he printed handbills and distributed them around the city, unaware that New York City had an anti-litter ordinance that prohibited such materials.

After the city informed Chrestensen that he could not distribute his handbills, he revised them so as to have his commercial message on one side and a political message on the other, claiming that if there was a political message on the handbill, it would get First Amendment protection. The city did not accept the claim of political speech because it considered it just a ruse to get around the city ordinance. When the case reached the U.S. Supreme Court, the court agreed with the city's viewpoint.[1]

Commercial advertising continued to remain unprotected until the mid-1970s, when the Supreme Court acknowledged it was worthy of limited First Amendment protection. In *Virginia State Board of Pharmacy v. Virginia Citizens Consumer Council,* the Court established the **commercial speech doctrine,** ruling that the fact that "the advertiser's interest is purely an economic one hardly disqualifies him from protection under the First Amendment." In addition, the Court ruled, First Amendment values also protect the consumers' right to receive the information.[2]

Despite the *Virginia State Board of Pharmacy* case, court rulings today continue to draw distinctions between commercial advertising that promotes products and services and political or opinion advertising that deals with issues and ideas. Commercial advertising is regulated by the Federal Trade Commission (FTC) and other regulatory bodies, while political advertising is regulated by the Federal Elections Commission (FEC), and in some cases, state election laws. The FEC's authority to regulate political advertising is considerably less than the FTC's authority to regulate commercial advertising, as many attempts to regulate political advertising are ruled by the courts to be in violation of the First Amendment. The justifications for not fully protecting commercial advertising are (1) commercial speech is not considered to carry as much social value as political speech and religious expression, and (2) commercial speech consists largely of statements of fact, which are easier to dispute than the opinions that comprise political speech.

Regulation of Commercial Advertising

Development of the Commercial Speech Doctrine

The history of commercial advertising in the United States can be divided into three time periods.

Throughout much of the 1800s, American merchants promoted their products through newspaper and magazine advertisements and flyers distributed door-to-door and displayed in public gathering places. Advertisers could make exaggerated or purely fictional claims, with little regulation by government agencies or professional regulatory organizations, and consumers who were misled or cheated had little recourse. "Caveat emptor" ("let the buyer beware") was the rule of the day.

In the early 1900s, however, the pendulum swung to the opposite extreme, as state governments adopted advertising regulations that were collectively known as "printer's ink statutes," named because the suggested regulations were first published in *Printer's Ink* magazine in 1911. Most of the state laws involved fines rather than imprisonment, but enforcement was vigorous. Shortly thereafter, the Federal Trade Commission was established, in part to regulate advertising on the national level.

While regulatory agencies still attempt to protect consumers from blatantly false and misleading advertising, the FTC, as well as the courts, believe that consumers bear some responsibility for protecting themselves by being skeptical of questionable advertising claims. In addition, court rulings have found that some commercial speech has value far beyond the promotion of products and services; it also provides consumers with important information to assist them in their purchasing decisions. By providing this limited First Amendment protection to advertising, the courts are protecting not only the advertisers' right to disseminate that information, but also the consumers' right to receive it.

Today, in addition to the FTC's regulations on advertising in general, numerous other agencies regulate specific aspects of advertising. The Federal Communications Commission (FCC) establishes and enforces specific regulations for advertising on television and radio. The Food and Drug Administration (FDA) regulates the advertising of food and pharmaceutical products in print and broadcast media. The U.S. Postal Service establishes and enforces regulations on the

The advertising of consumer products is subject to regulation by the Federal Trade Commission.

proportion of advertising to news in newspapers, magazines, and newsletters sent through the mail (the higher the percentage of advertising, the higher the mailing cost).

In addition to the authority of those agencies to regulate national advertising, all fifty states have revised their consumer-protection laws (originally passed in the mid-1900s) and have added new ones that regulate advertising at the state and local levels.

At the city and county level, advertising is regulated in the form of restrictions placed on handbills, illuminated signs, transit advertising, and outdoor advertising such as billboards and benches. The courts generally uphold such regulations as reasonable time, place, and manner restrictions.

False, Deceptive, and Misleading Advertising

One of the FTC's chief responsibilities is the enforcement of "truth in advertising" laws that deal with advertising that is false, deceptive, or misleading. These laws can be enforced through either prior restraint (taking the advertisement out of the publication or off the air) or punishment after the fact (a fine).

What is the difference between an advertisement that is "false" and one that is merely "misleading" or "deceptive"? The dividing line is difficult to detect, but here are some examples that may help to clarify the difference.

An advertisement is clearly false if it makes claims that are not true, such as a product's ability to achieve a certain result that in practice it clearly cannot. In order to substantiate such a claim of false advertising, however, the FTC would have to prove that the advertiser knew the product's limitations but published or broadcast the advertisement nevertheless. Other examples of outright **false advertising** include the mention of fictional endorsements or test results, such as "the American Cancer Society recommends eating product X daily" (if no such recommendation was made) or "scientists at X University tested our product and found that . . ." (if no such tests were actually conducted).

Conversely, an advertisement is "deceptive" if it makes no false statements, yet leaves out important information or is otherwise misleading. An example of **deceptive and misleading advertising** might be an advertisement that claims that product A costs less than product B, yet omits the fact that product A is sold in 32-ounce bottles while product B is sold in 48-ounce bottles.

To determine if an advertisement is deceptive, the FTC uses the **reasonable consumer standard,** meaning that each advertisement in question would be evaluated according to the likelihood that a "reasonable consumer" would be deceived. FTC guidelines say that an advertisement would not be deemed to be deceptive if "only a few gullible consumers would be deceived." The FTC admits that a company "cannot be liable for every possible reading of its claims, no matter how far-fetched," and that the law "could not help a consumer who thinks that all french fries are imported from France or that Danish pastry actually comes from Denmark."[3]

The first case to deal with deceptive advertising was *Federal Trade Commission v. Colgate-Palmolive Co.* (1965). Colgate-Palmolive produced television commercials for a shaving cream called Rapid Shave, which included demonstrations in which the product appeared to shave sand off sandpaper. But what was really happening was that the producers of the commercial had put loose sand on an ordinary sheet of glass and made it look as though it was sandpaper. The FTC ruled that it was a deceptive advertisement and ordered Colgate-Palmolive to take it off the air, but the company challenged the ruling to the Supreme Court, which ruled in favor of the FTC.[4] The ruling set a precedent and reinforced the FTC's authority to fine advertisers suspected of staging deceptive demonstrations and other types of deception.

Another major FTC court victory came in the 1976 case of *Beneficial Corp. v. FTC,* in which a Federal District Court ruled against a tax accounting firm that advertised that it could provide "instant tax refunds" to clients, when in fact the company was merely loaning the client the money until the refund check was received. The ad also omitted the fact that clients had to complete applications for and be qualified for the loans, thus making the loans not as "instant" as it was leading potential clients to believe.[5]

Today, the most common advertising areas for regulatory scrutiny are food products and nonprescription or "over the counter" drugs. For example, the FTC forced orange juice processor Tropicana to cancel a 2005 ad that claimed its product was "heart-healthy" because it lowers a person's cholesterol and blood pressure. The FTC had challenged the company to produce scientific evidence to support its claims, but the company could not.[6]

Likewise, an advertisement for a medication cannot claim or even imply that it prevents colds or flu when in actuality it can only treat the symptoms. On more serious issues, the Food and Drug Administration would not allow a food or pharmaceutical company to claim in its advertising that a certain product prevents the onset of cancer, heart disease, arthritis, or other ailments without scientific medical studies to document such benefits.

Another factor that advertisers must approach with caution is the inclusion of research information derived from government tests or reports. For example, if the Department of Transportation performs crash-test studies to determine which new cars are the safest and mentions that a specific product is either at or near the top, the manufacturer can quote that report in its advertising but must be careful to present the information fairly. The ad can claim that Car X was ranked first in its category or finished in the top ten for three years in a row (if true). The ad cannot, however, state or imply that the Department of Transportation encourages consumers to buy Car X, because the Department of Transportation is a neutral government agency and does not make such endorsements.

In addition to being scrutinized by the FTC, advertisements making questionable claims can also result in legal action being taken by competing companies. Early in 2005, for example, a manufacturer of dental floss filed suit against a company that claimed its mouthwash was as effective as dental floss in reducing plaque and gum disease. Fearing a decline in sales of its dental floss, Johnson & Johnson filed suit against Pfizer, manufacturer of Listerine, claiming that such ads were "false and misleading" because no tests had been conducted to determine the relative merits of the two products. A federal judge agreed with Johnson & Johnson's claim and ordered Pfizer to withdraw the ad.[7]

Advertising of Controversial Products and Services

Because of the commercial speech doctrine, the Supreme Court has ruled that in most circumstances, the government cannot prohibit the advertising of legal products or services. Through administrative agencies such as the Federal Trade Commission, however, the government can make time, place, and manner restrictions on commercial advertising.

The first case in this area was *Bigelow v. Virginia* (1975). The conflict began when Jeffrey Bigelow, the editor of a weekly newspaper in Virginia, accepted an advertisement for an abortion clinic. The clinic was located in New York, where abortions were legal. In Virginia, however, abortions were illegal, and a state law made it a misdemeanor to advocate abortion in lectures, advertisements, or publications, regardless of where the services were to be performed.

A trial court found Bigelow guilty and fined him $500, which was to be reduced to $150 if he promised to not accept similar ads in the future. Despite the nominal amount, Bigelow appealed, based on what he saw as a publisher's First Amendment right to determine advertising policy. The U.S. Supreme Court vacated his conviction and sent the case back to the Virginia trial court, which again found him guilty.

Bigelow appealed his case again, and the timing of his second appeal—coming shortly after the Court had legalized abortions in the 1973 case, *Roe v. Wade*, worked in his favor. The Court reversed his conviction again, this time on First Amendment grounds, determining that in his role as publisher, Bigelow had the right to accept advertising for services that were legal. The Court also noted that the ad was more than just commercial speech; by announcing that "abortions are now legal in New York," the ad was communicating information of public interest, thus performing a function tangential to that of political speech.[8]

Another advertising case of the same era was *Virginia State Board of Pharmacy v. Virginia Citizens Consumer Council* (1976), which began when a consumer advocacy group challenged a state law that prohibited pharmacies from advertising the prices of prescription drugs. The Virginia Citizens Consumer Council claimed that if pharmacists were allowed to advertise, it would encourage more competitive pricing of drugs. The Supreme Court sided with the consumers and struck down the law, not only because it sought to protect the pharmacists' right to provide information but because it also wanted to protect the rights of consumers to receive that information.[9]

Three years later, in *Central Hudson v. Public Service Commission* (1980), the Supreme Court ruled that a state ban on the advertising of utilities services was unconstitutional. During the energy crisis of the late 1970s, the state of New York banned advertising of electrical services as an attempt to limit consumption. There was little dispute over the ban during the crisis itself, but when the Public Service Commission (PSC) elected to keep the ban in place after the crisis had passed, the Central Hudson Electric Company challenged the ban on constitutional grounds. After the Supreme Court judged the rule to be unconstitutional,[10] the PSC dropped its objections to advertising by all public utilities in the state.

The Supreme Court did, however, leave the door open for the government to regulate advertising in the future, emphasizing that government would bear the burden of proof to demonstrate why it needed to regulate it. It established the **Central Hudson Test** for limitations on advertising. In order to regulate advertising, the Court ruled, the governmental agency attempting to do so would have to meet all four of the following criteria:

1. The speech in question must be ineligible for First Amendment protection because it is either inaccurate, reflects discriminatory employment practices, or deals with illegal products or services.
2. The government must have a substantial interest in regulating it, such as a concern for public health and safety. In a later case involving a city government's attempt to prohibit billboards, the Court ruled that the city's claim of "visual blight" was insufficient grounds to allow such a law to remain in place.
3. The regulation in question must advance that government interest.
4. The regulation must be sufficiently narrow.[11]

One of the few cases in which the Central Hudson Test has been used to regulate advertising occurred in the 1988 Supreme Court case of *Posadas de Puerto Rico Associates v. Tourism Company of Puerto Rico*. The plaintiff in the case was a company that owned casinos on the island of Puerto Rico; the defendant was a company employed by the island's government to regulate casino gambling. The regulatory company had an unusual policy on advertising: casinos could not advertise on the island itself, but could advertise in the mainland United States. After being fined by the company for violating the rule, Posadas appealed through the court system, and the case eventually reached the Supreme Court. In a 5–4 decision, the court ruled in favor of the regulatory company, ruling that its advertising policies were legal under the Central Hudson Test because of the potential harm of gambling and its alleged connection to organized crime.[12]

In a 1996 case, the Court seemed to back away from the Posadas ruling in the case of *44 Liquormart v. Rhode Island*. Focusing on the third part of the Central Hudson test, the Court raised the burden of proof that a state government would have to meet to justify advertising regulation. In this case, the Court ruled that the state of Rhode Island was unable to prove that its law restricting the advertising of alcohol would advance its interest of discouraging its citizens from drinking.[13]

The following year, the Court declined to hear the appeal of a case involving a city government's right to limit the advertising of controversial products and services. The conflict began when the city of Baltimore enacted an ordinance prohibiting alcohol and tobacco advertising on billboards. The city believed the ban was a reasonable "time, place, and manner" restriction because it allowed exceptions for sports stadiums and some downtown and industrial areas. Anheuser-Busch and other advertisers challenged the ordinance on First Amendment grounds, but lower courts ruled that the city's aim of reducing underage drinking and smoking was sufficient justification for the geographic limitations. In April 1997, the Supreme Court declined to review the case, leaving the ordinance in place.[14]

Advertising Aimed at Children

If advertising targets children, the federal government, specifically the Federal Trade Commission, claims that a higher regulatory standard should apply. Toward that end, the FCC regulates the nature of advertising aimed at children and limits the total number of minutes that can be allotted to advertising during children's programming.

That position is supported by various watchdog groups. In 2000, for example, children's advocates formed the Campaign for a Commercial-Free Childhood (CCFC), a group formed to monitor the advertising industry and encourage more responsible advertising aimed at children. CCFC specifically targeted food and soft-drink companies for subjecting children to what it called a culture of "rampant consumerism." Under protest from CCFC, the advertising industry in 2003 discontinued its annual "Golden Marbles" awards program that honored achievement in print and broadcast advertising aimed at children.[15] In response to the criticism it receives from CCFC and other watchdog groups, the advertising industry—led by executives representing major food producers—formed the Alliance for American Advertising. The alliance claims its mission is to help advertisers defend their First Amendment rights.

Advertising That Implies Discrimination

In addition to being punished for publishing or broadcasting ads deemed to be false or deceptive, media outlets can also be punished for accepting ads associated with illegal products, services, or activities, including those implying discrimination in housing or employment.

Before and during the civil rights movement of the 1960s, it was not uncommon to find newspaper employment ads using terms such as "white applicants only" or "colored need not apply." Such advertisements would be illegal today, but the courts have ruled that in addition to not stating the intent to discriminate, employment advertisements cannot even imply that such conditions exist.

In the 1973 case of *Pittsburgh Press v. Pittsburgh Commission on Human Relations,* for example, the Supreme Court ruled that a newspaper could not categorize job listings with headings such as "male interest" and "female interest." The Court based its ruling on two factors: (1) that employment advertising was commercial speech, and therefore not subject to First Amendment protection; and (2) the job labels condoned job discrimination, an illegal activity.[16]

Real estate advertising is subject to similar scrutiny. In the 1991 case of *Ragin v. New York Times,* for example, a Circuit Court of Appeals ruled in favor of a non-profit organization suing the newspaper for failure to include black models in real estate advertisements showing potential homeowners. By carrying ads showing only white families, the court ruled, the newspaper was allowing advertisers to imply that only similar families were welcome in the neighborhoods where the properties were located, and such discrimination violated the Fair Housing Act of 1968 as well as the Fourteenth Amendment and numerous other civil rights laws.

Classified newspaper advertising is subject to a great deal of regulatory scrutiny from governmental agencies such as the FTC, Equal Employment Opportunities Commission, and the Federal Housing Authority.

The court further ruled that assigning newspapers the responsibility of monitoring advertisements for racially discriminatory messages did not pose an "unconstitutional burden" and did not violate their First Amendment rights.[17]

Advertising of Professional Services

Professional associations such as the American Medical Association and American Bar Association, as well as their statewide chapters, typically discourage their members from advertising their services because they view such promotion as undignified. In most states, medical associations and bar associations have quasi-governmental authority to regulate the professions, meaning that association rules carry the force of law. The courts have ruled, however, that associations can-not prohibit such advertisements because to do so would violate the professionals' First Amendment rights.

The case of *Bates v. State Bar of Arizona* (1977) illustrates this principle. The conflict began when two young attorneys opened a practice to offer low-cost legal services to moderate-income families and advertised their services, including a description of their fee structure, in the *Arizona Republic,* one of the largest daily newspapers in the state. The state bar association suspended the lawyers from practicing for a week, but despite the nominal nature of the punishment, the attorneys appealed their punishment based on their First Amendment rights to advertise. The Arizona Supreme Court upheld the suspensions, but the U.S. Supreme Court reversed, ruling that no state government, or professional regulatory body sanctioned by that government, had the authority to prohibit advertising unless it was proved to be false or deceptive.

The bar association had argued that because the costs of legal services vary from one case to the next, any advertisement that included a schedule of fixed fees would be false and deceptive. The Court disagreed, however, ruling that the lawyers' right to disseminate information and potential clients' right to receive it outweighed any concern over potential falsity or deception.[18]

In a 1988 case, *Shapero v. Kentucky Bar Association*, the Supreme Court extended the concept of freedom to advertise to direct mail, ruling that the lawyer was within his First Amendment rights to solicit potential clients through the mail, even though the state bar association had previously barred the practice under its ethical code.[19]

The Court modified its stance in 1995, however, upholding a Florida Bar Association rule that prohibited personal injury attorneys from sending direct mail solicitations to victims and their families during the first thirty days following an accident or disaster. In *Florida Bar Association v. Went For It*, the Court cited the second part of the Central Hudson Test and determined that the bar association was exercising a substantial state interest in (1) protecting the privacy of individuals against intrusion by the lawyers, and (2) preserving public confidence in the legal profession.[20]

Liability for Accepting Advertising

A publication's liability for advertisements it accepts was debated in two cases involving *Soldier of Fortune* magazine. In both cases, family members of persons allegedly murdered by professional killers responding to advertisements in the magazine filed suit against its publisher, claiming that it contributed to the deaths by carrying the advertisements. But different federal appeals courts ruled differently in the cases. *Eimann v. Soldier of Fortune* (1989) began with the following advertisement:

> Ex-marines, 1967–69 'Nam vets, ex-DI, weapons specialist, jungle warfare, pilot, high-risk assignments, U.S. or overseas.

The placement of the ad was linked to at least one murder, and the victim's family sued the magazine, claiming it functioned as an accessory to murder as a result of accepting the ad. A Texas court ruled in favor of the magazine, however, agreeing with its claim that it would be "unreasonably burdened" if it had to determine in advance the risk of accepting such ads.[21]

But three years later, in *Braun v. Solider of Fortune Magazine* (1992), a Georgia court ruled in favor of the plaintiffs in a similar case, determining that the magazine had "violated a public duty" in not screening advertisements for such danger.[22] In that case, the ad read:

> Gun for hire. 37-year-old professional mercenary seeks jobs. Vietnam veteran. Discreet and very private. Bodyguard, courier, and other special skills. All jobs considered.

Right to Refuse Advertising

While the government cannot prohibit the advertising of legal products and services, courts have ruled that media outlets have the right to deny advertising space or time to companies whose products or services they view as harmful to society or too controversial. Many major television networks, as well as local stations, for example, have policies of not accepting advertising for controversial products such as firearms, alcohol, fireworks, or contraceptives, or services such as abortion.

The courts have ruled that such policies are permissible and do not violate the advertisers' First Amendment rights, mainly because those advertisers have alternative methods of promoting their products and services. The principle providing media outlets with this leeway is based on their First Amendment rights and dates back to the country's founding. In the late 1700s, for example, newspaper publisher Benjamin Franklin quipped that his newspaper "was not a stagecoach with seats on it for everyone."[23]

There are three exceptions to the principle of allowing the media to refuse advertising: (1) broadcasters are required by FCC and FTC rules to provide advertising opportunities (i.e., political speech) to legally qualified candidates for public office, (2) media outlets cannot conspire with each other to prohibit advertising (because of federal anti-trust laws), and (3) media outlets cannot refuse to accept an advertisement as retribution for that individual or company advertising elsewhere.

Regulation of Political Advertising

Today, courts generally rule that in political campaigns—either those involving candidates running for an office or a public referendum on an issue—spending money is analogous to speech, and is therefore worthy of First Amendment protection.

Common law also provides that television and radio stations are not responsible for libelous or distasteful content in political advertisements. Because of the large volume of political advertisements aired during a political campaign, the courts have ruled, broadcasters would be "unreasonably burdened" by a requirement that they verify the accuracy of ads before they aired. Instead, the FCC and other observers suggest that for candidates claiming that their opponents are airing unfair or inaccurate ads, a more practical recourse is to respond with ads of their own, rather than expecting the station or network to withdraw the opponent's ad.

This principle was tested in two cases—*Farmers Educational and Cooperative Union of America v. WDAY* (1959) and *Becker v. FCC* (1992).

In the *Farmers* case, the Supreme Court ruled that the candidate, party, or organization placing the ad—not the broadcaster—was responsible for its content. The Court added that it did not want broadcasters to "set themselves up as the sole arbiter of what is true and what is false."[24]

In the *Becker* case, which dealt with taste rather than truth, a Circuit Court of Appeals ruled that a television station was not responsible for the content of an anti-abortion advertisement that included images of aborted fetuses. Viewers had complained to the FCC that the ad had upset their children, and both the FCC and a Federal District Court ruled that the station should limit the ad to late-night hours when fewer children would be watching. The Circuit Court of Appeals overruled, however, determining that it was not the station's responsibility to evaluate the content of a political advertisement.[25]

Post-Watergate Campaign Finance Reform

Many of the country's current laws dealing with political campaigns and contributions resulted from the Watergate scandal of the early 1970s.

In 1974 Congress passed the Federal Election Campaign Act in an attempt to control how campaigns are financed. The act set limits on how candidates raise money and spend it, and how individuals and companies could contribute to campaigns. In the 1976 case of *Buckley v. Valeo*, however, the Supreme Court found parts of the law to be unconstitutional. The court drew a distinction between **contributions** (what an outside party donates to a candidate) and **expenditures** (what a candidate or organization spends). In its majority opinion in *Buckley*, the Court ruled that Congress had the authority to regulate the former but not the latter.

The Supreme Court referred to contributions and expenditures as "two sides of the same First Amendment coin." The Court based its decision on its belief that the limitations on contributions were acceptable because they limited undue influence on a political campaign, while restrictions on spending were not allowed because they limited expression.[26]

As a result of the Supreme Court ruling in *Buckley* and subsequent cases, more attention is paid to whether a political organization's activities are considered contributions or expenditures. If an organization purchases an advertisement on behalf of a candidate, but without the candidate's knowledge or approval, that is considered an expenditure and is therefore not subject to regulation. But if the purchase is coordinated between the candidate and the organization, it is considered a contribution to the campaign and is subject to campaign financing rules.

Two years after the Supreme Court's *Buckley* ruling, political advertising received another favorable ruling in the case of *First National Bank of Boston v. Bellotti*

(1978). The Commonwealth of Massachusetts attempted to punish a bank for violating its law prohibiting regulated companies from using their advertising to become involved in legal, political, or regulatory issues. But after the Supreme Court ruled in favor of the bank, the case became precedent for other cases in which state governments attempted to regulate political advertising. The case also gave birth to the term *corporate free speech*. The bottom line of the *Bellotti* ruling is that companies have the same "free speech" rights as individuals, and just as the government cannot restrict the free speech of individuals, it cannot restrict the free speech rights of companies.[27]

Campaign Finance Reform in the Twenty-First Century

While much political advertising deals either with issues or candidates, the most controversial ads are those that deal with both. Prior to 2002, organizations such as political parties, political action committees, nonprofit organizations, and industry associations could sponsor "issue ads" that appeared to deal with an issue but were actually intended to influence voters to draw inferences about the candidates associated with those issues. Those were known as "soft money" ads because they were a way for organizations to indirectly support or oppose a candidate without being subject to financial limitations or disclosure laws.

A typical issue ad might call attention to Senator X's record of voting in favor of tax breaks for certain types of companies. The ad might emphasize that the companies that received the tax breaks also violated environmental laws, thus implying that Senator X favors tax breaks for environmental lawbreakers. Even though the ad may not mention that Senator X is running for re-election, its intent is obvious.

The key to issue ads, which grew out of the post-Watergate political reform laws that were discussed in the previous section, was that ads could not use words or phrases such as *vote for, vote against, elect, support, defeat, reject,* or *Smith for Congress*. The language for that list, sometimes referred to as the "magic words," comes from the 1976 case of *Buckley v. Valeo*.[28]

In 2002, Congress passed the Bipartisan Campaign Reform Act, also known as the McCain-Feingold-Cochran bill in recognition of the three legislators who introduced it. The BCRA was aimed at reducing the influence of issue advertising and closing other loopholes. Proponents of the bill hoped it would address the problem of money influencing politics, but instead it only forced politicians and their financial supporters to find ways to circumvent the law.

One such method was through the so-called "527 ads," so named for the IRS section 527 designation for nonprofit organizations involved in political causes. Under the BCRA, such organizations cannot sponsor political ads that mention a "clearly identifiable candidate" within thirty days of a primary election or within sixty days of a general election. Within those windows, the organizations' political advertising can refer only to issues and not to candidates.

Another provision of the BCRA is a requirement that political ads on television and radio include an announcement by the candidate such as "I am (name), a candidate for (office), and I approved this message." The rationale was to prevent candidates and parties from broadcasting ads attacking an opponent and then denying responsibility. While the law applies only to candidates for national office, many states have passed similar laws for state and local elections.

Most of the BCRA's provisions were upheld by the Supreme Court in the 2003 case, *McConnell v. Federal Elections Commission*.[29]

A conflict tangentially related to the BCRA took place during the 2004 presidential election campaign. A political group supporting the re-election campaign of President George W. Bush sought to restrict the advertising of Michael Moore's documentary film *Fahrenheit 9/11* on the grounds that because the film itself was critical of the Bush Administration, television advertisements promoting the film were themselves politically motivated.

Citizens United filed complaint with the Federal Elections Commission stating that to advertise the film within sixty days of the November 3 election would violate the BCRA. The FEC, however, sided with Moore after the filmmaker responded that to limit such advertising would violate his First Amendment rights, as well as the rights of theaters wishing to advertise and show the film and individuals who wanted to watch it.

Filmmaker Michael Moore's documentary Fahrenheit 9/11 *was at the center of a 2004 case involving political advertising.*

Frequently Asked Questions about Advertising Regulation

1. *Why does the government not scrutinize the advertising industry more heavily than it does?* The Federal Trade Commission, the government agency responsible for enforcing truth-in-advertising laws, is one of the most overworked and under-staffed agencies in Washington. With a heavy workload and limited resources, the FTC sets its enforcement priorities based on the outrageousness of the false claims and the potential for harm. Also, when the term *advertising* is used in a general sense, it is presumed to be truthful in nature. Unless a regulatory agency has accused a specific advertisement of being false, it is given the "benefit of the doubt" and presumed to be truthful.

2. *If advertising gets less First Amendment protection than political speech, why is it so difficult to pass laws about advertising of controversial products and services?* According to common law, if a product is legal to manufacture, sell, purchase, distribute, own, or use, no government agency can make it illegal to advertise it. Government agencies are, however, permitted to make time, place, and manner restrictions on advertising in cases in which there is a compelling state interest. Those restrictions apply mainly to advertising that is purely commercial speech; advertising that constitutes political speech would be difficult for the government to regulate.

3. *Are there any rules that limit the number of advertisements that can be aired on television per hour?* While the FCC has established rules regarding the amount of advertising time that can be allotted during children's programming, there are no such rules for advertising aired during other times. The FCC has determined that marketplace demands can determine the appropriate number of length of commercials better than the government. FCC publications state that "if stations air more commercials than the public will tolerate, the market will regulate itself—viewers will not watch and advertisers will not buy time."[30]

Point/Counterpoint: Advertising Aimed at Children

Why Advertising Aimed at Children Should be Tightly Regulated

The Federal Trade Commission claims that children are "unqualified by age or experience to anticipate or appreciate the possibility that representations may be exaggerated or untrue."[31] The Children's Advertising Review Unit of the Better Business Bureau adds that "younger children have a limited capacity for evaluating the credibility of information they receive; advertisers therefore have a special responsibility to protect children from their own susceptibilities."[32]

Why Advertising Aimed at Children Should Not be Regulated Differently Than Other Types of Advertising

Advertising industry executives admit that while their speech is lower on the First Amendment hierarchy than political speech and therefore deserves less protection, it is not completely unprotected, and the fact that some consumers may not be any taller than the top of the television set does not take away their rights as potential receivers of that information. Advertisers also claim that it is the responsibility of parents—not the courts or the FTC—to help children evaluate the credibility of information they receive through the mass media.

Chapter Summary

Because it is a form of political speech, political advertising is protected by the First Amendment and is subject to little regulation. That regulation comes in the form of the Bipartisan Campaign Reform Act, a 2002 law that regulates contributions to political campaigns and how that money is spent on advertising messages.

Conversely, commercial advertising receives a lesser degree of First Amendment protection and is subject to regulation from federal, state, and local governments. At the federal level, the Federal Trade Commission and other administrative agencies regulate advertising in an attempt to protect consumers from illegal or unethical advertising practices. Many states have similar regulations in place, mostly related to consumer protection. City and county governments regulate outdoor advertising, mostly in an attempt to enhance the aesthetics of the community based on the principle of time, place, and manner.

Apart from cases of false advertising, however, many attempts at advertising regulation fail because of the commercial speech doctrine, a philosophy which prohibits the government from regulating truthful advertising of legal products and services.

CASE PROBLEM

The Case of the Cable Descrambler

You're the advertising manager at the *Mudville Daily Tribune*. One morning you're sitting at your desk and the local cable television provider—one of your biggest advertisers—calls and asks you to "look at the ad on the bottom right corner of page D-11." You turn to that page and find a quarter-page ad for a device that enables the user to descramble cable television signals and, essentially, obtain cable television signals for free. The ad was placed by an out-of-state company that provided only a post office box, a 1-800 telephone number, and a web address. The ad was paid for in advance, and the advertisers' check has already been cashed. The advertiser paid for twelve weeks, and the ad has already run for three.

The cable company insists that you no longer carry the ad and warns that if you don't, the company will cancel its advertising in the newspaper and will sue you for loss of subscriber revenue. Before you can even contact your newspaper's attorney, the company calls you back and indicates it plans to sue your newspaper for lost revenue, even if it agrees to no longer carry the ad.

You contact your newspaper's attorney, but he is on vacation and will not return for another week. In the meantime, the cable company has also placed an angry call to the publisher of the newspaper (your boss).

The publisher wants to see you immediately. You realize that the publisher will want to do something immediately and will not wait for the attorney to return from vacation. Which of the following recommendations would you make?

- **a.** Cancel the ad immediately, issue a partial refund to the advertiser, apologize to the cable company, and hope that will be enough to prevent a lawsuit.
- **b.** Allow the ad to run the remaining nine weeks, since it has already been pre-paid, but promise the cable company you will not renew the ad after that.
- **c.** Inform the cable company that you cannot be responsible for the content of every advertisement that runs in your newspaper, and one advertiser will not dictate policies regarding what other ads you will accept. You will allow the advertiser to renew the ad if it wishes to.
- **d.** Offer to settle the matter without going to court but insist that the cable company prove damages—a specific dollar amount lost due to local customers using the device to steal cable signals.

SOCRATIC DIALOGUE QUESTIONS

1. Could the Central Hudson Test be used to support laws restricting the advertising of tobacco products? Why or why not?

2. Government agencies such as the FCC and FTC and watchdog groups such as the Better Business Bureau suggest that advertisers who aim their messages at children are responsible for making sure those ads are not misleading. Should that responsibility lie only with the advertisers, or should parents also be partly responsible? What is your reaction to the positions taken by advocacy groups such as the Campaign for a Commercial-Free Childhood and Alliance for American Advertising?

3. Suppose you work in the advertising department of a newspaper or magazine. To what extent is your newspaper or magazine responsible if some of the products or services sold through your advertising turn out to be illegal or result in illegal acts?

4. Find at least one case in Chapter 12 with which you strongly disagree with the court ruling (in the final resolution of the case) and be prepared to share your opinion with the class.

GLOSSARY OF TERMS

Central Hudson Test   A four-part test for determining the constitutionality of government regulation of advertising; established in the 1980 Supreme Court case, *Central Hudson v. Public Service Commission.*

Commercial speech doctrine   The policy of providing some degree of First Amendment protection to commercial speech (advertising), but far less than is given to political speech.

Contributions   Direct gifts of money or services that are subject to limitations under state and federal election laws.

Deceptive and misleading advertising   Advertising that is not false per se, but may omit pertinent information.

Expenditures   Money spent by political candidates, parties, or similar organizations; not subject to limitation under state or federal election laws.

False advertising   Advertising deemed to be untrue on its face; it receives no First Amendment protection.

Reasonable consumer standard   A standard applied in cases of advertising accused of being deceptive; an advertisement is considered to be deceptive if a "reasonable consumer" would be deceived.

NOTES

1. *Valentine v. Chrestensen*, 316 U.S. 52 (1941).
2. *Virginia State Board of Pharmacy v. Virginia Citizens Consumer Council*, 425 U.S. 748 (1976).
3. Randy Bobbitt and Ruth Sullivan, *Developing the Public Relations Campaign*. Boston, Mass.: Allyn and Bacon, 2005, p. 204.
4. *Federal Trade Commission v. Colgate-Palmolive Co.*, 380 U.S. 374 (1965).
5. *Beneficial Corp. v. FTC*, 542 F.2d 611 (1976).
6. "Tropicana Settles False Ad Charges." *Pittsburgh Post-Gazette*, June 3, 2005, p. 8-E.
7. Larry Neumeister, "Judge: Listerine Ads False, Misleading." Associated Press report, January 8, 2005; *McNeil-PPC, Inc., v. Pfizer, Inc.*, 351 F. Supp. 2d 226 (2005).
8. *Bigelow v. Virginia*, 421 U.S. 809 (1975).
9. *Virginia State Board of Pharmacy v. Virginia Citizens Consumer Council*, 425 U.S. 748 (1976).
10. *Central Hudson v. Public Service Commission*, 447 U.S. 557 (1980).
11. *Central Hudson v. Public Service Commission*, 447 U.S. 557 (1980).
12. *Posadas de Puerto Rico Associates v. Tourism Company of Puerto Rico*, 478 U.S. 328 (1986).
13. *44 Liquormart v. Rhode Island*, 517 U.S. 484 (1996).
14. Tony Mauro, "Court Lets Billboard Ad Ban Stand." *USA Today*, April 27, 1997, p. 1-A.
15. "Leading Advocates For Children Challenge Alliance for American Advertising." *Progressive Newswire*, March 15, 2005.
16. *Pittsburgh Press v. Pittsburgh Commission on Human Relations*, 413 U.S. 376 (1973).
17. *Ragin v. New York Times*, 923 F.2d 995 (1991).
18. *Bates v. State Bar of Arizona*, 433 U.S. 350 (1977).
19. *Shapero v. Kentucky Bar Association*, 486 U.S. 466 (1988).
20. *Florida Bar Association v. Went For It*, 515 U.S. 618 (1995).
21. *Eimann v. Soldier of Fortune*, 880 F.2d 830 (1989).
22. *Braun v. Solider of Fortune Magazine*, 968 F.2d 1110 (1992).
23. Frank Luther Mott, *American Journalism*. New York, N.Y.: MacMillan, 1950, p. 55.
24. *Farmers Educational and Cooperative Union of America v. WDAY*, 360 U.S. 525 (1959).
25. *Becker v. FCC*, 95 F.3d 75 (1992).
26. *Buckley v. Valeo*, 424 U.S. 1 (1976).
27. *First National Bank of Boston v. Bellotti*, 435 U.S. 765 (1978).
28. *Buckley v. Valeo*, 424 U.S. 1 (1976).
29. *McConnell v. Federal Elections Commission*, 540 U.S. 93 (2003).
30. *Television Deregulation*, 98 F.C.C. 1105.
31. "Federal Trade Commission Policy Statement on Deception," October 14, 1983.
32. Roy L. Moore, Ronald T. Farrar, and Erik L. Collins, *Advertising and Public Relations Law*. Mahwah, N.J.: Lawrence Erlbaum Associates, 1998, p. 432.

13 Public Relations

At the core of all ethical communications must be the truth. Not even the best-researched, best-planned, and best-executed public relations campaigns could convince the American people that one plus one equals three.

Edward L. Bernays, 1990

LEARNING OBJECTIVES

As a result of reading this chapter, students should:

- Understand how many of the legal issues affecting journalists (libel, privacy, copyright) also affect public relations professionals.

- Understand how knowledge of such issues can help an individual public relations professional advise his or her clients regarding when it may be advisable to seek formal legal counsel.

- Understand how knowledge of these issues can help public relations professionals avoid legal problems that may affect them and/or their clients or employers.

Public Relations and the Law: Some General Rules

There are two general principles regarding the legal obligations of public relations professionals:

    1. *A practitioner's obligation to the law always takes priority over his or her obligation to a client or employer.* This means that public relations representatives must cooperate with law enforcement investigations or other legal matters involving a client or employer, regardless of any confidentiality agreements between the parties.

    2. *Communication between a public relations representative and his or her client is confidential in a general sense, but not privileged in a legal sense.* While professional communicators have a general obligation to maintain the confidences and privacy rights of clients or employers, that does not mean they can claim privilege in a legal proceeding. Unlike journalists, they may be forced to provide information about the activities of their clients or employers. The court system recognizes the need for confidentiality in relationships such as journalist–source, doctor–patient and lawyer–client, but does not extend it to the relationship between public relations representatives and their clients or employers.

A significant number of public relations professionals responding to a recent survey admitted that they were either "not at all familiar" or only "somewhat familiar" with the legal principles involved in public relations work. Results for specific legal issues included Securities and Exchange Commission regulations (86.7 percent either "not at all familiar" or "somewhat familiar"), commercial speech (86.7 percent), copyright (78.5 percent), access to information (75.6 percent), and libel (71.8 percent).

Public Relations and the First Amendment

Contributions to Political Candidates and Causes

Because companies often coordinate their contributions to political candidates and causes through their public relations departments, those professionals should be knowledgeable about state and federal laws that affect such contributions. Federal laws are discussed in the previous chapter.

Bill Stuffers

Many state governments have attempted to regulate the manner in which banks and public utilities communicate to their customers by including informational items or **bill stuffers** with statements and bills. When challenged in the court system, however, such laws are often declared unconstitutional because they infringe on the company's First Amendment free speech rights.

In a 1980 U.S. Supreme Court case, *Consolidated Edison Co. of New York v. Public Service Commission of New York,* the court ruled that the electric company could use bill stuffers to communicate with its customers regardless of content of the material. The ruling invalidated a state law that allowed banks and utilities to include non-controversial information in bill stuffers, but prohibited information that dealt with legal, political, or regulatory matters.[1]

In the 1986 U.S. Supreme Court case of *Pacific Gas & Electric Co. v. Public Utilities Commission of California,* the court invalidated a state law that required public utilities to provide an opportunity for their critics to respond to the company's bill stuffers with bill stuffers of their own. The law, called a "right of reply" rule, stated that any individual or group who objected to the content of a bill stuffer could produce its own stuffer, at its own expense, deliver it to the utilities company, and the company would be required to include it with the next month's bill.

The Supreme Court, however, ruled that the utilities do not have to provide such an opportunity. The state's Public Utilities Commission claimed the rule was analogous to the broadcasting industry standard of "equal time," but the Court ruled that bill stuffers are more like print journalism than broadcasting, and therefore could not be regulated.[2]

Differentiating between Advertising and Public Relations

Sometimes the line between commercial advertising and other forms of expression is difficult to detect, but whether a form of communication is deemed to be commercial speech or political speech determines to a large degree the level of First Amendment protection for which it is eligible.

Sporting goods manufacturer Nike found itself in such a conflict in 2002–2003. Like many American companies that outsource the manufacturing process to overseas labor markets, the sporting goods manufacturer is often accused of violating child labor standards and condoning "sweatshop" conditions. The company decided to strike back at its critics, claiming in news releases and letters to newspapers that its products were not produced under such conditions. Nike also wrote letters to university administrators on campuses where students had called for their institutions to boycott the company, which was a major provider of athletic equipment.

Consumer advocate Marc Kasky of San Francisco accused Nike of conducting a "misleading" public relations campaign that violated California's truth-in-advertising law. California's unusual advertising statute not only prohibited companies from disseminating false information (a determination usually left to the Federal Trade Commission), but allowed individuals to file charges against violators, even though they may not have been personally harmed. The case centered not on whether Nike's statements were true, but whether they were protected as free speech and whether individuals such as Kasky should be allowed to pursue such cases.

A California trial court sided with Nike, ruling that its messages aimed at responding to public criticism were statements of opinion rather than commercial messages. The California Supreme Court reversed that decision, claiming that every message a company disseminates is to some degree a commercial message and was therefore not fully protected by the First Amendment.

Nike appealed the decision to the U.S. Supreme Court. Harvard Law School professor Laurence Tribe, representing the company, argued that the suit should be thrown out because of the company's First Amendment right to defend itself in matters of public interest. He and other Nike supporters pointed out that the company was merely using the same communications methods as its critics, and therefore deserved an equal level of free speech protection.

Organizations lining up to help Nike by filing amicus curiae ("friends of the court") briefs included Microsoft, the Public Relations Society of America, Exxon

Protestors gather outside the Supreme Court building as the court decides the 2003 case involving sporting goods manufacturer Nike and its advertising. The court had to first decide if its response to its critics should be classified as commercial speech or political speech.

Mobil, the American Civil Liberties Union, and national news organizations that worried that if Nike lost the case, many companies would be reluctant to communicate with the media for fear of violating the law. Siding with Kasky were the Sierra Club, Public Citizen, and several consumer groups.

In the spring of 2003, the Supreme Court refused to hear the case, meaning that Kasky could continue to pursue it in the California court system. In declining to hear the case, Justice John Paul Stevens wrote that "the speech at issue represents a blending of commercial speech and debate on issues of public importance," and Justice Sandra Day O'Connor added that "none of this speech was advertising in the strictest sense of the term."[3] Later that year, Nike agreed to settle the case for $2 million, with $1.5 million being paid to Kasky's organization and $500,000 being spent to provide after-hours educational programs and other benefits for Nike's overseas employees.

Relationships with Freelancers

The 1975 case of *Community for Creative Non-Violence v. Reid* established the principle that in the absence of a "works for hire" agreement, freelancers retain the rights to their creative work after their employers have used them one time. This case did not involve public relations professionals but affects the profession because of its dependency on freelance writers, photographers, graphic artists, and other independent contractors.[4] This case is covered in more detail in Chapter 11.

Funding of Government Communication Activities

Because of a 1913 law known as the Gillett Amendment, government agencies and units cannot spend public money on promotional activities or legislative advocacy unless they are authorized to do so by law or congressional mandate. The rationale behind the law is to prevent government agencies from spending taxpayer money to implement advertising and public relations campaigns related to political issues in which they have a vested interest. The law does not prevent government agencies and branches of the military from employing public information officers, as those functions are authorized by law and there are no conflicts of interest.

Although the Gillett Amendment is a federal law and does not apply to states, many state legislatures have created similar laws restricting the expenditure of state funds. One example is found in the case of state universities that use public money to campaign for increases in financial support from state government. In essence, a university involved in such an activity is using taxpayer money to generate more taxpayer money, creating an inherent conflict of interest. Universities wanting to conduct such persuasive activities must therefore do so using privately raised funds.

Public Relations Representatives as Lobbyists

When public relations professionals represent their clients in advocating or opposing political or regulatory issues at the federal level, they are required to register with the federal government as **lobbyists.** Most states have similar regulations for public relations professionals working on state issues. In most states, the attorney general or secretary of state is the official in charge of the registration process.

For example, if a public relations representative is working in the public relations department at a public utility and wants to meet with state legislators in an attempt to influence government regulation, it is not as easy as making appointments and then showing up at their offices.

Registration has always been a requirement for full-time political operatives, but for public relations professionals, it was unheard of until a 1950 court case. In *United States v. Slaughter*, the U.S. Supreme Court took away the dividing line between full-time lobbyists and public relations professionals.[5] Even if lobbying is only a small part of their job duties, public relations representatives are required to work under the same rules as full-time lobbyists if they represent their clients in legislative matters.

Legal Problems in Investor Relations

Public Disclosure

Public disclosure is a large and complicated area of federal law that is subject to frequent change. It is often difficult to keep up with the changes, meaning that when in doubt, public relations representatives should not hesitate to contact their legal departments for guidance. Attorney and public relations expert Frank Walsh wrote in a 1991 book that "there is a great deal for the public relations professional to know, but perhaps the most important thing for them to know is when to talk to the company's attorney."[6]

Put simply, public disclosure refers to the requirement that any information about a company that may affect how its stock is evaluated by stockbrokers, analysts, or potential investors must be released in a manner that is timely, accurate, and in its correct context. Examples include quarterly or annual earnings, potential mergers and acquisitions, changes in leadership, new products or services, major expansion plans, employee layoffs, pending litigation (as plaintiff or defendant), or defaults on loans. There have been numerous cases in which companies have been fined by the Securities and Exchange Commission (SEC) or sued by stockholders because such information was not provided in a timely manner, was deemed to be misleading, or was not in its correct context. Analysts suggest that such news be released in the late afternoon or early evening after the stock markets have closed, as opposed to releasing it while the trading floors are open.

In a 1972 case, *SEC v. Pig 'n' Whistle Corporation*, a public relations agency distributed news releases for its client, a Chicago–based restaurant and motel chain. When the releases were found to include inaccurate and misleading information, the question arose as to which party was responsible—the agency or the client. The Federal District Court ruled that the responsibility belonged to both and that the agency's claim that it was only "doing what the client asked" was not a sufficient defense. The SEC claimed, and the court agreed, that the agency was responsible for knowing enough about a client's business and SEC regulations to verify the claims made in the news releases before they were distributed.[7]

The SEC requirement that public relations representatives are responsible for the accuracy of news releases does not mean representatives must cross-examine their clients in detail about the information they are asked to disseminate, but they should not blindly release questionable information without some level of scrutiny.

In addition to the *Pig 'n' Whistle* case, other major cases in this area are *SEC v. Texas Gulf Sulphur* (1968), *Zucker v. Sable* (1976), *Staffin v. Greenberg* (1982), and a 1984 conflict between Apple Computer Corporation and its stockholders.

Texas Gulf Sulphur was an American-owned chemical company that had drilling rights in a remote region in eastern Canada. One of its operating units discovered large deposits of copper, zinc, and other valuable minerals, but wanted to keep the discovery a secret for as long as possible so it could purchase additional land to expand its operation. Rumors of the discovery leaked out and eventually reached Wall Street, so the company issued a series of news releases that admitted the find but downplayed its value. Meanwhile, company officials, who knew how valuable the minerals were, bought additional stock, so the SEC prosecuted the company for releasing misleading information and omitting other pertinent details from the news releases. The company was found guilty and fined.[8]

In the Zucker case, the defendant was the Sable Corporation, the manufacturer of contact lenses and other health-related items. Sable issued a news release about a new type of soft contact lens that it was developing. Based on the news release, new investors purchased stock in the company, and existing stockholders bought additional stock. Both groups expected the stock price to rise as a result of the new product.

What was omitted from the news release was the fact that the product had not yet been submitted to the Food and Drug Administration for its approval—a process that often takes two years or more. By leaving out that important detail, the release implied that the product would be on the market immediately.

One angry stockholder sued the company, claiming the omission misled him and other stockholders. A Federal District Court ruled that while the company should have been more specific, that omission did not constitute an inaccuracy. Even though the company was found not financially liable, it spent thousands of dollars in legal fees and the prolonged litigation damaged it in the eyes of stock analysts and current and potential investors.[9]

In *Staffin v. Greenberg*, a company was able to defend itself against a stockholder lawsuit, but not before spending thousands of dollars in legal fees. Robert Staffin was a stockholder in a Pennsylvania company called Bluebird Inc., which dealt in wholesale meats. For many years, its stock price had remained stable, selling for about $10 per share—the same price that Staffin and other investors had paid for it. What Staffin and other stockholders did not know was that the company was about to be taken over by a British wholesale company, and the stock price was expected to take a significant jump.

There had been some rumors that the acquisition was going to take place, but each time the stockholders tried to find out information from the company, its public relations department either denied that the meetings were taking place or responded with information that made it look like the merger was less likely than it actually was. The company issued news releases and stockholder advisories that used phrases such as "still a long way off" and "may happen in the distant future."

Staffin and the other stockholders grew tired of waiting and in July of 1979 sold their stock for $10 a share—about what they paid for it. Less than a month later, Bluebird was taken over by the British company, and the stock jumped from $10 to $15 a share overnight. Staffin and the other stockholders sued the company, claiming that it violated SEC rules by releasing false and misleading information. A Federal District Court and Circuit Court of Appeals both ruled that it was a "close call," but decided in favor of the company. The SEC punished the company with a nominal fine and said that while some of the information was misleading, there was no "smoking gun" to indicate a conspiracy to hide truthful information. Even though the company did not lose the lawsuit, the SEC fine damaged its reputation among current and potential investors.[10]

An opposite situation took place in the Apple computer case. Instead of misleading information skewed toward the negative that influenced stockholders to sell, it was a case of misleading information skewed toward the positive, which influenced stockholders to buy more stock based on positive and over-optimistic comments by company leaders. The case involved a new software program called "Lisa," which was over-promoted in the company's stockholder communications, influencing outsiders to begin investing in the company and existing stockholders to purchase additional stock.

The software program was a failure, and stockholders later learned that company leaders knew it would fail but continued to promote it, hoping it would somehow work out. The case was settled out of court, with Apple paying the stockholders an undisclosed amount.[11]

Insider Trading

Members of a company's public relations staff, as well as employees of public relations agencies that represent publicly traded companies, are in a unique position because they have access to a great deal of company information. If an employee of a company or the agency that represents that company uses that information to illegally trade that company's stock, however, he or she may be in violation of the Securities and Exchange Act of 1934, a law to prevent **insider trading.** An individual becomes an "insider" if he or she is in a position to learn of business information that affects that organization's stock before that information becomes public knowledge. SEC rules prohibit such individuals from purchasing or selling stock until after the information becomes public.

Although not a widespread problem at present, a 1986 case—*SEC v. Franco*—is a constant reminder of the danger. Anthony Franco was owner of a public relations agency and at one point in the 1980s was president of the Public Relations Society of America (PRSA). He was found guilty of violating insider trading laws because he bought stock in one of his client companies based on information that was not generally available to other stockholders. He never admitted any wrongdoing, but did pay a fine and was forced to resign as president of PRSA.[12]

Public Relations Materials and Libel Law

As discussed in Chapter 6, *libel* is a legal term that refers to the defamation of a person's character or reputation in a published or broadcast form. Libel is most often associated with media such as newspapers, magazines, television, and radio, but can also be found in news releases, internal publications, and other public relations materials. One notable example is the 1979 case of *Hutchinson v. Proxmire*, in which a United States senator was sued by a researcher because of defamatory comments in the senator's news releases and newsletters.[13] The case did not involve public relations professionals, but it caught their attention because it involved materials commonly used in the profession.

Common Law Protections

While writers of news releases must follow the same rules as journalists with respect to libel, they also benefit from some degree of First Amendment protection. In addition to "truth," courts have applied the "fair comment" defense (customarily applied to editorials and other forms of opinion writing) to opinions expressed in news releases.

The 1986 case of *Karp v. Hill and Knowlton* began when Steven Karp, an executive with the Buckingham Corporation, left the liquor and wine company and formed his own competing company. Buckingham, a Hill and Knowlton client, filed suit against Karp, claiming that the former employee used confidential business information and conspired with the company's distributors to form the new venture. After a court ruled in favor of the company but before a financial award was determined, Hill and Knowlton issued a news release that repeated the company's claim of fraud and expressed its view that "substantial relief should be granted." One of the recipients of the news release was a beverage industry newsletter, which included that quote and other excerpts in its coverage of the case. Karp filed a libel suit against the public relations firm, but the court ruled that all statements in the release were either factual (as based on the findings of the court in the initial case) or were protected as fair comment.[14]

The same year, in *Parks v. Steinbrenner*, the New York Supreme Court ruled in favor of the New York Yankees in a libel suit filed by umpire Dallas Parks. The news release quoted the team's owner as calling Parks a "scab" who "had it in" for the Yankees and "misjudged" plays. The release added that Parks did not "measure up" to American League standards and criticized his decision to eject two Yankees players from a game. A trial court ruled in favor of Parks, but the New York Supreme Court overturned, examining the news release and determining that, like in the Karp case, all of its components were either statements of fact or opinion, both of which were protected.[15]

Internal Publications

Publications such as employee newsletters and magazines are another problem area. Numerous companies have been sued by employees for either libel or invasion

A company's internal newsletter may be subject of libel to privacy lawsuits if it contains defamatory material about the company's employees or uses their photographs without their permission.

of privacy because of defamatory or embarrassing information in the company's publications. Complicating the privacy problem is the fact that while legal concepts such as "private facts" and "false light" apply, the privacy defenses commonly used by professional journalists (such as "newsworthiness") do not.

Courts have ruled that news releases and employee newsletters are "tools of the trade" and are not eligible for the "newsworthiness" defense, nor are they eligible for the same level of First Amendment protection as newspapers and other public media. Therefore, companies that allow defamatory or embarrassing information to be published in a company newsletter or other internal publication can be sued by the employees affected and cannot claim "newsworthiness" or "press freedom" as a defense.

As discussed in Chapter 6, the courts demand a high burden of proof in libel cases, especially when the plaintiff is a public official or public figure or is involved in a matter of great public interest. The "actual malice" standard that helps newspapers defend themselves against libel suits does not help the public relations professional accused of libel because the plaintiffs in such cases tend to be private individuals. Examples include internal memos explaining the reasons for an employee's termination, a negative reference letter, an employee newsletter that depicts an employee in an unflattering manner, or other documents that disparage a competing company's products or employees.

Public Relations Materials and Appropriation

As discussed in Chapter 7, appropriation is the use of a person's name, photograph, image, likeness, or voice to endorse or promote a commercial product or service without the individual's consent. Public relations professionals who are responsible for producing organizational publications should be familiar with how appropriation law pertains to the photographs they choose for those publications.

For non-employees, the rule is simple: Organizations may not use that person's name, photograph, image, likeness, or voice to endorse a product or service unless that person provides his or her consent in writing. If a public official, professional athlete, show business personality, or other celebrity attends a company's event and a member of the communications staff takes photographs of the event, it is safe to use those photographs in the company newsletter or other publication provided they are presented in their correct context: the individual attended the company's event and shook hands and/or signed autographs for employees. But the company cannot use those photographs in print or broadcast advertisements to promote that company's products or services without written permission of the individual involved.

Nonprofit organizations must also be careful when using photographs of celebrities to endorse their causes. When a celebrity attends an event and consents to photographs, that consent should be looked upon as a short-term endorsement. Just because he or she agrees to be photographed and does not object to those photographs being published in the next issue of the newsletter does not mean those photographs can be used beyond that. Most celebrities who agree to attend such events will insist on written agreements that spell out for how long and for what purposes their photographs may be used.

For employees, the rules are even simpler. Organizations may not use their names, photographs, images, likenesses, or voices to endorse a product or service unless they provide their consent in writing. However, companies that frequently use photographs of employees in their internal publications or advertisements often have new employees sign consent forms as a condition of employment so that the company will not have to obtain individual signatures at the time the photographs are used. This process also gives the public relations departments consent to provide to the media photographs of employees who earn recognition within the company or industry.

In many cases, courts will recognize the concept of "implied consent," meaning that if a photographer asks an individual or group of people to pose for a photograph and explains that it is for the employee newsletter, written permission from the person or persons being photographed is not required. But if the photographs are candid or not posed, it is better to obtain written permission.

Minors cannot give consent to having their photograph used. When employees bring their children to a company event, the public relations department must have the parents' written permission to use the children's photographs in company publications.

Frequently Asked Questions about Public Relations and the Law

1. *I'm planning to pursue a career in public relations. Most of communication law seems to apply more to print and broadcast journalists. What do I need to know about communication law as it applies to the public relations field?* Unlike print and broadcast journalists, public relations professionals find there are few actions they can take that will result in legal consequences such as a monetary fine, prison sentence, or lawsuit. Two exceptions to this principle are insider trading and obstruction of justice. Insider trading, described earlier in this chapter, is a problem for public relations representatives because in most publicly traded companies they have access to valuable information that is not available to other employees. **Obstruction of justice** may occur when a public relations representative or other individual either fails to cooperate with a law enforcement investigation of his or her client or employer or otherwise attempts to hinder that investigation.

In most other areas, such as libel, privacy, or intellectual property, it is unlikely a public relations representative would be punished individually. What is much more common is for his or her client or employer to absorb the punishment—by either paying a fine or settling a lawsuit—because of something the public relations representative did or failed to do.

2. *I work for a public relations agency and am also invested in the stock market. Is it a conflict of interest for me to own stock in the companies that we represent?* Owning stock in companies that your public relations agency represents may result in a number of opportunities for conflicts of interest—both real and perceived. Because of the complexity of Securities and Exchange Commission rules and the possibility of "honest mistakes" resulting in charges of insider trading, many public relations agencies take the added precaution of prohibiting their employees from owning stock in the companies the agency represents. Even if your agency allows it, it is a bad idea. There are plenty of other good stocks to invest in.

3. *My company's management wants the public relations department to organize a contest or sweepstakes. What are some of the legal principles we need to know about?* If a company sponsors a contest, its attorneys should review contest materials such as entry forms, posters, news releases, and advertisements. Even if a purchase is not required, any contest that is merely associated with a commercial product or service is subject to Federal Trade Commission rules. To avoid legal problems, many companies hire experienced outside consultants to administer sweepstakes or other contests for them.

4. *Are there any laws that regulate how public relations agencies and their clients treat each other?* There are no specific laws regulating the relationship between public relations agencies and their clients. Therefore, clients or agencies who feel they have been cheated or misled in the agency-client relationship have no specific laws under which they can file lawsuits. Some, however, have been able to use the common-law principle of **unfair business practices** to file suit against the other party.

One example is a scenario in which a prospective client invites numerous public relations firms to submit competing proposals for a project. If the client likes one proposal but hires another agency to carry it out, the agency on the losing end can pursue legal action under the "unfair business practice" principle. In most such cases, courts tend to rule in favor of the agency on the losing end of the transaction. To avoid such problems, many agencies attach copyright protection to their written proposals, or require prospective clients to agree in advance to compensate the agency for its time if part or all of a proposal is accepted, but the agency is not hired to carry it out.

Point/Counterpoint: Public Relations Representatives and Privilege

Why the Relationships between Public Relations Professionals and Their Clients/Employers Should be Privileged

Professional communicators deserve the same level of protection as doctors and lawyers. Doctors must have the complete trust of their patients in order to provide quality health care, and lawyers must have the complete trust of their clients in order to provide quality legal representation. Public relations is no different—clients and employers must have trusting relationships with their outside public relations agencies and employees in order for those individuals to provide their best advice or service.

A public relations representative testifying in court against a client or employer is putting his or her career on the line. Whether his or her testimony is voluntary or mandated by the court, he or she cannot continue to work for the client or employer against whom the testimony was given. He or she should not be put in that awkward position.

Without privilege, public relations professionals are too vulnerable. Much like journalists working in states without shield laws, public relations representatives are "easy targets" for prosecutors, defense attorneys, and government officials who are simply looking for shortcuts rather than doing more thorough investigative work on their own. Shield laws protect journalists; public relations representatives should have similar protection.

Why the Relationships between Public Relations Professionals and Their Clients/Employers Should Not be Privileged

Granting privilege to public relations professionals may impede important government investigations. Public relations representatives often have inside knowledge of matters such as employment discrimination, insurance fraud, stock market irregularities, and environmental damage. They should be required to provide this information because those investigations serve the public interest.

Doctors and lawyers work in fields that are well-defined, while public relations is not well-defined. If public relations professionals are given privilege, a company in legal trouble could simply re-draw its organizational chart and claim that all of its employees work in public relations and are therefore immune to subpoenas and other court documents.

Granting privilege to public relations professionals may produce a "slippery slope" problem that results in legal privilege for everyone. What comes next—privilege for plumbers and hair stylists?

Compared to the work of lawyers and doctors, the work of public relations professionals is not that important. Individuals facing criminal charges have the constitutional right to legal representation, and patients have a moral right to quality health care. But no one has the constitutional or moral right to public relations advice. It's simply not as important as legal representation or health care.

Chapter Summary

Many of the legal issues typically associated with the journalism profession, such as libel, privacy, and copyright, also affect public relations professionals. While it is unlikely that public relations representatives would find themselves in legal trouble as individuals, their lack of knowledge of such issues may cause legal problems for their clients or employers, which in the end, will reflect poorly on them as professionals.

One example of an issue causing problems for individual public relations professionals, however, is insider trading. Employees of public relations agencies should therefore be knowledgeable about the laws regarding securities transactions and should avoid trading in stocks of companies their agency represents.

While it is impractical to expect public relations professionals to know every minor nuance of communication law, they should know enough to spot potential legal problems and to advise their clients or employers regarding when it may be advisable to seek formal legal counsel.

CASE PROBLEM

Public Relations Agencies and Competing Proposals

You're running a small company, and you're considering hiring an agency to come up with a long-term public relations plan. You contact four of the largest public relations firms in town and provide them with a request for proposals (RFP). Each agency submits a written response to your RFP and also comes into your conference room to do an in-person presentation.

Agencies A and B submit fairly weak proposals and you eliminate them early in the process. But Agency C and Agency D present an interesting scenario.

Agency C submitted an excellent written proposal and you can tell it's exactly what your company needs to do. The problem is that when the account executives came to do the in-person presentation, they turned out to be the most obnoxious people you've ever met. You just can't picture yourself working with them for the long-term because you fear there would be too many personality conflicts.

Agency D submitted a written proposal that was very ordinary, and at first glance, it appeared to be only slightly better than the proposals from Agencies A and B that you had already rejected. But when you met Agency D's representatives in person, they were very enthusiastic and the chemistry between your employees and their employees was very positive.

Then one of your employees suggests taking the good proposal from Agency C and hiring Agency D to carry it out.

Without consulting an attorney, which of the following do you believe?

    a. It is **already illegal** or **should be illegal** for a prospective client to do that.

    b. It is **perfectly legal** to do that. Although it is perhaps unfair to Agency C, the agency developed and submitted the proposal at its own risk and that's just part of being in a competitive business.

    c. It is legal to do that but certainly **unethical** and a lousy way to treat another business.

SOCRATIC DIALOGUE QUESTIONS

1. Should an employee be able to sue his or her employer for libel or invasion of privacy for damaging or embarrassing information published in the company newsletter? Why or why not? If your answer is yes, should the damage award be comparable to that resulting from a libel judgment against a daily newspaper?

2. Should public relations representatives and their clients enjoy the same level of confidentiality as doctors and patients, lawyers and clients, and clergy and parishioners? Why or why not? What are some of the similarities and differences in those relationships?

3. Find at least one case in Chapter 13 with which you strongly disagree with the court ruling (in the final resolution of the case) and be prepared to share your opinion with the class.

GLOSSARY OF TERMS

Bill stuffer   A way to communicate with customers by including informational items with statements and bills.

Insider trading   The illegal trading of stock based on information not available to the general public.

Lobbyist   A role in which public relations professionals represent their clients in advocating or opposing political or regulatory issues. Lobbyists are required to register with state and/or federal officials.

Obstruction of justice   Failure to cooperate with a government or law enforcement investigation or other intentional act intended to delay or impede an investigation.

Public disclosure   The Security and Exchange Commission requires that information that may affect how a company's stock is evaluated must be released in a timely manner and must be in its correct context and not misleading.

Unfair business practice   When there are no specific laws under which to file lawsuits, some have been able to use the common-law principle of unfair business practices to file suit against the other party.

NOTES

1. *Consolidated Edison Co. of New York v. Public Service Commission of New York,* 447 U.S. 530, (1980).
2. *Pacific Gas & Electric Co. v. Public Utilities Commission of California,* 475 U.S. 1 (1986).
3. "Nike Settlement Resolves Case, No Free Speech Issues at Heart." Associated Press report, September 13, 2003; "PR Utterances: Nike Settles Commercial Speech Case for $2 Million." *Crisis Counselor,* October 2003.
4. *Community for Creative Non-Violence v. Reid,* 490 U.S. 730 (1975).
5. "What You Need to Know About Governmental Relations and Lobbying." *Public Relations Journal,* October 1983, pp. 23–24.
6. Frank Walsh, *Public Relations and the Law.* Sarasota, Fla.: Institute for Public Relations Research and Education, 1991, p. 60.
7. *SEC v. Pig 'n' Whistle Corporation,* CCH Fed. Sec. L. Rep. (1972).
8. *SEC v. Texas Gulf Sulphur,* 401 F.2d 833 (1968).
9. *Zucker v. Sable,* 425 F. Supp. 658 (1976).
10. *Staffin v. Greenberg,* 672 F.2d 1196 (1982).
11. "Angry Stockholders Want to Take a Bite Out of Apple." Associated Press report, December 2, 1984.
12. *SEC v. Franco,* 1986 Lexis 909 (1986).
13. *Hutchinson v. Proxmire,* 443 U.S. 11 (1979).
14. *Karp v. Hill and Knowlton,* 12 Media L. Rep. 2093 (1986).
15. *Parks v. Steinbrenner,* 12 Media L. Rep. 2200 (1986).

APPENDIX A

Sources/Suggestions for Further Reading

Chapter 1   Getting Started

Brenner, Daniel L., and William L. Rivers, eds. *Free But Regulated: Conflicting Traditions in Media Law*. Ames, Iowa: Iowa State University Press, 1982.

Carter, T. Barton, Juliet L. Dee, Martin J. Gaynes, and Harvey L. Zuckman. *Mass Communications Law in a Nutshell*. St. Paul, Minn.: West Publishing, 1994.

Chamberlin, Bill, and Kent Middleton. *The Law of Public Communication*. White Plains: Longman Publishing Group, 1994.

Devol, Kenneth S. *Mass Media and the Supreme Court*. New York: Hastings House, 1990.

Dilts, John Paul, and Ralph Holsinger. *Media Law*. New York: McGraw-Hill, 1997.

Fraleigh, Douglas M., and Joseph S. Tuman. *Freedom of Speech in the Marketplace of Ideas*. New York: St. Martin's Press, 1997.

Frohnmayer, John. *Leaving Town Alive*. Boston: Houghton-Mifflin, 1993.

Hopkins, W. Wat, ed. *Communication and the Law*. Northport, Ala.: Vision Press, 2000.

Lang, James M. *Life on the Tenure Track: Lessons from the First Year*. Baltimore, Md.: Johns Hopkins University Press, 2005.

Moore, Roy L. *Mass Communication Law and Ethics*. Mahwah, N.J.: Lawrence Erlbaum Associates, 1999.

Nerone, John C., ed. *Last Rights: Revisiting Four Theories of the Press*. Urbana, Ill.: University of Illinois Press, 1995.

Overbeck, Wayne. *Major Principles of Media Law*. Fort Worth, Texas: Harcourt Brace, 1995.

Pember, Don. *Mass Media Law*. Dubuque, Iowa: Brown and Benchmark, 1996.

Siebert, Fred S., Theodore Peterson, and Wilbur Schramm. *Four Theories of the Press*. Freeport: Books for Libraries Press, 1973.

Wolfson, Nicholas. *Hate Speech, Sex Speech, Free Speech*. Westport, Conn.: Praeger Publishing, 1997.

Chapter 2   An Overview of the First Amendment

Chapter 3   The First Amendment and Political Speech

Berns, Walter. *The First Amendment and the Future of American Democracy*. Chicago: Gateway Editions, 1985.

Briggs, Tracey W. "When the First Amendment Hits Close to Home." *USA Today*, September 18, 2006, p. 7-D.

Brown, Charlene J., and Bill F. Chamberlin, *The First Amendment Reconsidered: New Perspectives on the Meaning of Freedom of Speech and Press*. New York: Longman, 1982.

Drucker, Susan, and Gary Gumpert. "Surveillance, Security in Post–September 11 America." *Free Speech Yearbook*, Vol. 39 (2001), pp. 83–96.

Emerson, Thomas L. *The System of Freedom of Expression*. New York: Vintage Books, 1971.

Emerson, Thomas L. *Toward a General Theory of the First Amendment*. New York: Vintage Books, 1967.

"The First Amendment: The Amendment That Keeps Us Free." Brochure from the Freedom Forum First Amendment Center, Nashville, Tenn.

Fraleigh, Douglas M., and Joseph S. Tuman, *Freedom of Speech in the Marketplace of Ideas*. New York: St. Martin's Press, 1987.

Freehling, William G. "Problem Solved? An Evaluation of the 1992 Military-Press Agreement." Paper presented at the 2001 Association for Education in Journalism and Mass Communication Conference, March 10, 2001.

Frohnmayer, John. *Out of Tune: Listening to the First Amendment*. Nashville, Tenn.: Freedom Forum Media Studies Center, 1994.

Greenawalt, Kent. *Fighting Words: Individuals, Communities and Liberties of Speech*. Princeton, N.J.: Princeton University Press, 1995.

Haiman, Franklyn S. *Speech and Law in a Free Society*. Chicago: University of Chicago Press, 1981.

Hentoff, Nat. *Free Speech for Me—But Not for Thee*. New York: HarperCollins, 1992.

Hentoff, Nat. *Living the Bill of Rights: How to be an Authentic American*. New York: HarperCollins, 1998.

Hopkins, W. Wat. "Cross-Burning Revisited: Will the Court Get it Right This Time?" Paper presented at the 2003 Association for Education in Journalism and Mass Communication Southeastern Conference, 2003.

Hudson, David. "The First Amendment: A Wartime Casualty?" First Amendment Center position paper, February 15, 2002.

Hudson, David L. "The Patriot Act: An Overview." Freedom Forum First Amendment Center position paper, March 15, 2002.

McKinnon, Catharine, Floyd Abrams, and Anthony Lewis. "A Conversation on the First Amendment." *New York Times Magazine*, March 13, 1994, p. 30.

Paulson, Ken. "Where Americans Stand on Freedom." Syndicated column, June 30, 2000.

Schauer, Frederick. *Free Speech: A Philosophical Enquiry*. New York: Cambridge Publishing, 1982.

Schudson, Michael. *The Sociology of News*. New York: W. W. Norton & Company, 2003.

Smith, Craig R., and David M. Hunsaker. *The Four Freedoms of the First Amendment*. Long Grove: Waveland Press, 2004.

Smolla, Rodney A. *Free Speech in an Open Society*. New York: Alfred A. Knopf, 1992.

Smolla, Rodney A. *A Year in the Life of the Supreme Court*. Durham, N.C.: Duke University Press, 1995.

"The State of the First Amendment 2005." Nashville, Tenn.: Freedom Forum First Amendment Center, 2005.

Stone, George, Richard A. Epstein, and Cass R. Sunstein. *The Bill of Rights in the Modern State*. Chicago: University of Chicago Press, 1992.

Terry, Carolyn. "The First Under Fire." *Presstime*, September 1995, pp. 36–42.

Trager, Robert L., and Donna L. Dickerson. *Freedom of Expression in the 21st Century*. Thousand Oaks, Calif.: Pine Forge Press, 1999.

Chapter 4   The First Amendment and Sexual Expression

Baird, Robert M., and Stuart E. Rosenbaum, eds. *Pornography: Private Right or Public Menace?* New York: Prometheus Books, 1998.

Clark, Charles C. "The Obscenity Debate." *CQ Researcher*, December 20, 1991, pp. 969–992.

Clark, Charles C. "Sex, Violence, and the Media." *CQ Researcher*, November 17, 1995, pp. 1017–1040.

Cline, Victor. *Where Do You Draw the Line?* Provo, Utah: Brigham Young University Press, 1974.

Copp, David, and Susan Wendell. *Pornography and Censorship.* Buffalo, N.Y.: Prometheus Books, 1983.

Crary, David. "Adult Porn Goes Mainstream, Stirs Furor." Associated Press report, April 2, 2006.

Downs, Donald Alexander. *The New Politics of Pornography.* Chicago, Ill.: University of Chicago Press, 1989.

Dworkin, Andrea, and Catharine MacKinnon, *Only Words.* Cambridge, Mass.: Harvard University Press, 1993.

Dwyer, Susan. *The Problem of Pornography.* Belmont, Calif.: Wadsworth Publishing, 1995.

"Everything You Always Wanted to Know About the Movie Rating System." Brochure provided by the National Association of Theatre Owners.

Flynt, Larry C. *An Unseemly Man: My Life as a Pornographer, Pundit, and Social Outcast.* Los Angeles, Calif.: Dove Books, 1996.

Funston, Richard, ed. *Judicial Crises: The Supreme Court in a Changing America.* New York: John Wiley and Sons, 1974.

Hart, Harold C., ed. *Censorship: For and Against.* New York, N.Y.: Hart Publishing Co., 1971.

Lane, Frederick. *Obscene Profits: The Entrepreneurs of Pornography in the Cyber Age.* New York: Taylor & Francis, Inc., 2001.

Linz, Daniel, and Neil Malamuth. *Pornography.* Newbury Park, Calif.: Sage Publications, 1998.

Strassen, Nadine. *Defending Pornography: Free Speech, Sex, and the Fight for Women's Rights.* New York: Scribner, 1995.

Terry, Carolyn. "The First Under Fire." *Presstime*, September 1995, pp. 36–42.

"Tough Talk on Entertainment." *Time*, June 12, 1995, pp. 32–35.

Trager, Robert, and Donna L. Dickerson. *Freedom of Expression in the 21st Century.* Thousand Oaks, Calif.: Pine Forge Press, 1999.

Wesson, Marianne, "Pornography as Speech and Product." *University of Chicago Law Review*, Vol. 60 (1993), p. 845.

Chapter 5   The First Amendment and Campus Issues

Arthur, John, and Amy Shapiro, ed. *Campus Wars: Multiculturalism and the Politics of Indifference.* Boulder, Colo.: Westview Press, 1995.

Berley, Marc. "Campuses Silence Free Speech." Syndicated column, April 2, 2001.

Bernstein, David E. *You Can't Say That!* Washington, D.C., Cato Institute, 2003.

Carlson, Tucker. "Banned! Today's Schoolbooks are a Lesson in Propaganda." *Reader's Digest,* October 2003, p. 43–44.

"Cyberlaw and the Student Media." Student Press Law Center, 1998.

Dardenne, Robert. *A Free and Responsible Student Press.* St. Petersburg, Fla.: The Poynter Institute, 2000.

Duscha, Julius, and Thomas Fischer, *The Campus Press: Freedom and Responsibility.* Washington, D.C.: American Association of State Colleges and Universities, 1973.

Estrin, Herman A., and Arthur M. Sanderson, ed. *Freedom and Censorship of the College Press.* Dubuque, Iowa: W. C. Brown Co., 1966.

Feldman, Samuel N. *The Student Journalist and Legal and Ethical Issues.* New York: Rosen Press, 1968.

Haiman, Franklyn. *Speech Acts and the First Amendment.* Carbondale, Ill.: Southern Illinois University Press, 1993.

Hentoff, Nat, and Stanley Fish. "Do Speech Codes Suppress Freedom of Expression?" *Taking Sides: Clashing Views on Controversial Issues in Media and Society.* Guilford, Conn.: McGraw Hill, 1999.

Kleiman, Howard M. "Student Electronic Media and the First Amendment." *Journalism & Mass Communication Educator,* Summer 1996, pp. 4–14.

Kors, Alan Charles, and Harvey A. Silverglate. *The Shadow University: The Betrayal of Liberty America's Campuses.* New York: HarperCollins, 1999.

Korwar, Arati. *War of Words: Speech Codes at Colleges and Universities in the United States.* Nashville, Tenn.: Freedom Forum Media Studies Center, 1995.

"The Latest Chapter: Book-Banning Attempts in Public Schools Decline Slightly." *Pittsburgh Post-Gazette,* September 5, 1996, p. A-16.

Law of the Student Press. Arlington, Va.: Student Press Law Center, 1994.

Lewis, Lionel. "The Limits of Faculty Freedom." *St. Petersburg Times,* December 29, 2002, p. 1-D.

"Making Schools Safe for the First Amendment." *Student Press Law Center Report,* Spring 2000.

McMurtrie, Beth. "War of Words." *Chronicle of Higher Education,* May 23, 2003, p. A-31.

Moore, Melanie A. "Free Speech on College Campuses: Protecting the First Amendment in the Marketplace of Ideas." *West Virginia Law Review,* Vol. 96 (1993–94), p. 511–548.

Nelson, Jack. *Captive Voices: The Report of the Commission of Inquiry Into High School Journalism.* New York: Schocken Books, 1974.

Paulson, Ken. "How Free is Campus Speech?" Syndicated column, April 24, 2001.

Philips, Susan. "Student Journalism: Are First Amendment Rights in Danger?" *CQ Researcher,* June 5, 1998, pp. 481–504.

Rubinstein, Ruth P. *Dress Codes: Meanings and Messages in American Culture.* Boulder, Colo.: Westview Press, 2001.

Shen, Fern. "Who Decides What Books You Can Read?" *Washington Post,* September 26, 2002.

Street, Scott. "Promoting Order of Squelching Campus Dissent?" *Chronicle of Higher Education,* January 12, 2001, p. A-38.

Terry, Carolyn. "The First Under Fire." *Presstime,* September 1995, pp. 36–42.

Trager, Robert L., and Donna L. Dickerson. *College Student Press Law.* National Council of College Publications Advisers, 1976.

"What Every Student Journalist Should Know." *Quill,* September 1997, pp. 44–49.

Wigal, Grace. "Hazelwood East School District v. Kuhlmeier: The Death of No Prior Restraint in an Official High School Newspaper." *West Virginia Law Review,* Vol. 91 (1989), p. 635.

Chapter 6   Defamation

Associated Press Stylebook and Libel Manual. New York: Associated Press, 1998.

Bobbitt, Randy. *West Virginia Media Law.* Charleston W. Va.: West Virginia Press Association, 1998.

Boylan, James. "Punishing the Press." *Columbia Journalism Review,* March/April 1997, pp. 24–27.

Colino, Stacey. "Long Arm of the Lawsuit SLAPPS at Dissenters." *In These Times,* March 28–April 3, 1990, pp. 11+.

Dill, Barbara. *The Journalist's Handbook on Libel and Privacy.* New York: Macmillan, 1986.

Gartner, Michael. "Naming the Victim." *Columbia Journalism Review,* July/August 1991, p. 54.

Goldsborough, Reid. "Warding Off Internet Legal Woes." *Public Relations Tactics,* July 2001, p. 6.

Gower, Karla. *Legal and Ethical Restraints in Public Relations.* Prospect Heights: Waveland Press, 2003.

Lee, Douglas. "Libel Judgments Climb as Respect for Media Falls." *First Amendment News,* August 1997, p. 1.

Libel Defense Resource Center, news releases, 2005 and 2006.

Miller, Teresa N., and Robert J. Schoop. "Letters of References: Information vs. Defamation." *A Legal Memorandum* (National Association of Secondary School Principals), Summer 2004, pp. 1–6.

Proposal for the Reform of Libel Law. Chicago: Annenberg Washington Program, 1988.

Prosser, William L. *The Law of Torts.* St. Paul, Minn.: West Publishing, 1964. *Restatement of Torts,* Second Edition. St. Paul, Minn.: American Law Institute, 1979.

Savage, David G. "Justices Refuse to Shield Reports of False Charges." *Los Angeles Times,* March 29, 2005.

Smolla, Rodney, and Michael J. Gaertner. "The Annenberg Libel Reform Proposal: The Case for Enactment." *William and Mary Law Review,* Fall 1989, pp. 25–65.

Smolla, Rodney. *Suing the Press.* New York: Oxford University Press, 1986.

"Ten Misconceptions About Libel Law." *Editor and Publisher,* June 21, 1997, pp. 90–91.

Terry, Carolyn. "The First Under Fire." *Presstime,* September 1995, pp. 36–42.

Touhy, John M., and Jeffrey W. Sarles, "Defamation Law," *National Law Journal,* September 8, 1997, p. B-6.

Chapter 7   Privacy

Alderman, Ellen, and Caroline Kennedy. *The Right to Privacy.* New York: Alfred A. Knopf, 1995.

"An Invasion of Privacy: The Media's Involvement in Law Enforcement Activities." Washington Legal Foundation Critical Issues Series, January 1998.

Baker, Russ. "Damning Undercover Tactics as Fraud." *Columbia Journalism Review,* March/April 1997, pp. 28–34.

Bellafante, Ginia. "Hide and Go Sue." *Time,* January 13, 1997, p. 81.

Biskupic, Joan. "High Court to Review Reporter Ride-Alongs." *Washington Post,* March 21, 1999, p. A-2.

Coronna, David. M. "The Right of Publicity." *Public Relations Journal,* February 1983, pp. 29–31.

Dill, Barbara. *The Journalist's Handbook on Libel and Privacy.* New York: Macmillan, 1986.

Riski, Richard J. "The Paparazzi Backlash." Paper presented at the Association for Education in Journalism and Mass Communications Spring Conference, March 2001.

Kirtley, Jane. "Is Reporter Ride-Along Doomed?" *West Virginia Press Association Newsletter,* June 1999, p. 4.

Lord, Lewis. "The Perils of 'Gotcha' Journalism." *U.S. News and World Report,* February 3, 1997, p. 11.

Mauro, Tony. "High Court Rulings Forever Change Relationship Between Media, Law Enforcement." *First Amendment News,* May 25, 1999.

"Network's Reporting Tactics Help Sink Media's Credibility." *USA Today,* October 22, 1999, pp. A-27.

Pollitt, Katha. "Naming and Blaming: Media Goes Wilding in Palm Beach." *The Nation,* June 24, 1991, pp. 833–838.

Prosser, William L. "Privacy." *California Law Review,* Vol. 48 (1960), p. 383.

Prosser, William L. *The Law of Torts.* St. Paul, Minn.: West Publishing, 1964.

Restatement of Torts, Second Edition. St. Paul, Minn.: American Law Institute, 1979.

Riski, Richard J. "The Paparazzi Backlash: Privacy and Newsgathering Through the Looking Glass." Paper presented at the Association for Education in Journalism and Mass Communication Southeast Colloquium, March 2001.

Schulz, David A. "Troubling Ruling Restricts News Gathering." *Editor & Publisher,* June 29, 1996, p. 5.

Smolla, Rodney. "Drawing Lines: Logic and Language Can Help When Separating Private From Public Information." *Presstime,* November 1992, p. 38.

Smolla, Rodney. *Jerry Falwell v. Larry Flynt: The First Amendment on Trial.* New York: St. Martin's Press, 1988.

Smolla, Rodney. *Suing the Press.* New York: Oxford University Press, 1986.

Warren, Samuel, and Louis D. Brandeis. "The Right to Privacy." *Harvard Law Review,* Vol. 4 (1890), p. 193.

"What's Fair?" *Media Studies Journal,* 1998.

Chapter 8   Problems News-Gathering

Boylan, James. "Punishing the Press." *Columbia Journalism Review,* March/April 1997, pp. 24–27.

"Closed Courtrooms." *Associated Press Stylebook and Libel Manual,* pp. 304–305.

"Covering the Courts." *Media Studies Journal,* 1998.

Farber, Myron. *Somebody Is Lying.* Garden City: Doubleday, 1982.

Freehling, William G. "Problem Solved? An Evaluation of the 1992 Military-Press Agreement." Paper presented at the 2001 Association for Education in Journalism and Mass Communication Conference, March 10, 2001.

Goodale, James C. *"Branzburg v. Hayes* and the Development of Qualified Privilege." *Hastings Law Review,* Vol. 26, p. 709 (1975).

Grady, Sandy. "Time for Supreme Court Reality TV." *USA Today,* September 13, 2005, p. 13-A.

Hernandez, Debra G. "Courtroom Cameras Debated." *Editor & Publisher,* February 17, 1996, pp. 11–13.

Kaiser, Robert G. "Because You Should Know: Governments Try to Hide What's Embarrassing." *Washington Post,* June 25, 2006, p. 7-E.

Lieberman, Jethro K. *How the Government Breaks the Law.* New York: Stein and Day, 1972.

Meyer, Philip. "What is a 'Journalist'?" *USA Today,* March 31, 2005, p. A-11.

Minow, Newton N., and Fred H. Cate. "Who Is an Impartial Juror in an Age of Mass Media?" *American University Review,* Winter 1991, pp. 631–664.

"Subpoenaed? Here's What You Can Do." *West Virginia Press Association Newsletter*, November 1996, p. 4.

"Supreme Court: No TV Cameras." *NewsMax,* September 2006, p. 32.

Tapscott, Mark. "Boondoggles Need Exposure." Syndicated column, December 8, 2004.

Taylor, Matthew P. "Dead Man Walking, But Who's Watching?" Paper presented at Association for Education in Journalism and Mass Communication Southeast Colloquium, March 8, 2003.

Wardle, Lynn D. "Allowing Cameras and Electronic Media in the Courtroom." Testimony before U.S. Senate Judiciary Committee, September 6, 2000.

Weisberg, Jacob. "Who is a Journalist? Anybody Who Wants to Be." Slate.com, March 9, 2005.

Whalen, Charles W. *Your Right to Know.* New York: Random House, 1973.

Who Is an Impartial Juror in an Age of Mass Media? Chicago: The Annenberg Washington Program, 1991.

Wilson, Theo. *Headline Justice.* New York: Thunder's Mouth Press, 1996.

Wise, David. *The Politics of Lying: Government Deception, Secrecy, and Power.* New York: Random House, 1973.

Yates, Carol. "What to Do When the Law Says, 'No Pictures.'" *News Photographer,* November 1993, p. 19.

Chapter 9   Broadcasting and Cable

Bittner, John R. *Law and Regulation of Electronic Media.* Englewood Cliffs, N.J.: Prentice-Hall, 1994.

Rivera-Sanchez, Milagros. "The Origins of the Ban on 'Obscene, Indecent, or Profane' Language of the Radio Act of 1927." *Journalism & Mass Communication Monographs,* February 1995, pp. 1–33.

Sadler, Roger L. *Electronic Media Law.* Thousand Oaks, Calif.: Sage Publications, 2005.

Sutel, Seth. "Court Throws Out FCC Media Ownership Rules." Associated Press report, June 25, 2004.

Chapter 10   Cyberspace Issues

Charles S. Clark, "Regulating the Internet." *CQ Researcher,* June 30, 1995, pp. 561–584.

Elmer-DeWitt, Philip. "On a Screen Near You: Cyberporn." *Time,* July 3, 1995, pp. 38–45.

"Free Speech Is Under Attack in Cyberspace." *Chronicle of Higher Education,* January 20, 1995.

Goldsborough, Reid. "Warding Off Internet Legal Woes." *Public Relations Tactics,* July 2001, p. 6.

Helle, Steven. "Libel in Cyberspace." *Editor & Publisher,* December 24, 1994, p. 16.

Lemisch, Jesse. "The First Amendment Is Under Attack in Cyberspace." *Chronicle of Higher Education,* January 20, 1995, pp. A-56+.

Levy, Steven. "No Place For Kids? A Parents' Guide to Sex on the Net." *Newsweek,* July 3, 1995, pp. 47+.

Mauro, Tony. "Long Arm of the Law Reaches Into Cyberspace." *First Amendment News,* February 1996, pp. 1–7.

Mauro, Tony. "First Amendment Community Cyber-Celebrates." *First Amendment News*, July 1996, pp. 1–6.

Miller, Leslie. "The Internet's Seamy Side: Online Sex, Once Found, Can Be Raunchy." *USA Today*, July 19, 1995, p. A-1.

Samoriski, Jan. *Issues In Cyberspace*. Boston: Allyn and Bacon, 2002.

"Saving Children or Sacrificing Rights?" *Freedom Forum News*, April 8, 1996, p. 1.

"Study of Enron Email Finds Porn, Racial Comments, Offensive Jokes." *Crisis Counselor*, December 1, 2004.

Chapter 11   Intellectual Property

Ahrens, Frank. "Movie Industry to Sue Pirates." *Washington Post*, November 5, 2004.

Biskupic, Joan. "Copyright Case to Determine Use of Classic Culture." *USA Today*, October 9, 2002, p. 5-A.

Bobbitt, Randy. *Who Owns What's Inside the Professor's Head? Universities, Faculty, and the Battle Over Intellectual Property*. Lewiston, N.Y.: Edwin Mellen Press, 2006.

Burt, Andrew. "Pirates of the Constitution." Syndicated column, July 21, 2003.

Carnes, Rick. "Stealing Hurts Songwriters." *USA Today*, March 30, 2005, p. A-12.

Crabb, Kelly Charles. *The Movie Business*. New York: Simon & Schuster, 2005.

Elias, Stephen. *Patent and Copyright Law: A Desk Reference to Intellectual Property Law*. Berkeley, Calif.: Nolo Press, 1999.

Finn, Michael. "Trademark Tribulations." *American Journalism Review*, September 1993, pp. 44–51.

Gilbert, Steven W., and Peter Lyman. "Intellectual Property in the Information Age." *Change*, May/June 1989, pp. 23–28.

Goldsborough, Reid. "Warding Off Internet Legal Woes." *Public Relations Tactics*, July 2001, p. 6.

Herskovitz, Marshall. "Whose Movie Is It Anyway?" Syndicated column, April 26, 2005.

"Industry Opposes File Sharing—But it Fought VCRs, Too." *USA Today*, March 30, 2005, p. A-12.

"Internet's Greedy Tune-Traders Must Not be Licensed to Steal." *Tampa Tribune*, May 27, 2005, p. A-10.

Lieberman, David. "How Dangerous Are Pirates?" *USA Today*, April 5, 2002, p 1-A.

McLeod, Kembrew. *Owning Culture: Authorship, Ownership, and Intellectual Property Law*. New York: Peter Lang, 2001.

McManis, Charles R. *Intellectual Property Law in a Nutshell*. St. Paul, Minn.: West Publishing, 1993.

Newcomb, Jonathan. "Stealing on the 'Net." *USA Today*, December 20, 1995.

Questions and Answers on Copyright for the Campus Community. Association of American Publishers, National Association of College Stores, and the Software Publishers Association, 1997.

Scott, M. M. "Intellectual Property Rights: A Ticking Time Bomb in Academia." *Academe*, May–June 1998, pp. 22–26.

Sharpe, Jo Ellen Meyers. "Whose Copyrights?" *Editor & Publisher*, February 14, 1998, pp. 14–15.

Slacks, Jarvis. "Is Downloading Dead?" *Wilmington Star-News* (North Carolina), March 3, 2005, pp. 16–17 (Currents).

Chapter 12 Advertising

Mauro, Tony. "Court Lets Billboard Ad Ban Stand." *USA Today*, April 29, 1997, p. A-1.

Mauro, Tony. "Court Upholds Advertisers' Free-Speech Rights." *First Amendment News*, June 1996, pp. 1–6.

Moore, Roy, Ronald T. Farrar, and Erik Collins. *Advertising and Public Relations Law*. Mahwah, N.J.: Erlbaum, 1998.

Neumeister, Larry. "Judge: Listerine Ads False, Misleading." Associated Press report, January 8, 2005.

Pinkerton, James. "Campaign Reform and Free Speech." Syndicated column, July 3, 2004.

"Tropicana Settles False Ad Charges." *Pittsburgh Post-Gazette*, June 3, 2005, p. E-8.

Whitaker, L. Paige. "Campaign Finance Reform: A Legal Analysis of Issue and Express Advocacy." Congressional Research Service Report, May 15, 1998.

Will, George F. "Soft Money is Just Free Speech." Syndicated column, April 19, 2006.

Chapter 13 Public Relations

Bobbitt, Randy, and Ruth Sullivan. *Developing the Public Relations Campaign: A Team-Based Approach*. Boston: Allyn and Bacon, 2005.

Coronna, David. M. "The Right of Publicity." *Public Relations Journal*, February 1983, pp. 29–31.

Gower Karla. *Legal and Ethical Restraints in Public Relations*. Prospect Heights: Waveland Press, 2003.

Moore, Roy, Ronald T. Farrar, and Erik Collins. *Advertising and Public Relations Law*. Mahwah, N.J.: Lawrence Erlbaum Associates, 1998.

Samples, John. "Stop Funding Government PR." Syndicated column, February 7, 2005.

Sneed, Don, Tim Wulfemeyer, and Harry W. Stonecipher. "Public Relations News Releases and Libel: Extending First Amendment Protections." *Public Relations Review*, Vol. 17, no. 2 (1991), pp. 131–144.

Walsh, Frank. *Public Relations and the Law*. Gainesville, Fla.: Institute for Public Relations Research and Education, 1991.

APPENDIX B

Legal Research and Writing

Court Reporters

Citation	Title and Description
ALR	American Law Reports. Cases from state courts.
ALR 2d	First edition covers cases 1919 through 1947;
ALR 3d	second edition, 1948–64; third edition, 1965 through 1979; fourth edition, 1980 through 1991;
ALR 4th	fifth edition, 1992 to present.
ALR 5th	
ALR FED	American Law Reports, Federal Courts Edition.
F.	Federal Reporter. Proceedings of U.S. Courts of
F.2d.	Appeals. First edition covers cases through 1923,
F.3d	second edition 1924–93, third edition 1993 to present.
F. Supp.	Federal Supplement. Proceedings of Federal District Courts.
L.Ed.	Lawyer's Edition. U.S. Supreme Court cases. Privately published.
Media L. Rep.	Media Law Reporter.
S. Ct.	Supreme Court Reporter. Published by West Publishing Co.
U.S.	U.S. Reports. Official government record of Supreme Court proceedings.
U.S.L.W.	United States Law Week. Privately published.

Books

If you intend to take a number of law classes, the first two books you should purchase are *Black's Law Dictionary* and the *Bluebook of Legal Citations*. Appendix A of this book provides a list of other books you should be able to find at your campus library or request through inter-library loan.

In addition to using keyword searches in your library card catalog, you may also wish to peruse the shelves. Assuming your campus library uses the Library of Congress cataloging system, you should look at the following ranges:

Freedom of expression and the First Amendment	PN 4770–PN 4775
Journalism and broadcasting law	KF 2740–KF 2760
High school and college issues	LB 3615–LB 3635
Legal issues in advertising and public relations	KF 1610–KF 1620

Internet Sources

Case law:

http://www.law.cornell.edu (Legal Information Institute)
http://supct.law.cornell.edu.edu:8080/supct/
http://www.law.emory.edu/FEDCTS
http://www.fastsearch.com/law/
http://www.law.vill.edu/Fed-Ct/fedcourt/html#usappeals
http://www.findlaw.com

Other legal references:

http://www.bolen.bc.ca/wwlia/diction/htm (legal dictionary)
http://www.laderapress.com (basic copyright information)
http://www.libweb.sonoma.edu/web/copyright/html
http://www.yahoo.com/law/
http://www.legalengine.com
http://www.yahoo.com/government/law/legal_research/libraries
http://www.yahoo.com/government/law/journals
http://www.spj.org/foia_opendoors.asp (public records law)

Organizations:

American Bar Association	www.abanet.org
American Civil Liberties Union	www.aclu.org
CNN Law Center	www.cnn.com/LAW
Cornell University Law School	www.law.cornell.edu
Electronic Frontier Foundation	www.eff.org
Freedom Forum	
First Amendment Center	www.freedomforum.org/first/
Libel Defense Resource Center	www.ldrc.com

National Law Center   www.nationallawcenter.org
Poynter Institute   www.poynter.org
Reporters Committee for
    Freedom of the Press   www.rcfp.org
Society of Professional Journalists www.spj.org
Student Press Law Center   www.splc.org

Writing about the Law

For legal professionals, professors, and students, the preferred style manual is *The Bluebook: A Uniform System of Citation*, published by the Harvard Law Review. If you can't locate a copy, here are some general notes on style:

Case names: In most publications, case names are italicized with the plaintiff listed first. *Smith v. Jones* (1993). The year is not italicized. Although you often hear the connector pronounced as "versus," it is spelled v., not vs.

Citations: When citing from court reporters (described earlier in this appendix), the proper form is the volume number, the title of the reporter, followed by the page number: 488 U.S. 572 (U.S. Reports, volume 488, page 572.). If you're referring to a case in a general sense, use the page number on which the case begins. If you're referring to a specific passage, add the page number where the passage is found: 488 U.S. 572 (at 590). When citing from a book, or an article in a law journal, academic journal, newspaper, or magazine, follow the style manual recommended by your professor (most likely APA, Turabian, Chicago, or MLA).

Capitals: Always capitalize the formal names of courts: The U.S. Supreme Court, Circuit Court of Appeals, Federal District Court. If referring to a court more generally, lowercase the word *court*, such as: federal courts or appeals courts. To reduce redundancy, on subsequent references refer to the U.S. Supreme Court as the Court. Constitutional amendments are capitalized when used formally: the First Amendment. But "the amendment" is acceptable on second reference.

Numbers: Spell out one through nine and use numerals for numbers 10 and higher. Exceptions: Ages, addresses, legal documents, proposed amendments to state constitutions, and casual expressions. Examples: A 5-year-old child. The victim's address was 7 Thomasville Drive. The voters rejected Proposition 8 and Amendment 9. She's one in a million (not one in 1,000,000).

Abbreviations: Spell out the names of all parties involved in a case on first reference: National Broadcasting Company, Cable News Network, Federal Trade Commission. Abbreviate on subsequent references: NBC, CNN, FTC.

Defining terms: The need to define terms used in your paper depends largely on the nature of your audience. If you're writing a paper for a communication law class, your professor will be familiar with the terms, so you don't need to define them. But if you're writing a paper on a legal topic for a sociology or political science class, you will probably need to define or paraphrase terms such as *writ of certiorari, hate speech, non-obscene sexual expression, actual malice,* and *privilege.*

CASE INDEX

SUBJECT INDEX

PHOTO CREDITS